FAULT-TOLERANT SYSTEMS

In Praise of Fault-Tolerant Systems

"Fault attacks have recently become a serious concern in the smart card industry. "Fault-Tolerant Systems" provides the reader with a clear exposition of these attacks and the protection strategies that can be used to thwart them. A must read for practitioners and researchers working in the field."

David Naccache, Ecole normale supérieure

"Understanding the fundamentals of an area, whether it is golf or fault tolerance, is a prerequisite to developing expertise in the area. Krishna and Koren's book can provide a reader with this underlying foundation for fault tolerance. This book is particularly timely because the design of fault-tolerant computing components, such as processors and disks, is becoming increasingly important to the mainstream computing industry."

Shubu Mukherjee, Director, FACT-AMI Group, Intel Corporation

"Professors Koren and Krishna, have written a modern, dual purpose text that first presents the basics fault tolerance tools describing various redundancy types both at the hardware and software levels followed by current research topics. It reviews fundamental reliability modeling approaches, combinatorial blocks and Markov chain techniques. Notably, there is a complete chapter on statistical simulation methods that offers guidance to practical evaluations as well as one on fault-tolerant networks. All chapters, which are clearly written including illuminating examples, have extensive reference lists whereby students can delve deeper into almost any topic. Several practical and commercial computing systems that incorporate fault tolerance are detailed. Furthermore, there are two chapters introducing current fault tolerance research challenges, cryptographic systems and defects in VLSI designs."

Robert Redinbo, UC Davis

"The field of Fault-Tolerant Computing has advanced considerably in the past ten years and yet no effort has been made to put together these advances in the form of a book or a comprehensive paper for the students starting in this area. This is the first book I know of in the past 10 years that deals with hardware and software aspects of fault-tolerant computing, is very comprehensive, and is written as a text for the course."

Kewal Saluja, University of Wisconsin, Madison

FAULT-TOLERANT SYSTEMS

Israel Koren

C. Mani Krishna

ELSEVIER

AMSTERDAM • BOSTON • HEIDELBERG • LONDON
NEW YORK • OXFORD • PARIS • SAN DIEGO
SAN FRANCISCO • SINGAPORE • SYDNEY • TOKYO

Morgan Kaufmann Publishers is an imprint of Elsevier

MORGAN KAUFMANN PUBLISHERS

Publisher	Denise Penrose
Publishing Services Manager	George Morrison
Production Editor	Dawnmarie Simpson
Assistant Editor	Kimberlee Honjo
Cover Design	Alisa Andreola
Cover Illustration	Yaron Koren
Text Design	Gene Harris
Composition	VTEX
Copyeditor	Graphic World Publishing Services
Proofreader	Graphic World Publishing Services
Indexer	Graphic World Publishing Services
Interior printer	The Maple–Vail Book Manufacturing Group
Cover printer	Phoenix Color, Inc.

Morgan Kaufmann Publishers is an imprint of Elsevier.
500 Sansome Street, Suite 400, San Francisco, CA 94111

This book is printed on acid-free paper.

Library of Congress Cataloging-in-Publication Data
Koren, Israel, 1945-
    Fault-tolerant systems / Israel Koren, C. Mani Krishna.
        p. cm.
    Includes bibliographical references and index.
    ISBN 0-12-088525-5 (alk. paper)
    1. Fault-tolerant computing. 2. Computer systems–Reliability.
    I. Krishna, C. M. II. Title.
    QA76.9.F38K67 2007
    004.2–dc22   2006031810

ISBN 13: 978-0-12-088525-1
ISBN 10: 0-12-088525-5

For information on all Morgan Kaufmann publications, visit our
Web site at *www.mkp.com* or *www.books.elsevier.com*

Printed in the United States

06 07 08 09 10   5 4 3 2 1

Contents

3 Information Redundancy   55

4 Fault-Tolerant Networks   109

Foreword

Systems used in critical applications such as health, commerce, transportation, utilities, and national security must be highly reliable. Ubiquitous use of computing systems and other electronic systems in these critical areas requires that computing systems have high reliability. High reliability is achieved by designing the systems to be fault-tolerant. Even though the high reliability requirements of computing systems gave the original impetus to the study of the design of fault-tolerant systems, trends in manufacturing of VLSI circuits and systems are also requiring the use of fault-tolerant design methods to achieve high yields from manufacturing plants. This is due to the fact that with reduced feature sizes of VLSI circuit designs and shortcomings of lithographic techniques used in fabrication the characteristics of the manufactured devices are becoming unpredictable. Additionally small sizes of devices make them susceptible to radiation induced failures causing run time errors. Thus it may be necessary to use fault tolerance techniques even in systems that are used in non-critical applications such as consumer electronics.

This book covers comprehensively the design of fault-tolerant hardware and software, use of fault-tolerance techniques to improve manufacturing yields and design and analysis of networks. Additionally it includes material on methods to protect against threats to encryption subsystems used for security purposes. The material in the book will help immensely students and practitioners in electrical and computer engineering and computer science in learning how to design reliable computing systems and how to analyze fault-tolerant computing systems.

Sudhakar M. Reddy
Distinguished Professor of Electrical and Computer Engineering
University of Iowa Foundation
Iowa City, Iowa

Preface

The purpose of this book is to provide a solid introduction to the rich field of fault-tolerant computing. Its intended use is as a text for senior-level undergraduate and first-year graduate students, as well as a reference for practicing engineers in the industry. Since it would be impossible to cover in one book all the fault-tolerance techniques and practices that have been developed or are currently in use, we have focused on providing the basics of the field and enough background to allow the reader to access more easily the rapidly expanding fault-tolerance literature. Readers who are interested in further details should consult the list of references at the end of each chapter. To understand this book well, the reader should have a basic knowledge of hardware design and organization, principles of software development, and probability theory.

The book has 10 chapters; each chapter has a list of relevant references and a set of exercises. Solutions to the exercises are available on-line and access to them is provided by the publisher upon request to instructors who adopt this book as a textbook for their class. Powerpoint slides for instructors are also available.

The book starts with an outline of preliminaries, in which we provide introductory information. This is followed by a set of six chapters that form the core of what we believe should be covered in any introduction to fault-tolerant systems.

Chapter 2 deals with hardware fault-tolerance; this is the discipline with the longest history (indeed, the idea of using hardware redundancy for fault-tolerance goes back to the very pioneers of computing, most notably von Neumann). We also include in this chapter an introduction to some of the probabilistic tools used in analyzing reliability measures.

Chapter 3 deals with information redundancy with the main focus on error detecting and correcting codes. Such codes, like hardware fault-tolerance, go back a very long way, and were motivated in large measure by the need to counter errors in information transmission. The same, or similar, techniques are being used today in other applications as well, principally in contemporary memory circuits. We have sought to provide a survey of only the more important coding techniques, and it was not intended to be comprehensive: indeed, a comprehensive survey of coding would require multiple volumes. Following this, we turn to the issue of managing information redundancy in storage, and end with algorithm-based fault-tolerance.

Chapter 4 covers fault-tolerant networks. With processors becoming cheaper, distributed systems are becoming more commonplace; we look at some key network topologies and consider how to quantify and enhance their fault-tolerance.

Chapter 5 describes techniques for software fault-tolerance. It is widely believed that software accounts for a majority of the failures seen in today's computer systems. As a field, software fault-tolerance is less mature than fault-tolerance using either hardware or information redundancy. It is also a much harder nut to crack. Software is probably the most complex artificial construct that people have created, and rendering it fault-tolerant is an arduous task. We cover such techniques as recovery blocks and N-version programming, together with a discussion of acceptance tests and ways to model software failure processes analytically.

In Chapter 6, we cover the use of time-redundancy through checkpointing. The majority of hardware failures are transient in nature; in other words, they are failures which simply go away after some time. An obvious response to such failures is to roll back the execution and re-execute the program. Checkpointing is a technique which allows us to limit the extent of such re-executions.

Chapter 7, which contains several case studies, rounds off the core of the book. There, we describe several real-life examples of fault-tolerant systems illustrating the usage of the various techniques presented in the previous chapters.

The remaining three chapters of the book deal with more specialized topics. In Chapter 8, we cover defect-tolerance in VLSI. As die sizes increase and feature sizes drop, it is becoming increasingly important to be able to tolerate manufacturing defects in a VLSI chip without affecting its functionality. We discuss the key approaches being used, as well as the underlying mathematical models.

In Chapter 9, we focus on cryptographic devices. The increasing use of computers in commerce, including smart cards and Internet shopping, has motivated the use of encryption in everyday applications. It turns out that injecting faults into cryptographic devices and observing the outputs is an effective way to attack secure systems and obtain their secret key. We present in this chapter the use of fault-detection to counter these types of security attacks.

Chapter 10, which ends the book, deals with simulation and experimental techniques. Simulating a fault-tolerant system to measure its reliability is often computationally very demanding. We provide in this chapter an outline of basic simulation techniques, as well as ways in which simulation can be accelerated. Also provided are basic statistical tools by which simulation output can be analyzed and an outline of experimental fault-injection techniques.

A companion web site (www.ecs.umass.edu/ece/koren/FaultTolerantSystems/) includes additional resources for the book such as lecture slides, the inevitable list of errors, and, more importantly, a link to an extensive collection of educational tools and simulators that can be of great assistance to the readers of the book. Elsevier also maintains an instructor web site that will house the solutions for those who adopt this book as a textbook for their class. The website can be found at http://textbooks.elsevier.com.

Acknowledgements

Many people have assisted us in putting this book together. Pride of place in these acknowledgments must go to Zahava Koren, who read through the manuscript in detail and provided many incisive comments. While the authors are responsible for any errors that still remain in this book, she is responsible for the absence of very many that do not. We also had very valuable feedback from the reviewers of this manuscript. Some of them chose to remain anonymous, so we cannot thank them individually. However, those who can be named are: Wendy Bartlett from HP Labs, Doug Blough from Georgia Institute of Technology, Mark Karpovski from Boston University, Cetin Kaya Koc from Oregon State University, Shubu Mukherjee from Intel, David Naccache from École normale supérieure, Nohpill Park from Oklahoma State University, Irith Pomeranz from Purdue University, Mihaela Radu from Rose Hulman Institute of Technology, Robert Redinbo from UC Davis, Kewal Saluja from University of Wisconsin at Madison, Jean-Pierre Seifert from Applied Security Research Group, Arun Somani from Iowa State University, and Charles Weinstock from Carnegie Mellon University.

We would like to thank the staff at Morgan Kaufman for their efforts on behalf of this project. In particular, Denise Penrose and Kim Honjo spent many hours in meetings and discussions with us on many issues ranging from the technical content of this book to its look and feel.

About the Authors

Israel Koren is a Professor of Electrical and Computer Engineering at the University of Massachusetts, Amherst. Previously, he held positions with the University of California at Santa Barbara, the University of Southern California at Los Angeles, the Technion at Haifa, Israel, and the University of California at Berkeley. He received a BSc (1967), an MSc (1970), and a DSc (1975) in electrical engineering from the Technion in Haifa, Israel. His research interests include fault-tolerant systems, VLSI yield and reliability, secure cryptographic systems, and computer arithmetic. He publishes extensively and has over 200 publications in refereed journals and conferences. He is an Associate Editor of the IEEE Transactions on VLSI Systems, the VLSI Design Journal, and the IEEE Computer Architecture Letters. He served as General Chair, Program Chair and Program Committee member for numerous conferences. He is the author of the textbook Computer Arithmetic Algorithms, 2nd edition, A.K. Peters, Ltd., 2002, and an editor and co-author of Defect and Fault-Tolerance in VLSI Systems, Plenum, 1989. Dr. Koren is a fellow of the IEEE Computer Society.

C. Mani Krishna is a Professor of Electrical and Computer Engineering at the University of Massachusetts, Amherst. He received his PhD in Electrical Engineering from the University of Michigan in 1984. He previously received a BTech in Electrical Engineering from the Indian Institute of Technology, Delhi, in 1979, and an MS from the Rensselaer Polytechnic Institute in Troy, NY, in 1980. Since 1984, he has been on the faculty of the Department of Electrical and Computer Engineering at the University of Massachusetts at Amherst. He has carried out research in a number of areas: real-time, fault-tolerant, and distributed systems, sensor networks, and performance evaluation of computer systems. He coauthored a book, Real-Time Systems, McGraw-Hill, 1997, with Kang G. Shin. He has also been an editor on volumes of readings in performance evaluation and real-time systems, and for special issues on real-time systems of IEEE Computer and the Proceedings of the IEEE.

Preliminaries

The past 50 years have seen computers move from being expensive computational engines used by government and big corporations to becoming an everyday commodity, deeply embedded in practically every aspect of our lives. Not only are computers visible everywhere, in desktops, laptops, and PDAs, it is also a commonplace that they are *invisible* everywhere, as vital components of cars, home appliances, medical equipment, aircraft, industrial plants, and power generation and distribution systems. Computer systems underpin most of the world's financial systems: given current transaction volumes, trading in the stock, bond, and currency markets would be unthinkable without them. Our increasing willingness, as a society, to place computers in life-critical and wealth-critical applications is largely driven by the increasing possibilities that computers offer. And yet, as we depend more and more on computers to carry out all of these vital actions, we are—implicitly or explicitly—gambling our lives and property on computers doing their jobs properly.

Computers (hardware plus software) are quite likely the most complex systems ever created by human beings. The complexity of computer hardware is still increasing as designers attempt to exploit the higher transistor density that new generations of technology make available to them. Computer software is far more complex still, and with that complexity comes an increased propensity to failure. It is probably fair to say that there is not a single large piece of software or hardware today that is free of bugs. Even the space shuttle, with software that was developed and tested using some of the best and most advanced techniques known to engineering, is now known to have flown with bugs that had the potential to cause catastrophe.

Computer scientists and engineers have responded to the challenge of designing complex systems with a variety of tools and techniques to reduce the number of faults in the systems they build. However, that is not enough: we need to build systems that will acknowledge the existence of faults as a fact of life, and incorpo-

1

rate techniques to tolerate these faults while still delivering an acceptable level of service. The resulting field of *fault tolerance* is the subject of this book.

1.1   Fault Classification

In everyday language, the terms *fault*, *failure*, and *error* are used interchangeably. In fault-tolerant computing parlance, however, they have distinctive meanings. A *fault* (or *failure*) can be either a hardware defect or a software/programming mistake (bug). In contrast, an *error* is a manifestation of the fault/failure/bug.

As an example, consider an adder circuit, with an output line stuck at 1; it always carries the value 1 independently of the values of the input operands. This is a fault, but not (yet) an error. This fault causes an error when the adder is used and the result on that line is supposed to have been a 0, rather than a 1. A similar distinction exists between programming mistakes and execution errors. Consider, for example, a subroutine that is supposed to compute $\sin(x)$ but owing to a programming mistake calculates the absolute value of $\sin(x)$ instead. This mistake will result in an execution error only if that particular subroutine is used and the correct result is negative.

Both faults and errors can spread through the system. For example, if a chip shorts out power to ground, it may cause nearby chips to fail as well. Errors can spread because the output of one unit is used as input by other units. To return to our previous examples, the erroneous results of either the faulty adder or the $\sin(x)$ subroutine can be fed into further calculations, thus propagating the error.

To limit such contagion, designers incorporate *containment zones* into systems. These are barriers that reduce the chance that a fault or error in one zone will propagate to another. For example, a fault-containment zone can be created by ensuring that the maximum possible voltage swings in one zone are insulated from the other zones, and by providing an independent power supply to each zone. In other words, the designer tries to electrically isolate one zone from another. An error-containment zone can be created, as we will see in some detail later on, by using redundant units/programs and voting on their output.

Hardware faults can be classified according to several aspects. Regarding their duration, hardware faults can be classified into *permanent*, *transient*, or *intermittent*. A *permanent fault* is just that: it reflects the permanent going out of commission of a component. As an example of a permanent fault think of a burned-out lightbulb. A *transient fault* is one that causes a component to malfunction for some time; it goes away after that time and the functionality of the component is fully restored. As an example, think of a random noise interference during a telephone conversation. Another example is a memory cell with contents that are changed spuriously due to some electromagnetic interference. The cell itself is undamaged: it is just that its contents are wrong for the time being, and overwriting the memory cell will make the fault go away. An *intermittent fault* never quite goes away entirely; it oscillates between being quiescent and active. When the fault is quiescent, the component functions normally; when the fault is active, the component malfunctions. An example for an intermittent fault is a loose electrical connection.

Another classification of hardware faults is into *benign* and *malicious* faults. A fault that just causes a unit to go dead is called *benign*. Such faults are the easiest to deal with. Far more insidious are the faults that cause a unit to produce reasonable-looking, but incorrect, output, or that make a component "act maliciously" and send differently valued outputs to different receivers. Think of an altitude sensor in an airplane that reports a 1000-foot altitude to one unit and a 8000-foot altitude to another unit. These are called *malicious* (or Byzantine) faults.

1.2 Types of Redundancy

All of fault tolerance is an exercise in exploiting and managing *redundancy*. Redundancy is the property of having more of a resource than is minimally necessary to do the job at hand. As failures happen, redundancy is exploited to mask or otherwise work around these failures, thus maintaining the desired level of functionality.

There are four forms of redundancy that we will study: hardware, software, information, and time. Hardware faults are usually dealt with by using hardware, information, or time redundancy, whereas software faults are protected against by software redundancy.

Hardware redundancy is provided by incorporating extra hardware into the design to either detect or override the effects of a failed component. For example, instead of having a single processor, we can use two or three processors, each performing the same function. By having two processors, we can detect the failure of a single processor; by having three, we can use the majority output to override the wrong output of a single faulty processor. This is an example of *static hardware redundancy*, the main objective of which is the immediate masking of a failure. A different form of hardware redundancy is *dynamic redundancy*, where spare components are activated upon the failure of a currently active component. A combination of static and dynamic redundancy techniques is also possible, leading to *hybrid hardware redundancy*.

Hardware redundancy can thus range from a simple duplication to complicated structures that switch in spare units when active ones become faulty. These forms of hardware redundancy incur high overheads, and their use is therefore normally reserved for critical systems where such overheads can be justified. In particular, substantial amounts of redundancy are required to protect against malicious faults.

The best-known form of information redundancy is error detection and correction coding. Here, extra bits (called check bits) are added to the original data bits so that an error in the data bits can be detected or even corrected. The resulting error-detecting and error-correcting codes are widely used today in memory units and various storage devices to protect against benign failures. Note that these error codes (like any other form of information redundancy) require extra hardware to process the redundant data (the check bits).

Error-detecting and error-correcting codes are also used to protect data communicated over noisy channels, which are channels that are subject to many transient failures. These channels can be either the communication links among widely separated processors (e.g., the Internet) or among locally connected processors that form a local network. If the code used for data communication is capable of only detecting the faults that have occurred (but not correcting them), we can retransmit as necessary, thus employing time redundancy.

In addition to transient data communication failures due to noise, local and wide-area networks may experience permanent link failures. These failures may disconnect one or more existing communication paths, resulting in a longer communication delay between certain nodes in the network, a lower data bandwidth between certain node pairs, or even a complete disconnection of certain nodes from the rest of the network. Redundant communication links (i.e., hardware redundancy) can alleviate most of these problems.

Computing nodes can also exploit time redundancy through re-execution of the same program on the same hardware. As before, time redundancy is effective mainly against *transient* faults. Because the majority of hardware faults are transient, it is unlikely that the separate executions will experience the same fault. Time redundancy can thus be used to detect transient faults in situations in which such faults may otherwise go undetected. Time redundancy can also be used when other means for detecting errors are in place and the system is capable of recovering from the effects of the fault and repeating the computation. Compared with the other forms of redundancy, time redundancy has much lower hardware and software overhead but incurs a high performance penalty.

Software redundancy is used mainly against software failures. It is a reasonable guess that *every* large piece of software that has ever been produced has contained faults (bugs). Dealing with such faults can be expensive: one way is to independently produce two or more versions of that software (preferably by disjoint teams of programmers) in the hope that the different versions will not fail on the same input. The secondary version(s) can be based on simpler and less accurate algorithms (and, consequently, less likely to have faults) to be used only upon the failure of the primary software to produce acceptable results. Just as for hardware redundancy, the multiple versions of the program can be executed either concurrently (requiring redundant hardware as well) or sequentially (requiring extra time, i.e., time redundancy) upon a failure detection.

1.3   Basic Measures of Fault Tolerance

Because fault tolerance is about making machines more dependable, it is important to have proper measures (yardsticks) by which to gauge such dependability. In this section, we will examine some of these yardsticks and their application.

A measure is a mathematical abstraction that expresses some relevant facet of the performance of its object. By its very nature, a measure only captures some subset of the properties of an object. The trick in defining a suitable measure is to keep this subset large enough so that behaviors of interest to the user are captured, and yet not so large that the measure loses focus.

1.3.1 Traditional Measures

We first describe the traditional measures of dependability of a single computer. These metrics have been around for a long time and measure very basic attributes of the system. Two of these measures are *reliability* and *availability*.

The conventional definition of reliability, denoted by $R(t)$, is the probability (as a function of the time t) that the system has been up continuously in the time interval $[0, t]$. This measure is suitable for applications in which even a momentary disruption can prove costly. One example is computers that control physical processes such as an aircraft, for which failure would result in catastrophe.

Closely related to reliability are the *Mean Time to Failure*, denoted by MTTF, and the *Mean Time Between Failures*, MTBF. The first is the average time the system operates until a failure occurs, whereas the second is the average time between two consecutive failures. The difference between the two is due to the time needed to repair the system following the first failure. Denoting the *Mean Time to Repair* by MTTR, we obtain

$$\mathrm{MTBF} = \mathrm{MTTF} + \mathrm{MTTR}$$

Availability, denoted by $A(t)$, is the average fraction of time over the interval $[0, t]$ that the system is up. This measure is appropriate for applications in which continuous performance is not vital but where it would be expensive to have the system down for a significant amount of time. An airline reservation system needs to be highly available, because downtime can put off customers and lose sales; however, an occasional (very) short-duration failure can be well tolerated.

The long-term availability, denoted by A, is defined as

$$A = \lim_{t \to \infty} A(t)$$

A can be interpreted as the probability that the system will be up at some random point in time, and is meaningful only in systems that include repair of faulty components. The long-term availability can be calculated from MTTF, MTBF, and MTTR as follows:

$$A = \frac{\mathrm{MTTF}}{\mathrm{MTBF}} = \frac{\mathrm{MTTF}}{\mathrm{MTTF} + \mathrm{MTTR}}$$

A related measure, *Point Availability*, denoted by $A_{\mathrm{p}}(t)$, is the probability that the system is up at the particular time instant t.

It is possible for a low-reliability system to have high availability: consider a system that fails every hour on the average but comes back up after only a second.

Such a system has an MTBF of just 1 hour and, consequently, a low reliability; however, its availability is high: $A = 3599/3600 = 0.99972$.

These definitions assume, of course, that we have a state in which the system can be said to be "up" and another in which it is not. For simple components, this is a good assumption. For example, a lightbulb is either good or burned out. A wire is either connected or has a break in it. However, for even simple systems, such an assumption can be very limiting. For example, consider a processor that has one of its several hundreds of millions of gates stuck at logic value 0. In other words, the output of this logic gate is always 0, regardless of the input. Suppose the rest of the processor is functional, and that this failed logic gate only affects the output of the processor about once in every 25,000 hours of use. For example, a particular gate in the divide unit when being faulty may result in a wrong quotient if the divisor is within a certain subset of values. Clearly, the processor is not fault-free, but would one define it as "down"?

The same remarks apply with even greater force to systems that degrade gracefully. By this, we mean systems with various levels of functionality. Initially, with all of its components operational, the system is at its highest level of functionality. As these components fail, the system degrades from one level of functionality to the next. Beyond a certain point, the system is unable to produce anything of use and fails completely. As with the previous example, the system has multiple "up" states. Is it said to fail when it degrades from full to partial functionality? Or when it fails to produce any useful output at all? Or when its functionality falls below a certain threshold? If the last, what is this threshold, and how is it determined?

We can therefore see that traditional reliability and availability are very limited in what they can express. There are obvious extensions to these measures. For example, we may consider the average computational capacity of a system with n processors. Let c_i denote the computational capacity of a system with i operational processors. This can be a simple linear function of the number of processors, $c_i = ic_1$, or a more complex function of i, depending on the ability of the application to utilize i processors. The *Average Computational Capacity* of the system can then be defined as $\sum_{i=1}^{n} c_i P_i(t)$, where $P_i(t)$ is the probability that exactly i processors are operational at time t. In contrast, the reliability of the system at time t will be

$$R(t) = \sum_{i=m}^{n} P_i(t)$$

where m is the minimum number of processors necessary for proper operation of the system.

1.3.2 Network Measures

In addition to the general system measures previously discussed, there are also more specialized measures, focusing on the network that connects the processors together. The simplest of these are classical node and line *connectivity*, which are

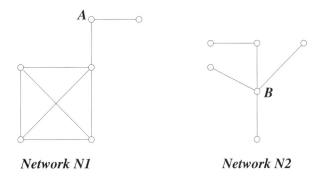

FIGURE 1.1 Inadequacy of classical connectivity.

defined as the minimum number of nodes and lines, respectively, that have to fail before the network becomes disconnected. This gives a rough indication of how vulnerable a network is to disconnection: for example, a network that can be disconnected by the failure of just one (critically positioned) node is potentially more vulnerable than another that requires at least four nodes to fail before it becomes disconnected.

Classical connectivity is a very basic measure of network reliability. Like reliability, it distinguishes between only two network states: connected and disconnected. It says nothing about how the network degrades as nodes fail before, or after, becoming disconnected. Consider the two networks shown in Figure 1.1. Both networks have the same classical node connectivity of 1. However, in a real sense, network $N1$ is much more "connected" than $N2$. The probability that $N2$ splinters into small pieces is greater than that for $N1$.

To express this type of "connectivity robustness," we can use additional measures. Two such measures are the average node-pair distance, and the network diameter (the maximum node-pair distance), both calculated given the probability of node and/or link failure. Such network measures, together with the traditional measures listed above, allow us to gauge the dependability of various networked systems that consist of computing nodes connected through a network of communication links.

1.4 Outline of This Book

The next chapter is devoted to hardware fault tolerance. This is the most established topic within fault-tolerant computing, and many of the basic principles and techniques that have been developed for it have been extended to other forms of fault tolerance. Techniques to evaluate the reliability and availability of fault-tolerant systems are introduced here, including the use of Markov models.

Next, several variations of information redundancy are covered, starting with the most widely used error detecting and correcting codes. Then, other forms of information redundancy are discussed, including storage redundancy (RAID systems), data replication in distributed systems, and, finally, the algorithm-based fault-tolerance technique that tolerates data errors in array computations using some error-detecting and error-correcting codes.

Many computing systems nowadays consist of multiple networked processors that are subject to interconnection link failures, in addition to the already-discussed single node/processor failures. We, therefore, present in this book suitable fault tolerance techniques for these networks and analysis methods to determine which network topologies are more robust.

Software mistakes/bugs are, in practice, unavoidable, and consequently, some level of software fault tolerance is a must. This can be as simple as acceptance tests to check the reasonableness of the results before using them, or as complex as running two or more versions of the software (sequentially or in parallel). Programs also tend to have their state deteriorate after running for long periods of time and eventually crash. This situation can be avoided by periodically restarting the program, a process called rejuvenation. Unlike hardware faults, software faults are very hard to model. Still, a few such models have been developed and several of them are described.

Hardware fault-tolerance techniques can be quite costly to implement. In applications in which a complete and immediate masking of the effect of hardware faults (especially, of transient nature) is not necessary, checkpointing is an inexpensive alternative. For programs that run for a long time and for which re-execution upon a failure might be too costly, the program state can be saved (once or periodically) during the execution. Upon a failure occurrence, the system can roll back the program to the most recent checkpoint and resume its execution from that point. Various checkpointing techniques are presented and analyzed in the book.

Case studies illustrating the use of many of the fault-tolerance techniques described previously are presented, including Tandem, Stratus, Cassini, and microprocessors from IBM and Intel.

Two fault-tolerance topics that are rapidly increasing in practical importance, namely, defect tolerant VLSI design and fault tolerance in cryptographic devices are discussed. The increasing complexity of VLSI chip design has resulted in a situation in which manufacturing defects are unavoidable. If nothing is done to remedy this situation, the expected *yield* (the fraction of manufactured chips which are operational) will be very low. Thus, techniques to reduce the sensitivity of VLSI chips to defects have been developed, some of which are very similar to the hardware redundancy schemes.

For cryptographic devices, the need for fault tolerance is two-fold. Not only is it crucial that such devices (e.g., smart cards) operate in a fault-free manner in whatever environment they are used, but more importantly, they must stay secure. Fault-injection-based attacks on cryptographic devices have become the simplest and fastest way to extract the secret key from the device. Thus, the incorporation of fault tolerance is a must in order to keep cryptographic devices secure.

An important part of the design and evaluation process of a fault-tolerant system is to demonstrate that the system does indeed function at the advertised level of reliability. Often the designed system is too complex to develop analytical expressions of its reliability. If a prototype of the system has already been constructed, then fault-injection experiments can be performed and certain dependability attributes measured. If, however, as is very common, a prototype does not yet exist, statistical simulation must be used. Simulation programs for complex systems must be carefully designed to produce accurate results. We discuss the principles that should be followed when preparing a simulation program, and show how simulation results can be analyzed to infer system reliability.

1.5 Further Reading

Several textbooks and reference books on the topic of fault tolerance have been published in the past. See, for example, [2,4,5,9,10,13–16]. Journals have published several special issues on fault-tolerant computing, e.g., [7,8]. The major conference in the field is the *Conference on Dependable Systems and Networks* (DSN) [3]; this is a successor to the *Fault-Tolerant Computing Symposium* (FTCS).

The concept of computing being invisible everywhere appeared in [19], in the context of *pervasive computing*, that is, computing that pervades everyday living, without being obtrusive.

The definitions of the basic terms and measures appear in most of the textbooks mentioned above and in several probability and statistics books. For example, see [18]. Our definitions of fault and error are slightly different from those used in some of the references. A generally used definition of an error is that it is that part of the system state that leads to system failure. Strictly interpreted, this only applies to a system with state, i.e., with memory. We use the more encompassing definition of anything that can be construed as a manifestation of a fault. This wider interpretation allows purely combinational circuits, which are stateless, to generate errors.

One measure of dependability that we did not describe in the text is to consider everything from the perspective of the application. This approach was taken to define the measure known as *performability*. The application is used to define "accomplishment levels" $L_1, L_2, \ldots, L_n$. Each of these represents a level of quality of service delivered by the application. For example, L_i may be defined as follows: "There are i system crashes during the time period $[0, T]$." Now, the performance of the computer affects this quality (if it did not, by definition, it would have nothing to do with the application!). The approach taken by performability is to link the performance of the computer to the accomplishment level that this enables. Performability is then a vector, $(P(L_1), P(L_2), \ldots, P(L_n))$, where $P(L_i)$ is the probability that the computer functions well enough to permit the application to reach up to accomplishment level L_i. For more on performability, see [6,11,12].

References

[1] A. Avizienis and J. Laprie, "Dependable Computing: From Concepts to Design Diversity," *Proceedings of the IEEE*, Vol. 74, pp. 629–638, May 1986.

[2] W. R. Dunn, *Practical Design of Safety-Critical Computer Systems*, Reliability Press, 2002.

[3] *Dependable Systems and Networks (DSN) Conference*, http://www.dsn.org.

[4] C. E. Ebeling, *An Introduction to Reliability and Maintainability Engineering*, McGraw-Hill, 1997.

[5] J.-C. Geffroy and G. Motet, *Design of Dependable Computing Systems*, Kluwer Academic Publishers, 2002.

[6] M.-C. Hsueh, R. K. Iyer, and K. S. Trivedi, "Performability Modeling Based on Real Data: A Case Study," *IEEE Transactions on Computers*, Vol. 37, pp. 478–484, April 1988.

[7] *IEEE Computer*, Vol. 23, No. 5, July 1990. [Special issue on fault-tolerant systems]

[8] *IEEE Transactions on Computers*, Vol. 41, February 1992; Vol. 47, April 1998; and Vol. 51, February 2002. [Special issues on fault-tolerant systems]

[9] P. Jalote, *Fault Tolerance in Distributed Systems*, PTR Prentice Hall, 1994.

[10] B. W. Johnson, *Design and Analysis of Fault-Tolerant Digital Systems*, Addison-Wesley, 1989.

[11] J. F. Meyer, "On Evaluating the Performability of Degradable Computing Systems," *IEEE Transactions on Computers*, Vol. 29, pp. 720–731, August 1980.

[12] J. F. Meyer, D. G. Furchtgott, and L. T. Wu, "Performability Evaluation of the SIFT Computer," *IEEE Transactions on Computers*, Vol. 29, pp. 501–509, June 1980.

[13] D. K. Pradhan (Ed.), *Fault Tolerant Computer System Design*, Prentice Hall, 1996.

[14] L. L. Pullum, *Software Fault Tolerance Techniques and Implementation*, Artech House, 2001.

[15] D. P. Siewiorek and R. S. Swarz, *Reliable Computer Systems: Design and Evaluation*, A. K. Peters, 1998.

[16] M. L. Shooman, *Reliability of Computer Systems and Networks: Fault Tolerance, Analysis, and Design*, Wiley-Interscience, 2001.

[17] A. K. Somani and N. H. Vaidya, "Understanding Fault-tolerance and Reliability," *IEEE Computer*, Vol. 30, pp. 45–50, April 1997.

[18] K. S. Trivedi, *Probability and Statistics with Reliability, Queuing, and Computer Science Applications*, John Wiley, 2002.

[19] M. Weiser, "The Computer for the Twenty-first Century," *Scientific American*, pp. 94–104, September 1991. Available at: http://www.ubiq.com/hypertext/weiser/SciAmDraft3.html.

Hardware Fault Tolerance

Hardware fault tolerance is the most mature area in the general field of fault-tolerant computing. Many hardware fault-tolerance techniques have been developed and used in practice in critical applications ranging from telephone exchanges to space missions. In the past, the main obstacle to a wide use of hardware fault tolerance has been the cost of the extra hardware required. With the continued reduction in the cost of hardware, this is no longer a significant drawback, and the use of hardware fault-tolerance techniques is expected to increase. However, other constraints, notably on power consumption, may continue to restrict the use of massive redundancy in many applications.

This chapter first discusses the rate at which hardware failures occur, as well as its effect on the reliability of a single component. We then extend the discussion to more complex systems consisting of multiple components, describe various resilient structures which have been proposed and implemented, and evaluate their reliability and/or availability. Next, we describe hardware fault-tolerance techniques that have been developed specifically for general-purpose processors. Finally, we discuss *malicious* faults and investigate the amount of redundancy needed for tolerating them.

2.1 The Rate of Hardware Failures

The single most important parameter used in the reliability analysis of hardware systems is the component failure rate, which is the rate at which an individual component suffers faults. This is the expected number of failures per unit time that a currently good component will suffer in a given future time interval. The failure rate depends on the current age of the component, any voltage or physical

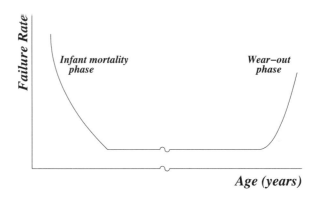

FIGURE 2.1   Bathtub curve.

shocks that it suffers, the ambient temperature, and the technology. The dependence on age is usually captured by what is known as the *bathtub curve* (see Figure 2.1). When components are very young, their failure rate is quite high. This
is due to the chance that some components with manufacturing defects slipped
through manufacturing quality control and were released. As time goes on, these
components are weeded out, and the component spends the bulk of its life showing a fairly constant failure rate. As it becomes very old, aging effects start to take
over, and the failure rate rises again.

The impact of the other factors can be expressed through the following empirical failure rate formula:

$$\lambda = \pi_L \pi_Q (C_1 \pi_T \pi_V + C_2 \pi_E) \tag{2.1}$$

where the notations are as follows:

λ Failure rate of component.

π_L Learning factor, associated with how mature the technology is.

π_Q Quality factor, representing manufacturing process quality control (ranging from 0.25 to 20.00).

π_T Temperature factor, with values ranging from 0.1 to 1000. It is proportional to $e^{-E_a/kT}$, where E_a is the activation energy in electron-volts
associated with the technology, k is the Boltzmann constant (0.8625×10^{-4} eV/K), and T is the temperature in Kelvin.

π_V Voltage stress factor for CMOS devices; can range from 1 to 10, depending on the supply voltage and the temperature; does not apply to other
technologies (where it is set to 1).

π_E Environment shock factor; ranges from very low (about 0.4), when the
component is in an air-conditioned office environment, to very high (13.0)
when it is in a harsh environment.

C_1, C_2 Complexity factors; functions of the number of gates on the chip and the number of pins in the package.

Further details can be found in *MIL-HDBK-217E*, which is a handbook produced by the U.S. Department of Defense.

Devices operating in space, which is replete with charged particles and can subject devices to severe temperature swings, can thus be expected to fail much more often than their counterparts in air-conditioned offices, so too can computers in automobiles (which suffer high temperatures and vibration) and industrial applications.

2.2 Failure Rate, Reliability, and Mean Time to Failure

In this section, we consider a single component of a more complex system, and show how reliability and Mean Time to Failure (MTTF) can be derived from the basic notion of failure rate. Consider a component that is operational at time $t = 0$ and remains operational until it is hit by a failure. Suppose now that all failures are permanent and irreparable. Let T denote the lifetime of the component (the time until it fails), and let $f(t)$ and $F(t)$ denote the probability density function of T and the cumulative distribution function of T, respectively. These functions are defined for $t \geqslant 0$ only (because the lifetime cannot be negative) and are related through

$$f(t) = \frac{\mathrm{d}F(t)}{\mathrm{d}t}, \qquad F(t) = \int_0^t f(\tau)\,\mathrm{d}\tau \tag{2.2}$$

$f(t)$ represents (but is not equal to) the momentary probability of failure at time t. To be exact, for a very small Δt, $f(t)\Delta t \approx \mathrm{Prob}\{t \leqslant T \leqslant t + \Delta t\}$. Being a density function, $f(t)$ must satisfy

$$f(t) \geqslant 0 \quad \text{for } t \geqslant 0 \quad \text{and} \quad \int_0^\infty f(t)\,\mathrm{d}t = 1$$

$F(t)$ is the probability that the component will fail at or before time t,

$$F(t) = \mathrm{Prob}\{T \leqslant t\}$$

$R(t)$, the reliability of a component (the probability that it will survive at least until time t), is given by

$$R(t) = \mathrm{Prob}\{T > t\} = 1 - F(t) \tag{2.3}$$

$f(t)$ represents the probability that a *new* component will fail at time t in the future. A more meaningful quantity is the probability that a good component of current age t will fail in the next instant of length $\mathrm{d}t$. This is a *conditional* probability, since we know that the component survived at least until time t. This conditional probability is represented by the *failure rate* (also called the *hazard rate*) of a component at time t, denoted by $\lambda(t)$, which can be calculated as follows:

$$\lambda(t) = \frac{f(t)}{1 - F(t)} \tag{2.4}$$

Since $\frac{dR(t)}{dt} = -f(t)$, we obtain

$$\lambda(t) = -\frac{1}{R(t)} \frac{dR(t)}{dt} \tag{2.5}$$

Certain types of components suffer no aging and have a failure rate that is constant over time, $\lambda(t) = \lambda$. In this case,

$$\frac{dR(t)}{dt} = -\lambda R(t)$$

and the solution of this differential equation (with $R(0) = 1$) is

$$R(t) = e^{-\lambda t} \tag{2.6}$$

Therefore, a constant failure rate implies that the lifetime T of the component has an exponential distribution, with a parameter that is equal to the constant failure rate λ

$$f(t) = \lambda e^{-\lambda t} \qquad F(t) = 1 - e^{-\lambda t} \qquad R(t) = e^{-\lambda t} \quad \text{for } t \geqslant 0$$

For an irreparable component, the MTTF is equal to its expected lifetime, $E[T]$ (where $E[\,]$ denotes the expectation or mean of a random variable)

$$\text{MTTF} = E[T] = \int_0^\infty t f(t)\, dt \tag{2.7}$$

Substituting $\frac{dR(t)}{dt} = -f(t)$ yields

$$\text{MTTF} = -\int_0^\infty t \frac{dR(t)}{dt}\, dt = -t R(t)\big|_0^\infty + \int_0^\infty R(t)\, dt = \int_0^\infty R(t)\, dt \tag{2.8}$$

(the term $-t R(t)$ is equal to zero when $t = 0$ and when $t = \infty$, since $R(\infty) = 0$).

For the case of a constant failure rate for which $R(t) = e^{-\lambda t}$,

$$\text{MTTF} = \int_0^\infty e^{-\lambda t}\, dt = \frac{1}{\lambda}$$

Although a constant failure rate is used in most calculations of reliability (mainly owing to the simplified derivations), there are cases for which this simplifying assumption is inappropriate, especially during the "infant mortality" and "wear-out" phases of a component's life (Figure 2.1). In such cases, the Weibull distribution is often used. This distribution has two parameters, λ and β, and has the following density function of the lifetime T of a component:

$$f(t) = \lambda \beta t^{\beta-1} e^{-\lambda t^{\beta}} \tag{2.9}$$

The corresponding failure rate is

$$\lambda(t) = \lambda \beta t^{\beta-1} \tag{2.10}$$

This failure rate is an increasing function of time for $\beta > 1$, is constant for $\beta = 1$, and is a decreasing function of time for $\beta < 1$. This makes it very flexible, and especially appropriate for the wear-out and infant mortality phases. The component reliability for a Weibull distribution is

$$R(t) = e^{-\lambda t^{\beta}} \tag{2.11}$$

and the MTTF of the component is

$$\text{MTTF} = \frac{\Gamma(\beta^{-1})}{\beta \lambda^{\beta^{-1}}} \tag{2.12}$$

where $\Gamma(x) = \int_0^\infty y^{x-1} e^{-y} \, dy$ is the Gamma function. The Gamma function is a generalization of the factorial function to real numbers, and satisfies

- $\Gamma(x) = (x-1)\Gamma(x-1)$ for $x > 1$;
- $\Gamma(0) = \Gamma(1) = 1$;
- $\Gamma(n) = (n-1)!$ for an integer n, $n = 1, 2, \ldots$.

Note that the Weibull distribution includes as a special case ($\beta = 1$) the exponential distribution with a constant failure rate λ.

With these preliminaries, we now turn to structures that consist of more than one component.

2.3 Canonical and Resilient Structures

In this section, we consider some canonical structures, out of which more complex structures can be constructed. We start with the basic series and parallel structures, continue with non-series/parallel ones, and then describe some of the many resilient structures that incorporate redundant components (next referred to as modules).

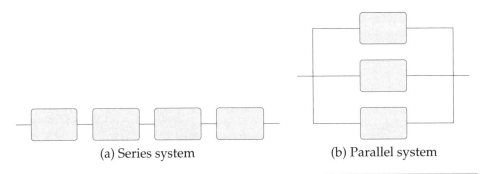

(a) Series system   (b) Parallel system

FIGURE 2.2   Series and parallel systems.

2.3.1 Series and Parallel Systems

The most basic structures are the series and parallel systems depicted in Figure 2.2. A *series system* is defined as a set of N modules connected together so that the failure of any one module causes the entire system to fail. Note that the diagram in Figure 2.2a is a reliability diagram and not always an electrical one; the output of the first module is not necessarily connected to the input of the second module. The four modules in this diagram can, for example, represent the instruction decode unit, execution unit, data cache, and instruction cache in a microprocessor. All four units must be fault-free for the microprocessor to function, although the way they are connected does not resemble a series system.

Assuming that the modules in Figure 2.2a fail independently of each other, the reliability of the entire series system is the product of the reliabilities of its N modules. Denoting by $R_i(t)$ the reliability of module i and by $R_s(t)$ the reliability of the whole system,

$$R_s(t) = \prod_{i=1}^{N} R_i(t) \tag{2.13}$$

If module i has a constant failure rate, denoted by λ_i, then, according to Equation 2.6, $R_i(t) = e^{-\lambda_i t}$, and consequently,

$$R_s(t) = e^{-\lambda_s t} \tag{2.14}$$

where $\lambda_s = \sum_{i=1}^{N} \lambda_i$. From Equation 2.14 we see that the series system has a constant failure rate equal to λ_s (the sum of the individual failure rates), and its MTTF is therefore $\mathrm{MTTF}_s = \frac{1}{\lambda_s}$.

A *parallel system* is defined as a set of N modules connected together so that it requires the failure of all the modules for the system to fail. This leads to the

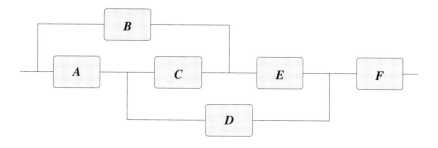

FIGURE 2.3   A non-series/parallel system.

following expression for the reliability of a parallel system, denoted by $R_p(t)$:

$$R_p(t) = 1 - \prod_{i=1}^{N} \left(1 - R_i(t)\right) \tag{2.15}$$

If module i has a constant failure rate λ_i, then

$$R_p(t) = 1 - \prod_{i=1}^{N} \left(1 - e^{-\lambda_i t}\right) \tag{2.16}$$

As an example, the reliability of a parallel system consisting of two modules with constant failure rates λ_1 and λ_2 is given by

$$R_p(t) = e^{-\lambda_1 t} + e^{-\lambda_2 t} - e^{-(\lambda_1 + \lambda_2)t}$$

Note that a parallel system does not have a constant failure rate; its failure rate decreases with each failure of a module. It can be shown that the MTTF of a parallel system with all its modules having the same failure rate λ is $\text{MTTF}_p = \sum_{k=1}^{N} \frac{1}{k\lambda}$.

2.3.2 Non-Series/Parallel Systems

Not all systems have a reliability diagram with a series/parallel structure. Figure 2.3 depicts a non-series/parallel system whose reliability cannot be calculated using either Equation 2.13 or 2.15. Each path in Figure 2.3 represents a configuration that allows the system to operate successfully. For example, the path ADF means that the system operates successfully if all three modules A, D and F are fault-free. A path in such reliability diagrams is valid only if all modules and edges are traversed from left to right. The path $BCDF$ in Figure 2.3 is thus invalid. No graph transformations that may result in violations of this rule are allowed.

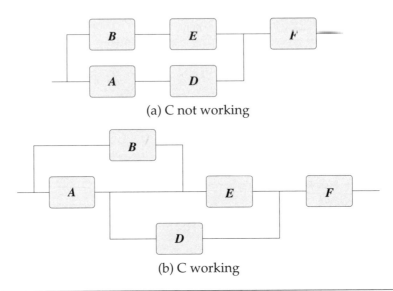

(a) C not working

(b) C working

FIGURE 2.4   Expanding the diagram in Figure 2.3 about module *C.*

In the following analysis, the dependence of the reliability on the time t is omitted for simplicity of notation, although it is implied that all reliabilities are functions of t.

We calculate the reliability of the non-series/parallel system in Figure 2.3 by expanding about a single module i. That is, we condition on whether or not module i is functional, and use the Total Probability formula.

$$R_{\text{system}} = R_i \cdot \text{Prob\{System works}|i \text{ is fault-free}\}$$

$$+ (1 - R_i) \cdot \text{Prob\{System works}|i \text{ is faulty}\} \qquad \textbf{(2.17)}$$

where, as before, R_i denotes the reliability of module i $(i = A, B, C, D, E, F)$. We can now draw two new diagrams. In the first, module i will be assumed to be working, and in the second, module i will be faulty. Module i is selected so that the two new diagrams are as close as possible to simple series/parallel structures for which we can then use Equations 2.13 and 2.15. Selecting module C in Figure 2.3 results in the two diagrams in Figure 2.4. The process of expanding is then repeated until the resulting diagrams are of the series/parallel type. Figure 2.4a is already of the series/parallel type, whereas Figure 2.4b needs further expansion about E. Note that Figure 2.4b should not be viewed as a parallel connection of A and B, connected serially to D and E in parallel; such a diagram will have the path $BCDF$, which is not a valid path in Figure 2.3. Based on Figure 2.4 we can write, using Equation 2.17,

$$R_{\text{system}} = R_C \cdot \text{Prob\{System works}|C \text{ is fault-free}\}$$

$$+ (1 - R_C)R_F \big[1 - (1 - R_A R_D)(1 - R_B R_E)\big] \qquad \textbf{(2.18)}$$

Expanding the diagram in Figure 2.4b about E yields

$$\text{Prob}\{\text{System works}|C \text{ is fault-free}\}$$
$$= R_E R_F \big[1 - (1 - R_A)(1 - R_B)\big] + (1 - R_E)R_A R_D R_F$$

Substituting this last expression in 2.18 results in

$$R_{\text{system}} = R_C \big[R_E R_F (R_A + R_B - R_A R_B) + (1 - R_E)R_A R_D R_F\big]$$
$$+ (1 - R_C)\big[R_F (R_A R_D + R_B R_E - R_A R_D R_B R_E)\big] \tag{2.19}$$

If $R_A = R_B = R_C = R_D = R_E = R_F = R$, then

$$R_{\text{system}} = R^3 \big(R^3 - 3R^2 + R + 2\big) \tag{2.20}$$

If the diagram of the non-series/parallel structure is too complicated to apply the above procedure, upper and lower bounds on R_{system} can be calculated instead.

An upper bound is given by

$$R_{\text{system}} \leqslant 1 - \prod (1 - R_{\text{path } i}) \tag{2.21}$$

where $R_{\text{path } i}$ is the reliability of the series connection of the modules along path i. The bound in Equation 2.21 assumes that all the paths are in parallel and that they are independent. In reality, two of these paths may have a module in common, and the failure of this module will result in both paths becoming faulty. That is why Equation 2.21 provides only an upper bound rather than an exact value. As an example, let us calculate the upper bound for Figure 2.3. The paths are ADF, BEF, and $ACEF$, resulting in

$$R_{\text{system}} \leqslant 1 - (1 - R_A R_D R_F)(1 - R_B R_E R_F)(1 - R_A R_C R_E R_F) \tag{2.22}$$

If $R_A = R_B = R_C = R_D = R_E = R_F = R$, then $R_{\text{system}} \leqslant R^3(R^7 - 2R^4 - R^3 + R + 2)$, which is less accurate than the exact calculation in Equation 2.20.

The upper bound can be used to derive the exact reliability, by performing the multiplication in Equation 2.22 (or Equation 2.21 in the general case) and replacing every occurrence of R_i^k by R_i. Since each module is used only once, its reliability should not be raised to any power greater than 1. The reader is invited to verify that applying this rule to the upper bound in Equation 2.22 yields the same exact reliability as in Equation 2.19.

A lower bound can be calculated based on minimal cut sets of the system diagram, where a minimal cut set is a minimal list of modules such that the removal (due to faults) of all modules from the set will cause a working system to fail. The lower bound is obtained by

$$R_{\text{system}} \geqslant \prod (1 - Q_{\text{cut } i}) \tag{2.23}$$

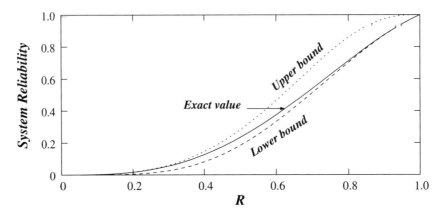

FIGURE 2.5   Comparing the exact reliability of the non-series/parallel system in Figure 2.3 to its upper and lower bounds.

where $Q_{\text{cut}\,i}$ is the probability that minimal cut i is faulty. In Figure 2.3, the minimal cut sets are F, AB, AE, DE, and BCD. Consequently,

$$R_{\text{system}} \geqslant R_F\big[1 - (1 - R_A)(1 - R_B)\big]\big[1 - (1 - R_A)(1 - R_E)\big]\big[1 - (1 - R_D)(1 - R_E)\big]$$
$$\times \big[1 - (1 - R_B)(1 - R_C)(1 - R_D)\big] \tag{2.24}$$

If $R_A = R_B = R_C = R_D = R_E = R_F = R$, then $R_{\text{system}} \geqslant R^5(24 - 60R + 62R^2 - 33R^3 + 9R^4 - R^5)$. Figure 2.5 compares the upper and lower bounds to the exact system reliability for the case in which all six modules have the same reliability R. Note that in this case, for the more likely high values of R, the lower bound provides a very good estimate for the system reliability.

2.3.3 *M*-of-*N* Systems

An M-of-N system is a system that consists of N modules and needs at least M of them for proper operation. Thus, the system fails when fewer than M modules are functional. The best-known example of this type of systems is the triplex, which consists of three identical modules whose outputs are voted on. This is a 2-of-3 system: so long as a majority (2 or 3) of the modules produce correct results, the system will be functional.

Let us now compute the reliability of an M-of-N system. We assume as before that the failures of the different modules are statistically independent and that there is no repair of failing modules. If $R(t)$ is the reliability of an individual module (the probability that the module is still operational at time t), the reliability of an M-of-N system is the probability that M or more modules are functional at

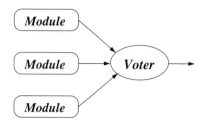

FIGURE 2.6   A Triple Modular Redundant (TMR) structure.

time t. The system reliability is therefore given by

$$R_{M\_of\_N}(t) = \sum_{i=M}^{N} \binom{N}{i} R^i(t)\big[1 - R(t)\big]^{N-i} \tag{2.25}$$

where $\binom{N}{i} = \frac{N!}{(N-i)!i!}$. The assumption that failures are independent is key to the high reliability of M-of-N systems. Even a slight extent of positively correlated failures can greatly diminish their reliability. For example, suppose q_{cor} is the probability that the entire system suffers a common failure. The reliability of the system now becomes

$$R^{cor}_{M\_of\_N}(t) = (1 - q_{cor}) \sum_{i=M}^{N} \binom{N}{i} R^i(t)\big[1 - R(t)\big]^{N-i} \tag{2.26}$$

If the system is not designed carefully, the correlated failure factor can dominate the overall failure probability.

In practice, correlated failure rates can be extremely difficult to estimate. In Equation 2.26, we assumed that there was a failure mode in which the entire cluster of N modules suffers a common failure. However, there are other modes as well, in which subsets of the N modules could undergo a correlated failure. There being $2^N - N - 1$ subsets containing two or more modules, it quickly becomes infeasible to obtain by experiment or otherwise the correlated failure probabilities associated with each of the subsets, even for moderate values of N.

Perhaps the most important M-of-N system is the *triplex*, or the Triple Modular Redundant (TMR) cluster shown in Figure 2.6. In such a system, $M = 2$ and $N = 3$, and a voter selects the majority output. If a single voter is used, that voter becomes a critical point of failure and the reliability of the cluster is

$$R_{TMR}(t) = R_{voter}(t) \sum_{i=2}^{3} \binom{3}{i} R^i(t)\big[1 - R(t)\big]^{3-i}$$

$$= R_{voter}(t)\big(3R^2(t)\big[1 - R(t)\big] + R^3(t)\big) = R_{voter}(t)\big(3R^2(t) - 2R^3(t)\big) \tag{2.27}$$

where $R_{voter}(t)$ is the reliability of the voter.

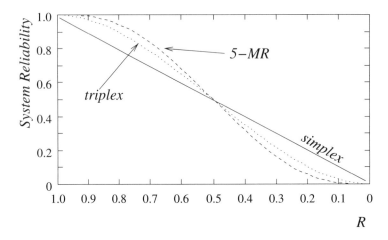

FIGURE 2.7   Comparing NMR reliability (for $N=3$ and 5) to that of a single module (voter failure rate is considered negligible).

The general case of TMR is called N-modular redundancy (NMR) and is an M-of-N cluster with N odd and $M = \lceil N/2 \rceil$.

In Figure 2.7, we plot the reliability of a simplex (a single module), a triplex (TMR), and an NMR cluster with $N = 5$. For high values of $R(t)$, the greater the redundancy, the higher the system reliability. As $R(t)$ decreases, the advantages of redundancy become less marked; until for $R(t) < 0.5$, redundancy actually becomes a disadvantage, with the simplex being more reliable than either of the redundant arrangements. This is also reflected in the value of MTTF_{TMR}, which (for $R_{\text{voter}}(t) = 1$ and $R(t) = e^{-\lambda t}$) can be calculated based on Equation 2.8 as

$$\text{MTTF}_{\text{TMR}} = \int_0^\infty \left(3R^2(t) - 2R^3(t)\right) dt = \int_0^\infty \left(3e^{-2\lambda t} - 2e^{-3\lambda t}\right) dt = \frac{5}{6\lambda}$$

$$< \frac{1}{\lambda} = \text{MTTF}_{\text{Simplex}}$$

In most applications, however, $R(t) \gg 0.5$ for realistic t and the system is repaired or replaced long before $R(t) < 0.5$, so a triplex arrangement does offer significant reliability gains.

Equation 2.27 was derived under the conservative assumption that every failure of the voter will lead to erroneous system output and that any failure of two modules is fatal. This is not necessarily the case. If, for example, one module has a permanent logical 1 on one of its outputs and a second module has a permanent logical 0 on its corresponding output, the TMR (or NMR) will still function properly. Clearly, a similar situation may arise regarding certain faults within the voter circuit. These are examples of compensating faults. Another case of faults that may be harmless are non-overlapping faults. For example, one module may have a faulty adder and another module a faulty multiplier. If the adder and multiplier circuits are disjoint, the two faulty modules are unlikely to generate wrong outputs simultaneously. If all compensating and non-overlapping faults are taken into account, the resulting reliability will be higher than that predicted by Equation 2.27.

2.3.4 Voters

A voter receives inputs $x_1, x_2, \ldots, x_N$ from an M-of-N cluster and generates a representative output. The simplest voter is one that does a bit-by-bit comparison of the outputs, and checks if a majority of the N inputs are identical. If so, it outputs the majority. This approach only works when we can guarantee that every functional module will generate an output that matches the output of every other functional module, bit by bit. This will be the case if the modules are identical processors, use identical inputs and identical software, and have mutually synchronized clocks.

If, however, the modules are different processors or are running different software for the same problem, it is possible for two correct outputs to diverge slightly, in the lower significant bits. Hence, we can declare two outputs x and y as practically identical if $|x - y| < \delta$ for some specified δ. (Note that "practically identical" is not transitive; if A is practically identical to B and B is practically identical to C, this does not necessarily mean that A is practically identical to C.)

For such approximate agreement, we can do *plurality* voting. A *k-plurality voter* looks for a set of at least k practically identical outputs (this is a set in which each member is practically identical to all other members) and picks any of them (or the median) as the representative. For example, if we set $\delta = 0.1$ and the five outputs were $1.10, 1.11, 1.32, 1.49, 3.00$, then the subset $\{1.10, 1.11\}$ would be selected by a 2-plurality voter.

In our discussion so far, we have implicitly assumed that each output has an equal chance of being faulty. In some cases that may not be true; the hardware (or software) producing one output may have a different failure probability than does the hardware (or software) producing another output. In this case, each output is assigned a weight that is related to its probability of being correct. The voter then does weighted voting and produces an output that is associated with over half the sum of all weights.

2.3.5 Variations on *N*-Modular Redundancy

Unit-Level Modular Redundancy

In addition to applying replication and voting at the level of the entire system, the same idea can be applied at the subsystem level as well. Figure 2.8 shows how triple-modular replication can be applied at the individual unit level for a system consisting of four units. In such a scheme, the voters are no longer as critical as in NMR. A single faulty voter will cause no more harm than a single faulty unit, and

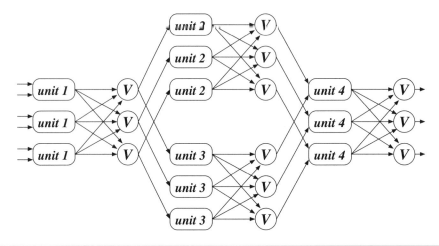

FIGURE 2.8   Subsystem-level TMR.

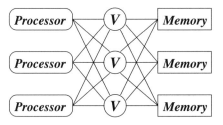

FIGURE 2.9   Triplicated voters in a processor/memory TMR.

the effect of either one will not propagate beyond the next level of units. Clearly, the level at which replication and voting are applied can be further lowered at the expense of additional voters, increasing the overall size and delay of the system.

Of particular interest is the triplicated processor/memory system shown in Figure 2.9. Here, all communications (in either direction) between the triplicated processors and triplicated memories go through majority voting. This organization is more reliable than a single majority voting of a triplicated processor/memory structure.

Dynamic Redundancy

The above variations of NMR employ considerable amounts of hardware in order to instantaneously mask errors that may occur during the operation of the system. However, in many applications, temporary erroneous results are acceptable as long as the system is capable of detecting such errors and reconfiguring itself by replacing the faulty module with a fault-free spare module. An example of such a dynamic (or active) redundancy scheme is depicted in Figure 2.10, in which the

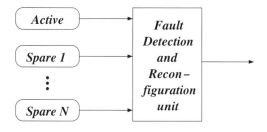

FIGURE 2.10 Dynamic redundancy.

system consists of one active module, N spare modules, and a *Fault Detection and Reconfiguration* unit that is assumed to be capable of detecting any erroneous output produced by the active module, disconnecting the faulty active module, and connecting instead a fault-free spare (if one exists).

Note that if all the spare modules are active (powered), we expect them to have the same failure rate as the single active module. This dynamic redundancy structure is, therefore, similar to the basic parallel system in Figure 2.2, and its reliability is given by

$$R_{\text{dynamic}}(t) = R_{\text{dru}}(t)\left(1 - \left[1 - R(t)\right]^{N+1}\right) \tag{2.28}$$

where $R(t)$ is the reliability of each module, and $R_{\text{dru}}(t)$ is the reliability of the detection and reconfiguration unit. If, however, the spare modules are not powered (in order to conserve energy), they may have a negligible failure rate when not in operation. Denoting by c the *coverage factor*, defined as the probability that the faulty active module will be correctly diagnosed and disconnected and a good spare will be successfully connected, we can derive the system reliability for very large N by arguing as follows.

Failures to the active module occur at rate λ. The probability that a given such failure cannot be recovered from is $1 - c$. Hence, the rate at which unrecoverable failures occur is $(1 - c)\lambda$. The probability that no unrecoverable failure occurs to the active processor over a duration t is therefore given by $e^{-(1-c)\lambda t}$; the reliability of the reconfiguration unit is given by $R_{\text{dru}}(t)$. We therefore have:

$$R_{\text{dynamic}}(t) = R_{\text{dru}}(t)e^{-(1-c)\lambda t} \tag{2.29}$$

Hybrid Redundancy

An NMR system is capable of masking permanent and intermittent failures, but as we have seen, its reliability drops below that of a single module for very long mission times if no repair or replacement are taking place. The objective of hybrid redundancy is to overcome this by adding spare modules that will be used to replace active modules once they become faulty. Figure 2.11 depicts a hybrid system consisting of a core of N processors constituting an NMR, and a set of K spares. The outputs of the active primary modules are compared (by the *Compare*

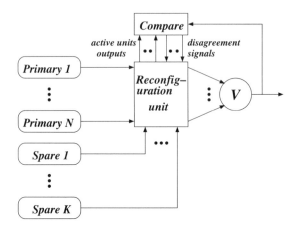

FIGURE 2.11   Hybrid redundancy.

unit) to the output of the voter to identify a faulty primary (if any). The *Compare* unit then generates the corresponding disagreement signal, which will cause the *Reconfiguration unit* to disconnect the faulty primary and connect a spare module instead.

The reliability of a hybrid system with a TMR core and K spares is

$$R_{\text{hybrid}}(t) = R_{\text{voter}}(t)R_{\text{rec}}(t)\big(1 - mR(t)\big[1 - R(t)\big]^{m-1} - \big[1 - R(t)\big]^m\big) \tag{2.30}$$

where $m = K + 3$ is the total number of modules, and $R_{\text{voter}}(t)$ and $R_{\text{rec}}(t)$ are the reliability of the voter and the comparison and reconfiguration circuitry, respectively. Equation 2.30 assumes that any fault in either the voter or the comparison and reconfiguration circuit will cause a system failure. In practice, not all faults in these circuits are fatal, and the reliability of the hybrid system will be higher than what is predicted by Equation 2.30. A more accurate value of $R_{\text{hybrid}}(t)$ can be obtained through a detailed analysis of the voter and the comparison and reconfiguration circuits and the different ways in which they can fail.

Sift-Out Modular Redundancy

As in NMR, all N modules in the *Sift-out Modular Redundancy* scheme (see Figure 2.12) are active, and the system is operational as long as there are at least two fault-free modules. Unlike NMR, this system uses comparator, detector, and collector circuits instead of a majority voter. The comparator compares the outputs of all pairs of modules, so that $E_{ij} = 1$ if the outputs of modules i and j do not match. Based on these signals, the detector determines which modules are faulty and generates the logical outputs $F_1, F_2, \ldots, F_N$, where $F_i = 1$ if module i has been determined to be faulty and 0 otherwise. Finally, the collector unit produces the system output, which is the OR of the outputs of all fault-free modules. This way, a

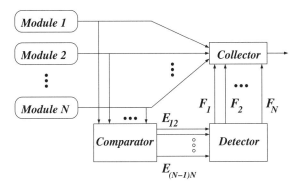

FIGURE 2.12 Sift-out structure.

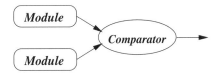

FIGURE 2.13 Duplex system.

module whose output disagrees with the outputs of the other modules is switched out and no longer contributes to the system output. The implementation of this scheme is simpler than that of hybrid redundancy.

Care must be taken, however, not to be too aggressive in the purging (sifting-out) process. The vast majority of failures tend to be transient and disappear on their own after some time. It is preferable, therefore, to only purge a module if it produces incorrect outputs over a sustained interval of time.

2.3.6 Duplex Systems

A duplex system is the simplest example of module redundancy. Figure 2.13 shows an example of a duplex system consisting of two processors and a comparator. Both processors execute the same task, and if the comparator finds that their outputs are in agreement, the result is assumed to be correct. The implicit assumption here is that it is highly unlikely for both processors to suffer identical hardware failures that result in their both producing identical wrong results. If, on the other hand, the results are different, there is a fault, and higher-level software has to decide how it is to be handled.

The fact that the two processors disagree does not, by itself, allow us to identify the failed processor. This can be done using one of several methods, some of which we will consider below. To derive the reliability of the duplex system we denote, as before, by c the *coverage factor*, which is the probability that a faulty processor will be correctly diagnosed, identified, and disconnected.

Assuming that the two processors are identical, each with a reliability $R(t)$, the reliability of the duplex system is

$$R_{\text{duplex}}(t) = R_{\text{comp}}(t)\big(R^2(t) + 2cR(t)[1 - R(t)]\big) \tag{2.31}$$

where R_{comp} is the reliability of the comparator. Assuming a fixed failure rate of λ for each processor and an ideal comparator ($R_{\text{comp}}(t) = 1$), the MTTF of the duplex system is

$$\text{MTTF}_{\text{duplex}} = \frac{1}{2\lambda} + \frac{c}{\lambda}$$

The main difference between a duplex and a TMR system is that in a duplex, the faulty processor must be identified. We discuss next the various ways in which this can be done.

Acceptance Tests

The first method for identifying the faulty processor is to carry out a check of each processor's output and is known as an *acceptance test*. One example of an acceptance test is a *range test*, which checks if the output is in the expected range. This is a basic and simple test, which usually works very well. For example, if the output of a processor is supposed to indicate the predicted pressure in a container (for gases or liquids), we would know the range of pressures that the container can hold. Any output outside those values results in the output being flagged as faulty. We are therefore using semantic information of the task to predict which values of output indicate an error.

The question is now how to determine the range of acceptable values. The narrower this range, the greater the probability that an incorrect output will be identified as such but so is the probability that a correct output will be misidentified as erroneous. We define the *sensitivity* of a test as the conditional probability that the test detects an error given that the output is actually erroneous, and the *specificity* of a test as the conditional probability that the output is erroneous, given that the acceptance test declares an error. A narrow range acceptance test will have high *sensitivity* but low *specificity*, which means that the test is very likely not to miss an erroneous output but at the same time it is likely to get many false-positive results (correct results that the test declares faulty).

The reverse happens when we make this range very wide: then we have low sensitivity but high specificity. We will consider this problem again when we discuss recovery block approaches to software fault tolerance in Chapter 5.

Range tests are the simplest, but by no means the only, acceptance test mechanism. Any other test that can discriminate reasonably accurately between a correct and an incorrect output can be used. For instance, suppose we want to check the correctness of a square-root operation; since $(\sqrt{x})^2 = x$, we can square the output and check if it is the same as the input (or sufficiently close, depending on the level of precision used).

Hardware Testing

The second method of identifying the failed processor is to subject both processors to some hardware/logic test routines. Such diagnostic tests are regularly used to verify that the processor circuitry is functioning properly, but running them can identify the processor that produced the erroneous output only if a permanent fault is present in that processor. Since most hardware faults are transient, hardware testing has a low probability of identifying the processor that failed to produce the correct output.

Even if the hardware fault is permanent, running hardware tests does not guarantee that the fault will be detected. In practice, hardware tests are never perfect, and there is a non-zero probability that the test passes as good a processor which is actually faulty. The test sensitivity, or the probability of the test identifying a faulty processor as such, is in the case of hardware tests often called the *test coverage*.

Forward Recovery

A third method for identifying the faulty processor in a duplex is to use a third processor to repeat the computations carried out by the duplex. If only one of the three processors (the duplex plus this new processor) is faulty, then whichever processor the third disagrees with is the faulty one.

It is also possible to use a combination of these methods. The acceptance test is the quickest to run but is often the least sensitive. The result of the acceptance test can be used as a provisional indication of which processor is faulty, and this can be confirmed by using either of the other two approaches.

Pair-and-Spare System

Several more complicated resilient structures have been proposed that use the duplex as their building block. The first such system that we describe is the pair-and-spare system (see Figure 2.14), in which modules are grouped in pairs, and each pair has a comparator that checks if the two outputs are equal (or sufficiently close). If the outputs of the two primary modules do not match, this indicates an error in at least one of them but does not indicate which one is in error. Running diagnostic tests, as described in the previous section, will result in a disruption in service. To avoid such a disruption, the entire pair is disconnected and the computation is transferred to a spare pair. The two members of the switched-out pair can now be tested offline to determine whether the error was due to a transient or permanent fault. In the case of a transient fault, the pair can eventually be marked as a good spare.

Triplex–Duplex System

Another duplex-based structure is the triplex–duplex system. Here, processors are tied together to form duplexes, and then, a triplex is formed out of these duplexes. When the processors in a duplex disagree, both of them are switched out of

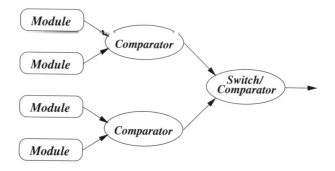

FIGURE 2.14   A pair-and-spare structure consisting of two duplexes.

the system. The triplex–duplex arrangement allows for the error masking of voting combined with a simpler identification of faulty processors. Furthermore, the triplex can continue to function even if only one duplex is left functional, because the duplex arrangement allows the detection of faults. Deriving the reliability of a triplex–duplex system is reasonably simple and is left for the reader as an exercise.

2.4   Other Reliability Evaluation Techniques

Most of the structures that we have described so far have been simple enough to allow reliability derivations using straightforward, and relatively simple, combinatorial arguments. Analysis of more complex resilient structures requires more advanced reliability evaluation techniques, some of which are described next.

2.4.1 Poisson Processes

Consider non-deterministic events of some sort, occurring over time with the following probabilistic behavior:

For a time interval of very short length Δt,

1. The probability of one event occurring during the interval Δt is, for some constant λ, $\lambda \Delta t$ plus terms of order Δt^2.

2. The probability of more than one event occurring during Δt is negligible (of the order of Δt^2).

3. The probability of no events occurring during the interval Δt is $1 - \lambda \Delta t$ plus terms of order Δt^2.

Let $N(t)$ denote the number of events occurring in an interval of length t, and let $P_k(t) = \text{Prob}\{N(t) = k\}$ be the probability of exactly k events occurring during an interval of length t ($k = 0, 1, 2, \ldots$). Based on (1)–(3), we have

$$P_k(t + \Delta t) \approx P_{k-1}(t) \lambda \Delta t + P_k(t)(1 - \lambda \Delta t) \quad \text{(for } k = 1, 2, \ldots)$$

and

$$P_0(t + \Delta t) \approx P_0(t)(1 - \lambda \Delta t)$$

These approximations become more accurate as $\Delta t \to 0$, and lead to the differential equations:

$$\frac{\mathrm{d} P_k(t)}{\mathrm{d} t} = \lambda P_{k-1}(t) - \lambda P_k(t) \quad \text{(for } k = 1, 2, \ldots)$$

and

$$\frac{\mathrm{d} P_0(t)}{\mathrm{d} t} = -\lambda P_0(t)$$

Using the initial condition $P_0(0) = 1$, the solution to this set of differential equations is

$$P_k(t) = \text{Prob}\{N(t) = k\} = e^{-\lambda t} \frac{(\lambda t)^k}{k!} \quad \text{(for } k = 0, 1, 2, \ldots)$$

A process $N(t)$ with this probability distribution is called a Poisson process with rate λ. A Poisson process with rate λ has the following properties:

1. The expected number of events occurring in an interval of length t is λt.

2. The length of time between consecutive events is an exponentially distributed random variable with parameter λ and mean value $1/\lambda$.

3. The numbers of events occurring in disjoint intervals of time are independent of one another.

4. The sum of two independent Poisson processes with rates λ_1 and λ_2 is itself a Poisson process with rate $\lambda_1 + \lambda_2$.

As an example for the use of the Poisson process we consider a duplex system, consisting of two active identical processors with an unlimited number of spares. The two active processors are subject to failures occurring at a constant rate of λ per processor. The spares, however, are assumed to always be functional (they have a negligible failure rate so long as they are not active).

When a failure occurs in an active processor, it must be detected and a new processor inducted into the duplex to replace the one that just failed. As before, we define the coverage factor c as the probability of successful detection and induction. We, however, assume for simplicity that the comparator failure rate is negligible and that the induction process of a new processor is instantaneous.

Let us now calculate the reliability of this duplex system over the time interval $[0, t]$. We first concentrate on the failure process in one of the two processors. When a processor fails (due to a permanent fault), it is diagnosed and replaced instantaneously. Due to the constant failure rate λ, the time between two consecutive failures of the same processor is exponentially distributed with parameter λ. This implies that $N(t)$, the number of failures that occur in this one processor during the time interval $[0, t]$, is a Poisson process with the rate λ.

Since the duplex has two active processors, the number of failures that occur in the duplex is the sum of the numbers of failures of the two processors, and hence, it is also a Poisson process (denoted by $M(t)$) with rate 2λ. The probability that k failures occur in the duplex over an interval of duration t is thus

$$\text{Prob}\{k \text{ failures in duplex}\} = \text{Prob}\{M(t) = k\} = e^{-2\lambda t} \frac{(2\lambda t)^k}{k!} \qquad (2.32)$$

For the duplex system not to fail, each of these failures must be detected and the processor successfully replaced. The probability of one such success is the coverage factor c, and the probability that the system will survive k failures is c^k. The reliability of the duplex over the interval $[0, t]$ is therefore

$$R_{\text{duplex}}(t) = \sum_{k=0}^{\infty} \text{Prob}\{k \text{ failures in duplex}\} \cdot c^k = \sum_{k=0}^{\infty} e^{-2\lambda t} \frac{(2\lambda t)^k c^k}{k!}$$

$$= e^{-2\lambda t} \sum_{k=0}^{\infty} \frac{(2\lambda t c)^k}{k!} = e^{-2\lambda t} e^{2\lambda t c}$$

$$= e^{-2\lambda(1-c)t} \qquad (2.33)$$

In our derivation, we have used the fact that

$$e^x = 1 + x + \frac{x^2}{2!} + \cdots = \sum_{k=0}^{\infty} \frac{x^k}{k!}$$

We could have obtained the expression in 2.33 more directly using the type of reasoning we employed in the analysis of hybrid redundancy. To reiterate, the steps are as follows:

1. Individual processors fail at a rate λ, and so processor failures occur in the duplex at the rate 2λ.

2. Each processor failure has a probability c of being successfully dealt with, and a probability $1 - c$ of causing failure to the duplex.

3. As a result, failures that crash the duplex occur with rate $2\lambda(1 - c)$.

4. The reliability of the system is thus $e^{-2\lambda(1-c)t}$.

Similar derivations can be made for *M*-of-*N* systems in which failing processors are identified and replaced from an infinite pool of spares. This is left for the reader as an exercise. The extension to the case with only a finite set of spares is simple: the summation in the reliability expression is capped at that number of spares, rather than going to infinity.

2.4.2 Markov Models

In complex systems in which constant failure rates are assumed but combinatorial arguments are insufficient for analyzing the reliability of the system, we can use *Markov models* for deriving expressions for the system reliability. In addition, Markov models provide a structured approach for the derivation of reliabilities of systems that may include coverage factors and a repair process.

A *Markov chain* is a special type of a stochastic process. In general, a stochastic process $X(t)$ is an infinite number of random variables, indexed by time t. Consider now a stochastic process $X(t)$ that must take values from a set (called the *state space*) of discrete quantities, say the integers $0, 1, 2, \ldots$. The process $X(t)$ is called a *Markov chain* if

$$\text{Prob}\{X(t_n) = j \mid X(t_0) = i_0, X(t_1) = i_1, \ldots, X(t_{n-1}) = i_{n-1}\} = \text{Prob}\{X(t_n) = j \mid X(t_{n-1}) = i_{n-1}\}$$

for every $t_0 < t_1 < \cdots < t_{n-1} < t_n$

If $X(t) = i$ for some t and i, we say that the chain is in state i at time t. We will deal only with continuous time, discrete state Markov chains, for which the time t is continuous ($0 \leqslant t < \infty$) but the state $X(t)$ is discrete and integer valued. For convenience, we will use as states the integers $0, 1, 2, \ldots$. The Markov property implies that in order to predict the future trajectory of a Markov chain, it is sufficient to know its present state. This freedom from the need to store the entire history of the process is of great practical importance: it makes the problem of analyzing Markovian stochastic processes tractable in many cases.

The probabilistic behavior of a Markov chain can be described as follows. Once it moves into some state i, it stays there for a length of time that has an exponential distribution with parameter λ_i. This implies a constant *rate* λ_i of leaving state i. The probability that, when leaving state i, the chain will move to state j (with $j \neq i$) is denoted by p_{ij} ($\sum_{j \neq i} p_{ij} = 1$). The rate of transition from state i to state j is thus $\lambda_{ij} = p_{ij} \lambda_i$ ($\sum_{j \neq i} \lambda_{ij} = \lambda_i$).

We denote by $P_i(t)$ the probability that the process will be in state i at time t, given it started at some initial state i_0 at time 0. Based on the above notations, we can derive a set of differential equations for $P_i(t)$ ($i = 0, 1, 2, \ldots$).

For a given time instant t, a given state i, and a very small interval of time Δt, the chain can be in state i at time $t + \Delta t$ in one of the following cases:

1. It was in state i at time t and has not moved during the time interval Δt. This event has a probability of $P_i(t)(1 - \lambda_i \Delta t)$ plus terms of order Δt^2.

2. It was at some other state j at time t ($j \neq i$) and moved from j to i during the interval Δt. This event has a probability of $P_j(t)\lambda_{ji}\Delta t$ plus terms of order Δt^2.

The probability of more than one transition during Δt is negligible (of order Δt^2) if Δt is small enough. Therefore, for small Δt,

$$P_i(t + \Delta t) \approx P_i(t)(1 - \lambda_i \Delta t) + \sum_{j \neq i} P_j(t)\lambda_{ji}\Delta t$$

Again, this approximation becomes more accurate as $\Delta t \to 0$, and results in

$$\frac{dP_i(t)}{dt} = -\lambda_i P_i(t) + \sum_{j \neq i} \lambda_{ji} P_j(t)$$

and, since $\lambda_i = \sum_{j \neq i} \lambda_{ij}$,

$$\frac{dP_i(t)}{dt} = -\sum_{j \neq i} \lambda_{ij} P_i(t) + \sum_{j \neq i} \lambda_{ji} P_j(t)$$

This set of differential equations (for $i = 0, 1, 2, \ldots$) can now be solved, using the initial conditions $P_{i_0}(0) = 1$ and $P_j(0) = 0$ for $j \neq i_0$ (since i_0 is the initial state).

Consider, for example, a duplex system that has a single active processor and a single standby spare that is connected only when a fault has been detected in the active unit. Let λ be the fixed failure rate of each of the processors (when active) and let c be the coverage factor. The corresponding Markov chain is shown in Figure 2.15. Note that because the integers assigned to the different states are arbitrary, we can assign them in such a way that they are meaningful and thus easier to remember. In this example, the state represents the number of good processors (0, 1, or 2, with the initial state being 2 good processors). The differential equations describing this Markov chain are:

$$\frac{dP_2(t)}{dt} = -\lambda P_2(t)$$

$$\frac{dP_1(t)}{dt} = \lambda c P_2(t) - \lambda P_1(t)$$

$$\frac{dP_0(t)}{dt} = \lambda(1 - c)P_2(t) + \lambda P_1(t) \tag{2.34}$$

Solving 2.34 with the initial conditions $P_2(0) = 1$, $P_1(0) = P_0(0) = 0$ yields

$$P_2(t) = e^{-\lambda t} \qquad P_1(t) = c\lambda t e^{-\lambda t} \qquad P_0(t) = 1 - P_1(t) - P_2(t)$$

and as a result,

$$R_{\text{system}}(t) = 1 - P_0(t) = P_2(t) + P_1(t) = e^{-\lambda t} + c\lambda t e^{-\lambda t} \tag{2.35}$$

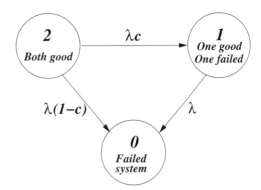

FIGURE 2.15 The Markov model for the duplex system with an inactive spare.

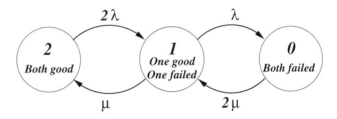

FIGURE 2.16 The Markov model for a duplex system with repair.

This expression can also be derived based on combinatorial arguments. The derivation is left to the reader as an exercise.

Our next example of a duplex system that can be analyzed using a Markov model is a system with two active processors, each with a constant failure rate of λ and a constant repair rate of μ. The Markov model for this system is depicted in Figure 2.16.

As in the previous example, the state is the number of good processors. The differential equations describing this Markov chain are

$$\frac{dP_2(t)}{dt} = -2\lambda P_2(t) + \mu P_1(t)$$

$$\frac{dP_1(t)}{dt} = 2\lambda P_2(t) + 2\mu P_0(t) - (\lambda + \mu)P_1(t)$$

$$\frac{dP_0(t)}{dt} = \lambda P_1(t) - 2\mu P_0(t) \tag{2.36}$$

Solving 2.36 with the initial conditions $P_2(0) = 1$, $P_1(0) = P_0(0) = 0$ yields

$$P_2(t) = \frac{\mu^2}{(\lambda + \mu)^2} + \frac{2\lambda\mu}{(\lambda + \mu)^2}e^{-(\lambda+\mu)t} + \frac{\lambda^2}{(\lambda + \mu)^2}e^{-2(\lambda+\mu)t}$$

$$P_1(t) = \frac{2\lambda\mu}{(\lambda+\mu)^2} + \frac{2\lambda(\lambda-\mu)}{(\lambda+\mu)^2}e^{-(\lambda+\mu)t} + \frac{2\lambda^2}{(\lambda+\mu)^2}e^{-2(\lambda+\mu)t}$$

$$P_0(t) = 1 - P_1(t) - P_2(t) \tag{2.37}$$

Note that we solve only for $P_1(t)$ and $P_2(t)$; using the boundary condition that the probabilities must sum up to 1 (for every t) gives us $P_0(t)$ and reduces by one the number of differential equations to be solved.

Note also that this system does not fail completely; it is not operational while at state 0 but is then repaired and goes back into operation. For a system with repair, calculating the availability is more meaningful than calculating the reliability. The (point) availability, or the probability that the system is operational at time t, is

$$A(t) = P_1(t) + P_2(t)$$

The reliability $R(t)$, on the other hand, is the probability that the system never enters state 0 at any time during $[0,t]$ and cannot be obtained out of the above expressions. To obtain this probability, we must modify the Markov chain slightly by removing the transition out of state 0, so that state 0 becomes an *absorbing* state. This way, the probability of ever entering the state in the interval $[0,t]$ is reduced to the probability of being in state 0 at time t. This probability can be found by writing out the differential equations for this new Markov chain, solving them, and calculating the reliability as $R(t) = 1 - P_0(t)$.

Since in most applications processors are repaired when they become faulty, the long-run availability of the system, A, is a more relevant measure than the reliability. To this end, we need to calculate the long-run probabilities, $P_2(\infty)$, $P_1(\infty)$, and $P_0(\infty)$. These can be obtained either from Equation 2.37 by letting t approach ∞ or from Equation 2.36 by setting all the derivatives $\frac{dP_i(t)}{dt}$ ($i = 0, 1, 2$) to 0 and using the relationship $P_2(\infty) + P_1(\infty) + P_0(\infty) = 1$. The availability in the long-run, A, is then

$$A = P_2(\infty) + P_1(\infty) = \frac{\mu^2}{(\lambda+\mu)^2} + \frac{2\lambda\mu}{(\lambda+\mu)^2} = \frac{\mu(\mu+2\lambda)}{(\lambda+\mu)^2} = 1 - \left(\frac{\lambda}{\lambda+\mu}\right)^2$$

2.5   Fault-Tolerance Processor-Level Techniques

All the resilient structures described so far can be applied to a wide range of modules, from very simple combinatorial logic modules to the most complex microprocessors or even complete processor boards. Still, duplicating complete processors that are not used for critical applications introduces a prohibitively large overhead and is not justified. For such cases, simpler techniques with much smaller overheads have been developed. These techniques rely on the fact that processors execute stored programs and upon an error, the program (or part of it) can be re-executed as long as the following two conditions are satisfied: the error is

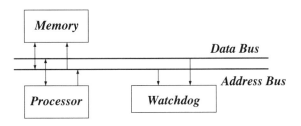

FIGURE 2.17   Error detection using a watchdog processor.

detected, and the cause of the error is a short-lived transient fault that will most likely disappear before the program is re-executed.

The simplest technique of this type mandates executing every program twice and using the results only if the outcomes of the two executions match. This *time redundancy* approach will clearly reduce the performance of the computer by as much as 50%.

The above technique does not require any means for error detection. If a mechanism (and suitable circuitry) is provided to detect errors during the execution of an instruction, then that instruction can be re-executed, preferably after a certain delay to allow the transient fault to disappear. Such an *instruction retry* has a considerably lower performance overhead than the brute force re-execution of the entire program.

A different technique for low-cost concurrent error detection without relying on time redundancy is through the use of a small and simple processor that will monitor the behavior of the main processor. Such a monitoring processor is called a *watchdog processor* and is described next.

2.5.1 Watchdog Processor

A watchdog processor (see Figure 2.17) performs concurrent system-level error detection by monitoring the system buses connecting the processor and the memory. This monitoring primarily targets control flow checking, verifying that the main processor is executing the correct blocks of code and in the right order. Such monitoring can detect hardware faults and software faults (mistakes/bugs) that cause either an erroneous instruction(s) to be executed or a wrong program path to be taken.

To perform the monitoring of the control flow, the watchdog processor must be provided with information regarding the program(s) that are to be checked. This information is used to verify the correctness of the program(s) execution by the main processor in real-time. The information that is provided to the watchdog processor is derived from the Control Flow Graph (CFG), which represents the control flow of the program to be executed by the main processor (see an example of a five-node CFG in Figure 2.18a). A node in this graph represents a block of branch-free instructions; no branches are allowed from and into the block. An

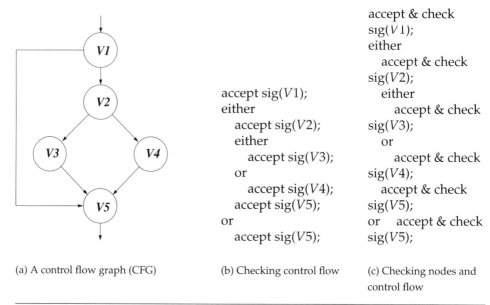

(a) A control flow graph (CFG)

(b) Checking control flow

```
accept sig(V1);
either
    accept sig(V2);
    either
        accept sig(V3);
    or
        accept sig(V4);
    accept sig(V5);
or
    accept sig(V5);
```

(c) Checking nodes and control flow

```
accept & check
sig(V1);
either
    accept & check
    sig(V2);
    either
        accept & check
        sig(V3);
    or
        accept & check
        sig(V4);
    accept & check
    sig(V5);
or  accept & check
    sig(V5);
```

FIGURE 2.18   A control flow graph (a) and the corresponding watchdog check programs for assigned signatures (b) and for calculated signatures (c).

edge represents a permissible flow of control, often corresponding to a branch instruction. Labels (called *signatures*) are assigned to the nodes of the CFG and are stored in the watchdog processor. During the execution of the program, run-time signatures of the executed blocks are generated and compared with the reference ones stored in the watchdog processor. If a discrepancy is detected, an error signal is generated.

The signatures of the nodes in the CFG can be either assigned or calculated. Assigned signatures can simply be successive integers that are stored in the watchdog processor along with the CFG. During execution, the signatures of the currently executed nodes are forwarded to the watchdog processor by the main processor. The watchdog processor can then verify that the path taken by the program corresponds to a valid path of the given CFG. The program that the watchdog processor will execute for the CFG in Figure 2.18a is shown in Figure 2.18b, where sig(*Vi*) is the signature assigned to node *Vi*. This check program will detect an invalid program path such as {V1, V4}. Note, however, that an error in one or more instructions within a node will not be detected by this scheme.

To increase the error detection capabilities of the watchdog processor and allow it to detect errors in individual instructions, calculated signatures can be used instead of assigned ones. For a given node, a signature can be calculated from the instructions included in the node by adding (modulo 2) all the instructions in the node or using a checksum (see Chapter 3) or another similar code. As before, these signatures are stored in the watchdog processor and then compared with the run-time signatures calculated by the watchdog processor while monitoring the instructions executed by the main processor. The program that the watchdog processor will execute for the CFG in Figure 2.18a with calculated signatures is shown in Figure 2.18c.

Note that most data errors will not be detected by the watchdog processor, since the majority of such errors will not cause the program to change its execution path. The functionality of the watchdog processor can, in principle, be extended to cover a larger portion of data errors by including *assertions* in the program executed by the watchdog processor. Assertions are reasonableness checks that verify expected relationships among the variables of the program and, as such, are a generalization of acceptance tests. These assertions must be prepared by the application programmer and could be made part of the application software rather than delegated to the watchdog processor. The performance benefits of having the watchdog processor rather than the main processor check the assertions may be offset by the need to frequently forward the values of the relevant application variables from the main processor to the watchdog processor. In addition, the design of the watchdog processor becomes more complicated since it needs now to be capable of executing arithmetic and logical operations that would otherwise not be required. If assertions are not used, then the watchdog processor must be supplemented by other error-detection techniques (e.g., parity codes described in Chapter 3) to cover data errors.

One of the quoted advantages of using a watchdog processor for error detection is that the checking circuitry is independent of the checked circuitry, thus providing protection against common or correlated errors. Such a protection can also be achieved in duplex structures through the use of design diversity; for example, implementing one of the processors in complementary logic or simply using processors from different manufacturers. Separation between the watchdog processor and the main processor is becoming harder to achieve in current high-end microprocessors in which simple monitoring of the processor-memory bus is insufficient to determine which instructions will eventually be executed and which have been fetched speculatively and will be aborted. Furthermore, the current trend to support simultaneous multithreading greatly increases the complexity of designing a watchdog processor. A different technique for concurrent error checking for a processor supporting simultaneous multithreading is described next.

2.5.2 Simultaneous Multithreading for Fault Tolerance

We start this section with a brief overview of simultaneous multithreading. For a more detailed description, the reader is invited to consult any good book on computer architecture.

High-end processors today improve speed by exploiting both pipelining and parallelism. Parallelism is facilitated by having multiple functional units, with the attempt to overlap the execution of as many instructions as possible. However, because of data and control dependencies, most programs have severe limits on how much parallelism can actually be uncovered within each thread of execution. Indeed, a study of some benchmarks found that on average only about 1.5 instructions can be overlapped. Therefore, most of the time the majority of the functional units will be idle. It is to remedy this problem that the approach of simultaneous multithreading (SMT) was born.

The key idea behind SMT is the following. If data and control dependencies limit the amount of parallelism that can be extracted out of individual threads, allow the processor to execute multiple threads *simultaneously*. Note that we are not talking about rapid context switches to swap processes in and out: instructions from *multiple* threads are being executed at the same time (in the same clock cycle). To support such increased functionality, the architecture must be augmented suitably. A program counter register is needed for each of the threads that the system is simultaneously executing. If the instruction set specifies a k-register architecture and we want to execute n threads simultaneously, at least nk physical registers are needed (so that there is one k-register set for each of the n threads). These are just the externally-visible registers: most high-end architectures have a larger number of internal registers that are not "visible" to the instruction set to facilitate register renaming and thereby improve performance. Unlike the nk architectural registers, the internal renaming registers are shared by all simultaneously executing threads, which also share a common issue queue. A suitable policy must be implemented for fetching and issuing instructions and for assigning internal registers and other resources so that no thread is starved.

How is this different from just running the workload on a multiprocessor consisting of n traditional processors? The answer lies in the way the resources can be assigned. In the traditional multiprocessor, each processor will be running an individual thread, which will have access to just the functional units and rename registers associated with that processor. In the SMT, we have a set of threads that have access to a pool of functional units and rename registers. The usage of these entities will depend on the available parallelism within each thread at the moment; it can change with time, as the resource requirements and inherent parallelism levels change in each simultaneously executing thread.

To take advantage of the multithreading capability for fault-detection purposes, *two* independent threads are created for every thread that the application wants to run. These threads execute identical code, and care is taken to ensure that they receive exactly the same inputs. If all is well, they must both produce the same output: a divergence in output signals a fault, and appropriate steps must be taken for recovery. The idea is to provide almost the same amount of protection against transient faults as can be obtained from a traditional approach that runs a total of two copies of the program independently.

To reduce the performance penalty of re-execution, the second execution of the program always trails the first. Call these two executions the leading and the trailing copies of the program, respectively. The advantage of doing this is that information can be passed from the leading to the trailing copy to make the trailing

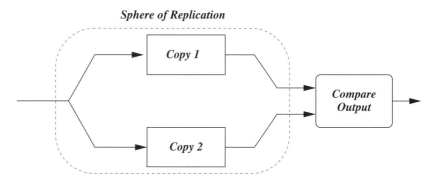

FIGURE 2.19 Sphere of replication.

copy run faster and consume less computational resources. For example, the leading copy can tell the trailing copy the outcome of conditional branches so that the trailer never makes an incorrect branch guess, or the leading copy can make loading faster for the trailer.

To support the two independent but identical threads, two different sets of several hardware components must be assigned to these threads. For example, two sets of the architectural registers must be used so that a fault in a register being used by one thread will have no impact on the execution of the other thread.

This leads to the concept of the *sphere of replication*. Items that are replicated for the two threads are said to be within this sphere; items that are not replicated are outside. Data flows across the surface of this sphere (see Figure 2.19). Items that are replicated use such redundancy as a means for fault tolerance and are within the sphere of replication; items that are not must use some other means (such as error-correcting codes) to protect against the impact of faults. We can decide what items fall within the sphere of replication based on the cost or overhead that they entail and the effectiveness with which other fault-tolerance techniques can protect them should they be kept outside it. For example, providing two copies of the instruction and data caches may be too expensive, and so, one can rely instead on error-correcting codes to protect their contents.

2.6 Byzantine Failures

We have so far classified failures according to their temporal behavior: are they permanent or do they go away after some time? We will now introduce another important classification, based on how the failed unit behaves.

It is usually assumed that when a unit fails, it goes dead. The picture many people have in their minds is that of a lightbulb, which fails by burning out. If all devices behaved that way when they failed, dealing with failures would be relatively simple. However, devices in general, and processors in particular, can suffer

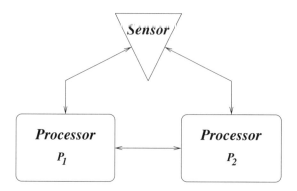

FIGURE 2.20   Network for Byzantine example.

malicious failures in which they produce arbitrary outputs. Such failures are known as *Byzantine* failures, and are described below. These failures cause no problem in an *M*-of-*N* system with voting since the voter acts as a centralizing entity, masking out the erroneous outputs. However, when processors are used in a truly distributed way without such a centralizing entity, Byzantine failures can cause subtle problems.

To see this, consider the following example. A sensor is providing temperature information to two processors through point-to-point links between them (see Figure 2.20). The sensor has suffered a Byzantine failure and tells processor P_1 that the temperature is 25° while telling P_2 that it is 45°. Now, is there any way in which P_1 and P_2 can figure out that the sensor is faulty? The best they can do is to exchange the messages they have received from the sensor: P_1 tells P_2 that it got 25°, and P_2 tells P_1 that it got 45°. At this point, both processors know that something is wrong in the system, but neither can figure out which unit is malfunctioning. As far as P_1 is concerned, the input it received from the sensor contradicts the input from P_2; however, it has no way of knowing whether it is the sensor or P_2 that is faulty. P_2 has a similar problem. No number of additional communications between P_1 and P_2 can solve this problem.

This is known as the *Byzantine Generals* problem, since an early paper in this field used as a model a general communicating his attack plans to his lieutenants by messengers. A traitorous commander could send contradictory messages to his lieutenants, or one or more of the lieutenants could be disloyal and misrepresent the commander's orders and get some divisions to attack and others to retreat. The objective is to get all the loyal lieutenants to agree on the commander's order. If the commanding general is loyal, the order the loyal lieutenants agree on must be the order that the commander sent. Traitorous officers can lie about the order they received.

The solution to this problem is the Byzantine Generals algorithm (also known as the Interactive Consistency algorithm). The model is that of a single entity (such as a sensor or processor) disseminating the value of some variable to a set of receivers. The receivers can communicate among themselves to exchange information about the value they received from the original source. If a unit is functional, it will be truthful in all its messages; a faulty unit may behave arbitrarily. This arbitrary behavior includes the possibility of sending out contradictory messages. All communications are time-bounded, i.e., the absence of a message can be detected by a time-out mechanism. The goal of the algorithm is to satisfy the following *interactive consistency* conditions:

IC1. All functional (non-faulty) units must arrive at an agreement of the value that was transmitted by the original source.

IC2. If the original source is functional, the value they agree on must be the value that was sent out by the original source.

There are many algorithms to solve the Byzantine Generals problem. We will present here the original algorithm, because it is the simplest. More recent algorithms are referenced in the Further Reading section.

The algorithm is recursive. Let there be N units in all (one original source and $N - 1$ receivers), of which up to m may be faulty. It is possible to show that interactive consistency can only be obtained when $N \geqslant 3m + 1$. If $N \leqslant 3m$, no algorithm can be constructed that satisfies the interactive consistency conditions.

The algorithm $Byz(N,m)$ consists of the following three steps:

Step 1. The original source disseminates the information to each of the $N - 1$ receivers.

Step 2. If $m > 0$, each of the $N - 1$ receivers now acts as an original source to disseminate the value that it received in the previous step. To do this, each receiver runs the $Byz(N - 1, m - 1)$ algorithm, and sends out its received value to the other $N - 2$ receivers. If a unit does not get a message from another unit, it assumes the default message was sent and so enters the default into its records. If $m = 0$, this step is bypassed.

Step 3. At the end of the preceding step, each receiver has a vector, containing the agreed values received (a) from the original source, and (b) from each of the other receivers (if $m > 0$). If $m > 0$, each receiver takes a vote over the values contained in its vector, and this is used as the value that was transmitted by the original source. If no majority exists, a default value is used. If $m = 0$, the receiver simply uses the value it received from the original source.

Note that we assume that all units have a timer available to them and a timeout mechanism to detect the absence (or loss) of a message. Otherwise, a faulty node could cause the entire system to be suspended indefinitely by remaining silent.

Let us consider some examples of this algorithm. We will use the following notations:

■ If A and B are units, then $A.B(n)$ means that A sent B the message n.

- If U is a string of units $A_1, A_2, \ldots, A_m$, and B is a unit, then $U.B(n)$ means that B received the message n from A_m who claims to have received it from A_{m-1} and so on.

- A message that is not sent is denoted by φ. For example, $A.B(\varphi)$ means that the message that A was supposed to send B was never sent.

For example, $A.B.C(n)$ represents the fact that B told C that the value it received from A was n. Similarly, $A.B.C.D(n)$ means that D received the message n from C who claims to have received it from B who, in turn, claims to have received it from A. The string of units thus represents a chain along which the given message, n, has passed. For example, Black.White.Green(341) means that Green received the message 341 from White who claims to have received it from Black.

EXAMPLE

Consider the degenerate case of the algorithm when $m = 0$, i.e., no fault tolerance is provided. In such a case, step 2 is bypassed, and the interactive consistency vector consists of a single value: the one that has been received from the original source. ■

EXAMPLE

Consider now the case where $m = 1$. We must have at least $3m + 1 = 4$ units participating in this algorithm. Our model in this example consists of a sensor, S, and three receivers, R_1, R_2, and R_3. Suppose the sensor is faulty and sends out inconsistent messages to the receivers: $S.R_1(1)$, $S.R_2(1)$, $S.R_3(0)$. All the receivers are functional, and the default is assumed to be 1.

In the second step of the algorithm, R_1, R_2, and R_3 each acts as the source for the message it received from the sensor and runs $Byz(3,0)$ on it. That is, the following messages are sent:

$$
\begin{array}{ll}
S.R_1.R_2(1) & S.R_1.R_3(1) \\
S.R_2.R_1(1) & S.R_2.R_3(1) \\
S.R_3.R_1(0) & S.R_3.R_2(0)
\end{array}
$$

Define an Interactive Consistency Vector (ICV) at receiver R_i as $(x_1^i, x_2^i, \ldots, x_{N-1}^i)$, where

$$
x_j^i = \begin{cases} \text{Report of } R_j \text{ as determined by } R_i & \text{if } i \neq j \\ \text{Value received from the original source} & \text{if } i = j \end{cases}
$$

At the end of this step, the ICVs are each $(1,1,0)$ at every receiver. Taking the majority vote over this yields 1, which is the value used by each of them. ■

■ EXAMPLE

Let $N = 7, m = 2$, but this time let receivers R_1 and R_6 be faulty and the other units (S, R_2, R_3, R_4, R_5) be functional. The messages sent out in the first round by S are consistent: $S.R_1(1)$, $S.R_2(1)$, $S.R_3(1)$, $S.R_4(1)$, $S.R_5(1)$, and $S.R_6(1)$. Each of the receivers now executes $Byz(6, 1)$ in step 2 of the $Byz(7, 2)$ algorithm. Consider R_1 first. This unit is faulty and can send out any message it likes (or even nothing at all). Suppose it sends out the following messages in step 1 of the $Byz(6, 1)$ algorithm for all receivers to agree on its value:

$$S.R_1.R_2(1) \quad S.R_1.R_3(2) \quad S.R_1.R_4(3) \quad S.R_1.R_5(4) \quad S.R_1.R_6(0)$$

In step 2 of this $Byz(6, 1)$ algorithm, each of the remaining receivers $(R_2, R_3, R_4, R_5, R_6)$ uses the $Byz(5, 0)$ algorithm to disseminate the message it received from R_1. The following are the messages:

$$
\begin{array}{llll}
S.R_1.R_2.R_3(1) & S.R_1.R_2.R_4(1) & S.R_1.R_2.R_5(1) & S.R_1.R_2.R_6(1) \\
S.R_1.R_3.R_2(2) & S.R_1.R_3.R_4(2) & S.R_1.R_3.R_5(2) & S.R_1.R_3.R_6(2) \\
S.R_1.R_4.R_2(3) & S.R_1.R_4.R_3(3) & S.R_1.R_4.R_5(3) & S.R_1.R_4.R_6(3) \\
S.R_1.R_5.R_2(4) & S.R_1.R_5.R_3(4) & S.R_1.R_5.R_4(4) & S.R_1.R_5.R_6(4) \\
S.R_1.R_6.R_2(1) & S.R_1.R_6.R_3(8) & S.R_1.R_6.R_4(0) & S.R_1.R_6.R_5(\varphi)
\end{array}
$$

Note that R_6 being maliciously faulty is free to send out anything it likes. The ICVs maintained at each of the receivers in connection with the $S.R_1(1)$ message are:

$$\text{ICV}_{S.R_1}(R_2) = (1, 2, 3, 4, 1)$$

$$\text{ICV}_{S.R_1}(R_3) = (1, 2, 3, 4, 8)$$

$$\text{ICV}_{S.R_1}(R_4) = (1, 2, 3, 4, 0)$$

$$\text{ICV}_{S.R_1}(R_5) = (1, 2, 3, 4, 0)$$

$\text{ICV}_{S.R_1}(R_6)$ is irrelevant, since R_6 is faulty. Also, note that since R_5 received nothing from R_6, its value is recorded as the default, say 0.

When R_2, R_3, R_4, and R_5 examine their ICVs, they find no majority and therefore assume the default value for $S.R_1$. This default is zero, and so each of these receivers records that the message that S sent R_1 is agreed to be 0.

Similarly, agreement can be reached on the message that S sent to each of the other receivers (the reader is encouraged to write out the messages). This completes the generation of the ICVs connected with the original $Byz(7, 2)$ algorithm. ■

Let us now prove that algorithm Byz does indeed satisfy the Interactive Consistency conditions, IC1 and IC2 if $N \geqslant 3m + 1$. We proceed by induction on m. The induction hypothesis is that the theorem holds for all $m \leqslant M$ for some $M \geqslant 0$. We now consider two cases.

Case 1. The original source is non-faulty.

We show by induction that whenever the original source is nonfaulty, algorithm $Byz(N, m)$ satisfies IC2 if there are more than $2k + m$ nodes and at most k faulty elements. The proof is by induction on m. Assume the result holds for all $m \leqslant M$ and consider the case $m = M + 1$.

In the first step, the original source sends out its message to each of the other processors. Since the source is nonfaulty, all processors receive consistent messages.

In the second step, each processor runs $Byz(N - 1, m - 1)$ to disseminate the message it received from the original source. Since $N > 2k + m$, we have $N - 1 > 2k + m - 1$. Hence, by the induction hypothesis, executing $Byz(N - 1, m - 1)$ is sufficient to permit all correct processors to disseminate the messages they received.

Now, set $k = m$. Since there are at most m faulty elements, a majority of the processors is functional. Hence, the majority vote on the values disseminated will result in a consistent value being produced by each correct processor.

Case 2. The original source is faulty.

If the original source is faulty, at most $m - 1$ other processors can be faulty.

In step 1, the original source can send out any message it likes to each of the other processors. There are $N - 1 \geqslant 3(m - 1) + 1$ other processors. Hence, when these processors run $Byz(N - 1, m - 1)$ among the $N - 1$ other processors, by the induction hypothesis, each processor will have consistent entries in its ICV for each of them. The only entry in the ICV that can differ is that corresponding to the original source. Therefore, when the majority function is applied to each ICV, the result is the same, and the proof is completed.

We have shown that $N \geqslant 3m + 1$ is a sufficient condition for Byzantine agreement. We did this by construction, i.e., by presenting an algorithm that achieved consistency under these conditions. It also turns out that this condition is necessary. That is, under the condition of two-party messages and arbitrary failures, it is impossible for *any* algorithm to guarantee that conditions IC1 and IC2 will be met if $N < 3m$.

2.6.1 Byzantine Agreement with Message Authentication

The Byzantine Generals problem is hard because faulty processors could lie about the message they received. Let us now remove this possibility by providing some mechanism to *authenticate* the messages. That is, suppose each processor can append to its messages an unforgeable signature. Before forwarding a message, a processor appends its own signature to the message it received. The recipient can check the authenticity of each signature. Thus, if a processor receives a message that has been forwarded through processors A and B, it can check to see whether the signatures of A and B have been appended to the message and if they are valid. Once again, we assume that all processors have timers so that they can time out any (faulty) processor that remains silent.

In such a case, maintaining interactive consistency becomes very easy. Here is an algorithm that does so:

Algorithm. $AByz(N, m)$

Step A1. The original source signs its message ψ and sends it out to each of the processors.

Step A2. Each processor i that receives a signed message $\psi : A$, where A is the set of signatures appended to the message ψ, checks the number of signatures in A. If this number is less than $m + 1$, it sends out $\psi : A \cup \{i\}$ (i.e., what it received plus its own signature) to each of the processors not in set A. It also adds this message, ψ, to its list of received messages.

Step A3: When a processor has seen the signatures of every other processor (or has timed out), it applies some decision function to select from among the messages it has received.

Let us now show that the algorithm maintains Byzantine agreement for any number of processors. Clearly, if $N \leqslant m + 2$, the problem becomes trivial.

As before, we consider two cases.

Case 1. The original source is functional.

In such a case, an identical signed message (say, μ) is transmitted by the original source to every processor in the system. Since nobody can forge the original source's signature, no processor will accept any message other than μ in step A2 (any corruption of a message will, by definition, be detected). As a result, it will correctly select μ as the message disseminated by the original source.

Case 2. The original source is faulty.

In this case, different messages may be sent out to different processors, each with the original source's correct signature. We now show that the list of received messages (minus the signatures) is the same at each nonfaulty processor.

Let us proceed by contradiction. Suppose this is not true, and in particular, the sets at nonfaulty processors i and j (call them Ψ_i and Ψ_j) are different. Let ψ_1 be a message in Ψ_i but not in Ψ_j.

Since processor i did not pass on ψ_1 to processor j, ψ_1 must have had at least $m + 1$ signatures appended to it. Let ℓ be one of these signatures. When processor ℓ received ψ_1, j's signature was not appended to ψ_1, and the list of signatures would have been less than $m + 1$ long. Hence, processor ℓ would have forwarded the message to j, and so $\psi_1 \in \Psi_j$, establishing the desired contradiction.

2.7   Further Reading

An excellent introduction to the basics of hardware fault tolerance can be found in [24]. Some basic definitions can be found in [2]. Hardware failure rate models are described in [27]. The topic of hardware/logic circuits testing is covered in many textbooks, e.g., [1,8].

Readers who are weak in probability theory may have found some of the reliability derivations difficult to understand. A very readable source for the mathematical background associated with such probabilistic calculations is [26]. The textbook [6] is quite dated, but is still very useful as a detailed and advanced introduction to reliability models. [10] contains a description of reliability models in addition to a guide to statistical methods.

One approach to representing the dependence of overall system reliability on the health of individual modules is *fault trees*. For details, see [5,29].

Voting techniques have been the focus of some work in the literature: a good comprehensive reference is [14] with more recent work reported in [3,7,19]. Compensating faults in NMR structures were introduced in [23] and an analysis of hybrid redundancy with compensating faults appears in [12]. The sift-out modular redundancy is described in [25].

Various techniques for processor error checking by watchdog processors have been described in the literature. An excellent survey with an extensive list of references appears in [16]. The capabilities of watchdog processors were extended to include checking of memory accesses in [18]. Other signatures generation schemes for checking the program control flow based on the use of M-of-N codes (see Chapter 3), have been described in [28]. The exploitation of multithreading techniques for fault tolerance is discussed in [17,22,30].

There is an extensive bibliography on Byzantine Generals algorithms. See, for example, [9,11,13,15,20]. A good survey can be found in [4].

2.8   Exercises

1. The lifetime (measured in years) of a processor is exponentially distributed, with a mean lifetime of 2 years. You are told that a processor failed sometime in the interval [4, 8] years. Given this information, what is the conditional probability that it failed before it was 5 years old?

2. The lifetime of a processor (measured in years) follows the Weibull distribution, with parameters $\lambda = 0.5$ and $\beta = 0.6$.

   a. What is the probability that it will fail in its first year of operation?

   b. Suppose it is still functional after $t = 6$ years of operation. What is the conditional probability that it will fail in the next year?

   c. Repeat parts a and b for $\beta = 2$.

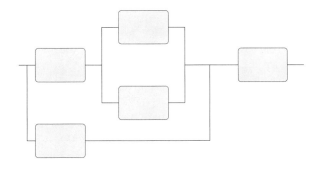

FIGURE 2.21 A 5-module series-parallel system.

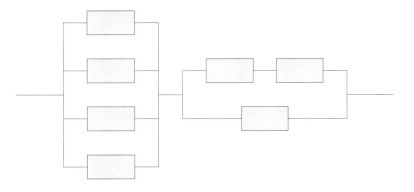

FIGURE 2.22 A 7-module series-parallel system.

    d. Repeat parts a and b for $\beta = 1$.

3. To get a feel for the failure rates associated with the Weibull distribution, plot them for the following parameter values as a function of the time, t:

    a. Fix $\lambda = 1$ and plot the failure rate curves for $\beta = 0.5, 1.0, 1.5$.

    b. Fix $\beta = 1.5$ and plot the failure rate curves for $\lambda = 1, 2, 5$.

4. Write the expression for the reliability $R_{\text{system}}(t)$ of the series/parallel system shown in Figure 2.21, assuming that each of the five modules has a reliability of $R(t)$.

5. The lifetime of each of the seven blocks in Figure 2.22 is exponentially distributed with parameter λ. Derive an expression for the reliability function of the system, $R_{\text{system}}(t)$, and plot it over the range $t = [0, 100]$ for $\lambda = 0.02$.

6. Consider a triplex that produces a 1-bit output. Failures that cause the output of a processor to be permanently stuck at 0 or stuck at 1 occur at constant rates λ_0 and λ_1, respectively. The voter never fails. At time t, you carry out a calculation the correct output of which should be 0. What is the probability that the triplex will produce an incorrect result? (Assume that stuck-at faults are the only ones that a processor can suffer from, and that these are permanent faults; once a processor has its output stuck at some logic value, it remains stuck at that value forever).

7. Write the expression for the reliability of a 5MR system and calculate its MTTF. Assume that failures occur as a Poisson process with rate λ per node, that failures are independent and permanent, and that the voter is failure-free.

8. Consider an NMR system that produces an eight-bit output. $N = 2m + 1$ for some m. Each processor fails at a constant rate λ and the failures are permanent. A failed processor produces any of the 2^8 possible outputs with equal probability. A majority voter is used to produce the overall output, and the voter is assumed never to fail. What is the probability that, at time t, a majority of the processors produce the same incorrect output after executing some program?

9. Design a majority voter circuit out of two- and three-input logic gates. Assume that you are voting on 1-bit inputs.

10. Derive an expression for the reliability of the voter you designed in the previous question. Assume that, for a given time t, the output of each gate is stuck-at-0 or stuck-at-1 with probability P_0 and P_1, respectively (and is fault-free with probability $1 - P_0 - P_1$). What is the probability that the output of your voter circuit is stuck-at-0 (stuck-at-1) given that the three inputs to the voter are fault-free and do change between 000 and 111?

11. Show that the MTTF of a parallel system of N modules, each of which suffers permanent failures at a rate λ, is $\text{MTTF}_p = \sum_{k=1}^{N} \frac{1}{k\lambda}$.

12. Consider a system consisting of two subsystems in series. For improved reliability, you can build subsystem i as a parallel system with k_i units, for $i = 1, 2$. Suppose permanent failures occur at a constant rate λ per unit.

    a. Derive an expression for the reliability of this system.

    b. Obtain an expression for the MTTF of this system with $k_1 = 2$ and $k_2 = 3$.

13. List the conditions under which the processor/memory TMR configuration shown in Figure 2.9 will fail, and compare them to a straightforward TMR configuration with three units, in which each unit consists of a processor and a memory. Denote by R_p, R_m, and R_v the reliability of a processor, a memory, and a voter, respectively, and write expressions for the reliability of the two TMR configurations.

14. Write expressions for the upper and lower bounds and the exact reliability of the following non-series/parallel system shown in Figure 2.23 (denote by $R_i(t)$ the reliability of module i). Assume that D is a bidirectional unit.

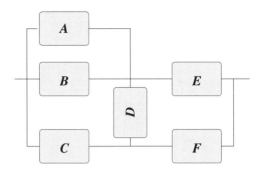

FIGURE 2.23 A 6-module non-series/parallel system.

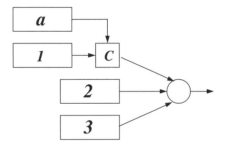

FIGURE 2.24 A TMR with a spare.

15. The system shown in Figure 2.24 consists of a TMR core with a single spare a that can serve as a spare only for module 1. Assume that modules 1 and a are active. When either of the two modules 1 or a fails, the failure is detected by the perfect comparator C, and the single operational module is used to provide an input to the voter.

a. Assuming that the voter is perfect as well, which one of the following expressions for the system reliability is correct (where each module has a reliability R and the modules are independent).

1. $R_{\text{system}} - R^4 + 4R^3(1 - R) + 3R^2(1 - R)^2$

2. $R_{\text{system}} = R^4 + 4R^3(1 - R) + 4R^2(1 - R)^2$

3. $R_{\text{system}} = R^4 + 4R^3(1 - R) + 5R^2(1 - R)^2$

4. $R_{\text{system}} = R^4 + 4R^3(1 - R) + 6R^2(1 - R)^2$

   b. Write an expression for the reliability of the system if instead of a perfect comparator for modules 1 and a, there is a coverage factor c (c is the probability that a failure in one module is detected, the faulty module is correctly identified, and the operational module is successfully connected to the voter that is still perfect).

16. A duplex system consists of two active units and a comparator. Assume that each unit has a failure rate of λ and a repair rate of μ. The outputs of the two active units are compared, and when a mismatch is detected, a procedure to locate the faulty unit is performed. The probability that upon a failure, the faulty unit is correctly identified and the fault-free unit (and consequently, the system) continues to run properly is the coverage factor c. Note that when a coverage failure occurs, the entire system fails and both units have to be repaired (at a rate μ each). When the repair of one unit is complete, the system becomes operational and the repair of the second unit continues, allowing the system to return to its original state.

   a. Show the Markov model for this duplex system.

   b. Derive an expression for the long-term availability of the system assuming that $\mu = 2\lambda$.

17. **a.** Your manager in the Reliability and Quality Department asked you to verify her calculation of the reliability of a certain system. The equation that she derived is

$$R_{\text{system}} = R_C\left[1 - (1 - R_A)(1 - R_B)\right]\left[1 - (1 - R_D)(1 - R_E)\right]$$
$$+ (1 - R_C)\left[1 - (1 - R_A R_D)(1 - R_B R_E)\right]$$

   However, she lost the system diagram. Can you draw the diagram based on the expression above?

   b. Write expressions for the upper and lower bounds on the reliability of the system and calculate these values and the exact reliability for the case $R_A = R_B = R_C = R_D = R_E = R = 0.9$.

18. A duplex system consists of a switching circuit and two computing units: an active unit with a failure rate of λ_1 and a standby idle unit that has a lower failure rate $\lambda_2 < \lambda_1$ while idle. The switching circuit frequently tests the active unit, and when a fault is detected, the faulty unit is switched out, and the second unit is switched in and becomes fully operational with a failure rate λ_1. The probability that upon a failure, the fault is correctly detected and the fault-free idle unit resumes the computation successfully is denoted by c (the coverage factor). Note that when a coverage failure occurs, the entire system fails.

   a. Show the Markov model for this duplex system (hint: three states are sufficient).

b. Write the differential equations for the Markov model and derive an expression for the reliability of the system.

19. You have a processor susceptible only to transient failures which occur at a rate of λ per second. The lifetime of a transient fault (measured in seconds) is exponentially distributed with parameter μ. Your fault-tolerance mechanism consists of running each task twice on this processor, with the second execution starting τ seconds after the first. The executions take s seconds each ($\tau > s$). Find the probability that the output of the first execution is correct, but that of the second execution is incorrect.

References

[1] M. Abramovici, M. A. Breuer, and A. D. Friedman, *Digital Systems Testing and Testable Design*, revised edition, IEEE Computer Society Press, 1995.

[2] A. Avizienis, J.-C. Laprie, and B. Randell, "Dependability and its Threats—A Taxonomy," *IFIP Congress Topical Sessions*, pp. 91–120, August 2004.

[3] D. E. Bakken, Z. Zhan, C. C. Jones, and D. A. Karr, "Middleware Support for Voting and Data Fusion," *International Conference on Dependable Systems and Networks*, pp. 453–462, June–July 2001.

[4] M. Barborak, M. Malek, and A. Dahbura, "The Consensus Problem in Fault-Tolerant Computing," *ACM Computing Surveys*, Vol. 25, pp. 171–220, June 1993.

[5] R. E. Barlow, *Reliability and Fault Tree Analysis*, Society for Industrial and Applied Mathematics, 1982.

[6] R. E. Barlow and F. Proschan, *Mathematical Theory of Reliability*, Society of Industrial and Applied Mathematics, 1996.

[7] D. M. Blough and G. F. Sullivan, "Voting Using Predispositions," *IEEE Transactions on Reliability*, Vol. 43, pp. 604–616, December 1994.

[8] M. L. Bushnell and V. D. Agrawal, *Essentials of Electronic Testing for Digital, Memory, and Mixed-Signal VLSI Circuits*, Kluwer Academic Publishers, 2000.

[9] D. Dolev, "The Byzantine Generals Strike Again," *Journal of Algorithms*, Vol. 3, pp. 14–30, 1982.

[10] C. E. Ebeling, *An Introduction to Reliability and Maintainability Engineering*, McGraw-Hill, 1997.

[11] M. J. Fischer and N. A. Lynch, "A Lower Bound for the Time to Assure Interactive Consistency," *Information Processing Letters*, Vol. 14, pp. 183–186, June 1982.

[12] I. Koren and E. Shalev, "Reliability Analysis of Hybrid Redundancy Systems," *IEE Proceedings on Computer and Digital Techniques*, Vol. 131, pp. 31–36, January 1984.

[13] L. Lamport, R. Shostak, and M. Pease, "The Byzantine Generals Algorithm," *ACM Transactions on Programming Languages and Systems*, Vol. 4, pp. 382–401, July 1982.

[14] P. R. Lorczak, A. K. Caglayan, and D. E. Eckhardt, "A Theoretical Investigation of Generalized Voters for Redundant Systems," *Nineteenth Fault Tolerant Computing Symposium*, pp. 444–451, 1989.

[15] N. A. Lynch, M. J. Fischer, and R. J. Fowler, "A Simple and Efficient Byzantine Generals Algorithm," *Second Symposium on Reliability in Distributed Software and Database Systems*, pp. 46–52, July 1982.

[16] A. Mahmood and E. J. McCluskey, "Concurrent Error Detection using Watchdog Processors—A Survey," *IEEE Transactions on Computers*, Vol. 37, pp. 160–174, February 1988.

[17] S. S. Mukherjee, M. Kontz, and S. K. Reinhardt, "Detailed Design and Evaluation of Redundant Multithreading Alternatives," *International Symposium on Computer Architecture*, pp. 99–110, 2002.

[18] M. Namjoo and E. J. McCluskey, "Watchdog Processors and Capability Checking," *12th International Symposium on Fault Tolerant Computing*, pp. 245–248, 1982.

[19] B. Parhami, "Voting Algorithms," *IEEE Transactions on Reliability*, Vol. 43, pp. 617–629, December 1994.

[20] M. Pease, R. Shostak, and L. Lamport, "Reaching Agreement in the Presence of Faults," *Journal of the ACM*, Vol. 27, pp. 228–234, April 1980.

[21] S. K. Reinhardt and S. S. Mukherjee, "Transient Fault Detection via Simultaneous Multithreading," *International Symposium on Computer Architecture*, pp. 25–36, 2000.

[22] E. Rotenberg, "AR-SMT: A Microarchitectural Approach to Fault Tolerance in Microprocessors," *Fault-Tolerant Computing Systems Symposium*, pp. 84–91, 1999.

[23] D. P. Siewiorek, "Reliability Modeling of Compensating Module Failures in Majority Voting Redundancy," *IEEE Transactions on Computers*, Vol. C-24, pp. 525–533, May 1975.

[24] D. P. Siewiorek and R. S. Swarz, *Reliable Computer Systems: Design and Evaluation*, A. K. Peters, 1998.

[25] P. T. de Sousa and F. P Mathur, "Sift-out Modular Redundancy," *IEEE Transactions on Computers*, Vol. C-27, pp. 624–627, July 1978.

[26] K. S. Trivedi, *Probability and Statistics with Reliability, Queuing, and Computer Science Applications*, John Wiley, 2002.

[27] U.S. Department of Defense, *Military Standardization Handbook: Reliability Prediction of Electronic Equipment*, MIL-HDBK-217E, 1986.

[28] S. Upadhyaya and B. Ramamurthy, "Concurrent Process Monitoring with No Reference Signatures," *IEEE Transactions on Computers*, Vol. 43, pp. 475–480, April 1994.

[29] W. E. Vesely, *Fault Tree Handbook*, Nuclear Regulatory Commission, 1987.

[30] T. N. Vijaykumar, I. Pomeranz, and K. Cheng, "Transient-Fault Recovery Using Simultaneous Multithreading," *International Symposium on Computer Architecture*, pp. 87–98, 2002.

Information Redundancy

Errors in data may occur when the data are being transferred from one unit to another, from one system to another, or even while the data are stored in a memory unit. To tolerate such errors, we introduce redundancy into the data: this is called *information redundancy*. The most common form of information redundancy is *coding*, which adds check bits to the data, allowing us to verify the correctness of the data before using it and, in some cases, even allowing the correction of the erroneous data bits. Several commonly used error-detecting and error-correcting codes are discussed in Section 3.1.

Introducing information redundancy through coding is not limited to the level of individual data words but can be extended to provide fault tolerance for larger data structures. The best-known example of such a use is the Redundant Array of Independent Disks (RAID) storage system. Various RAID organizations are presented in Section 3.2, and the resulting improvements in reliability and availability are analyzed.

In a distributed system where the same data sets may be needed by different nodes in the system, data replication may help with data accessibility. Keeping a copy of the data on just a single node could cause this node to become a performance bottleneck and leave the data vulnerable to the failure of that node. An alternative approach would be to keep identical copies of the data on multiple nodes. Several schemes for managing the replicated copies of the same data are presented in Section 3.3.

We conclude this chapter with a description of *algorithm-based fault tolerance* which can be an efficient information redundancy technique for applications that process large arrays of data elements.

3.1 Coding

Coding is an established area of research and practice, especially in the communication field, and many textbooks on this topic are available (see the Further Reading section). Here, we limit ourselves to a brief survey of the more common codes.

When coding, a d-bit data word is encoded into a c-bit *codeword*, which consists of a larger number of bits than the original data word, i.e., $c > d$. This encoding introduces information redundancy, that is, we use more bits than absolutely needed. A consequence of this information redundancy is that not all 2^c binary combinations of the c bits are valid codewords. As a result, when attempting to *decode* the c-bit word to extract the original d data bits, we may encounter an invalid codeword and this will indicate that an error has occurred. For certain encoding schemes, some types of errors can even be corrected and not just detected.

A code is defined as the set of all permissible codewords. Key performance parameters of a code are the number of erroneous bits that can be detected as erroneous, and the number of errors that can be corrected. The overhead imposed by the code is measured in terms of both the additional bits that are required and the time needed to encode and decode.

An important metric of the space of codewords is the *Hamming distance*. The Hamming distance between two codewords is the number of bit positions in which the two words differ. Figure 3.1 shows the eight 3-bit binary words. Two words in this figure are connected by an edge if their Hamming distance is 1. The words 101 and 011 differ in two bit positions and have, therefore, a Hamming distance of 2; one has to traverse two edges in Figure 3.1 to get from node 101 to node 011. Suppose two valid codewords differ in only the least significant bit position, for example, 101 and 100. In this case, a single error in the least significant bit in

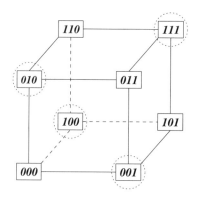

FIGURE 3.1   Hamming distances in the 3-bit word space.

either one of these two codewords will go undetected, since the erroneous word is also an existing codeword. In contrast, a Hamming distance of two (or more) between two codewords guarantees that a single-bit error in any of the two words will not change it into the other.

The *code distance* is the minimum Hamming distance between any two valid codewords. The code that consists of the four codewords {001, 010, 100, 111}, marked by circles in Figure 3.1, has a distance of 2 and is, therefore, capable of detecting any single-bit error. The code that consists only of the codewords {000, 111} has a distance of 3 and is, therefore, capable of detecting any single- or double-bit error. If double-bit errors are not likely to happen, this code can be used to *correct* any single-bit error. In general, to detect up to k-bit errors, the code distance must be at least $k + 1$, whereas to correct up to k-bit errors, the code distance must be at least $2k + 1$. The code {000, 111} can be used to encode a single data bit with 0 (for example) encoded as 000 and 1 as 111. This code is similar to the TMR redundancy technique, which was discussed in Chapter 2. In principle, many redundancy techniques can be considered as coding schemes. A duplex, for example, can be considered as a code whose valid codewords consist of two identical data words. For a single data bit, the codewords will be 00 and 11.

Another important property of codes is *separability*. A *separable* code has separate fields for the data and the check bits. Therefore, decoding for a separable code simply consists of selecting the data bits and disregarding the check bits. The check bits must still be processed separately to verify the correctness of the data. A nonseparable code, on the other hand, has the data and check bits integrated together, and extracting the data from the encoded word requires some processing, thus incurring an additional delay. Both types of codes are covered in this chapter.

3.1.1 Parity Codes

Perhaps the simplest codes of all are the parity codes. In its most basic form, a parity-coded word includes d data bits and an extra (check) bit that holds the parity. In an even (odd) parity code, this extra bit is set so that the total number of 1s in the whole $(d + 1)$-bit word (including the parity bit) is even (odd). The overhead fraction of the parity code is $1/d$.

A parity code has a Hamming distance of 2 and is guaranteed to detect all single-bit errors. If a bit flips from 0 to 1 (or vice versa), the overall parity will no longer be the same, and the error can be detected. However, simple parity cannot correct any bit errors.

Since the parity code is a separable code, it is easy to design parity encoding and decoding circuits for it. Figure 3.2 shows circuits to encode and decode 5-bit data words. The encoder consists of a five-input modulo-2 adder, which generates a 0 if the number of 1s is even. The output of this adder is the parity signal for the even parity code. The decoder generates the parity from the received data bits and compares this generated parity with the received parity bit. If they match, the output of the rightmost Exclusive-OR (XOR) gate is a 0, indicating that no error

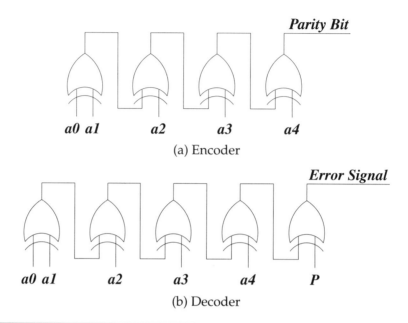

Parity Bit

a0 a1   a2   a3   a4

(a) Encoder

Error Signal

a0 a1   a2   a3   a4   P

(b) Decoder

FIGURE 3.2   Even parity encoding and decoding circuits.

has been detected. If they do not match, the output is a 1, indicating an error. Note that double-bit errors cannot be detected by a parity check. However, all three (and in general, any odd number of) bit errors will be detected.

The choice of even parity or odd parity depends on which type of all-bits unidirectional error (i.e., all-0s or all-1s error) is more probable. If, for example, we select the even parity code, the parity bit generated for the all zeroes data word will be 0. In such a case, an all-0s failure will go undetected because it is a valid codeword. Selecting the odd parity code will allow the detection of the all-0s failure. If, on the other hand, the all-1s failure is more likely than is the all-0s failure, we have to make sure that the all-1s word (data and parity bit) is invalid. To this end, we should select the odd parity code if the total number of bits (including the parity bit) is even and vice versa.

Several variations of the basic parity code have been proposed and implemented. One of these is the parity-bit-per-byte technique. Instead of having a single parity bit for the entire data word, we assign a separate parity bit to every byte (or any other group of bits). This will increase the overhead from $1/d$ to m/d, where m is the number of bytes (or other equal-sized groups). On the other hand, up to m errors will be detected as long as they occur in different bytes. If the all-0s and all-1s failures are likely to happen, we can select the odd parity code for one byte and the even parity code for another byte. A variation of the above is the *byte-interlaced* parity code. For example, suppose that $d = 64$ and denote the data bits by $a_{63}, a_{62}, \ldots, a_0$. Use eight parity bits such that the first will be the parity bit

$$
\begin{array}{ccccccc}
0 & 0 & 0 & 1 & 1 & 1 & \mathbf{1} \\
1 & 0 & 1 & 0 & 1 & 1 & \mathbf{0} \\
1 & 1 & 0 & 0 & 0 & 0 & \mathbf{0} \\
0 & 0 & 0 & 1 & 1 & 1 & \mathbf{1} \\
1 & 1 & 1 & 1 & 1 & 1 & \mathbf{0} \\
\mathbf{1} & \mathbf{0} & \mathbf{0} & \mathbf{1} & \mathbf{0} & \mathbf{0} & \mathbf{0}
\end{array}
$$

FIGURE 3.3   Example of overlapping parity.

of a_{63}, a_{55}, a_{47}, a_{39}, a_{31}, a_{23}, a_{15} and a_{7}, i.e., all the most significant bits in the eight bytes. Similarly, the remaining seven parity bits will be assigned so that the corresponding groups of bits are interlaced. Such a scheme is beneficial when shorting of adjacent bits is a common failure mode (e.g., in a bus). If, in addition, the parity type (odd or even) is alternated between the groups, the unidirectional errors (all-0s and all-1s) will also be detected.

An extension of the parity concept can render the code error correcting as well. The simplest such scheme involves organizing the data in a two-dimensional array as shown in Figure 3.3. The parity bits are shown in boldface. The bit at the end of a row represents the parity over this row; a bit at the bottom row is the parity bit for the corresponding column. The even parity scheme is followed for both rows and columns in Figure 3.3. A single-bit error anywhere will result in a row and a column being identified as erroneous. Because every row and column intersect in a unique bit position, the erroneous bit can be identified and corrected.

The above was an example of *overlapping parity*, in which each bit is "covered" by more than one parity bit. We next describe the general theory associated with overlapping parity. Our aim is to be able to identify every single erroneous bit. Suppose there are d data bits in all. How many parity bits should be used and which bits should be covered by each parity bit?

Let r be the number of parity bits (check bits) that we add to the d data bits resulting in codewords of size $d + r$ bits. Hence, there are $d + r$ error states, where in state i the ith bit of the codeword is erroneous (keep in mind that we are dealing only with single-bit errors: this scheme will not detect all double-bit errors). In addition, there is the state in which no bit is erroneous, resulting in $d + r + 1$ states to be distinguished.

We detect faults by performing r parity checks, that is, for each parity bit, we check whether the overall parity of this parity bit and the data bits covered by it is correct. These r parity checks can generate up to 2^r different check outcomes. Hence, the minimum number of parity bits is the smallest r that satisfies the following inequality

$$2^r \geqslant d + r + 1 \tag{3.1}$$

How do we decide which data bits will be covered by each parity bit? We associate each of the $d + r + 1$ states with one of the 2^r possible outcomes of the r parity checks. This is best illustrated by an example.

State	Erroneous parity check(s)	Syndrome
TABLE 3.1 ■ Example of assignment of parity values to states		
No errors	None	000
Bit 0 (p_0) error	p_0	001
Bit 1 (p_1) error	p_1	010
Bit 2 (p_2) error	p_2	100
Bit 3 (a_0) error	p_0, p_1	011
Bit 4 (a_1) error	p_0, p_2	101
Bit 5 (a_2) error	p_1, p_2	110
Bit 6 (a_3) error	p_0, p_1, p_2	111

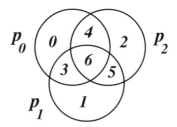

FIGURE 3.4   The assignment of parity bits in Table 3-1.

■ EXAMPLE

Suppose we have $d = 4$ data bits, $a_3a_2a_1a_0$. From Equation 3.1 we know that $r = 3$ is the minimum number of parity bits, which we denote by $p_2p_1p_0$. There are $4 + 3 + 1 = 8$ states that the codeword can be in. The complete 7-bit codeword is $a_3a_2a_1a_0p_2p_1p_0$, i.e., the least significant bit positions 0, 1, and 2 are parity bits and the others are data bits. Table 3-1 shows one possible assignment of parity check outcomes to the states, which is also illustrated in Figure 3.4. The assignment of no errors in the parity checks to the "no errors" state is obvious, as is the assignment for the next three states for which only one parity check is erroneous. The assignment of the bottom four states (corresponding to an error in a data bit) to the remaining four outcomes of the parity checks can be done in 4! ways. One of these is shown in Table 3-1 and Figure 3.4. For example, if the two checks of p_0 and p_2 (and only these) are in error, that indicates a problem with bit position 4, which is a_1.

A parity bit will cover all bit positions whose error is indicated by the corresponding parity check. Thus, p_0 covers positions $0, 3, 4$, and 6 (see Figure 3.4), i.e., $p_0 = a_0 \oplus a_1 \oplus a_3$. Similarly, $p_1 = a_0 \oplus a_2 \oplus a_3$ and $p_2 = a_1 \oplus a_2 \oplus a_3$. For example, for the data bits $a_3a_2a_1a_0 = 1100$, the generated parity bits are $p_2p_1p_0 = 001$.

Suppose now that the complete codeword 1100001 experiences a single-bit error and becomes 1000001. We recalculate the three parity bits, obtaining $p_2p_1p_0 = 111$. Calculating the difference between the new generated values of the parity bits and their previous values (by performing a bitwise XOR operation) yields 110. This difference, which is called the *syndrome*, indicates which parity checks are in error. The syndrome 110 indicates, based on Table 3-1, that bit a_2 is in error and the correct data should be $a_3a_2a_1a_0 = 1100$. This code is called a $(7,4)$ Hamming single error correcting (SEC) code.

The syndrome (which is the result of the parity checks) can be calculated directly from the bits $a_3a_2a_1a_0p_2p_1p_0$ in one step. This is best represented by the following matrix operation in which all the additions are modulo-2. The matrix below is called the *parity check matrix*:

$$
\begin{array}{c}
a_3\,a_2\,a_1\,a_0\,p_2\,p_1\,p_0 \\
\begin{bmatrix}
1 & 1 & 1 & 0 & 1 & 0 & 0 \\
1 & 1 & 0 & 1 & 0 & 1 & 0 \\
1 & 0 & 1 & 1 & 0 & 0 & 1
\end{bmatrix}
\end{array}
\begin{bmatrix}
a_3 \\
a_2 \\
a_1 \\
a_0 \\
p_2 \\
p_1 \\
p_0
\end{bmatrix}
= \begin{bmatrix} s_2\,s_1\,s_0 \end{bmatrix}
$$

For all the syndromes generated this way (see Table 3-1), except for 011 and 100, we can subtract 1 from the calculated syndrome to obtain the index of the bit in error. We can modify the assignment of states to the parity check outcomes so that the calculated syndrome will for all cases (except, clearly, the no-error case) provide the index of the bit in error after subtracting 1. For the example above, the order $a_3a_2a_1p_2a_0p_1p_0$ will provide the desired syndromes. If we modify the bit position indices so that they start with 1 and thus avoid the need to subtract a 1, we obtain the following parity check matrix:

$$
\begin{bmatrix}
1 & 1 & 1 & 1 & 0 & 0 & 0 \\
1 & 1 & 0 & 0 & 1 & 1 & 0 \\
1 & 0 & 1 & 0 & 1 & 0 & 1
\end{bmatrix}
$$
$$
\begin{array}{ccccccc}
7 & 6 & 5 & 4 & 3 & 2 & 1 \\
a_3 & a_2 & a_1 & p_2 & a_0 & p_1 & p_0
\end{array}
$$

Note that now the bit position indices of all the parity bits are powers of 2 (i.e., 1, 2, and 4), and the binary representations of these indices form the parity check matrix. ∎

If $2^r > d + r + 1$, we need to select $d + r + 1$ out of the 2^r binary combinations to serve as syndromes. In such a case, it is best to avoid those combinations that

$$
\begin{array}{c}
a_2\,a_1\,a_0\,p_2\,p_1\,p_0 \\
\left[\begin{array}{cccccc}
1 & 0 & 1 & 1 & 0 & 0 \\
1 & 1 & 0 & 0 & 1 & 0 \\
1 & 1 & 1 & 0 & 0 & 1
\end{array}\right]
\end{array}
\qquad
\begin{array}{c}
a_2\,a_1\,a_0\,p_2\,p_1\,p_0 \\
\left[\begin{array}{cccccc}
0 & 1 & 1 & 1 & 0 & 0 \\
1 & 0 & 1 & 0 & 1 & 0 \\
1 & 1 & 0 & 0 & 0 & 1
\end{array}\right]
\end{array}
$$

(a)   (b)

FIGURE 3.5   Two possible parity check matrices for $d = 3$.

include a large number of 1s. This will result in a parity check matrix that includes fewer 1s, leading to simpler circuits for the encoding and decoding operations. For example, for $d = 3$ we set $r = 3$, but only seven out of the eight 3-bit binary combinations are needed. Figure 3.5 shows two possible parity check matrices: (a) uses the combination 111 whereas (b) does not. As a result, the encoding circuit for the matrix in (a) will require a single XOR gate for generating p_1 and p_2 but two XOR gates for generating p_0. In contrast, the encoding circuit for the matrix in (b) needs a single XOR gate for generating each parity bit.

The code in Table 3-1 is capable of correcting a single-bit error but cannot detect a double-error. For example, if two errors occur in 1100001, yielding 1010001 (a_2 and a_1 are erroneous), the resulting syndrome is 011, indicating erroneously that bit a_0 should be corrected. One way to improve the error detection capabilities is to add an extra check bit that will serve as the parity bit of all the other data and check bits. The resulting code is called an (8,4) single-error correcting/double-error detecting (SEC/DED) Hamming code. The generation of the syndrome for this code is shown below.

$$
\begin{array}{c}
a_3\,a_2\,a_1\,a_0\,p_3\,p_2\,p_1\,p_0 \\
\left[\begin{array}{cccccccc}
1 & 1 & 1 & 1 & 1 & 1 & 1 & 1 \\
1 & 1 & 1 & 0 & 0 & 1 & 0 & 0 \\
1 & 1 & 0 & 1 & 0 & 0 & 1 & 0 \\
1 & 0 & 1 & 1 & 0 & 0 & 0 & 1
\end{array}\right]
\end{array}
\left[\begin{array}{c}
a_3 \\ a_2 \\ a_1 \\ a_0 \\ p_3 \\ p_2 \\ p_1 \\ p_0
\end{array}\right]
= \left[\, s_3\,s_2\,s_1\,s_0 \,\right]
$$

As before, the last three bits of the syndrome indicate the bit in error to be corrected, as long as the first bit, s_3, is equal to 1. Since p_3 is the parity bit of all the other data and check bits, a single-bit error changes the overall parity, and as a result, s_3 must be equal to 1. If s_3 is zero and any of the other syndrome bits is nonzero, a double or greater error is detected. For example, if one error occurs in 11001001 yielding 10001001, the calculated syndrome is 1110, indicating, as before, that a_2 is in error. If, however, two errors occur, resulting in 10101001, the calculated syndrome is 0011, indicating that an uncorrectable error has occurred. In general, an even number of errors is detectable whereas an odd (and larger than 1) number of errors is indistinguishable from a single-bit error, leading to an erroneous correction.

Current memory circuits that have SEC/DED support (not all do) use either a $(39,7)$ or a $(72,8)$ Hamming code. Since errors in two or more physically adjacent memory cells are quite likely, the bits in a single memory word are often assigned to non-adjacent memory cells to reduce the probability of an uncorrectable double error in the same word.

A disadvantage of the above SEC/DED Hamming code is that the calculation of the additional check bit, which is the parity bit of all other check and data bits, may slow down encoding and decoding. One way to avoid this penalty but still have the ability to detect double errors is to assign to the data and check bits only syndromes that include an odd number of 1s. Note that in the original SEC Hamming code, each parity bit has a syndrome that includes a single 1. By restricting ourselves to the use of syndromes that include an odd number of 1s (for any single-bit error), a double error will result in a syndrome with an even number of 1s, indicating an error that cannot be corrected. A possible parity check matrix for such an $(8,4)$ SEC/DED Hamming code is shown below.

$$
\begin{array}{cccccccc}
a_3 & a_2 & a_1 & a_0 & p_3 & p_2 & p_1 & p_0
\end{array}
$$
$$
\begin{bmatrix}
0 & 1 & 1 & 1 & 1 & 0 & 0 & 0 \\
1 & 0 & 1 & 1 & 0 & 1 & 0 & 0 \\
1 & 1 & 0 & 1 & 0 & 0 & 1 & 0 \\
1 & 1 & 1 & 0 & 0 & 0 & 0 & 1
\end{bmatrix}
$$

Limiting ourselves to odd syndromes implies that we use only 2^{r-1} out of the 2^r possible combinations. This is equivalent to saying that we need an extra check bit beyond the minimum required for a SEC Hamming code, and the total number of check bits is the same as for the original SEC/DED Hamming code.

If the number of data bits is very large, the probability of having an error that is not correctable by an SEC code increases. To reduce this probability, we may partition the D data bits into, say, D/d equal slices (of d bits each) and encode each slice separately using an appropriate $(d+r, d)$ SEC Hamming code. This, however, will increase the overhead, r/d, imposed by the SEC code. We have therefore a tradeoff between the probability of an uncorrectable error and the overhead. If f is the probability of a bit error and if bit errors occur independently of one another, the probability of more than one bit error in a field of $d + r$ bits is given by

$$
\Phi(d, r) = 1 - (1-f)^{d+r} - (d+r)f(1-f)^{d+r-1}
$$
$$
\approx \frac{(d+r)(d+r-1)}{2}f^2 \quad \text{if } f \ll 1 \tag{3.2}
$$

d	r	Overhead r/d	$\Psi(D,d,r)$

TABLE 3-2 ■ The overhead versus probability of an uncorrectable error tradeoff for an overlapping parity code with a total of $D = 1024$ data bits and a bit error probability of $f = 10^{-11}$

d	r	Overhead r/d	$\Psi(D,d,r)$
2	3	1.5000	0.5120E-16
4	3	0.7500	0.5376E-16
8	4	0.5000	0.8448E-16
16	5	0.3125	0.1344E-15
32	6	0.1875	0.2250E-15
64	7	0.1094	0.3976E-15
128	8	0.0625	0.7344E-15
256	9	0.0352	0.1399E-14
512	10	0.0195	0.2720E-14
1024	11	0.0107	0.5351E-14

The probability that there is an uncorrectable error in any one of the D/d slices is given by

$$\Psi(D,d,r) = 1 - \left(1 - \Phi(d,r)\right)^{D/d}$$
$$\approx (D/d)\Phi(d,r) \quad \text{if } \Phi(d,r) \ll 1 \qquad (3.3)$$

Some numerical results illustrating the tradeoff are provided in Table 3-2.

3.1.2 Checksum

Checksum is primarily used to detect errors in data transmission through communication channels. The basic idea is to add up the block of data that is being transmitted and to transmit this sum as well. The receiver then adds up the data it received and compares this sum with the checksum it received. If the two do not match, an error is indicated.

There are several variations of checksums. Assume the data words are d bits long. In the *single-precision* version, the checksum is a modulo-2^d addition. In the *double-precision* version, it is a modulo-2^{2d} addition. Figure 3.6 shows an example of each. In general, the single-precision checksum catches fewer errors than the double-precision version, since we only keep the rightmost d bits of the sum. The *residue* checksum takes into account the carry out of the dth bit as an end-around carry (i.e., the carryout is added to the least significant bit of the checksum) and is therefore somewhat more reliable. The *Honeywell* checksum, by concatenating words together into pairs for the checksum calculation (performed modulo-2^{2d}), guards against errors happening in the same position. For example, consider the situation in Figure 3.7. Because the line carrying a_3 is stuck at 0, the receiver will find that the transmitted checksum and its own computed checksum match in the

0000	0000	0000	
0101	0101	0101	
1111	1111	1111	00000101
0010	0010	0010	11110010
0110	00010110	0111	11110111
(a) Single-precision	(b) Double-precision	(c) Residue	(d) Honeywell

FIGURE 3.6 Variations of checksum coding (boxed quantities are the computed checksums).

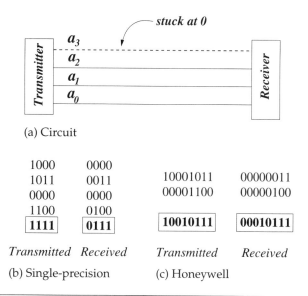

(a) Circuit

1000	0000
1011	0011
0000	0000
1100	0100
1111	**0111**

Transmitted   *Received*

(b) Single-precision

10001011	00000011
00001100	00000100
10010111	**00010111**

Transmitted   *Received*

(c) Honeywell

FIGURE 3.7 Honeywell versus single-precision checksum (boxed quantities indicate transmitted/received checksum).

single-precision checksum. However, the Honeywell checksum, when computed on the received data, will differ from the received checksum and the error will be detected. All the checksum schemes allow error detection but not error location, and the entire block of data must be retransmitted if an error is detected.

3.1.3 *M*-of-*N* Codes

The *M*-of-*N* code is an example of a unidirectional error-detecting code. As the term implies, in unidirectional errors all the affected bits change in the same direction, either from 0 to 1 or from 1 to 0 but not in both directions.

In an *M*-of-*N* code, every *N*-bit codeword has exactly *M* bits that are 1, resulting in $\binom{M}{N}$ codewords. Any single-bit error will change the number of 1s to either

Digit	Codeword
0	00011
1	00101
2	00110
3	01001
4	01010
5	01100
6	10001
7	10010
8	10100
9	11000

TADLE 3 3 ■ The 2 of 5 code for decimal digits

$M + 1$ or $M - 1$ and will be detected. Unidirectional multiple errors would also be detected. A simple instance of an M-of-N code is the 2-of-5 code, which consists of 10 codewords and can serve to encode the decimal digits. An example of a 2-of-5 code is shown in Table 3-3. There are 10! different ways of assigning the 10 codewords to the decimal digits. The assignment shown in the table preserves the binary order. The main advantage of M-of-N codes is their conceptual simplicity. However, encoding and decoding become relatively complex operations because such codes are, in general, nonseparable, unlike the parity and checksum codes.

Still, separable M-of-N codes can be constructed. For example, an M-of-$2M$ code can be constructed by adding M check bits to the given M data bits so that the resulting $2M$-bit codeword has exactly M 1s. Such codes are easy to encode and decode but have a greater overhead (100% or more) than do the nonseparable ones. For example, to encode the 10 decimal digits, we start with 4 bits per digit, leading to a 4-of-8 code, which has a much higher level of redundancy than does the 2-of-5 code.

3.1.4 Berger Code

The M-of-$2M$ code for detecting unidirectional errors is a separable code but has a high level of information redundancy. A unidirectional error detecting code that is separable and has a much lower overhead is the Berger code. To encode, count the number of 1s in the word, express this count in binary representation, complement it, and append this quantity to the data. For example, suppose we are encoding 11101. There are four 1s in it, which is 100 in binary. Complementing results in 011 and the codeword will be 11101011.

The overhead of the Berger code can be computed as follows. If there are d data bits, then there can be at most d 1s in it, which can take up to $\lceil \log_2(d + 1) \rceil$ bits to

TABLE 3-4 ■ Berger code overhead		
d	r	Overhead
8	4	0.5000
15	4	0.2667
16	5	0.3125
31	5	0.1613
32	6	0.1875
63	6	0.0952
64	7	0.1094
127	7	0.0551
128	8	0.0625
255	8	0.0314
256	9	0.0352

count. The overhead per data bit is therefore given by

$$\frac{\lceil \log_2(d+1) \rceil}{d}$$

This overhead is tabulated for some values of d in Table 3-4. If $d = 2^k - 1$ for an integer k, then the number of check bits, denoted by r, is $r = k$ and the resulting code is called a maximum-length Berger code. For the unidirectional error detection capability provided, the Berger code requires the smallest number of check bits out of all known separable codes.

3.1.5 Cyclic Codes

In cyclic codes, encoding of data consists of multiplying (modulo-2) the data word by a constant number, and the coded word is the product that results. Decoding is done by dividing by the same constant: if the remainder is nonzero, it indicates that an error has occurred. These codes are called cyclic because for every codeword $a_{n-1}, a_{n-2}, \ldots, a_0$, its cyclic shift $a_0, a_{n-1}, a_{n-2}, \ldots, a_1$ is also a codeword. For example, the 5-bit code consisting of {00000, 00011, 00110, 01100, 11000, 10001, 00101, 01010, 10100, 01001, 10010, 01111, 11110, 11101, 11011, 10111} is cyclic.

Cyclic codes have been the focus of a great deal of research and are widely used in both data storage and communication. We will present only a small sampling of this work: the theory of cyclic codes rests on advanced algebra, which is outside the scope of this book. Interested readers are directed to the ample coding literature (see the Further Reading section).

Suppose k is the number of bits of data that we are seeking to encode. The encoded word of length n bits is obtained by multiplying the given k data bits by a number that is $n - k + 1$ bits long.

$$\begin{array}{r} 1110 \\ \times \quad 11 \\ \hline 1110 \\ 1110 \\ \hline 10010 \end{array}$$

FIGURE 3.8   Encoding the data word 1110.

In cyclic coding theory, the multiplier is represented as a polynomial, called the *generator* polynomial. The 1s and 0s in the $(n - k + 1)$-bit multiplier are treated as the coefficients of an $(n - k)$-degree polynomial. For example, if the 5-bit multiplier is 11001, the generator polynomial is $G(x) = 1 \cdot X^4 + 1 \cdot X^3 + 0 \cdot X^2 + 0 \cdot X^1 + 1 \cdot X^0 = X^4 + X^3 + 1$. A cyclic code using a generator polynomial of degree $n - k$ and total number of encoded bits n is called an (n, k) cyclic code. An (n, k) cyclic code can detect all single errors and also all runs of adjacent bit errors, so long as these runs are shorter than $n - k$. These codes are therefore very useful in such applications as wireless communication, where the channels are frequently noisy and subject the transmission to bursts of interference that can result in runs of adjacent bit errors. For a polynomial of degree $n - k$ to serve as a generator polynomial of an (n, k) cyclic code, it must be a factor of $X^n - 1$. The polynomial $X^4 + X^3 + 1$ is a factor of $X^{15} - 1$ and can thus serve as a generator polynomial for a $(15, 11)$ cyclic code. Another factor of $X^{15} - 1$ is $X^4 + X + 1$, which can generate another $(15, 11)$ cyclic code. The polynomial $X^{15} - 1$ has five prime factors, namely,

$$X^{15} - 1 = (X + 1)(X^2 + X + 1)(X^4 + X + 1)(X^4 + X^3 + 1)(X^4 + X^3 + X^2 + X + 1)$$

Any one of these five factors and any product of two (or more) of these factors can serve as a generating polynomial for a cyclic code. For example, the product of the first two factors is $(X + 1)(X^2 + X + 1) = X^3 + 1$, and it can generate a $(15, 12)$ cyclic code. When multiplying $X + 1$ and $X^2 + X + 1$, note that all additions are performed modulo-2. Also note that subtraction in modulo-2 arithmetic is identical to addition, and thus, $X^{15} - 1$ is identical to $X^{15} + 1$.

The 5-bit cyclic code mentioned at the beginning of this section has the generator polynomial $X + 1$ satisfying $X^5 - 1 = (X + 1)(X^4 + X^3 + X^2 + X + 1)$ and is a $(5, 4)$ cyclic code. We can verify that $X + 1$ is the generator polynomial for the above $(5, 4)$ cyclic code by multiplying all 4-bit data words (0000 through 1111) by $X + 1$ or 11 in binary. For example, the codeword corresponding to the data word 0110 is 01010, as we now show. The data word 0110 can be represented as $X^2 + X$, and when multiplied by $X + 1$, results in $X^3 + X^2 + X^2 + X = X^3 + X$, which represents the 5-bit codeword 01010. The multiplication by the generator polynomial can also be performed directly in binary arithmetic rather than using polynomials. For example, the codeword corresponding to the data word 1110 is obtained by multiplying 1110 by 11 in modulo-2 arithmetic as shown in Figure 3.8. Note that this cyclic code is not separable. The data bits and check bits within the codeword 10010 are not separable.

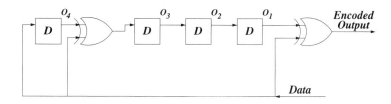

FIGURE 3.9 **Encoding circuit for the** (15,11) **cyclic code with the generating polynomial** $X^4 + X^3 + 1$.

$$
\begin{array}{r}
10001100101 \\
\times \quad 11001 \\
\hline
10001100101 \\
00000000000 \\
00000000000 \\
10001100101 \\
10001100101 \\
\hline
110000100011101
\end{array}
$$

FIGURE 3.10 **Example of modulo-2 multiplication for encoding the 11-bit input 10001100101.**

One of the most significant reasons for the popularity of cyclic codes is the fact that multiplication and division by the generator polynomial can be implemented in hardware using simple shift registers and XOR gates. Such a simple implementation allows fast encoding and decoding. Let us start with an example: consider the generator polynomial $X^4 + X^3 + 1$ (corresponding, as we have seen, to the multiplier 11001). Consider the circuit shown in Figure 3.9, where the square boxes are delay elements, which hold their input for one clock cycle.

The reader will find that this circuit does indeed multiply (modulo-2) serial inputs by 11001. To see why this should be, consider the multiplication shown in Figure 3.10. Focus on the boxed column. It shows how the fifth bit of the product is the modulo-2 sum of the corresponding bits of the multiplicand shifted 0 times, 3 times, and 4 times. If the multiplicand is fed in serially, starting with the least significant bit and we add the multiplicand shifted as shown above, we arrive at the product. It is precisely this shifting that is done by the delay elements of the circuit. Table 3-5 illustrates the operation of the encoding circuit in which i_3 is the input to the O_3 delay element.

We now consider the process of decoding, which is done through division by the generator polynomial. Let us first illustrate the decoding process through division by the constant 11001 as shown in Figure 3.11a. The final remainder is zero, indicating that no error has been detected. If a single error occurs and we receive 110000100**1**11101 (the boldface **1** is the bit in error), the division will generate a

TABLE 3-5 ■ The operation of the encoder in Figure 3.9 for the example in Figure 3.10					
Shift clock	**Input data**	O_4	i_3	$O_3 O_2 O_1$	**Encoded output**
1	1	0	1	000	1
2	0	1	1	100	0
3	1	0	1	110	1
4	0	1	1	111	1
5	0	0	0	111	1
6	1	0	1	011	0
7	1	1	0	101	0
8	0	1	1	010	0
9	0	0	0	101	1
10	0	0	0	010	0
11	1	0	1	001	0
12	0	1	1	100	0
13	0	0	0	110	0
14	0	0	0	011	1
15	0	0	0	001	1

```
110000100011101 : 11001 = 10001100101        110000100111101 : 11001 = 10001100110
11001                                        11001
─────                                        ─────
  10100                                         10100
  11001                                         11001
  ─────                                         ─────
   11010                                         11011
   11001                                         11001
   ─────                                         ─────
     11111                                         10111
     11001                                         11001
     ─────                                         ─────
       11001                                         11100
       11001                                         11001
       ─────                                         ─────
       00000                                         01011
```

(a) Error free   (b) A single-bit error (in boldface)

FIGURE 3.11   Decoding through division.

nonzero remainder as shown in Figure 3.11b. To show that every single error can be detected, note that a single error in bit position i can be represented by X^i, and the received codeword that includes such an error can be written as $D(X)G(X) + X^i$, where $D(X)$ is the original data word and $G(X)$ is the generator polynomial. If $G(X)$ has at least two terms, it does not divide X^i, and consequently, dividing $D(X)G(X) + X^i$ by $G(X)$ will generate a nonzero remainder.

The above (15,11) cyclic code can be shown to have a Hamming distance of 3, thus allowing the detection of all double-bit errors irrespective of their bit positions. The situation is different when three-bit errors occur. Suppose first that

```
110000111010101 : 11001 =  10001101101      110000011011101 : 11001 =  10001110011
11001                                        11001
  10111                                        10011
  11001                                        11001
   11100                                        10100
   11001                                        11001
    10110                                        11011
    11001                                        11001
     11111                                        10110
     11001                                        11001
      11001                                        11111
      11001                                        11001
       00000                                        00110
```

(a) Three nonadjacent errors (in boldface)   (b) Three adjacent errors (in boldface)

FIGURE 3.12   Decoding through division with 3-bit errors.

the 3-bit errors occur in nonadjacent bit positions, producing, for example, 11000 01**11**0 10101 instead of 11000 01000 11101. Repeating the above division for this codeword results in the quotient and remainder shown in Figure 3.12a. The final remainder is zero, and consequently, the 3-bit errors were not detected, although the final result is erroneous. If, however, the 3-bit errors are adjacent, e.g., 11000 00**11**0 11101, we obtain the quotient and remainder shown in Figure 3.12b. The nonzero remainder indicates an error.

To implement a divider circuit, we should realize that division can be achieved through multiplication in the feedback loop. We illustrate this through the following example.

■ E X A M P L E

Let the encoded word be denoted by the polynomial $E(X)$, and use the previously defined notation of $G(X)$ and $D(X)$ for the generator polynomial and the original data word, respectively. If no bit errors exist, we will receive $E(X)$ and can calculate $D(X)$ from $D(X) = \frac{E(X)}{G(X)}$ and the remainder will be zero. In such a case, we can rewrite the division as

$$E(X) = D(X) \cdot G(X) = D(X)\{X^4 + X^3 + 1\}$$

$$= D(X)\{X^4 + X^3\} + D(X)$$

$$\text{thus} \quad D(X) = E(X) - D(X)\{X^4 + X^3\}$$

$$= E(X) + D(X)\{X^4 + X^3\}$$

(because addition = subtraction in modulo-2)

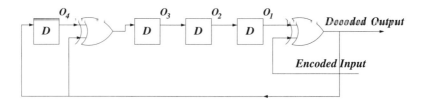

FIGURE 3.13   Decoding circuit for the $(15, 11)$ **cyclic code with the generating polynomial** $X^4 + X^3 + 1$.

TABLE 3-6 ■ The operation of the decoder in Figure 3.13 for the input 110000100011101						
Shift clock	Encoded input	i_4	O_4	i_3	$O_3 O_2 O_1$	Decoded output
1	1	1	0	1	000	1
2	0	0	1	1	100	0
3	1	1	0	1	110	1
4	1	0	1	1	111	0
5	1	0	0	0	111	0
6	0	1	0	1	011	1
7	0	1	1	0	101	1
8	0	0	1	1	010	0
9	1	0	0	0	101	0
10	0	0	0	0	010	0
11	0	1	0	1	001	1
12	0	0	1	1	100	0
13	0	0	0	0	110	0
14	1	0	0	0	011	0
15	1	0	0	0	001	0

With this last expression, we can construct the feedback circuit for division (see Figure 3.13). We start with all delay elements holding 0, produce first the seven quotient bits that constitute the data bits, and then the four remainder bits. If these remainder bits are nonzero, we know that an error has occurred. Table 3-6 illustrates the decode operation in which i_3 is the input to the O_3 delay element. The reader can verify that any error in the received sequence $E(X)$ will result in a nonzero remainder. ■

In many data transmission applications, there is a need to make sure that all burst errors of length 16 bits or less will be detected. Therefore, cyclic codes of the type $(16+k, k)$ are used. The generating polynomial of degree 16 should be selected so that the maximum number of data bits is sufficiently large, allowing the use of the same code (and the same encoding and decoding circuits) for data blocks of many different sizes. Two generating polynomials of degree 16 are commonly used for this purpose. These are the CRC-16 polynomial (where CRC stands for Cyclic Redundancy Check),

$$G(X) = (X+1)(X^{15} + X + 1) = X^{16} + X^{15} + X^2 + 1$$

and the CRC-CCITT polynomial,

$$G(X) = (X+1)(X^{15} + X^{14} + X^{13} + X^{12} + X^4 + X^3 + X^2 + X + 1)$$
$$= X^{16} + X^{12} + X^5 + 1$$

In both cases, the degree-16 polynomial divides $X^n - 1$ for $n = 2^{15} - 1$ (but not for any smaller value of n) and thus can be used for blocks of data of size up to $2^{15} - 1 = 32,767$ bits. Note that shorter blocks can still use the same cyclic code. Such blocks can be viewed as blocks of size 32,767 bits with a sufficient number of leading 0s that can be ignored in the encoding or decoding operations. Also note that both CRC polynomials have only four nonzero coefficients, greatly simplifying the design of the encoding and decoding circuits.

The CRC-32 code shown below is widely used for data transfers over the Internet:

$$G(X) = X^{32} + X^{26} + X^{23} + X^{22} + X^{16} + X^{12} + X^{11}$$
$$+ X^{10} + X^8 + X^7 + X^5 + X^4 + X^2 + X + 1$$

allowing the detection of burst errors consisting of up to 32 bits for blocks of data of size up to $n = 2^{32} - 1$ bits.

For data transmissions of long blocks, it is more efficient to employ a separable encoding that will allow the received data to be used immediately without having to wait for all the bits of the codeword to be received and decoded. A separable cyclic code will allow performing the error detection independently of the data processing itself. Fortunately, there is a simple way to generate a separable (n,k) cyclic code. Instead of encoding the given data word $D(X) = d_{k-1}X^{k-1} + d_{k-2}X^{k-2} + \cdots + d_0$ by multiplying it by the generator polynomial $G(X)$ of degree $n - k$, we first append $(n - k)$ zeroes to $D(X)$ and obtain $\bar{D}(X) = d_{k-1}X^{n-1} + d_{k-2}X^{n-2} + \cdots + d_0X^{n-k}$. We then divide $\bar{D}(X)$ by $G(X)$, yielding

$$\bar{D}(X) = Q(X)G(X) + R(X)$$

where $R(X)$ is a polynomial of degree smaller than $n - k$. Finally, we form the codeword $C(X) = \bar{D}(X) - R(X)$, which will be transmitted. This n-bit codeword has $G(X)$ as a factor, and consequently, if we divide $C(X)$ by $G(X)$, a nonzero remainder will indicate that errors have occurred. In this encoding, $\bar{D}(X)$ and $R(X)$ have no terms in common, and thus, the first k bits in $C(X) = \bar{D}(X) - R(X) = \bar{D}(X) + R(X)$

are the original data bits while the remaining $n - k$ are the check bits, making the encoding separable.

■ EXAMPLE

We illustrate the procedure described above through the $(5,4)$ cyclic code that uses the same generator polynomial $X+1$ as before. For the data word 0110 we obtain $\bar{D}(X) = X^3 + X^2$. Dividing $\bar{D}(X)$ by $X+1$ yields $Q(X) = X^2$ and $R(X) = 0$. Thus, the corresponding codeword is $X^3 + X^2$, or in binary 01100, where the first four bits are the data bits and the last one the check bit. Similarly, for the data word 1110, we obtain

$$\bar{D}(X) = X^4 + X^3 + X^2 = \left(X^3 + X + 1\right)(X+1) + 1$$

yielding the codeword 11101. The reader can verify that the same 16 codewords as before are generated, $\{00000, 00011, 00110, 01100, 11000, 10001, 00101, 01010, 10100, 01001, 10010, 01111, 11110, 11101, 11011, 10111\}$, but the correspondence between the data words and the codewords has changed. ■

3.1.6 Arithmetic Codes

Arithmetic error codes are those codes that are preserved under a set of arithmetic operations. This property allows us to detect errors which may occur during the execution of an arithmetic operation in the defined set. Such concurrent error detection can always be attained by duplicating the arithmetic unit, but duplication is often too costly to be practical.

We say that a code is preserved under an arithmetic operation $\star$ if for any two operands X and Y, and the corresponding encoded entities X' and Y', there is an operation $\circledast$ for the encoded operands satisfying

$$X' \circledast Y' = (X \star Y)' \tag{3.4}$$

This implies that the result of the arithmetic operation $\circledast$, when applied to the encoded operands X' and Y', will yield the same result as encoding the outcome of applying the original operation $\star$ to the original operands X and Y. Consequently, the result of the arithmetic operation will be encoded in the same code as the operands.

We expect arithmetic codes to be able to detect all single-bit faults. Note, however, that a single-bit error in an operand or an intermediate result may well cause a multiple-bit error in the final result. For example, when adding two binary numbers, if stage i of the adder is faulty, all the remaining $(n - i)$ higher order digits may become erroneous.

There are two classes of arithmetic codes: separable and nonseparable. The simplest nonseparable codes are the AN codes, formed by multiplying the operands by a constant A. In other words, X' in Equation 3.4 is $A \cdot X$, and the operations $\circledast$ and $\star$ are identical for addition and subtraction. For example, if $A = 3$, we multiply each operand by 3 (obtained as $2X + X$) and check the result of an add or subtract operation to see whether it is an integer multiple of 3. All error magnitudes that are multiples of A are undetectable. Therefore, we should not select a value of A that is a power of the radix 2 (the base of the number system). An odd value of A will detect every single digit fault, because such an error has a magnitude of 2^i. Setting $A = 3$ yields the least expensive AN code that still enables the detection of all single errors.

For example, the number $0110_2 = 6_{10}$ is represented in the AN code with $A = 3$ by $010010_2 = 18_{10}$. A fault in bit position 3 may result in the erroneous number $011010_2 = 26_{10}$. This error is easily detectable, since 26 is not a multiple of 3.

The simplest separable codes are the residue code and the inverse residue code. In each of these, we attach a separable check symbol $C(X)$ to every operand X. For the residue code, $C(X) = X \bmod A = |X|_A$, where A is called the check modulus. For the inverse residue code, $C(X) = A - (X \bmod A)$. For both separable codes, Equation 3.4 is replaced by

$$C(X) \circledast C(Y) = C(X \star Y) \tag{3.5}$$

This equality clearly holds for addition and multiplication because the following equations apply:

$$|X + Y|_A = \big||X|_A + |Y|_A\big|_A$$
$$|X \cdot Y|_A = \big||X|_A \cdot |Y|_A\big|_A \tag{3.6}$$

■ **EXAMPLE**

If $A = 3$, $X = 7$, and $Y = 5$, the corresponding residues are $|X|_A = 1$ and $|Y|_A = 2$. When adding the two operands, we obtain $|7 + 5|_3 = 0 = ||7|_3 + |5|_3|_3 = |1 + 2|_3 = 0$. When multiplying the two operands, we get $|7 \cdot 5|_3 = 2 = ||7|_3 \cdot |5|_3|_3 = |1 \cdot 2|_3 = 2$. ■

For division, the equation $X - S = Q \cdot D$ is satisfied, where X is the dividend, D the divisor, Q the quotient, and S the remainder. The corresponding residue check is therefore

$$\big||X|_A - |S|_A\big|_A = \big||Q|_A \cdot |D|_A\big|_A$$

■ EXAMPLE

If $A = 3$, $X = 7$, and $D = 5$, the results are $Q = 1$ and $S = 2$. The corresponding residue check is $||7|_3 - |2|_3|_3 = ||5|_3 \cdot |1|_3|_3 = 2$. The subtraction in the left-hand-side term is done by adding the complement to the modulus 3, i.e., $|1 - 2|_3 = |1 + |3 - 2|_3|_3 = |1 + 1|_3 = 2$. ■

A residue code with A as a check modulus has the same undetectable error magnitudes as the corresponding AN code. For example, if $A = 3$, only errors that modify the result by some multiple of 3 will go undetected, and consequently, single-bit errors are always detectable. In addition, the checking algorithms for the AN code and the residue code are the same: in both we have to compute the residue of the result modulo-A. Even the increase in word length, $|\log_2 A|$, is the same for both codes. The most important difference is due to the property of separability. The arithmetic unit for the check symbol $C(X)$ in the residue code is completely separate from the main unit operating on X, whereas only a single unit (of a higher complexity) exists in the case of the AN code. An adder with a residue code is depicted in Figure 3.14. In the error detection block shown in this figure, the residue modulo-A of the $X + Y$ input is calculated and compared to the result of the mod A adder. A mismatch indicates an error.

The AN and residue codes with $A = 3$ are the simplest examples of a class of arithmetic (separable and nonseparable) codes that use a value of A of the form $A = 2^a - 1$, for some integer a. This choice simplifies the calculation of the remainder when dividing by A (which is needed for the checking algorithm), and this is why such codes are called *low-cost* arithmetic codes. The calculation of the remainder when dividing by $2^a - 1$ is simple, because the equation

$$\left|z_i r^i\right|_{r-1} = |z_i|_{r-1}, \quad r = 2^a \tag{3.7}$$

allows the use of modulo-$(2^a - 1)$ summation of the groups of size a bits that compose the number (each group has a value $0 \leqslant z_i \leqslant 2^a - 1$, see below).

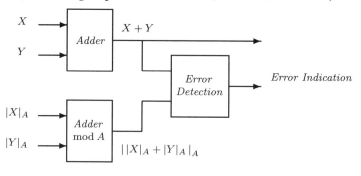

FIGURE 3.14   An adder with a separate residue check.

■ EXAMPLE

To calculate the remainder when dividing the number $X = 11110101011$ by $A = 7 = 2^3 - 1$, we partition X into groups of size 3, starting with the least significant bit. This yields $X = (z_3, z_2, z_1, z_0) = (11, 110, 101, 011)$. We then add these groups modulo-7; i.e., we "cast out" 7s and add the end-around-carry whenever necessary. A carry-out has a weight of 8, and because $|8|_7 = 1$, we must add an end-around-carry whenever there is a carry-out as illustrated below.

$$
\begin{array}{rll}
 & 11 & z_3 \\
+ & 110 & z_2 \\
\hline
1 & 001 & \\
+ & 1 & \text{end-around carry} \\
\hline
 & 010 & \\
+ & 101 & z_1 \\
\hline
 & 111 & \\
+ & 011 & z_0 \\
\hline
1 & 010 & \\
 & 1 & \text{end-around carry} \\
\hline
+ & 011 & \\
\end{array}
$$

The residue modulo-7 of X is 3, which is the correct remainder of $X = 1963_{10}$ when divided by 7. ■

Both separable and nonseparable codes are preserved when we perform arithmetic operations on unsigned operands. If we wish to include signed operands as well, we must require that the code be complementable with respect to R, where R is either 2^n or $2^n - 1$ and n is the number of bits in the encoded operand. The selected R will determine whether two's complement (for which $R = 2^n$) or one's complement (for which $R = 2^n - 1$) arithmetic will be employed. For the AN code, $R - AX$ must be divisible by A, and thus A must be a factor of R. If we insist on A being odd, it excludes the choice $R = 2^n$, and only one's complement can be used.

■ EXAMPLE

For $n = 4$, R is equal to $2^n - 1 = 15$ for one's complement and is divisible by A for the AN code with $A = 3$. The number $X = 0110$ is represented by $3X = 010010$, and its one's complement 101101 ($= 45_{10}$) is divisible by 3. However, the two's complement of $3X$ is 101110 ($= 46_{10}$) and is not divisible by 3. If $n = 5$, then for one's complement R is equal to 31, which is not divisible by A. The number $X = 00110$ is represented by $3X = 0010010$, and its one's complement is 1101101 ($= 109_{10}$), which is not divisible by 3. ∎

For the residue code with the check modulus A, the equation $A - |X|_A = |R - X|_A$ has to be satisfied. This implies that R must be an integer multiple of A, again allowing only one's complement arithmetic to be used. However, we may modify the procedure so that two's complement (with $R = 2^n$) can also be employed:

$$\left|2^n - X\right|_A = \left|2^n - 1 - X + 1\right|_A = \left|2^n - 1 - X\right|_A + |1|_A \qquad (3.8)$$

We therefore need to add a correction term $|1|_A$ to the residue code when forming the two's complement. Note that A must still be a factor of $2^n - 1$.

■ **EXAMPLE**

For the residue code with $A = 7$ and $n = 6$, $R = 2^6 = 64$ for two's complement and $R - 1 = 63$ is divisible by 7. The number $001010_2 = 10_{10}$ has the residue 3 modulo-7. The two's complement of 001010 is 110110. The complement of $|3|_7$ is $|4|_7$, and adding the correction term $|1|_7$ yields 5, which is the correct residue modulo-7 of 110110 ($= 54_{10}$). ∎

A similar correction is needed when we add operands represented in two's complement and a carry-out (of weight 2^n) is generated in the main adder. Such a carry-out is discarded according to the rules of two's complement arithmetic. To compensate for this, we need to subtract $|2^n|_A$ from the residue check. Since A is a factor of $(2^n - 1)$, the term $|2^n|_A$ is equal to $|1|_A$.

■ **EXAMPLE**

If we add to $X = 110110$ (in two's complement) the number $Y = 001101$, a carry-out is generated and discarded. We must therefore subtract the correction term $|2^6|_7 = |1|_7$ from the residue check with the modulus $A = 7$, obtaining

$$
\begin{array}{ll}
\quad\; 110110 = X & \qquad 101 = |X|_7 \\
+ \;\; 001101 = Y & + \;\; 110 = |Y|_7 \\
\hline
1 \;\;\; 000011 & 1 \;\;\; 011 \\
\end{array}
$$

$$
\begin{array}{l}
\qquad\qquad\quad 1 \;\; \text{end-around carry} \\
\hline
\qquad\qquad\quad 100 \\
- \;\;\; 1 \;\; \text{correction term} \\
\hline
\qquad\qquad\quad 011
\end{array}
$$

where 3 is clearly the correct residue of the result 000011 modulo-7. ∎

The above modifications result in an interdependence between the main arithmetic unit and the check unit that operates on the residues. Such an interdependence may cause a situation in which an error from the main unit propagates to the check unit and the effect of the fault is masked. However, it has been shown that the occurrence of a single-bit error is always detectable.

Error correction can be achieved by using two or more residue checks. The simplest case is the bi-residue code, which consists of two residue checks A_1 and A_2. If n is the number of bits in the operand, select a and b such that n is the least common multiple of a, b. If $A_1 = 2^a - 1$ and $A_2 = 2^b - 1$ are two low-cost residue checks, then any single-bit error can be corrected.

3.2 Resilient Disk Systems

An excellent example of employing information redundancy through coding at a higher level than individual data words is the RAID structure. RAID stands for Redundant Arrays of Independent (or Inexpensive) Disks. We describe next five RAID structures.

3.2.1 RAID Level 1

RAID1 consists of mirrored disks. In place of one disk, there are two disks, each being a copy of the other. If one disk fails, the other can continue to serve access requests. If both disks are working, RAID1 can speed up read accesses by dividing them among the two disks. Write accesses are, however, slowed down, because both disks must finish the update before the operation can complete.

Let us assume that the disks fail independently, each at a constant rate λ, and that the time to repair each is exponentially distributed with mean $1/\mu$. We will now compute the reliability and availability of a RAID1 system.

To compute the reliability, we set up a three-state Markov chain as shown in Figure 3.15 (Markov chains are explained in Chapter 2). The state of the system is the number of disks that are functional: it can vary between 0 (failed system) and 2 (both disks up). The unreliability at time t is the probability of being in the failed state, $P_0(t)$. The differential equations associated with this Markov chain are as follows:

$$\frac{\mathrm{d}P_2(t)}{\mathrm{d}t} = -2\lambda P_2(t) + \mu P_1(t)$$

$$\frac{\mathrm{d}P_1(t)}{\mathrm{d}t} = -(\lambda + \mu)P_1(t) + 2\lambda P_2(t)$$

$$P_0(t) = 1 - P_1(t) - P_2(t)$$

Solving these simultaneous differential equations with the initial conditions $P_2(0) = 1$; $P_0(0) = P_1(0) = 0$, we can obtain the probability that the disk system fails sometime before t. The expressions for the state probabilities are rather complex and not very illuminating. We will make use of an approximation, whereby

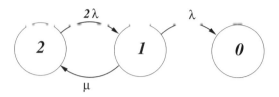

FIGURE 3.15   Markov chain for RAID1 reliability calculation.

we compute the Mean Time to Data Loss (MTTDL), and then use the fact that $\mu \gg \lambda$ (the repair rate is much greater than the failure rate).

The MTTDL is computed in the following way. State 0 will be entered if the system enters state 1 and then makes a transition to state 0. If we start in state 2 at time 0, the mean time before state 1 is entered is $1/2\lambda$. The mean time spent staying in state 1 is $1/(\lambda + \mu)$. Following this, the system can either go back to state 2, which it does with probability $q = \mu/(\mu + \lambda)$ or to state 0, which it does with probability $p = \lambda/(\mu + \lambda)$. The probability that n visits are made to state 1 before the system transits to state 0 is clearly $q^{n-1}p$, because we would have to make $n - 1$ transitions from 1 to 2, followed by a transition from 1 to 0. The mean time to enter state 0 in this case is given by

$$T_{2\to0}(n) = n\left(\frac{1}{2\lambda} + \frac{1}{\lambda + \mu}\right) = n\,\frac{3\lambda + \mu}{2\lambda(\lambda + \mu)}$$

Hence,

$$\begin{aligned}
\mathrm{MTTDL} &= \sum_{n=1}^{\infty} q^{n-1}pT_{2\to0}(n) \\
&= \sum_{n=1}^{\infty} nq^{n-1}pT_{2\to0}(1) \\
&= T_{2\to0}(1)/p \\
&= \frac{3\lambda + \mu}{2\lambda^2}
\end{aligned}$$

If $\mu \gg \lambda$, we can approximate the transition into state 0 by regarding the aggregate of states 1 and 2 as a single state, from which there is a transition of rate 1/MTTDL to state 0. Hence, the reliability can be approximated by the function

$$R(t) \approx e^{-t/\mathrm{MTTDL}} \tag{3.9}$$

Figure 3.16 shows the unreliability of the system (probability of data loss) over time for a variety of mean disk lifetimes and mean disk repair times. It is worth noting the substantial impact of the mean repair time on the probability of data loss.

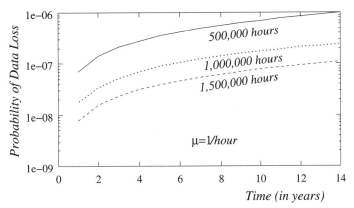

Curve labels indicate mean lifetime of a single disk

(a) Impact of mean disk lifetime

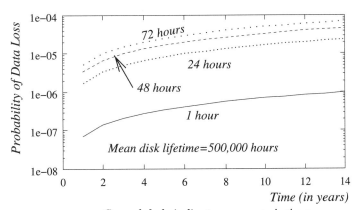

Curve labels indicate mean repair times

(b) Impact of mean disk repair time

FIGURE 3.16   Unreliability of RAID1 system.

A calculation of the long-term availability of the disk system can be done based on a Markov chain identical to that shown in Figure 2.16, yielding

$$A = \frac{\mu(\mu + 2\lambda)}{(\lambda + \mu)^2}$$

3.2.2 RAID Level 2

Level 2 RAID consists of a bank of data disks in parallel with Hamming-coded disks. Suppose there are d data disks and c code disks. Then, we can think of the ith bit of each disk as bits of a $(c + d)$-bit word. Based on the theory of Hamming codes, we know that we must have $2^c \geqslant c + d + 1$ in order to permit the correction of one bit per word.

We will not spend more time on RAID2 because other RAID designs impose much less overhead.

3.2.3 RAID Level 3

RAID3 is a modification of RAID2 and arises from the observation that each disk has error-correction coding per sector. Hence, if a sector is bad, we can identify it as such. RAID3 consists of a bank of d data disks together with one parity disk. The data are bit-interleaved across the data disks, and the ith position of the parity disk contains the parity bit associated with the bits in the ith position of each of the data disks. An example of a five-disk RAID3 system is shown in Figure 3.17.

For error-detection and error-correction purposes, we can regard the ith bit of each disk as forming a $(d + 1)$-bit word, consisting of d data and 1 parity bits. Suppose one such word has an incorrect bit in the jth bit position. The error-correcting code for that sector in the jth disk will indicate a failure, thus locating the fault. Once we have located the fault, the remaining bits can be used to restore the faulty bit.

For example, let the word be 01101, where 0110 are the data bits and 1 is the parity bit. If even parity is being used; we know that a bit is in error. If the fourth disk (disk 3 in the figure) indicates an error in the relevant sector and the other disks show no such errors, we know that the word should be 01111, and the correction can be made appropriately.

The Markov chains for the reliability and availability of this system are almost identical to those used in RAID1. In RAID1, we had two disks per group; here, we have $d + 1$. In both cases, the system fails (we have data loss) if two or more disks fail. Hence, the Markov chain for computing reliability is as shown in Figure 3.18. The analysis of this chain is similar to that of RAID1: the mean time to data loss

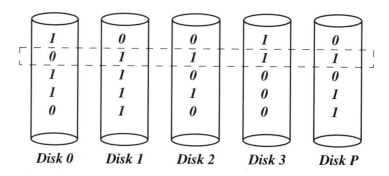

FIGURE 3.17   **A RAID3 system with 4 data disks and an even-parity disk.**

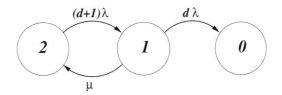

FIGURE 3.18   Markov chain for RAID3 reliability calculation.

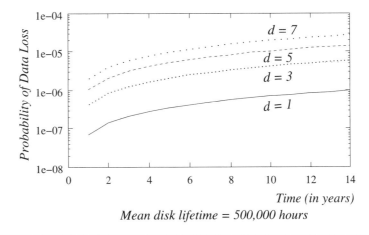

Mean disk lifetime = 500,000 hours

FIGURE 3.19   Unreliability of RAID3 system.

for this group is

$$\text{MTTDL} = \frac{(2d+1)\lambda + \mu}{d(d+1)\lambda^2} \tag{3.10}$$

and the reliability is given approximately by

$$R(t) \approx e^{-t/\text{MTTDL}} \tag{3.11}$$

Figure 3.19 shows some numerical results for various values of d. The case $d = 1$ is identical to the RAID1 system. The reliability drops as d increases, as is to be expected.

3.2.4 RAID Level 4

RAID4 is similar to RAID3, except that the unit of interleaving is not a single bit but a block of arbitrary size, called a *stripe*. An example of a RAID4 system with four data disks and a parity disk is shown in Figure 3.20. The advantage of RAID4 over RAID3 is that a small read operation may be contained in just a single data disk, rather than interleaved over all of them. As a result, small read operations

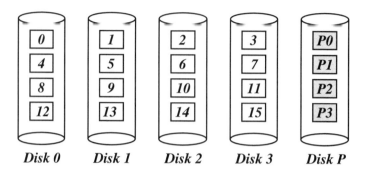

FIGURE 3.20   A RAID4 system with four data disks and a parity disk (each rectangle in the figure contains a block (stripe) of data).

are faster in RAID4 than in RAID3. A similar remark applies to small write operations: in such an operation, both the affected data disk and the parity disk must be updated. The updating of the parity is quite simple: the parity bit toggles if the corresponding data bit that is being written is different from the one being overwritten.

The reliability model for RAID4 is identical to that of RAID3.

3.2.5 RAID Level 5

This is a modification of the RAID4 structure and arises from the observation that the parity disk can sometimes be the system bottleneck: in RAID4, the parity disk is accessed in each write operation. To get around this problem, we can simply interleave the parity blocks among the disks. In other words, we no longer have a disk dedicated to carrying parity bits. Every disk has some data blocks and some parity blocks. An example of a five-disk RAID5 system is shown in Figure 3.21.

The reliability model for RAID5 is obviously the same as for RAID4: it is only the performance model that is different.

3.2.6 Modeling Correlated Failures

In the analysis we have presented so far, we have assumed that the disks fail independently of one another. In this section, we will consider the impact of correlated failures.

Correlated failures arise because power supply and control are typically shared among multiple disks. Disk systems are usually made up of *strings*. Each string consists of disks that are housed in one enclosure, and they share power supply, cabling, cooling, and a controller. If any of these items fails, the entire string can fail.

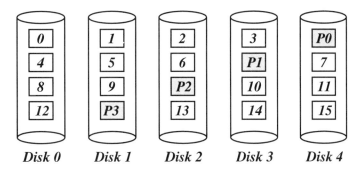

FIGURE 3.21 Distributed parity blocks in a five-disk RAID5 system.

Let λ_{str} be the rate of failure of the support elements (power, cabling, cooling, control) of a string. If a RAID group is controlled by a single string, then the aggregate failure rate of the group is given by

$$\lambda_{total} = \lambda_{indep} + \lambda_{str} \tag{3.12}$$

where λ_{indep} is approximately the inverse of the MTTDL, assuming independent disk failures. If the disk repair rate is much greater than the disk failure rate, data loss due to independent disk failures can be well modeled by a Poisson process. The sum of two independent Poisson processes is itself a Poisson process: we can therefore regard the aggregate failure process as Poisson with rate λ_{total}. The reliability is therefore given by

$$R_{total}(t) = e^{-\lambda_{total}t} \tag{3.13}$$

The dramatic impact of string failures in a RAID1 system is shown in Figure 3.22. (The impact for RAID3 and higher levels is similar). Figures of 150,000 hours for the mean string lifetime have been quoted in the literature, and at least one manufacturer claims mean disk lifetimes of 1,000,000 hours. Grouping together an entire RAID array as a single string therefore increases the unreliability by several orders of magnitude.

To get around this, one can have an orthogonal arrangement of strings and RAID groups, as depicted in Figure 3.23. In such a case, the failure of a string affects only one disk in each RAID group. Because each RAID can tolerate the failure of up to one disk, this reduces the impact of string failures.

The orthogonal system can be modeled approximately as follows. Every data loss is caused by a sequence of events. If this sequence started with a single disk failure or by a string failure, we say the failure is *triggered* by an individual or string failure, respectively.

Since both string and disk failure rates are very low, we can without significant error, model separately failures triggered by individual and string failures. We will find the (approximate) failure rate due to each. Adding these two fail-

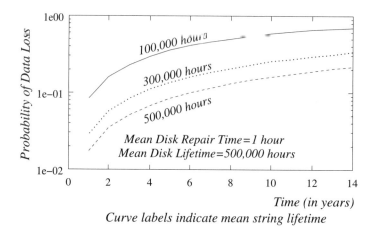

FIGURE 3.22   Impact of string failure rate on RAID1 system.

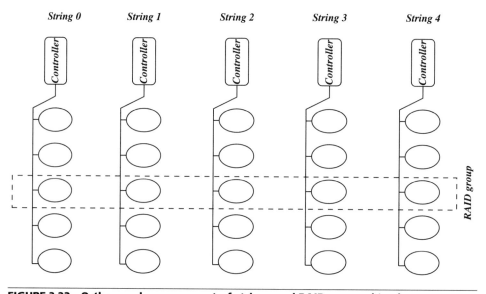

FIGURE 3.23   Orthogonal arrangement of strings and RAID groups ($d = 4$).

ure rates will give us the approximate overall failure rate, which can then be used to determine the MTTDL and the probability of data loss over any given time.

We next construct an approximate model that computes MTTDL and the reliability of the system at any time t. This model allows any general distribution for the repair times.

There is a total of $d+1$ disks per RAID group, which in the orthogonal arrangement means $d+1$ strings, and g groups of disks. The total number of disks is therefore $(d+1)g$. Unlike our previous derivation, we will no longer assume that repair times are exponentially distributed: all we ask is that their distributions be known. Let $f_{\text{disk}}(t)$ denote the density function of the disk repair time.

The approximate rate at which individual failures trigger data loss in a given disk is given by $\lambda_{\text{disk}}\pi_{\text{indiv}}$, where λ_{disk} is the failure rate of a single disk and π_{indiv} is the probability that a given individual failure triggers data loss. To calculate π_{indiv}, recall that it is the probability that another disk fails in the affected RAID group while the previous failure has not yet been repaired. But this failure happens at the rate $d(\lambda_{\text{disk}} + \lambda_{\text{str}})$, since the second disk failure can happen either due to an individual disk, or string, failure. Let τ denote the (random) disk repair time. The probability of data loss conditioned on the event that the repair of the first disk takes time τ is

$$\text{Prob}\{\text{Data loss}|\text{the repair takes } \tau\} = 1 - e^{-d(\lambda_{\text{disk}}+\lambda_{\text{str}})\tau}$$

τ has the density function $f_{\text{disk}}(\cdot)$; hence, the unconditional probability of data loss is

$$\pi_{\text{indiv}} = \int_0^\infty \text{Prob}\{\text{Data loss}|\text{the repair takes } \tau\} \cdot f_{\text{disk}}(\tau)\, d\tau$$

$$= \int_0^\infty \left(1 - e^{-d(\lambda_{\text{disk}}+\lambda_{\text{str}})\tau}\right) f_{\text{disk}}(\tau)\, d\tau$$

$$= \int_0^\infty f_{\text{disk}}(\tau)\, d\tau - \int_0^\infty e^{-d(\lambda_{\text{disk}}+\lambda_{\text{str}})\tau} f_{\text{disk}}(\tau)\, d\tau$$

$$= 1 - F_{\text{disk}}^*\left(d[\lambda_{\text{disk}} + \lambda_{\text{str}}]\right) \tag{3.14}$$

where $F_{\text{disk}}^*(\cdot)$ is the Laplace transform of $f_{\text{disk}}(\cdot)$. Since there are $(d+1)g$ data disks in all, the approximate rate at which data loss is triggered by individual disk failure is given by

$$\Lambda_{\text{indiv}} \approx (d+1)g\lambda_{\text{disk}}\left\{1 - F_{\text{disk}}^*\left(d[\lambda_{\text{disk}} + \lambda_{\text{str}}]\right)\right\} \tag{3.15}$$

Why is this approximate and not exact? Because $(d+1)g\lambda_{\text{disk}}$ is the rate at which individual disk failures occur *in a fault-free system*. Since the probability is very high that the system is entirely fault-free (if the repair times are much smaller than the time between failures and the size of the system is not excessively large), this is usually a good approximation. It does have the merit of not imposing any limitations on the distribution of the repair time.

Let us now turn to computing Λ_{str}, the rate at which data loss is triggered by a string failure. The total rate at which strings fail (if all strings are up) is $(d+1)\lambda_{\text{str}}$. When a string fails, we have to repair the string itself and then make any necessary repairs to the individual disks, which may have been affected by the string failure. We will make the *pessimistic* approximation that failure can happen if another failure occurs in *any* of the groups or any of the disks before *all* of the groups are fully restored. This is pessimistic because there are instances that are counted as causing data loss that, in fact, do not do so. For example, we will count as causing a data failure the occurrence of two string failures in the same string, the second occurring before the first has been repaired. We can also make the *optimistic* assumption that the disks affected by the triggering string failure are all immune to a further failure before the string and all its affected disks are fully restored. The difference between the failure rates predicted by these two assumptions will give us an idea of how tight the pessimistic bound happens to be.

Let τ be the (random) time taken to repair the failed string and all of its constituent disks that may have been affected by it. Let $f_{\text{str}}(\cdot)$ be the probability density function of this time. Then, under the pessimistic assumption, additional failures occur at the rate $\lambda_{\text{pess}} = (d+1)\lambda_{\text{str}} + (d+1)g\lambda_{\text{disk}}$. Under the optimistic assumption, additional failures occur at the rate $\lambda_{\text{opt}} = d\lambda_{\text{str}} + dg\lambda_{\text{disk}}$.

A data loss will therefore be triggered in the pessimistic model with the conditional (upon τ) probability $p_{\text{pess}} = 1 - e^{-\lambda_{\text{pess}}\tau}$ and in the optimistic model with the conditional (upon τ) probability $p_{\text{opt}} = 1 - e^{-\lambda_{\text{opt}}\tau}$. Integrating on τ, we obtain the unconditional pessimistic and optimistic estimates: $\pi_{\text{pess}} = 1 - F^*_{\text{str}}(\lambda_{\text{pess}})$ and $\pi_{\text{opt}} = 1 - F^*_{\text{str}}(\lambda_{\text{opt}})$, respectively, where $F^*_{\text{str}}(\cdot)$ is the Laplace transform of $f_{\text{str}}(\cdot)$. The pessimistic and optimistic rates at which a string failure triggers data loss are therefore given by

$$\Lambda_{\text{str\_pess}} = (d+1)\lambda_{\text{str}}\pi_{\text{pess}}$$

$$\Lambda_{\text{str\_opt}} = (d+1)\lambda_{\text{str}}\pi_{\text{opt}} \tag{3.16}$$

The rate at which data loss happens in the system is therefore approximately:

$$\Lambda_{\text{data\_loss}} \approx \begin{cases} \Lambda_{\text{indiv}} + \Lambda_{\text{str\_pess}} & \text{under the pessimistic assumption} \\ \Lambda_{\text{indiv}} + \Lambda_{\text{str\_opt}} & \text{under the optimistic assumption} \end{cases} \tag{3.17}$$

From this, we immediately have that

$$\text{MTTDL} \approx \frac{1}{\Lambda_{\text{data\_loss}}}, \qquad R(t) \approx e^{-\Lambda_{\text{data\_loss}}t} \tag{3.18}$$

as approximations of the MTTDL and reliability of the system, respectively.

3.3 Data Replication

Data replication in distributed systems is another example of how information redundancy can be used for improved fault tolerance at the system level. Data

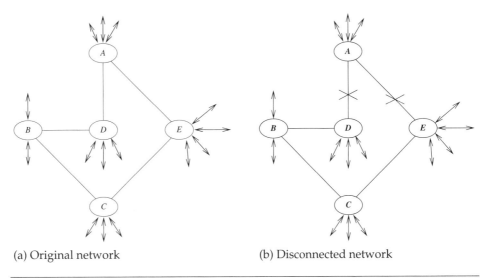

(a) Original network   (b) Disconnected network

FIGURE 3.24   Disconnection endangers the correct operation of data replication.

replication consists of holding identical copies of data on two or more nodes in a distributed system. As with a RAID system, a suitably managed data replication scheme can offer both fault tolerance and improved performance (because one can, for example, read data from nearby copies). However, it is important that the data replicates be kept consistent, despite failures in the system.

Consider, for example, a situation in which we keep five copies of the data: one copy on each of the five nodes of a distributed system, connected as shown in Figure 3.24a. Suppose that a read or a write request may arrive to any of the five nodes on the bidirectional links in the figure. As long as all five copies are kept consistent, a read operation can be sent to any of the nodes. However, suppose two of the links fail, as shown in Figure 3.24b. Then, node A is disconnected from nodes B and C. If a write operation updates the copy of the datum held in A, this write cannot be sent to the other nodes and they will no longer be consistent with A. Any read of their data will therefore result in stale data being used.

In what follows we describe two approaches to managing the replication of data through the assignment of weights (votes) to the individual copies: a non-hierarchical scheme and a hierarchical one. Such votes allow us to prefer copies that reside on more reliable and better connected nodes. We will assume that all faulty nodes can be recognized as such: no malicious behavior takes place.

3.3.1 Voting: Non-Hierarchical Organization

We next present a *voting* approach to handling data replication. To avoid confusion, we emphasize that we do not vote on multiple copies of data. If we read r copies of some data structure, we select one with the latest timestamp. We assume that data coding is used to detect/correct data errors in storage or transmission. Voting is not used for this purpose but solely to specify minimum sets of nodes that need to be updated for a write operation or that need to be accessed for a read operation to be completed.

The simplest voting scheme is the following. Assign v_i votes to copy i of that datum and let S denote the set of all nodes with copies of the datum. Define v to be the sum of all the votes, $v = \sum_{i \in S} v_i$. Define integers r and w with the following properties:

$$r + w > v, \qquad w > v/2$$

Let $V(X)$ denote the total number of votes assigned to copies in set X of nodes. The following strategy ensures that all reads are of the latest data.

To complete a read, it is necessary to read from all nodes of a set $R \subset S$ such that $V(R) \geqslant r$. Similarly, to complete a write, we must find a set $W \subset S$ such that $V(W) \geqslant w$, and execute that write on every copy in W.

This procedure works because for any sets R and W such that $V(R) \geqslant r$ and $V(W) \geqslant w$, we must have $R \cap W \neq \emptyset$ (because $r + w > v$). Hence, any read operation is guaranteed to read the value of at least one copy which has been updated by the latest write. Furthermore, for any two sets W_1, W_2 such that $V(W_1), V(W_2) \geqslant w$, we must have $W_1 \cap W_2 \neq \emptyset$. This prevents different writes to the same datum from being done concurrently and guarantees that there exists at least one node that gets both updates.

Any set R such that $V(R) \geqslant r$ is said to be a *read quorum*, and any set W such that $V(W) \geqslant w$ is called a *write quorum*.

How would this system work for the example shown in Figure 3.24? Assume we give one vote to each node: the sum of all votes is thus $v = 5$. We must have $w > 5/2$, so $w \in \{3, 4, 5\}$. Since $r + w > v$, we must have $r > v - w$. The following combinations are permissible:

$$(r, w) \in \{(1,5), (2,5), (3,5), (4,5), (5,5), (2,4), (3,4), (4,4), (5,4), (3,3)\}$$

Consider the case $(r, w) = (1, 5)$. A read operation can be successfully completed by reading any one of the five copies; however, to complete a write, we have to update every one of the five copies. This ensures that every read operation gets the latest update of the data. If we pick $w = 5$, it makes no sense to set $r > 1$, which would needlessly slow down the read operation. In this case, we can still continue to read from each node even after the failures disconnect the network, as shown in Figure 3.24b. However, it will be impossible to update the datum, since we cannot, from any source, reach all five copies to update them.

As another example, consider $(r, w) = (3, 3)$. This setting has the advantage of requiring just three copies to be written before a data update is successfully completed. However, read operations now take longer because each overall read operation requires reading three copies rather than one. With this system, after the network disconnection, read or write operations coming into node A will not be served. However, the four nodes that are left connected can continue to read and write as usual.

The selected values of r and w will affect the performance of the system. If, for instance, there are many more reads than writes, we may choose to keep r low to speed up the read operations. However, selecting $r = 1$ requires setting $w = 5$, which means that writes can no longer happen if even one node is disconnected. Picking $r = 2$ allows $w = 4$: the writes can still be done if four out of the five nodes are connected. We therefore have a tradeoff between performance and reliability.

The problem of assigning votes to nodes in such a way that availability is maximized is very difficult (the system availability is the probability that both read and write quorums are available). We therefore present two heuristics that usually produce good results (although not necessarily optimal). These heuristics allow us to use a general model that includes node and link failures. Assume that we know the availability of each node i: $a_n(i)$ and of each link j: $a_\ell(j)$. Denote by $L(i)$ the set of links incident on node i.

Heuristic 1. Assign to node i a vote $v(i) = a_n(i) \sum_{j \in L(i)} a_\ell(j)$ rounded to the nearest integer. If the sum of all votes assigned to nodes is even, give one extra vote to one of the nodes with the largest number of votes.

Heuristic 2. Let $k(i, j)$ be the node that is connected to node i by link j. Assign to node i a vote $v(i) = a_n(i) + \sum_{j \in L(i)} a_\ell(j) a_n(k(i, j))$ rounded to the nearest integer. As with Heuristic 1, if the sum of the votes is even, give one extra vote to one of the nodes with the largest number of votes.

As an example, consider the system in Figure 3.25. The initial assignment due to Heuristic 1 is as follows:

$$v(A) = \text{round}(0.7 \times 0.7) = 0$$

$$v(B) = \text{round}(0.8 \times 1.8) = 1$$

$$v(C) = \text{round}(0.9 \times 1.6) = 1$$

$$v(D) = \text{round}(0.7 \times 0.9) = 1$$

Note that Heuristic 1 gives node A 0 votes. This means that A and its links are so unreliable compared to the rest that we may as well not use it. The votes add up to 3, and so the read and write quorums must satisfy the requirements:

$$r + w > 3, \qquad w > 3/2$$

Consequently, $w \in \{2, 3\}$. If we set $w = 2$, we have $r = 2$ as the smallest read quorum. The possible read quorums are therefore $\{BC, CD, BD\}$; these are also the possible write quorums.

If we set $w = 3$, we have $r = 1$ as the smallest read quorum. The possible read quorums are then $\{B, C, D\}$, and there is only one write quorum: BCD.

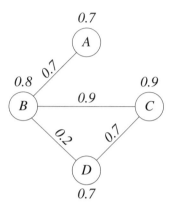

FIGURE 3.25 **Vote assignment example (numbers indicate availabilities).**

Under Heuristic 2, we have the following vote assignment:

$$v(A) = \text{round}(0.7 + 0.7 \times 0.8) = 1$$

$$v(B) = \text{round}(0.8 + 0.7 \times 0.7 + 0.9 \times 0.9 + 0.2 \times 0.7) = 2$$

$$v(C) = \text{round}(0.9 + 0.9 \times 0.8 + 0.7 \times 0.7) = 2$$

$$v(D) = \text{round}(0.7 + 0.2 \times 0.8 + 0.7 \times 0.9) = 1$$

Since the votes add up to an even number, we give B an extra vote, so that the final vote assignment becomes: $v(A) = 1$, $v(B) = 3$, $v(C) = 2$, $v(D) = 1$. The votes now add up to 7, so that the read and write quorums must satisfy

$$r + w > 7, \qquad w > 7/2$$

Consequently, $w \in \{4,5,6,7\}$. Table 3-7 shows read and write quorums associated with $r + w = 8$. We invite the reader to augment the table by listing the availability associated with each given (r,w) pair: this is, of course, the probability that at least one read and one write quorum can be mustered despite node and/or link failures. We illustrate the process by solving the problem for $(r, w) = (4,4)$. The availability in this case is the probability that at least one of the quorums AB, BC, BD, ACD can be used. We compute this probability by first calculating the availabilities of the individual quorums. Quorum AB can be used if A, B, and the single path connecting them are up. The probability of this occurring is

$$\text{Prob}\{AB \text{ can be used}\} = a_n(A)a_n(B)a_l(l_{AB}) = 0.7 \cdot 0.8 \cdot 0.7 = 0.392$$

where $a_l(l_{AB})$ is the availability of the link l_{AB} connecting the two nodes A and B. Quorum BC will be usable if B, C and at least one of the two paths connecting

TABLE 3-7 ■ Read and write quorums under heuristic 2			
r	w	**Read quorums**	**Write quorums**
4	4	AB, BC, BD, ACD	AB, BC, BD, ACD
3	5	B, AC, CD	BC, ABD
2	6	B, C, AD	ABC, BCD
1	7	A, B, C, D	ABCD

them are up. This probability can be calculated as follows:

$$\text{Prob}\{BC \text{ can be used}\} = a_n(B)a_n(C)\big[a_l(l_{BC}) + a_l(l_{BD})a_n(D)a_l(l_{DC})\big(1 - a_l(l_{BC})\big)\big]$$
$$= 0.8 \cdot 0.9[0.9 + 0.2 \cdot 0.7 \cdot 0.7 \cdot 0.1] = 0.655$$

Similarly, we can calculate the availabilities of the quorums BD and ACD. However, to compute the system availability, we cannot just add up the availabilities of the individual quorums because the events "quorum i is up" are not mutually exclusive. Instead, we would have to calculate the probabilities of all intersections of these events and then substitute them in the inclusion and exclusion formula, which is quite a tedious task. An easier and more methodical way of computing the system availability is to list all possible combinations of system components' states, and add up the probabilities of those combinations for which a quorum exists. In our example, the system has eight components (nodes and links), each of which can be in one of two states: "up" and "down," with $2^8 = 256$ system states in all. The probability of each state is a product of eight terms, each taking one of the following forms: $a_n(i)$, $(1 - a_n(i))$, $a_l(j)$, or $(1 - a_l(j))$. For each such state, we can establish whether a read quorum or a write quorum exists, and the availability of the system is the sum of the probabilities of the states in which both read and write quorums exist.

For $(r, w) = (4, 4)$, the lists of read quorums and write quorums are identical. For any other value of (r, w), these lists are different, and to calculate the availability of the system, we must take into consideration the relative frequencies of read and write operations and multiply these by the probabilities that a read quorum and a write quorum exists, respectively.

A write quorum must consist of more than half the total number of votes. A system that is not easily or rapidly repaired, however, could degrade to the point at which no connected cluster exists that can muster a majority of the total votes. In such a case, no updates can be carried out to any data even if a sufficiently large portion of the system remains operational.

This problem can be countered by dynamic vote assignment. Instead of keeping the read and write quorums static, we alter them to adjust to prevailing system conditions. In the discussion that follows, we assume that each node has exactly one vote. It is not difficult to relax this restriction.

For each datum, the algorithm consists of maintaining *version numbers*, VN_i, with each copy of that datum at each node i. Every time a node updates a datum,

1. If an update request arrives at node i, node i computes the following quantities:

   - $M = \max\{VN_j, j \in S_i\}$ (where S_i is the set of nodes with which node i can communicate, including i itself), i.e., the maximum version number of the concerned datum, among all the nodes with which node i can communicate.

   - $I = \{j | VN_j = M, j \in S_i\}$, i.e., the set of all nodes whose version number is equal to the maximum.

   - $N = \max\{SC_j, j \in I\}$, i.e., the maximum update sites cardinality associated with all the nodes in I.

2. If $\|I\| > N/2$, then node i can raise a write quorum and is allowed to carry out the update on all nodes in I; otherwise the update is not allowed. The update is carried out and the version number of each copy of that datum in I is incremented, i.e., VN_i is incremented for each $i \in I$. Also, for each $i \in I$, we set $SC_i = \|I\|$. This entire step must be done atomically: all these operations must be done at each node in I, or none of them can be done.

FIGURE 3.26   Algorithm for dynamic vote assignment ($\|I\|$ is the cardinality of set I).

the corresponding version number is incremented. Assume that an update arrives at a node. This can only be executed if a write quorum can be gathered. The *update sites cardinality* at node i, denoted by SC_i, is the number of nodes that participated in the VN_ith update of that datum. When the system starts operation, SC_i is initialized to the total number of nodes in the system. The algorithm in Figure 3.26 shows how the dynamic vote assignment procedure works.

The following example illustrates the algorithm. Suppose we start with seven nodes, all carrying copies of some datum. The state at time t_0 is as follows:

	A	B	C	D	E	F	G
VN	5	5	5	5	5	5	5
SC	7	7	7	7	7	7	7

Suppose now that at time t_0 a failure occurs in the system, disconnecting the system into two connected components: $\{A, B, C, D\}$ and $\{E, F, G\}$. No element in one component can communicate with any element in the other. Suppose E receives an update request at time $t_1 > t_0$. Since $SC_E = 7$, E has to find more than $7/2$ (i.e., four or more) nodes (including itself), to consummate that update. However, E can only communicate with two other nodes, F and G, and so the update request must be rejected.

At time $t_2 > t_0$, an update request arrives at node A, which is connected to three other nodes, and so the request can be honored. The update is carried out on A, B, C, and D, and the new state becomes the following:

	A	B	C	D	E	F	G
VN	6	6	6	6	5	5	5
SC	4	4	4	4	7	7	7

At time $t_3 > t_2$, there is a further failure: the connected components of the network become $\{A,B,C\}$, $\{D\}$, $\{E,F,G\}$. At time $t_4 > t_3$, an update request arrives at C. The write quorum at C consists of just three elements now (i.e., the smallest number greater than $SC_C/2$), and so the update can be successfully completed at nodes A,B, and C. The state is now:

	A	B	C	D	E	F	G
VN	7	7	7	6	5	5	5
SC	3	3	3	4	7	7	7

What protocols must be followed to allow nodes to rejoin the components after having been disconnected from them? We leave their design to the reader.

3.3.2 Voting: Hierarchical Organization

The obvious question that now arises is whether there is a way to manage data replication that does not require that $r + w > v$. If v is large (which can happen if a large number of copies is to be maintained), then data operations can take a long time. One solution is to have a hierarchical voting scheme as follows.

We construct an m-level tree in the following way. Let all the nodes holding copies of the data be the leaves at level $m - 1$. We then add virtual nodes at the higher levels up to the root at level 0. All the added nodes are only virtual groupings of the real nodes. Each node at level i will have the same number of children, denoted by ℓ_{i+1}. As an example, consider Figure 3.27. In this tree, $\ell_1 = \ell_2 = 3$.

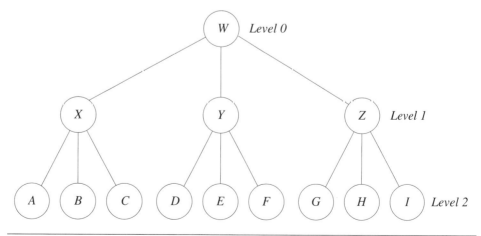

FIGURE 3.27   A tree for hierarchical quorum generation ($m = 3$).

We now assign one vote to each node in the tree and define the read and write quorum sizes, r_i and w_i, respectively, at level i to satisfy the inequalities:

$$r_i + w_i > \ell_i, \qquad w_i > \ell_i/2$$

Then, the following algorithm is used to recursively assemble a read and write quorum at the leaves of the tree. *Read-mark* the root at level 0. Then, at level 1, read-mark r_1 nodes. When proceeding from level i to level $i+1$, read-mark r_{i+1} children of each of the nodes read-marked at level i. It is not allowed to read-mark a node that does not have at least r_{i+1} nonfaulty children: if this was done, we need to backtrack and undo the marking of that node. Proceed like this until $i = m - 1$. The leaves that have been read-marked form a read-quorum. Forming a write-quorum is similar.

For the tree in Figure 3.27, let us select $w_i = 2$ for $i = 1, 2$, and set $r_i = \ell_i - w_i + 1 = 2$. Starting at the root, read-mark two of its children, say X and Y. Now, read-mark two children for X and Y, say A, B for X, and D, E for Y. The read quorum is the set of read-marked leaves, namely, A, B, D, and E.

Suppose D had been faulty. Then, it cannot be part of the read-quorum, so we have to pick another child of Y, namely, F, to be in the read-quorum. If two of Y's children had been faulty, we cannot read-mark Y and have to backtrack and try read-marking Z instead.

As an exercise, the reader should list read quorums generated by other values for r_i and w_i. For example, try $r_1 = 1$, $w_1 = 3$, $r_2 = 2$, $w_2 = 2$.

Note that the read quorum consists of just four copies. Similarly, we can generate a write quorum with four copies. If we had tried the non-hierarchical approach with one vote per node, our read and write quorums would have had to satisfy the conditions $r + w > 9$; $w > 9/2$. Hence, the write quorum in the non-hierarchical approach is of size at least 5, whereas that for the tree approach is 4.

Given each read and write quorum, the topology of the interconnection network, and the probability of node and link failures, we can, for each assignment of r_i and w_i, list the probability that read and write quorums will exist in any given system.

How can we prove that this approach does, in fact, work? We do so by showing that every possible read quorum has to intersect with every possible write quorum in at least one node. This is not difficult to do, and we leave it as an exercise to the reader.

3.3.3 Primary-Backup Approach

Another scheme for managing data replicas is the primary-backup approach, in which one node is designated as the primary, and all accesses are through that node. The other nodes are designated as backups. Under normal operation, all writes to the primary are also copied to the functional backups. When the primary fails, one of the backup nodes is chosen to take its place.

Let us now consider the details of this scheme. We start by describing how things work in the absence of failures. All requests from users (*clients* in the client-server terminology) are received by the primary server. It forwards the request to the copies and waits until it receives an acknowledgment from all of them. Once the acknowledgments are in, the primary fulfills the client's request.

All client requests must pass through the primary; it is the primary that serializes them determining the order in which they are served. All messages from the primary are numbered, so that they can be processed by the backups in the order in which they are sent. This is extremely important, because changing the order in which requests are served could result in entering an incorrect state.

■ EXAMPLE

The primary receives a request, R_d, to deposit $1000 in Mr. Smith's bank account. This is followed by a request, R_t, to transfer $500 out of his account. He had $300 in his bank balance to begin with.

Suppose the primary receives R_d first and then R_t. It forwards these messages in that order to each of the backups. Suppose backup B_1 receives R_d first and then R_t. B_1 can process them in that order, leaving $800 in Mr. Smith's account. Now, suppose backup B_2 receives R_t first and then R_d. R_t cannot be honored: Mr. Smith does not have enough money in his account. Hence, the transfer request is denied in the copy of the account held by B_2. B_1 and B_2 are now no longer consistent. ■

In the absence of failures, it is easy to see that all the copies will be consistent if we follow this procedure. We now need to augment it to consider the case of failure. We will limit ourselves here to fail-stop failures, which are failures that result in silence. Byzantine failures (in which nodes can send back lying messages and do arbitrary things to their copies of the data) are not covered.

Start by considering network failures. If the network becomes disconnected as a result of these failures, then it is only the component that is reachable by the primary that can take part in this algorithm. All others will fall out of date and will need to be reinitialized when the network is repaired.

Next, consider the loss of messages in the network. This can be handled by using a suitable communication algorithm, which retransmits messages until an acknowledgment is received. Hence, we can assume in what follows that if a message is transmitted, it will ultimately be received, unless we have a node failure.

Now, let us turn to node failures. Suppose one of the backups has failed and never returns an acknowledgment. The primary has to wait to receive an acknowledgment from each of the backups; if a backup fails, it may have to wait forever. This problem is easy to remedy: introduce a timeout feature. If the primary does not receive an acknowledgment from the backup within a specified period, the primary assumes the backup is faulty and proceeds to remove it from the group of backups. Obviously, the value that is used for the timeout depends on the interconnection network and the speed of the processing.

Next, consider the failure of the primary itself, and let us see how this affects the processing of some request, R. How complicated it can be to handle this case depends on when the primary goes down. If it fails before forwarding any copies of R to any of its backups, there is no possibility of inconsistency among the backup copies: all we have to do then is to designate one of the backups as the new primary. This can be done by numbering the primary and each of the backups and always choosing the smallest-numbered functional copy to play the part of the primary.

If it fails after forwarding copies of R to all of its backups, then again there is no inconsistency among the backup copies: they have all seen identical copies of R. All that remains then is to choose one of the backups to be the new primary.

The third case is the most complex: the primary fails after sending out messages to some, but not all, of its backups. Such a situation obviously needs some corrective action to maintain consistency among the backups. This is a little complicated and requires us to introduce the concept of a *group view*. To begin with, when the system starts with the primary and all backups fully functional and consistent, the group view consists of all of these copies. Each element in this set is aware of the group view, in other words, each backup knows the full set of backups to whom the primary is forwarding copies of requests. Call this initial group view G_0. At any point in time, there is a prevailing group view, which is modified as nodes fail and are repaired (as described below).

Messages as received by the backups are classified by them as either *stable* or *unstable*. A stable message is one that has been acknowledged by all the backups in the current group view. Until an acknowledgment has been observed, the message is considered to be unstable.

Suppose now that backup B_i detects that the primary has failed. We will discuss below how such failure might be detected. Then, B_i sends out a message announcing its findings to the other nodes in the current group view. A new group view is then constructed, from which the primary node is excluded and a new primary is designated.

Before each node can install the new group view, it transmits to the other nodes in the old group view all the unstable messages in its buffer. This is followed by an *end-of-stream* message, announcing that all of its unstable messages have been sent. When it has received from every node in the new view an acknowledgment of these messages, it can proceed to assume that the new group view is now established.

What if another node fails when this is going on? This will result in a waited-for-acknowledgment never being received: a timeout can be used to declare as faulty nodes that do not acknowledge messages, and the procedure of constructing yet another group view can be repeated.

This leaves us with the question of how the failure of a primary is to be discovered. There are many ways in which this can be done. For example, one may have each node run diagnostics on other nodes. Alternatively, we could require that the primary broadcast a message ("I am alive") at least once every T seconds, for some suitable T. If this requirement is not fulfilled, that could be taken as indicating that the primary is faulty.

Finally, we should mention that this procedure allows for nodes to be repaired. Such a node would make its database consistent with that of the nodes in the prevailing group view and announce its accession to the group through a message. The nodes would then go through the procedure of changing the group view to accommodate this returning node.

3.4 Algorithm-Based Fault Tolerance

Algorithm-Based Fault Tolerance (ABFT) is an approach to provide fault detection and diagnosis through data redundancy. The data redundancy is not implemented at either the hardware or operating system level. Instead, it is implemented at the application software level and as a result, its exact implementation will differ from one class of applications to another. Implementing data redundancy is more efficient when applied to large arrays of data rather than to many independent scalars. Consequently, ABFT techniques have been developed for matrix-based and signal processing applications such as matrix multiplication, matrix inversion, LU decomposition and the Fast Fourier Transform. We will illustrate the ABFT approach through its application to basic matrix operations.

Data redundancy in matrix operations is implemented using a checksum code. Given an $n \times m$ matrix A, we define the *column checksum matrix* A_C as

$$A_C = \begin{bmatrix} A \\ eA \end{bmatrix}$$

where $e = [1\ 1\ \cdots\ 1]$ is a row vector containing n 1s. In other words, the elements in the last row of A_C are the checksums of the corresponding columns of A. Similarly, we define the *row checksum matrix* A_R as

$$A_R = [A \quad Af]$$

where $f = [1\ 1\ \cdots\ 1]^T$ is a column vector containing m 1s. Finally, the *full* $(n+1) \times (m+1)$ *checksum matrix* A_F is defined as

$$A_F = \begin{bmatrix} A & Af \\ eA & eAf \end{bmatrix}$$

Based on the discussion in Section 3.1, it should be clear that the column or row checksum matrix can be used to detect a single fault in any column or row of A, respectively, whereas the full checksum matrix can be used to locate an erroneous single element of A. If the computed checksums are accurate (overflows are not discarded), locating the erroneous element allows us to correct it as well.

The above column, row, and full checksums can be used to detect (or correct) errors in various matrix operations. For example, we can replace the matrix addition $A + B = C$ by $A_C + B_C = C_C$ or $A_R + B_R = C_R$ or $A_F + B_F = C_F$. Similarly, instead of calculating $AB = C$, we may compute $AB_R = C_R$ or $A_C B = C_C$ or $A_C B_R = C_F$.

To allow locating and correcting errors even if only a column or row checksum matrix is used (rather than the full checksum matrix), a second checksum value is added to each column or row, respectively. The resulting matrices are called column, row, and full-weighted matrices and are shown below:

$$
A_C = \begin{bmatrix} A \\ eA \\ e_w A \end{bmatrix} \qquad A_R = \begin{bmatrix} A & Af & Af_w \end{bmatrix} \qquad A_F = \begin{bmatrix} A & Af & Af_w \\ eA & eAf & eAf_w \\ e_w A & e_w Af & e_w Af_w \end{bmatrix}
$$

where $e_w = [1\ 2\ \cdots\ 2^{n-1}]$ and $f_w = [1\ 2\ \cdots\ 2^{m-1}]^{\mathrm{T}}$.

This Weighted-Checksum Code (WCC) can correct a single error even if only two rows or two columns are added to the original matrix. For example, suppose that A_C is used and an error in column j is detected. Denote by WCS1 and WCS2 the values of the unweighted checksum eA and the weighted checksum $e_w A$ in column j, respectively. We then calculate the error in the unweighted checksum $S_1 = \sum_{i=1}^{n} a_{i,j} - \text{WCS1}$ and the error in the weighted checksum $S_2 = \sum_{i=1}^{n} 2^{i-1} a_{i,j} - \text{WCS2}$. If only one of these two error syndromes S_1 and S_2 is nonzero, then the corresponding checksum value is erroneous. If both S_1 and S_2 are nonzero, $S_2/S_1 = 2^{k-1}$ implies that the element $a_{k,j}$ is erroneous and can be corrected through $a'_{k,j} = a_{k,j} - S_1$.

The weighted checksum encoding scheme can be further extended to increase its error detection and correction capabilities by adding extra rows and/or columns with weights of the form $e_{w_d} = [1^{d-1}\ 2^{d-1}\ \cdots\ (2^{n-1})^{d-1}]$ and $f_{w_d} = [1^{d-1}\ 2^{d-1}\ \cdots\ (2^{m-1})^{d-1}]^{\mathrm{T}}$. Note that for $d = 1$ and $d = 2$, we obtain the above two (unweighted and weighted) checksums. If all the weights for $d = 1, 2, \ldots, v$ are used, the resulting weighted checksum encoding scheme has a Hamming distance of $v + 1$, and as a result, is capable of detecting up to v errors and correcting up to $\lfloor v/2 \rfloor$. We will focus below only on the case of $v = 2$.

For large values of n and m, the unweighted and weighted checksums can become very large and cause overflows. For the unweighted checksum, we can use the single-precision checksum scheme using two's complement arithmetic and discarding overflows. Discarding overflows implies that the sum will be calculated modulo-2^{ℓ}, where ℓ is the number of bits in a word. If only a single element of the matrix A is erroneous, the error cannot exceed $2^{\ell} - 1$, and the modulo-2^{ℓ} calculation performed for the single-precision checksum will provide the correct value of the syndrome S_1.

The weighted checksum uses the weights $[1 \ 2 \ \cdots \ 2^{m-1}]$ and would need more than ℓ bits. We can reduce the largest value that the weighted checksum can assume by using a weight vector e_w with smaller weights. For example, instead of $[1 \ 2 \ \cdots \ 2^{n-1}]$, we can use $[1 \ 2 \ \cdots \ n]$. For these weights, if both error syndromes S_1 and S_2 for column j are nonzero, $S_2/S_1 = k$ implies that the element $a_{k,j}$ is erroneous and it can be corrected as before through $a'_{k,j} = a_{k,j} - S_1$.

If floating-point arithmetic is used for the matrix operations, an additional complexity arises. Floating-point calculations may have roundoff errors that can result in a nonzero error syndrome S_1 even if all the matrix elements were computed correctly. Thus, we must set an error bound δ such that $S_1 < \delta$ will not signal a fault. The proper value of δ depends on the type of data, the type of calculations performed, and the size of the matrix. Setting δ too low will lead to roundoff errors misinterpreted as faults (causing false alarms), whereas setting it too high can reduce the probability of fault detection. One way to deal with this problem is to partition the matrix into submatrices and assign checksums to each submatrix separately. The smaller size of these submatrices will greatly simplify the selection of a value for δ, which will provide a good tradeoff between the probability of a false alarm and the probability of fault detection. Partitioning into submatrices will slightly increase the complexity of the calculations but will allow the detection of multiple faults even if only two (unweighted and weighted) checksums are used.

3.5 Further Reading

Many textbooks on the topic of coding theory are available. See, for example, [7–11,20,22,25,33,35,37,38,43–45,52,56–58]. Cyclic codes are discussed in detail in [7, 9,11,22,33,35,37,38,43–45,49,52,56,57]. There are several websites that include descriptions of various codes and even software implementations of some of them [13,15,31,39,46,59]. Arithmetic codes are discussed in [3,4,30,48] and unidirectional codes are covered in [12,49].

Descriptions of RAID structures are widely available in textbooks on computer architecture. See also [14,23,42].

An excellent source for voting algorithms is [28]. Pioneering work in this area appears in [18] and [55]. Further key contributions are presented in [6,17]. Hierarchical voting is described in [32]. See also [47] for a discussion of the tradeoff between message overheads and data availability and [26,27] for dynamic vote assignment, as well as [1,36] on quorums when servers may suffer Byzantine faults. The tradeoff between the load of a quorum system and its availability has been studied in [41]. The primary/backup approach to data-replica management can be found in [16,19,28,40,54]. The references also discuss another approach to replica management, where no single node is designated as the primary, but each copy can manage client requests. This is called *active replication* or the *state-machine approach*.

Algorithm-based fault tolerance was first proposed in [24] and further developed in [5,29]. Alternative weights for the checksum codes are presented in [2,34] and extending the approach to floating-point calculations is discussed in [50,60]. Round-off errors in floating-point operations are described in [30].

3.6   Exercises

1. Prove that it is possible to find at most 28 8-bit binary words such that the Hamming distance between any two of them is at least 3.

2. To an n-bit word with a single-parity bit (for a total of $(n+1)$ bits), a second parity bit for the $(n+1)$-bit word has been added. How would the error detection capabilities change?

3. Show that the Hamming distance of an M-of-N code is 2.

4. Compare two parity codes for data words consisting of 64 data bits: (1) a $(72,8)$ Hamming code and (2) a single-parity bit per byte. Both codes require 8 check bits. Indicate the error correction and detection capabilities, the expected overhead, and list the types of multiple errors that are detectable by these two codes.

5. Show that a code can detect all unidirectional errors if and only if no two of its codewords are ordered. Two binary N-bit words X and Y are *ordered* if either $x_i \leqslant y_i$ for all $i \in \{1,2,\ldots,N\}$ or $x_i \geqslant y_i$ for all $i \in \{1,2,\ldots,N\}$.

6. A communication channel has a probability of 10^{-3} that a bit transmitted on it is erroneous. The data rate is 12,000 bits per second (bps). Data packets contain 240 information bits, a 32-bit CRC for error detection, and 0, 8, or 16 bits for error correction coding (ECC). Assume that if 8 ECC bits are added, all single-bit errors can be corrected, and if 16 ECC bits are added all double-bit errors can be corrected.

   a. Find the throughput in information bits per second of a scheme consisting of error detection with retransmission of bad packets (i.e., no error correction).

   b. Find the throughput if eight ECC check bits are used, so that single-bit errors can be corrected. Uncorrectable packets must be retransmitted.

   c. Finally find the throughput if 16 ECC check bits are appended, so that 2-bit errors can be corrected. As in (b), uncorrectable packets must be retransmitted. Would you recommend increasing the number of ECC check bits from 8 to 16?

7. Derive all codewords for the separable 5-bit cyclic code based on the generating polynomial $X+1$ and compare the resulting codewords to those for the nonseparable code.

8. a. Show that if the generating polynomial $G(X)$ of a cyclic code has more than one term, all single-bit errors will be detected.

   b. Show that if $G(X)$ has a factor with three terms, all double-bit errors will be detected.

   c. Show that if $G(X)$ has $X + 1$ as a factor, all odd numbers of bit errors will be detected. That is, if $E(X)$ contains an odd number of terms (errors), it does not have $X + 1$ as a factor. Also show that CRC-16 and CRC-CCITT contain $X + 1$ as a factor. What are the error detection capabilities of these cyclic codes?

9. Given that $X^7 - 1 = (X + 1)g_1(X)g_2(X)$, where $g_1(X) = X^3 + X + 1$,

   a. Calculate $g_2(X)$.

   b. Identify all the $(7, k)$ cyclic codes that can be generated based on the factors of $X^7 - 1$. How many different such cyclic codes exist?

   c. Show all the codewords generated by $g_1(X)$ and their corresponding data words.

10. Given a number X and its residue modulo-3, $C(X) = |X|_3$; how will the residue change when X is shifted by one bit position to the left if the shifted-out bit is 0? Repeat this for the case where the shifted-out bit is 1. Verify your rule for $X = 01101$ shifted five times to the left.

11. Show that a residue check with the modulus $A = 2^a - 1$ can detect all errors in a group of $a - 1$ (or fewer) adjacent bits. Such errors are called *burst errors* of length $a - 1$ (or less).

12. You have a RAID1 system in which failures occur at individual disks at a constant rate λ per disk. The repair time of disks is exponentially distributed with rate μ. Suppose we are in an earthquake-prone area, where building-destroying earthquakes occur according to a Poisson process with rate λ_e. If the building is destroyed, so too is the entire RAID system. Derive an expression for the probability of data loss for such a system as a function of time. Assuming that the mean time between such earthquakes is 50 years, plot the probability of data loss as a function of time using the parameters $1/\lambda = 500,000$ hours and $1/\mu - 1$ hour.

13. For a RAID level 3 system with d data disks and one parity disk, as d increases the overhead decreases but the unreliability increases. Suggest a measure for cost-effectiveness and find the value of d which will maximize your proposed measure.

14. Given a RAID level 5 system with an orthogonal arrangement of $d + 1$ strings and $g = 8$ RAID groups, compare the MTTDL for different values of d from 4 to 10. Assume an exponential repair time for single disks and for strings of disks with rates of 1/hour and 3/hour, respectively. Also assume failure ratoc for cinglo dicks and ctrings of disks of 10^{-6}/hour and $5 \cdot 10^{-6}$/hour, respectively.

15. Derive expressions for the reliability and availability of the network shown in Figure 3.24a for the case $(r, w) = (3, 3)$ where a single vote is assigned to each node in the nonhierarchical organization. In this case, both read and write operations can take place if at least three of the five nodes are up. Assume that failures occur at each node according to a Poisson process with rate λ, but the links do not fail. When a node fails, it is repaired (repair includes loading up-to-date data) and the repair time is an exponentially distributed random variable with mean $1/\mu$. Derive the required expressions for the system reliability and availability using the Markov chains (see Chapter 2) shown in Figure 3.28a and b, respectively, where the state is the number of nodes that are down.

16. In Figure 3.28, a Markov chain is provided for the case in which nodes can be repaired in an exponentially distributed time. Suppose instead that the repair time was a fixed, deterministic time. How would this complicate the model?

17. For the model shown in Question 15, suppose $\lambda = 10^{-3}$ and $\mu = 1$. Calculate the reliability and availability of each of the following configurations: $(r, w) = (3, 3), (2, 4), (1, 5)$.

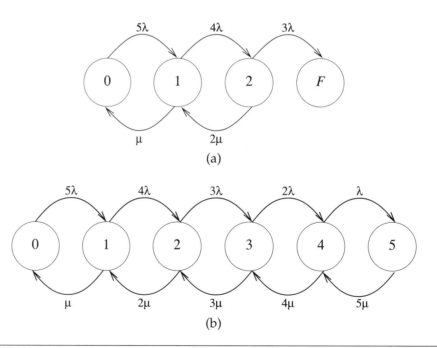

(a)

(b)

FIGURE 3.28   Markov chains for Questions 15–16 ($(r, w) = (3, 3)$).

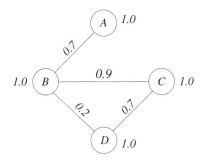

FIGURE 3.29 An example network (numbers indicate availabilities).

18. For the example shown in Figure 3.29, the four nodes have an availability of 1, while the links have the availabilities indicated in the figure. Use Heuristic 2 to assign votes to the four nodes, write down the possible values for w and the corresponding minimal values of r, and calculate the availability for each possible value of (r, w). Assume that read operations are twice as frequent as write operations.

19. Prove that in the hierarchical quorum generation approach in Section 3.3.2, every possible read quorum intersects with every possible write quorum in at least one node.

20. Consider the tree shown in Figure 3.27. If p is the probability that a leaf node is faulty, obtain an expression for the probability that read and write quorums exist. Assume that $r_1 = r_2 = w_1 = w_2 = 2$ and that nodes at levels 0 and 1 do not fail.

21. Show how checksums can be used to detect and correct errors in a scalar by matrix multiplication for the following example. Assume a 3×3 matrix:

$$A = \begin{bmatrix} 1 & 2 & 3 \\ 4 & 5 & 6 \\ 7 & 8 & 9 \end{bmatrix}$$

Show the corresponding column-weighted matrix A_C and assume that during the multiplication of A_C by the scalar 2 a single error has occurred resulting in the following output:

$$2 \cdot A = \begin{bmatrix} 2 & 4 & 6 \\ 8 & 10 & 12 \\ 14 & 17 & 18 \end{bmatrix}$$

References

[1] L. Alvisi, D. Malkhi, E. Pierce, M. K. Reiter, and R. N. Wright, "Dynamic Byzantine Quorum Systems," *International Conference on Dependable Systems and Networks (DSN '00)*, pp. 283–292, 2000.

[2] C. J. Anfinson and F. T. Luk, "A Linear Algebraic Model of Algorithm-Based Fault Tolerance," *IEEE Transactions on Computers*, Vol. 37, pp. 1599–1604, December 1988.

[3] A. Avizienis, "Arithmetic Error Codes: Cost and Effectiveness Studies for Application in Digital System Design," *IEEE Transactions on Computers*, Vol. C-20, pp. 1322–1331, November 1971.

[4] A. Avizienis, "Arithmetic Algorithms for Error-Coded Operands," *IEEE Transactions on Computers*, Vol. C-22, pp. 567–572, June 1973.

[5] P. Banerjee and J. A. Abraham, "Bounds on Algorithm-Based Fault Tolerance in Multiple Processor Systems," *IEEE Transactions on Computers*, Vol. C-35, pp. 296–306, April 1986.

[6] D. Barbara and H. Garcia-Molina, "The Reliability of Voting Mechanisms," *IEEE Transactions on Computers*, Vol. C-36, pp. 1197–1208, October 1987.

[7] J. Baylis, *Error-Correcting Codes*, Chapman and Hall, 1998.

[8] E. Berlekamp (ed), *Key Papers in the Development of Coding Theory*, IEEE Press, 1974.

[9] E. Berlekamp, *Algebraic Coding Theory*, 2nd edition, Aegean Park Press, 1984.

[10] R. Blahut, *Theory and Practice of Error Control Codes*, Addison-Wesley, 1983.

[11] R. Blahut, *Algebraic Codes for Data Transmission*, Cambridge University Press, 2003.

[12] B. Bose and D. J. Lin, "Systematic Unidirectional Error-Detecting Codes," *IEEE Transactions on Computers*, Vol. C-34, pp. 1026–1032, November 1985.

[13] J. Chen, ECC Resources: http://www.ece.umn.edu/users/jchen/ecc.html.

[14] P. M. Chen, E. K. Lee, G. A. Gibson, R. H. Katz, and D. A. Patterson, "RAID: High-performance, Reliable Secondary Storage," *ACM Computing Surveys*, Vol. 26, pp. 145–185, 1994.

[15] ECC Technologies, Inc.: http://members.aol.com/mnecctek/index.html.

[16] A. Cherif and T. Katayama, "Replica Management for Fault-Tolerant Systems," *IEEE Micro*, Vol. 18, pp. 54–65, 1998.

[17] H. Garcia-Molina and D. Barbara, "How to Assign Votes in a Distributed System," *Journal of the ACM*, Vol. 32, pp. 841–860, October 1985.

[18] D. K. Gifford, "Weighted Voting for Replicated Data," *Seventh ACM Symposium on Operating Systems*, pp. 150–162, 1979.

[19] R. Guerraoui and A. Schiper, "Software-Based Replication for Fault Tolerance," *IEEE Computer*, Vol. 30, pp. 68–74, April 1997.

[20] R. Hamming, *Coding and Information Theory*, Prentice Hall, 1980.

[21] M. Herlihy, "Dynamic Quorum Adjustment for Partitioned Data," *ACM Transactions on Database Systems*, Vol. 12, 1987.

[22] R. Hill, *A First Course in Coding Theory*, Oxford University Press, 1986.

[23] M. Holland, G. A. Gibson, and D. P. Siewiorek, "Architectures and Algorithms for Online Failure Recovery in Redundant Disk Arrays," *Distributed and Parallel Databases*, Vol. 2, pp. 295–335, July 1994.

[24] K.-H. Huang and J. A. Abraham, "Algorithm-Based Fault Tolerance for Matrix Operations," *IEEE Transactions on Computers*, Vol. 33, pp. 518–528, June 1984.

[25] C. W. Huffman and V. Pless, *Fundamentals of Error-Correcting Codes*, Cambridge University Press, 2003.

[26] S. Jajodia and D. Mutchler, "Dynamic Voting," *ACM SIGMOD International Conference on Management of Data*, pp. 227–238, 1987.

[27] S. Jajodia and D. Mutchler, "Dynamic Voting Algorithms for Maintaining the Consistency of a Replicated Database," *ACM Transactions on Database Systems*, Vol. 15, pp. 230–280, June 1990.

[28] P. Jalote, *Fault Tolerance in Distributed Systems*, Prentice Hall, 1994.

[29] J. Y. Jou and J. A. Abraham, "Fault Tolerant Matrix Arithmetic and Signal Processing on Highly Concurrent Computing Structures," *Proceedings of the IEEE*, Vol. 74, pp. 732–741, May 1986.

[30] I. Koren, *Computer Arithmetic Algorithms*, A. K. Peters, 2002.

[31] I. Koren, Fault Tolerant Computing Simulator: http://www.ecs.umass.edu/ece/koren/fault-tolerance/simulator/.

[32] A. Kumar, "Hierarchical Quorum Consensus: A New Algorithm for Managing Replicated Data," *IEEE Transactions on Computers*, Vol. 40, pp. 996–1004, September 1991.

[33] S. Lin and D. J. Costello, *Error Control Coding: Fundamentals and Applications*, 2nd edition, Prentice Hall, 1983.

[34] F. T. Luk and H. Park, "An Analysis of Algorithm-Based Fault Tolerance Techniques," *Journal of Parallel and Distributed Computing*, Vol. 5, pp. 172–184, 1988.

[35] F. MacWilliams and N. Sloane, *The Theory of Error-Correcting Codes*, North-Holland, 1977.

[36] D. Malkhi and M. Reiter, "Byzantine Quorum Systems," *Distributed Computing*, Vol. 11, pp. 203–213, 1998.

[37] R. McEliece, *The Theory of Information and Coding*, 2nd edition, Cambridge University Press, 2002.

[38] R. H. Morelos-Zaragoza, *The Art of Error Correcting Coding*, Wiley & Sons, 2002.

[39] R. Morelos-Zaragoza, The Error Correcting Codes (ECC) Home Page: http://www.eccpage.com/.

[40] S. Mullender (Ed.), *Distributed Systems*, Addison-Wesley, 1993.

[41] M. Naor and A. Wool, "The Load, Capacity, and Availability of Quorum Systems," *SIAM Journal of Computing*, Vol. 27, pp. 423–447, 1998.

[42] D. A. Patterson, G. A. Gibson, and R. H. Katz, "A Case for Redundant Arrays of Inexpensive Disks," *International Conference on Management of Data*, pp. 109–116, 1988.

[43] W. Peterson and E. Weldon, *Error-Correcting Codes*, 2nd edition, MIT Press, 1972.

[44] V. Pless, *Introduction to the Theory of Error-Correcting Codes*, 3rd edition, Wiley, 1998.

[45] O. Pretzel, *Error-Correcting Codes and Finite Fields*, Oxford University Press, 1992.

[46] Radio Design Group, Reed–Solomon Error Correction Software: http://www.radiodesign.com/rs_sale.htm.

[47] S. Rangarajan, S. Setia, and S. K. Tripathi, "A Fault Tolerant Algorithm for Replicated Data Management," *IEEE Transactions on Parallel and Distributed Systems*, Vol. 6, pp. 1271–1282, December 1995.

[48] T. R. N. Rao, "Bi-Residue Error-Correcting Codes for Computer Arithmetic," *IEEE Transactions on Computers*, Vol. C-19, pp. 398–402, May 1970.

[49] T. R. N. Rao and E. Fujiwara, *Error-Control Coding for Computer Systems*, Prentice Hall, 1989.

[50] J. Rexford and N. K. Jha, "Partitioned Encoding Schemes for Algorithm-Based Fault Tolerance in Massively Parallel Systems," *IEEE Transactions on Parallel and Distributed Systems*, Vol. 5, pp. 649–653, June 1994.

[51] M. A. Soderstrand, W. K. Jenkins, G. A. Jullien, and F. J. Taylor, *Residue Number System Arithmetic: Modern Applications in Digital Signal Processing*, IEEE Press, 1986.

[52] P. Sweeney, *Error Control Coding: From Theory to Practice*, Wiley, 2002.

[53] N. S. Szabo and R. I. Tanaka, *Residue Arithmetic and Its Application to Computer Technology*, McGraw-Hill, 1967.

[54] A. S. Tanenbaum and M. van Steen, *Distributed Systems: Principles and Paradigms*, Prentice Hall, 2002.

[55] R. H. Thomas, "A Majority Consensus Approach to Concurrency Control for Multiple Copy Databases," *ACM Transactions on Database Systems*, Vol. 4, pp. 180–209, June 1979.

[56] L. Vermani, *Elements of Algebraic Coding Theory*, Chapman and Hall, 1996.

[57] A. Viterbi and J. Omura, *Principles of Digital Communication and Coding*, McGraw-Hill, 1979.

[58] D. Welsh, *Codes and Cryptography*, Oxford University Press, 1988.

[59] R. Williams, A Painless Guide to CRC Error Detection Algorithms: http://www.ross.net/crc/crcpaper.html.

[60] S. Yajnik and N. K. Jha, "Graceful Degradation in Algorithm-Based Fault Tolerance Multiprocessor Systems," *IEEE Transactions on Parallel and Distributed Systems*, Vol. 8, pp. 137–153, February 1997.

CHAPTER 4

Fault-Tolerant Networks

Interconnection networks are widely used today. The simplest example is a network connecting processors and memory modules in a shared-memory multiprocessor, in which processors perform read or write operations in the memory modules. Another example is a network connecting a number of processors (typically with their own local memory) in a distributed system, allowing the processors to communicate through messages while executing parts of a common application. In these two types of network, the individual components (processors and memories) are connected through a collection of links and switchboxes, where a switchbox allows a given component to communicate with several other components without having a separate link to each of them.

A third type of networks, called *wide-area networks*, connects large numbers of processors that operate independently (and typically execute different and unrelated applications), allowing them to share various types of information. In such networks, the term *packet* is often used instead of message (a message may consist of several packets, each traversing the network independently), and they consist of more complicated switchboxes called *routers*. The best known example of this kind of network is the Internet.

The network's links and switchboxes establish one or more paths between the sender of the message (the *source*) and its receiver (the *destination*). These links and switchboxes can be either unidirectional or bidirectional. The specific organization, or *topology*, of the network may provide only a single path between a given source and a given destination, in which case any fault of a link or switchbox along the path will disconnect the source–destination pair. Fault tolerance in networks is thus achieved by having multiple paths connecting source to destination, and/or spare units that can be switched in to replace the failed units.

Many existing network topologies contain multiple paths for some or all source–destination pairs, and there is a need to evaluate the resilience to faults provided by such redundancy, as well as the degradation in the network operation as faults accumulate.

We begin this chapter by presenting several measures of resilience/fault-tolerance in networks. Then, we turn to several well-known network topologies used in distributed or parallel computing, analyze their resilience in the presence of failures, and describe ways of increasing their fault tolerance. We restrict ourselves in this chapter to networks meant for use in parallel and distributed computer systems. This field of network fault tolerance is large, and we will only be providing a brief sampling in this chapter. Pointers for further reading can be found toward the end.

There is a vast literature on adaptive routing and recovery from lost packets in the field of wide-area networks: for that material, the reader should consult one of the many available books on computer networking.

4.1 Measures of Resilience

To quantify the resilience of a network or its degradation in the presence of node and link failures, we need measures, several of which are presented in this section. We start with generic, graph-theoretical measures and then list several measures specific to fault tolerance.

4.1.1 Graph-Theoretical Measures

Representing the network as a graph, with processors and switchboxes as nodes and links as edges, we can apply resilience measures used in graph theory. Two such measures are:

■ **Node and Link Connectivity.** Perhaps the simplest consideration with respect to any network in the presence of faults is whether the network as a whole is still connected in spite of the failures, or whether some nodes are cut off and cannot communicate with the rest. Accordingly, the node (link) *connectivity* of a graph is defined as the minimum number of nodes (links) that must be removed from the graph in order to disconnect it. (When a node is removed, all links incident on it are removed as well.) Clearly, the higher the connectivity, the more resilient the network is to faults.

■ **Diameter Stability.** The *distance* between a source and a destination node in a network is defined as the smallest number of links that must be traversed in order to forward a message from the source to the destination. The *diameter* of a network is the longest distance between any two nodes. Even if the network has multiple paths for every source–destination pair, we must expect the distance between nodes to increase as links or nodes fail. *Diameter stability* focuses on how rapidly the diameter increases as nodes fail in the network (recall that the term nodes refers not only to processors but to switchboxes as well). A deterministic instance of such a measure is the *persistence*, which is the smallest number of nodes that must fail in order for the diameter to increase. For example, the persistence of a cycle graph is 1: the failure of just one node causes a cycle of n nodes to become a path of $n-1$ nodes, and the diameter jumps from $\lfloor n/2 \rfloor$ to $n-2$. A probabilistic measure of diameter stability is the vector

$$\mathbf{DS} = (p_{d+1}, p_{d+2}, \ldots)$$

where p_{d+i} is the probability that the diameter of the network increases from d to $d+i$ as a result of faults that occur according to some given probability distribution. In these terms, p_∞ is the probability of the diameter becoming infinite, namely, the graph being disconnected.

4.1.2 Computer Networks Measures

The following measures express the degradation of the dependability and performance of a computer network in the presence of faults better than the rather generic measures listed above.

- **Reliability.** We define $R(t)$, the network *reliability* at time t, as the probability that all the nodes are operational and can communicate with each other over the entire time interval $[0, t]$. If no redundancy exists in the network, $R(t)$ is the probability of no faults occurring up to time t. If the network has spare resources in the form of redundant nodes and/or multiple paths between source–destination pairs, the fact that the network is operational at time t means that any failed processing node has been successfully replaced by a spare, and even if some links failed, every source–destination pair can still communicate over at least one fault-free path.

  If a specific source–destination pair is of special interest, we define the *path reliability*—sometimes called *terminal reliability*—as the probability that an operational path has existed for this source–destination pair during the entire interval $[0, t]$.

  An important point to emphasize here is that the reliability (and for that matter, also the graph-theoretical measures listed above) does not include the option of repairing the network (other than switching in a spare), although the management of most actual networks involves the repair or replacement of any faulty component. The reason for that omission is that the reliability measure is intended to give an assessment of the resilience of the network, possibly compared to other similar networks. Also, in many cases repair is not always possible or immediate and may be very expensive. If repair is an integral component of the system's management, *availability* (as defined in Chapter 2) can be used instead of reliability.

■ **Bandwidth.** The meaning of *bandwidth* depends on its context. For a communications engineer, the bandwidth of a channel often stands for the range of frequencies that it can carry. The term can also mean the maximum rate at which messages can flow in a network. For example, a particular link could be specified as being able to carry up to 10 Mbits per second. One can also use the term in a probabilistic sense: for a certain pattern of accesses to a file system, we can use the bandwidth to mean the average number of bytes per second that can be accessed by this system.

The maximum rate at which messages can flow in a network (the theoretical upper bound of the bandwidth) usually degrades as nodes or links fail in a network. In assessing a network, we are often interested in how this expected maximum rate depends on the failure and repair rates.

■ **Connectability.** The node and link connectivity as defined above are rather simplistic measures of network vulnerability and say nothing about how the network degenerates before it becomes completely disconnected. A more informative measure is *connectability*: the connectability at time t, denoted by $Q(t)$, is defined as the expected number at time t of source–destination pairs which are still connected in the presence of a failure process. This measure is especially applicable to a shared memory multiprocessor, where $Q(t)$ denotes the expected number of processor-memory pairs that are still communicating at time t.

4.2 Common Network Topologies and Their Resilience

We present in this section examples of two types of network. The first type connects a set of input nodes (e.g., processors) to a set of output nodes (e.g., memories) through a network composed only of switchboxes and links. As examples for this type, we use the multistage and crossbar networks with bandwidth and connectability as measures for their resilience. The second type is a network of computing nodes that are interconnected through links. No separate switchboxes exist in these networks; instead, the nodes serve as switches as well as processors and are capable of forwarding messages that pass through them on the way to their final destination. The networks we use as examples for this type are the mesh and the hypercube, and the applicable measures for these networks are the reliability/path reliability or the availability, if repair is considered.

4.2.1 Multistage and Extra-Stage Networks

Multistage networks are commonly used to connect a set of input nodes to a set of output nodes through either unidirectional or bidirectional links. These networks

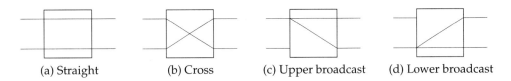

(a) Straight   (b) Cross   (c) Upper broadcast   (d) Lower broadcast

FIGURE 4.1   2 × 2 **switchbox settings.**

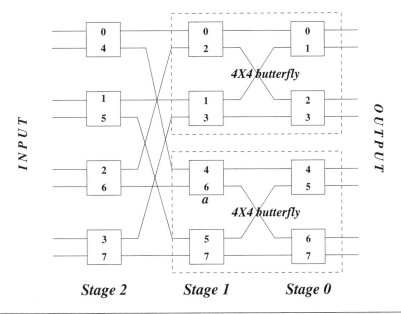

FIGURE 4.2   An 8 × 8 **butterfly network.**

are typically built out of 2 × 2 switchboxes. These are switches that have two inputs and two outputs each, and can be in any of the following four settings (see Figure 4.1):

- **Straight.** The top input line is connected to the top output, and the bottom input line to the bottom output.

- **Cross.** The top input line is connected to the bottom output, and the bottom input line to the top output.

- **Upper Broadcast.** The top input line is connected to both output lines.

- **Lower Broadcast.** The bottom input line is connected to both output lines.

A well-known multistage network is the *butterfly*. As an example see the three-stage butterfly connecting eight inputs to eight outputs shown in Figure 4.2. We have numbered each line in every switchbox such that a switchbox in stage *i* has lines numbered 2^i apart. Output line j of every stage goes into input line j of the following stage, for $j = 0, \ldots, 7$. Such a numbering scheme is probably the easiest way to remember the butterfly structure.

A $2^k \times 2^k$ butterfly network connects 2^k inputs to 2^k outputs and is made up of k stages of 2^{k-1} switchboxes each. The connections follow a recursive pattern from the input end to the output. For example, the 8×8 butterfly network shown in Figure 4.2 is constructed out of two 4×4 butterfly networks plus an input stage consisting of four switchboxes. In general, the input stage of a k-stage butterfly ($k \geqslant 3$) has the top output line of each switchbox connected to an input line of one $2^{k-1} \times 2^{k-1}$ butterfly, and the bottom output line of each switchbox connected to an input line of another $2^{k-1} \times 2^{k-1}$ butterfly. The input stage of a two-stage butterfly (see the 4×4 butterfly in Figure 4.2) has the top output line of each of its two switchboxes connected to one 2×2 switchbox, and the bottom output line to the second 2×2 switchbox.

An examination of the butterfly quickly reveals that the butterfly is not fault tolerant: there is only one path from any given input to any specific output. In particular, if a switchbox in stage i were to fail, there would be 2^{k-i} inputs which could no longer connect to any of 2^{i+1} outputs. The node and link connectivities are therefore each equal to 1. For example, if the switchbox in stage 1 that is labeled a in Figure 4.2 fails, the $2^{3-1} = 4$ inputs 0, 2, 4, and 6 will become disconnected from the $2^{1+1} = 4$ outputs 4, 5, 6, and 7.

One way to render the network fault tolerant is to introduce an extra stage, by duplicating stage 0 at the input. In addition, bypass multiplexers are provided to route around switchboxes in the input and output stages. If a switchbox in these stages is faulty, such a multiplexer can be used to route around the failure. An 8×8 extra-stage butterfly is shown in Figure 4.3. This network can remain connected despite the failure of up to one switchbox anywhere in the system. Suppose, for example, that the stage-0 switchbox carrying lines 2, 3 fails. Then, whatever switching it would have done can be duplicated by the extra stage, while the failed box is bypassed by the multiplexer. Or, suppose that the switchbox in stage 2 carrying lines 0, 4 fails. Then, the extra stage can be set so that input line 0 is switched to output line 1, and input line 4 to output line 5, thus bypassing the failed switchbox. Proving formally that this network can tolerate up to one switchbox failure is quite easy and is left as an exercise for the reader. This proof is based on the fact that because the line numbers in any stage-i box are 2^i apart, the numbers in any box other than at the output and extra stages are both of the same (even or odd) parity.

The network we have depicted connects a set of input nodes to a set of output nodes. The input and output nodes may be the same nodes, in which case node i provides data at line i of the input side and obtains data from line i of the output side. When the sets are disjoint (e.g., a set of processors is connected to a set of memory modules), we can have two networks, one in each direction. Figure 4.4 illustrates these configurations.

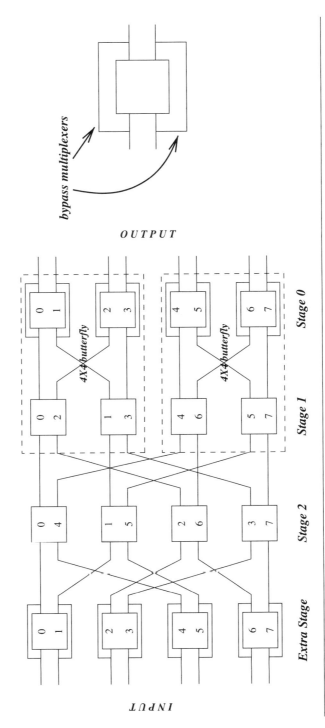

FIGURE 4.3   An 8 × 8 extra-stage butterfly network.

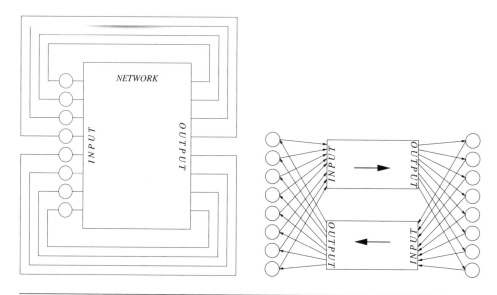

FIGURE 4.4   Two possible configurations for multistage networks.

Analysis of the Butterfly Network

In what follows we analyze the resilience of a k-stage butterfly interconnection network that connects $N = 2^k$ processors to $N = 2^k$ memory units in a shared-memory architecture.

Let us start by deriving the bandwidth of this network in the absence of failures. The bandwidth in this context is defined as the expected number of access requests from the processors that reach the memory modules. We will assume that every processor generates in each cycle, with probability p_r, a request to a memory module. This request is directed to any of the N memory modules with equal probability, $1/N$. Hence, the probability that a given processor generates a request to a specific memory module i ($i \in \{0, 1, \ldots, N-1\}$) is p_r/N. For simplicity, assume that each processor makes a request that is independent of its previous requests. Even if its previous request was not satisfied, the processor will generate a new, independent request. This is obviously an approximation: in practice, a processor will repeat its request until it is satisfied.

Because of the symmetry of the butterfly network and our assumption that all N processors generate requests to all N memories in a uniform fashion, all N output lines of a stage, say stage i, will carry a memory request with the same probability. Let us denote this probability by $p_r^{(i)}$, $i = 0, 1, \ldots, k-1$. We calculate this probability stage by stage, starting at the inputs (processors) where $i = k-1$ and working our way to the outputs (memories) where $i = 0$.

Starting from $i = k-1$, the memory requests of each processor (at a probability of p_r) will, on the average, be equally divided between the two output lines of the switchbox to which the processor is connected. That is, the probability that a certain output line of a switchbox at stage $(k-1)$ will carry a request generated by one of the two processors is $p_r/2$. Because a request on that output line can be generated by either of the two processors, $p_r^{(k-1)}$ is the probability of the union of the two corresponding events (each with probability $p_r/2$). Using the basic laws of probability, we can write

$$p_r^{(k-1)} = \frac{p_r}{2} + \frac{p_r}{2} - \left(\frac{p_r}{2}\right)^2 = p_r - \frac{p_r^2}{4}$$

Using a similar argument to derive an expression for $p_r^{(i-1)}$ when given $p_r^{(i)}$ yields the following recursive equation:

$$p_r^{(i-1)} = p_r^{(i)} - \frac{(p_r^{(i)})^2}{4}$$

Here, too, we rely of the statistical independence of the requests carried by the two input lines to a switchbox, since the two routes they traverse are disjoint.

The bandwidth of the network is the expected number of requests that make it to the memory end, which is

$$\text{BW} = N p_r^{(0)} \tag{4.1}$$

This approach can be extended to nonsymmetric access patterns, in which different memory modules are requested with differing probabilities.

We can now extend this analysis to include the possibility of faulty lines. Assume that a faulty line acts as an open circuit. For any link, let q_ℓ be the probability that it is faulty and $p_\ell = 1 - q_\ell$ the probability that it is fault-free. Note that we have omitted the dependence on time to simplify the notation.

We assume that the failure probability of a switchbox is incorporated into that of its incident links, and thus, in what follows we assume that only links can fail. The probability that a request at the input line to a switchbox at stage $(i-1)$ will propagate to one of the corresponding outputs in stage i is $p_\ell \, p_r^{(i)}/2$. The resulting recursive equation is therefore

$$p_r^{(i-1)} = p_\ell \, p_r^{(i)} - \left(p_\ell \, p_r^{(i)}\right)^2 / 4$$

Setting $p_r^{(k)} = p_r$, we now calculate $p_r^{(0)}$ recursively, and substitute it in Equation 4.1.

Let us now turn to calculating the expected number of connected processor-memory pairs in a k-stage, $2^k \times 2^k$ network, which we call *network connectability*. We are focusing here on the properties of the network and not on the health of the processors and memories. There are $k+1$ links and k switchboxes that need to be traversed in a k-stage network. We make here a distinction between switchbox failures and link failures and denote by q_s the probability that a switchbox fails ($p_s = 1 - q_s$). Because links and switchboxes are assumed to fail independently, and all $k + 1$ links and all k switchboxes on the input–output path must be up for a given processor-memory pair to be connected, the probability that this happens is $(1 - q_\ell)^{k+1}(1 - q_s)^k = p_\ell^{k+1} p_s^k$. Since there are 2^{2k} input–output pairs, the expected number of pairs that are connected is given by

$$Q = 2^{2k} p_\ell^{k+1} p_s^k$$

The network connectability measure does not provide any indication as to how many *distinct* processors and memories are still accessible. We say that a processor is *accessible* if it is connected to at least one memory; an *accessible* memory is defined similarly. To calculate the number of accessible processors, we obtain the probability that a given processor is able to connect to *any* memory. For this calculation, we again confine ourselves to link failures and assume that switchboxes do not fail. We can calculate this probability recursively, starting at the output stage. Denote by $\phi(i)$ the probability that at least one fault-free path exists from a switchbox in stage i to the output end of the network.

Consider $\phi(0)$. This is the probability that at least one line out of a switchbox at the output stage is functional: this probability is $1 - q_\ell^2$.

Consider $\phi(i)$, $i > 0$. From any switchbox in stage i, we have links to two switchboxes in stage $(i - 1)$. Consider the top outgoing link. A connection to the output end exists through this link if and only if that link is functional *and* the stage-$(i - 1)$ switchbox that it leads to is connected to the output end. The probability of this is $p_\ell \, \phi(i - 1)$. Since the two outgoing links from any switchbox are part of link-disjoint paths to the output end, the probability of a stage-i switchbox being disconnected from the output end is $(1 - p_\ell \, \phi(i - 1))^2$. Hence, the probability that it is not disconnected is given by

$$\phi(i) = 1 - \left(1 - p_\ell \, \phi(i - 1)\right)^2$$

The probability that a given processor can connect to the output end is given by $p_\ell \, \phi(k)$. Since there are 2^k processors, the expected number of accessible processors that can connect to at least one memory, denoted by A_c, is thus

$$A_c = 2^k p_\ell \, \phi(k)$$

The butterfly network is symmetric, and so this is also the expression for the expected number of accessible memories.

In this analysis, we have focused on link failures and ignored switchbox failures. As an exercise, we leave to the reader the task of extending the analysis by accounting for the possibility of switchbox failures.

Analysis of the Extra-Stage Network

The analysis of the nonredundant network was simplified by the independence between the two inputs to any switch. The incorporation of redundancy (in the form of additional switchboxes in the extra stage) into the multistage interconnection network in Figure 4.3, resulting in two (or more) paths connecting any given processor-memory pair, introduces dependency among the links. The analysis is further complicated by the existence of the bypass multiplexers at the input and output stages. We will therefore not present here the derivation of an expression for the bandwidth of the extra-stage network. A pointer to such analysis is provided in the Further Reading section.

The derivation of an expression for the network connectability Q is, however, relatively simple and will be presented next. As in the previous section, Q is expressed as the expected number of connectable processor-memory pairs. We first have to obtain the probability that at least one fault-free path between a given processor-memory pair exists.

Each processor-memory pair in the extra-stage network is connected by two disjoint paths (except for both ends), hence

Prob{At least one path is fault-free}

$= $ Prob{First path is fault-free} $+$ Prob{Second path is fault-free}

$-$ Prob{Both paths are fault-free}   **(4.2)**

This probability can assume one of the following two expressions (see, for example, the paths connecting processor 0 to memory 0 and the paths connecting processor 0 to memory 1 in Figure 4.3):

$$A = \left(1 - q_\ell^2\right)p_\ell^k\left(1 - q_\ell^2\right) + p_\ell^{k+2} - p_\ell^{2k+2}\left(1 - q_\ell^2\right)^2$$
$$B = 2\left(1 - q_\ell^2\right)p_\ell^{k+1} - p_\ell^{2k+2}\left(1 - q_\ell^2\right)^2$$

where $\left(1 - q_\ell^2\right)$ is the probability that, for a switchbox with a bypass multiplexer, at least one out of the original horizontal link and its corresponding bypass link is operational. Since there are 2^{k+1} pairs, we can now write

$$Q = (A + B)2^{k+1}/2 = (A + B)2^k$$

4.2.2 Crossbar Networks

The structure of a multistage network limits the communication bandwidth between the inputs and outputs. Even if the processors (connected to the network inputs) attempt to access different memories (connected to the network outputs), they sometimes cannot all do so owing to the network's limitations. For example,

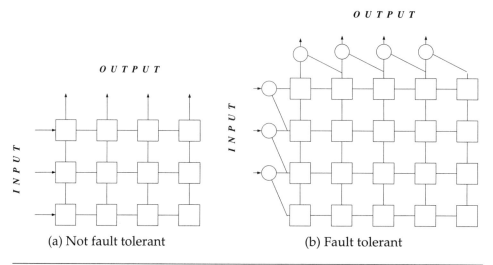

FIGURE 4.5   A 3 × 4 **crossbar.**

if processor 0 (in Figure 4.2) is accessing memory 0, processor 4 is unable to access any of the memories 1, 2, or 3. A crossbar, shown in Figure 4.5a, offers a higher bandwidth. As can be seen from Figure 4.5, if there are N inputs and M outputs, there is one switchbox associated with each of the NM input/output pairings. In particular, the switchbox in row i and column j is responsible for connecting the network input on row i to the network output on column j: we call this the (i,j) switchbox.

Each switchbox is capable of doing the following:

■ Forward a message incoming from its left link to its right link (i.e., propagate it along its row).

■ Forward a message incoming from its bottom link to its top link (i.e., propagate it along its column).

■ Turn a message incoming from its left link to its top link.

Each link is assumed to be able to carry one message; each switchbox can process up to two messages at the same time. For example, a switchbox can be forwarding messages from its left to its right link at the same time as it forwards messages from its bottom link to its top link.

The routing strategy is rather obvious. For example, if we want to send a message from input 3 to output 5, we will proceed as follows. The input will first arrive to switchbox $(3,1)$, which will forward it to $(3,2)$ and so on, until it reaches switchbox $(3,5)$. This switchbox will turn the message into column 5 and forward it to box $(2,5)$, which will send it to box $(1,5)$, which will send it to its destination.

It is easy to see that any input–output combination can be realized as long as there is no collision at the output (no two inputs are competing for access to the same output line).

The higher bandwidth that results from this is especially desirable when both inputs and outputs are connected to high-speed processors, rather than relatively slow memories. This higher performance comes at a price: as mentioned above, an $N \times M$ crossbar with N inputs and M outputs needs NM switchboxes, whereas an $N \times N$ multistage network (where $N = 2^k$) requires only $\frac{N}{2} \log_2 N$ switchboxes.

It is obvious from Figure 4.5a that the crossbar is not fault tolerant: the failure of any switchbox will disconnect certain input–output pairs. Redundancy can be introduced to make the crossbar fault tolerant: an example is shown in Figure 4.5b. We add a row and a column of switchboxes and augment the input and output connections so that each input can be sent to either of two rows, and each output can be received on either of two columns. If any switchbox becomes faulty, the row and column to which it belongs are retired, and the spare row and column are pressed into service.

The connectability of the crossbar (the original structure and the fault-tolerant variation) can be analyzed to identify its dependence on the failure probabilities of the individual components. We demonstrate next the calculation of the connectability Q of the original crossbar, using the same assumptions and notation as for the multistage network. We assume that processors are connected to the inputs and memories to the outputs. As before, assume that q_ℓ is the probability that a link is faulty, $p_\ell = 1 - q_\ell$, and the switchboxes are fault-free. The probability of switchbox failures can be taken into account, if necessary, by suitably adjusting the link failure probabilities. Counting from 1, for input i to be connectable to output j, we have to go through a total of $i + j$ links. The probability that all of them are fault-free is p_ℓ^{i+j}. Hence,

$$Q = \sum_{i=1}^{N} \sum_{j=1}^{M} p_\ell^{i+j} = p_\ell^2 \frac{1 - p_\ell^N}{1 - p_\ell} \frac{1 - p_\ell^M}{1 - p_\ell} \tag{4.3}$$

Calculating Q for the fault-tolerant crossbar and the bandwidth for both designs is more complicated and is left as an exercise for the interested reader.

4.2.3 Rectangular Mesh and Interstitial Mesh

The multistage and crossbar networks discussed above are examples of networks constructed out of switchboxes and links and connecting a set of input nodes to a set of output nodes. A two-dimensional $N \times M$ rectangular mesh network is a simple example of a network topology in which all the nodes are computing nodes and there are no separate switchboxes (see Figure 4.6). Most of the NM computing nodes (except the boundary nodes) have four incident links. To send a message to a node that is not an immediate neighbor, a path from the source of the message to

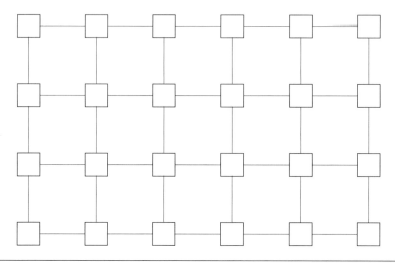

FIGURE 4.6   A 4 × 6 **mesh network.**

its destination must be identified and the message has to be forwarded by all the intermediate nodes along that path.

A conventional two-dimensional rectangular mesh network is unable to tolerate any faults in any of its nodes without losing the mesh property (that each internal node has four neighbors). We can introduce redundancy into the network and provide some tolerance to failures; one approach is shown in Figure 4.7. The modified mesh includes spare nodes that can be switched in to take the place of any of their neighbors that have failed. The scheme shown in Figure 4.7 is called $(1, 4)$ *interstitial redundancy.* In this scheme, each primary node has a single spare node, while each spare node can serve as a spare for four primary nodes: the redundancy overhead is 25%. The main advantage of the interstitial redundancy is the physical proximity of the spare node to the primary node which it replaces, reducing in this way the delay penalty resulting from the use of a spare.

Another version of interstitial redundancy is shown in Figure 4.8. This is an example of a $(4, 4)$ interstitial redundancy in which each primary node has four spare nodes and each spare node can serve as a spare for four primary nodes. This scheme provides a higher level of fault tolerance at the cost of a higher redundancy overhead of almost 100%.

Let us now turn to the reliability of meshes. We will focus on the case in which, as mentioned above, nodes are themselves processors engaging in computation, in addition to being involved in message-passing. In the context of this dual role of processors and switches, reliability no longer means just being able to communicate from one entry point of the network to another; it means instead the ability of the mesh, or a subset of it, to maintain its mesh property.

The algorithms that are executed by mesh-structured computers are often designed so that their communication structure matches that of the mesh. For ex-

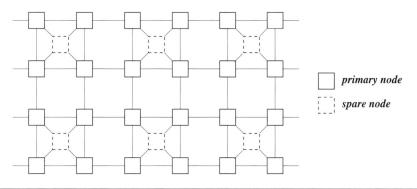

FIGURE 4.7 A mesh network with $(1, 4)$ **interstitial redundancy.**

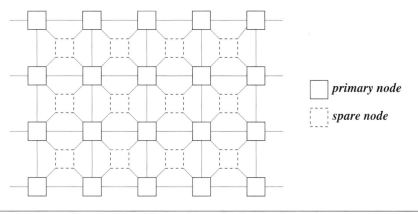

FIGURE 4.8 A mesh network with $(4, 4)$ **interstitial redundancy.**

ample, an iterative algorithm designed for mesh structures and used to solve the differential equation (for some function $f(x, y)$)

$$\frac{\partial^2 f(x, y)}{\partial x^2} + \frac{\partial^2 f(x, y)}{\partial y^2} = 0$$

requires that each node average the values held by its neighbors. Thus, if the mesh structure is disrupted, the system will not be able to efficiently carry out such mesh-structured computations. It is from this point of view that the reliability of the mesh is defined as the probability that the mesh property is retained.

The reliability of the $(1, 4)$ interstitial scheme can be evaluated as follows. Let $R(t)$ be the reliability of every primary or spare node, and let the mesh be of size $N \times M$ with both N and M even numbers. In such a case, the mesh contains $N \times M/4$ clusters of four primary nodes with a single spare node. The reliability of a cluster, assuming that all links are fault-free, is

$$R_{\text{cluster}}(t) = R^5(t) + 5R^4(t)\big(1 - R(t)\big)$$

and the reliability of the $N \times M$ interstitial mesh is

$$R_{\text{IM}}(t) = \big(R^5(t) + 5R^4(t)[1 - R(t)]\big)^{NM/4}$$

This should be compared to the reliability of the original $N \times M$ mesh, which under the same assumptions is $R_{\text{mesh}}(t) = R^{NM}(t)$. The assumption of fault-free links can be justified, for example, in the case in which redundancy is added to each link, making the probability of its failure negligible compared to that of a computing node.

Other measures of dependability can be defined for the mesh network (or its variations). For example, suppose that an application that is about to run on the mesh requires an $n \times m$ submesh for its execution where $n < N$ and $m < M$. In this case, the probability of being able to allocate an $n \times m$ fault-free submesh out of the $N \times M$ mesh in the presence of faulty nodes is of interest. Unfortunately, deriving a closed-form expression for this probability is very difficult because of the need to enumerate all possible positions of a fault-free $n \times m$ submesh within an $N \times M$ mesh with faulty nodes. Such an expression can, however, be developed if the allocation strategy of submeshes is restricted. For example, suppose that only nonoverlapping submeshes within the mesh can be allocated. This strategy limits the number of possible allocations to $k = \lfloor \frac{N}{n} \rfloor \times \lfloor \frac{M}{m} \rfloor$ places. This now becomes a 1-of-k system (see Chapter 2), yielding

$$\text{Prob}\{\text{A fault-free } n \times m \text{ submesh can be allocated}\} = 1 - \big[1 - R^{nm}(t)\big]^k$$

where $R(t)$ is the reliability of a node. If nodes can be repaired, the availability is the more suitable measure. A Markov chain can be constructed to evaluate the availability of a node and, consequently, of a certain size submesh.

4.2.4 Hypercube Network

A hypercube network of n dimensions, H_n, consists of 2^n nodes and is constructed recursively as follows. A zero-dimension hypercube, H_0, consists of just a single node. H_n is constructed by taking two H_{n-1} networks and connecting their corresponding nodes together. The edges that are added to connect corresponding nodes in the two H_{n-1} networks are called *dimension-$(n-1)$* edges. Figure 4.9 shows some examples of hypercubes.

A node in a dimension-n hypercube has n edges incident upon it. Sending a message from one node to another is quite simple if the nodes are named (numbered) in the following way. When the name is expressed in binary and nodes i and j are connected by a dimension-k edge, the names of i and j differ in only the

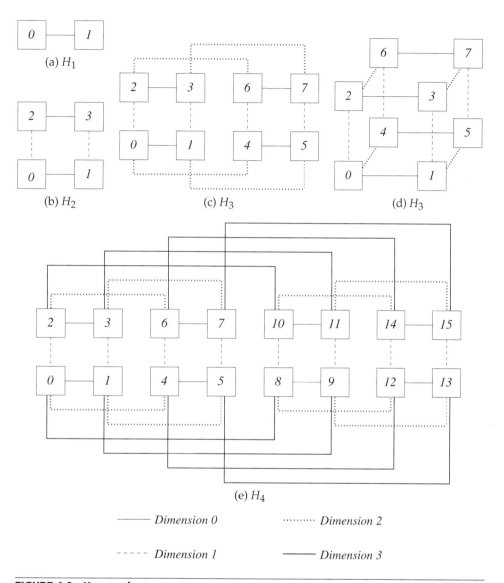

FIGURE 4.9   Hypercubes.

kth-bit position. Thus, we know that because nodes 0000 and 0010 differ in only bit position 1 (the least significant bit is in position 0), they must be connected by a dimension-1 edge.

This numbering scheme makes routing straightforward. Suppose a message has to travel from node 14 to node 2 in an H_4 network. Because 14 is 1110 in binary and 2 is 0010, the message will have to traverse one edge each in the dimensions in which the corresponding bit positions differ, which are dimensions 2 and 3. Thus, if it first travels from node 1110 on a dimension-3 edge, it arrives at node 0110. Leaving this node on a dimension-2 edge, the message arrives at its destination, 0010. Clearly, another alternative is to go first on a dimension-2 edge arriving at 1010 and then on a dimension-3 edge to 0010.

More generally, if X and Y are the node addresses of the source and destination in binary, then the distance between them is the number of bits in which their addresses differ. Going from X to Y can be accomplished by traveling once along each dimension in which they differ. More precisely, let $X = x_{n-1}\cdots x_0$ and $Y = y_{n-1}\cdots y_0$. Define $z_i = x_i \oplus y_i$, where $\oplus$ is the XOR operator. Then, the message must traverse an edge in every dimension i for which $z_i = 1$. Thus, $Z = z_{n-1}\cdots z_0$ is a routing vector, which specifies which dimension edges have to be traversed in order to get to the destination.

H_n (for $n \geqslant 2$) can clearly tolerate link failures because there are multiple paths from any source to any destination. However, node failures can disrupt the operation of a hypercube network. Several ways of adding spare nodes to a hypercube have been proposed. One way is to increase the number of communication ports of each node from n to $(n + 1)$ and connect these extra ports through additional links to one or more spare nodes. For example, if two spare nodes are used, each will serve as a spare for 2^{n-1} nodes, which are the nodes in an H_{n-1} subcube. Such spare nodes may require a large number of ports, namely, 2^{n-1}. This number of ports can be reduced by using several crossbar switches, the outputs of which will be connected to the corresponding spare node. The number of ports of the spare node can thus be reduced to $n + 1$, which will also be the degree of all other nodes. Figure 4.10 shows an H_4 hypercube with two spare nodes and with all 18 nodes having five ports.

Another way of incorporating node redundancy into the hypercube is by duplicating the processor in a few selected nodes. Each of these additional processors can serve as a spare, not only for the processor within the same node but also for any of the processors in the neighboring nodes. For example, nodes 0, 7, 8, and 15 in H_4 (see Figure 4.9e) can be modified to duplex nodes so that every node in the hypercube has a spare at a distance no larger than 1. In this as well as in the previous redundancy scheme, the replacement of a faulty processor by a spare processor will result in an additional communication delay that will be experienced by any node communicating with a spare node.

We now show how to calculate the reliability of this network. Assuming that the nodes and links fail independently of one another, the reliability of the H_n hypercube is the product of the reliabilities of the 2^n nodes and the probability that every node can communicate with every other node despite possible link failures. Since, for even moderately large n, multiple paths connect every source–destination pair in H_n, an exact evaluation of the latter probability would require a substantial enumeration.

Let us instead show how to obtain a good lower bound on the network reliability. We will start by assuming that the nodes are perfectly reliable: this will allow

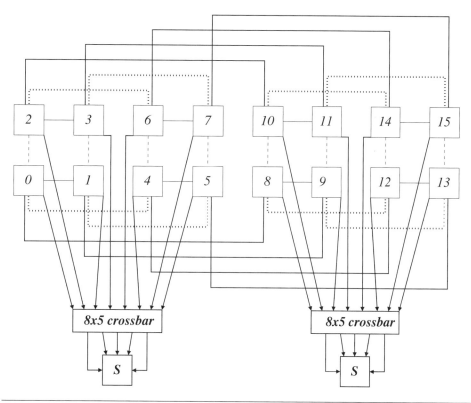

FIGURE 4.10   A hypercube with spare nodes.

us to focus on link failures. Once the network reliability is obtained under this assumption, we can then introduce node failures by multiplying by the probability that all the nodes are functional.

Denote by q_c and q_ℓ the probability of a failure (before time t) of a node and a link, respectively (recall that t is omitted for expression simplicity). Denote the network reliability of H_n under these conditions by $NR(H_n, q_\ell, q_c)$. Throughout we assume that the failures of individual components are independent of one another.

Our lower bound calculation will consist of listing three cases, under each of which the network is connected. These cases are mutually exclusive; we will add their probabilities to obtain our lower bound.

Our approach exploits the recursive nature of the hypercube. H_n can be regarded as two copies of H_{n-1}, with corresponding nodes connected by a link. Let us therefore decompose H_n in this way into two H_{n-1} hypercubes, A and B; H_n consists of these two networks plus dimension-$(n-1)$ links (the link dimensions of H_n are numbered 0 to $n-1$). We then consider the following three mutually exclusive cases, each of which results in a connected H_n. Keep in mind that we are assuming $q_c = 0$ to begin with. Also, when we say that a particular network is operational, we mean that all its nodes are functional and it is connected.

Case 1. Both A and B are operational and at least one dimension-$(n-1)$ link is functional.

$$\text{Prob\{Case 1\}} = \left[\text{NR}(H_{n-1}, q_\ell, 0)\right]^2 \left(1 - q_\ell^{2^{n-1}}\right)$$

Case 2. One of $\{A, B\}$ is operational and the other is not. All dimension-$(n-1)$ links are functional.

$$\text{Prob\{Case 2\}} = 2\,\text{NR}(H_{n-1}, q_\ell, 0)\left[1 - \text{NR}(H_{n-1}, q_\ell, 0)\right](1 - q_\ell)^{2^{n-1}}$$

Case 3. One of $\{A, B\}$ is operational and the other is not. Exactly one dimension-$(n-1)$ link is faulty. This link is connected in the nonoperational H_{n-1} to a node that has at least one functional link to another node.

$$\text{Prob\{Case 3\}} = 2\,\text{NR}(H_{n-1}, q_\ell, 0)\left[1 - \text{NR}(H_{n-1}, q_\ell, 0)\right]$$
$$\times 2^{n-1} q_\ell (1 - q_\ell)^{2^{n-1}-1}\left(1 - q_\ell^{n-1}\right)$$

In the Exercises, you are asked to show that each of these cases results in a connected H_n and that the cases are mutually exclusive.

We therefore have

$$\text{NR}(H_n, q_\ell, 0) = \text{Prob\{Case 1\}} + \text{Prob\{Case 2\}} + \text{Prob\{Case 3\}}$$

The base case is hypercubes of dimension 1: such a system consists of two nodes and one link, yielding

$$\text{NR}(H_1, q_\ell, 0) = 1 - q_\ell$$

We may also start with a hypercube of dimension 2, for which

$$\text{NR}(H_2, q_\ell, 0) = (1 - q_\ell)^4 + 4q_\ell(1 - q_\ell)^3$$

Finally, we consider the case $q_c \neq 0$. From the definition of network reliability, it follows immediately that

$$\text{NR}(H_n, q_\ell, q_c) = (1 - q_c)^{2^n}\,\text{NR}(H_n, q_\ell, 0) \tag{4.4}$$

4.2.5 Cube-Connected Cycles Networks

The hypercube topology has multiple paths between nodes and a low overall diameter of n for a network of 2^n nodes. However, these are achieved at the price of a high node degree. A node must have n ports, which implies that a new node design is required whenever the size of the network increases. An alternative is the Cube-Connected Cycles (CCC) which keeps the degree of a node fixed at three

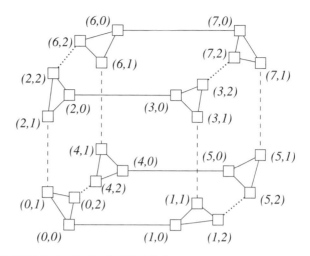

FIGURE 4.11 A $CCC(3,3)$ **(cube-connected cycles) network.**

or less. A CCC network that corresponds to the H_3 hypercube (see Figure 4.9d) is shown in Figure 4.11. Each node of degree three in H_3 is replaced by a cycle consisting of three nodes. In general, each node of degree n in the hypercube H_n is replaced by a cycle containing n nodes where the degree of every node in the cycle is 3. The resulting $CCC(n,n)$ network has $n2^n$ nodes. In principle, each cycle may include k nodes with $k \geqslant n$ with the additional $k - n$ nodes having a degree of 2. This will yield a $CCC(n,k)$ network with $k2^n$ nodes. The extra nodes of degree 2 have a very small impact on the properties that are of interest to us, and we will therefore restrict ourselves to the case $k = n$.

By extending the labeling scheme of the hypercube, we can represent each node of the CCC by $(i;j)$, where i (an n-bit binary number) is the label of the node in the hypercube that corresponds to the cycle and j ($0 \leqslant j \leqslant n - 1$) is the position of the node within the cycle. Two nodes, $(i;j)$ and $(i';j')$, are linked by an edge in the CCC if and only if either

1. $i = i'$ and $j - j' = \pm 1 \bmod n$, or

2. $j = j'$ and i differs from i' in precisely the jth bit.

The former case is a link along the cycle and the latter corresponds to the dimension-j edge in the hypercube. For example, nodes 0 and 2 in H_3 (see Figure 4.9d) are connected through a dimension-1 edge that corresponds to the edge connecting nodes $(0, 1)$ and $(2, 1)$ in Figure 4.11.

The lower degree of nodes in the CCC compared to the hypercube results in a bigger diameter. Instead of a diameter of size n for the hypercube, the diameter of

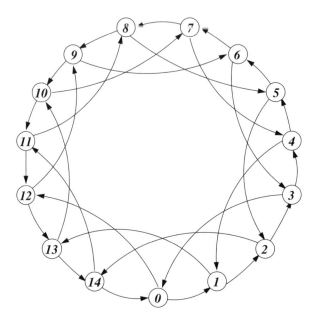

FIGURE 4.12   A 15-node chordal network with a skip distance of 3.

the $CCC(n, n)$ is

$$2n + \left\lfloor \frac{n}{2} \right\rfloor - 2 \approx 2.5n$$

The routing of messages in the *CCC* is also more complicated than that in hypercubes (discussed in Section 4.3.1). The fault tolerance of the *CCC* is, however, higher because the failure of a single node in the *CCC* will only have an effect similar to that of a single faulty link in the hypercube. A closed form expression for the reliability of the *CCC* has not yet been derived.

4.2.6 Loop Networks

The cycle topology (also called loop network) that is replicated in the *CCC* network can serve as an interconnection network with the desirable properties of a simple routing algorithm and a small node degree. However, an *n*-node loop with all its edges unidirectional has a diameter of $n - 1$, which means that a message from one node to the other will, on the average, have to be relayed by $n/2$ intermediate nodes. Moreover, a unidirectional loop network is not fault tolerant; a single node or link failure will disconnect the network.

To reduce the diameter and improve the fault tolerance of the loop network, extra links can be added. These extra links are called *chords*, and one way of adding these unidirectional chords is shown in Figure 4.12. Each node in such a chordal network has an additional backward link connecting it to a node at a distance s, called the *skip distance*. Thus, node i ($0 \leqslant i \leqslant n - 1$) has a forward link to node $(i + 1) \bmod n$ and a backward link to node $(i - s) \bmod n$. The degree of every node in this chordal network is 4 for any value of n.

Different topologies can be obtained by varying the value of s, and we can select s so that the diameter of the network is minimized. To this end, we need an expression for the diameter, denoted by D, as a function of the skip distance s. The diameter is the longest distance that a message must traverse from a source node i to a destination node j: it obviously depends on the routing scheme that is being used. Suppose we use a routing scheme that attempts to reduce the length of the path between i and j by using the backward chords (that allow skipping of intermediate nodes) as long as this is advantageous. If we denote by b the number of backward chords that are being used, then the number of nodes skipped is bs. If the maximum value of b, denoted by b', is reached, then the use of an additional backward chord will take us back to the source i (or even further). Thus, b' should satisfy $b's + b' \geqslant n$. To calculate the diameter D, we therefore use b' backward chords, where

$$b' = \left\lfloor \frac{n}{s+1} \right\rfloor$$

To these b' links, we may need to add a maximum of $s - 1$ forward links, and thus,

$$D = \left\lfloor \frac{n}{s+1} \right\rfloor + (s - 1) \tag{4.5}$$

We wish now to find a value of s that will yield a minimal D. Depending upon the value of n, there may exist several values of s that minimize D. The value $s = \lfloor \sqrt{n} \rfloor$ is optimal for most values of n yielding $D_{\text{opt}} \approx 2\sqrt{n} - 1$. For example, if $n = 15$ as in Figure 4.12, the optimal s that minimizes the diameter D is $s = \lfloor \sqrt{15} \rfloor = 3$ (the value that is used in the figure). The corresponding diameter is $D = \lfloor \frac{15}{4} \rfloor + 2 = 5$.

Analyzing the improvement in the reliability/fault tolerance of the loop network as a result of the extra chords is quite complicated. We can instead calculate the number of paths between the two farthest nodes in the network. If this number is maximized, it is likely that the reliability is close to optimal. We focus on the paths that are of the same length and consist of b' backward chords and $(s - 1)$ forward links but use the backward chords and forward links in a different order. The number of such paths is

$$\binom{b' + s - 1}{s - 1}$$

If we search for a value of s that will maximize the number of alternative paths of the minimum length between the two farthest nodes, we get $s = \lceil \sqrt{n} \rceil$. However, for most values of n, $s = \lfloor \sqrt{n} \rfloor$ also yields the same number of paths. In summary, we conclude that in most cases, the value of s that minimizes the diameter also

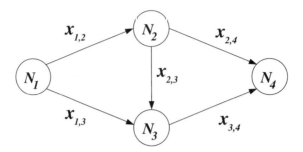

FIGURE 4.13   A four-node network.

maximizes the number of alternate paths and thus improves the reliability of the network.

4.2.7 Ad Hoc Point-to-Point Networks

The interconnection networks that we have considered so far have regular structures and the resulting symmetry greatly simplified the analysis of their resilience. The computing nodes in a distributed computer system are quite often interconnected through a network that has no regular structure. Such interconnection networks, also called *point-to-point networks*, have typically more than a single path between any two nodes, and are therefore inherently fault tolerant. For this type of network, we would like to be able to calculate the *path reliability*, defined as the probability that there exists an operational path between two specific nodes, given the various link failure probabilities.

███ E X A M P L E

Figure 4.13 shows a network of five directed links connecting four nodes. We are interested in calculating the path reliability for the source–destination pair $N_1 - N_4$. The network includes three paths from N_1 to N_4, namely, $P_1 = \{x_{1,2}, x_{2,4}\}$, $P_2 = \{x_{1,3}, x_{3,4}\}$ and $P_3 = \{x_{1,2}, x_{2,3}, x_{3,4}\}$. Let $p_{i,j}$ denote the probability that link $x_{i,j}$ is operational and define $q_{i,j} = 1 - p_{i,j}$. (Here too we omit the dependence on time to simplify the notation.) We assume that the nodes are fault-free; if the nodes can fail, we incorporate their probability of failure into the failure probability of the outgoing links. Clearly, for a path from N_1 to N_4 to exist, at least one of P_1, P_2, or P_3 must be operational. We may not, however, add the three probabilities Prob$\{P_i$ is operational$\}$, because some events will be counted more than once. The key to calculating the path reliability is to construct a set of *disjoint* (or mutually exclusive) events and then add up their probabilities. For this example, the disjoint events that allow N_1 to send a message to N_4 are (a) P_1 is up, (b) P_2 is up but P_1 is down, and (c) P_3 is up but both P_1 and P_2 are down. The path reliability is thus

$$R_{N_1,N_4} = p_{1,2}p_{2,4} + p_{1,3}p_{3,4}[1 - p_{1,2}p_{2,4}] + p_{1,2}p_{2,3}p_{3,4}[q_{1,3}q_{2,4}]$$

■

For this simple network, it is relatively easy to identify the links that must be faulty so that the considered paths are down and the events become disjoint. In the general case, however, the identification of such links can be very complicated, and using the inclusion and exclusion probability formula, detailed next, becomes necessary.

Suppose for a given source–destination pair, say N_s and N_d, m paths $P_1, P_2, \ldots, P_m$ exist from the source to the destination. Denote by E_i the event in which path P_i is operational. The expression for the path reliability is

$$R_{N_s,N_d} = \text{Prob}\{E_1 \cup E_2 \cup \cdots \cup E_m\} \tag{4.6}$$

The events $E_1, \ldots, E_m$ are not disjoint, but they can be decomposed into a set of disjoint events as follows:

$$E_1 \cup E_2 \cup \cdots \cup E_m = E_1 \cup \left(E_2 \cap \overline{E_1}\right) \cup \left(E_3 \cap \overline{E_1} \cap \overline{E_2}\right) \cup \cdots \cup \left(E_m \cap \overline{E_1} \cap \overline{E_2} \cap \cdots \cap \overline{E_{m-1}}\right) \tag{4.7}$$

where $\overline{E_i}$ denotes the event that path P_i is faulty. The events on the right hand side of Equation 4.7 are disjoint, and their probabilities can therefore be added to yield the path reliability:

$$R_{N_s,N_d} = \text{Prob}\{E_1\} + \text{Prob}\left\{E_2 \cap \overline{E_1}\right\} + \cdots + \text{Prob}\left\{E_m \cap \overline{E_1} \cap \overline{E_2} \cap \cdots \cap \overline{E_{m-1}}\right\} \tag{4.8}$$

This expression can be rewritten using conditional probabilities

$$R_{N_s,N_d} = \text{Prob}\{E_1\} + \text{Prob}\{E_2\}\,\text{Prob}\left\{\overline{E_1} \,\middle|\, E_2\right\} + \cdots$$
$$+ \text{Prob}\{E_m\}\,\text{Prob}\left\{\overline{E_1} \cap \overline{E_2} \cap \cdots \cap \overline{E_{m-1}} \,\middle|\, E_m\right\} \tag{4.9}$$

The probabilities $\text{Prob}\{E_i\}$ are easily calculated. The difficulty is in calculating the probabilities $\text{Prob}\{\overline{E_1} \cap \cdots \cap \overline{E_{i-1}} \,|\, E_i\}$. We can rewrite the latter as $\text{Prob}\{\overline{E_{1|i}} \cap \cdots \cap \overline{E_{i-1|i}}\}$, where $\overline{E_{j|i}}$ is the event in which P_j is faulty given that P_i is operational. To identify the links that must fail so that the event $\overline{E_{j|i}}$ occurs, we define the conditional set

$$P_{j|i} = P_j - P_i = \{x_k \,|\, x_k \in P_j \text{ and } x_k \notin P_i\}$$

We will illustrate the use of these equations through the following example.

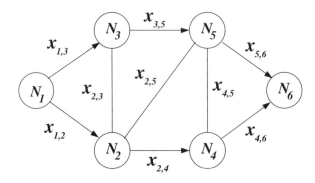

FIGURE 4.14   A six-node network.

▪ E X A M P L E

The six-node network shown in Figure 4.14 has nine links, out of which six are unidirectional and three bidirectional. We are interested in calculating the path reliability for the pair N_1–N_6. The list of paths leading from N_1 to N_6 includes the following:

$$P_1 = \{x_{1,3}, x_{3,5}, x_{5,6}\} \qquad P_8 = \{x_{1,2}, x_{2,3}, x_{3,5}, x_{5,6}\}$$
$$P_2 = \{x_{1,2}, x_{2,5}, x_{5,6}\} \qquad P_9 = \{x_{1,2}, x_{2,4}, x_{4,5}, x_{5,6}\}$$
$$P_3 = \{x_{1,2}, x_{2,4}, x_{4,6}\} \qquad P_{10} = \{x_{1,3}, x_{2,3}, x_{2,4}, x_{4,5}, x_{5,6}\}$$
$$P_4 = \{x_{1,3}, x_{3,5}, x_{4,5}, x_{4,6}\} \qquad P_{11} = \{x_{1,3}, x_{2,3}, x_{2,5}, x_{4,5}, x_{4,6}\}$$
$$P_5 = \{x_{1,3}, x_{2,3}, x_{2,4}, x_{4,6}\} \qquad P_{12} = \{x_{1,3}, x_{3,5}, x_{2,5}, x_{2,4}, x_{4,6}\}$$
$$P_6 = \{x_{1,3}, x_{2,3}, x_{2,5}, x_{5,6}\} \qquad P_{13} = \{x_{1,2}, x_{2,3}, x_{3,5}, x_{4,5}, x_{4,6}\}$$
$$P_7 = \{x_{1,2}, x_{2,5}, x_{4,5}, x_{4,6}\}$$

Note that these paths are ordered so that the shortest ones are at the top and the longest ones at the bottom. This simplifies the calculation of the path reliability, as will become apparent next.

The conditional set $P_{1|2}$ is $P_{1|2} = P_1 - P_2 = \{x_{1,3}, x_{3,5}\}$. The set $\{x_{1,3}, x_{3,5}\}$ must fail in order for P_1 to be faulty while P_2 is working. The second term in Equation 4.9 corresponding to P_2 will thus be $p_{1,2}p_{2,5}p_{5,6}(1 - p_{1,3}p_{3,5})$.

For calculating the other terms in Equation 4.9, the intersection of several conditional sets must be considered. For example, for P_4 the conditional sets are $P_{1|4} = \{x_{5,6}\}$, $P_{2|4} = \{x_{1,2}, x_{2,5}, x_{5,6}\}$, and $P_{3|4} = \{x_{1,2}, x_{2,4}\}$. Because $P_{2|4}$ will fail when $P_{1|4}$ fails, we can discard $P_{2|4}$ and focus on $P_{1|4}$ and $P_{3|4}$. Both P_1 and P_3 must be faulty while P_4 is working. The fourth term in Equation 4.9 corresponding to P_4 will therefore be $p_{1,3}p_{3,5}p_{4,5}p_{4,6}(1 - p_{5,6})(1 - p_{1,2}p_{2,4})$.

A more complicated situation is encountered when calculating the third term in Equation 4.9 for P_3. Here, $P_{1|3} = \{x_{1,3}, x_{3,5}, x_{5,6}\}$, $P_{2|3} = \{x_{2,5}, x_{5,6}\}$, and the two conditional sets are not disjoint. Both P_1 and P_2 will be faulty if one of the following disjoint events occur: (1) $x_{5,6}$ is faulty, (2) $x_{5,6}$ is working and either $x_{1,3}$ is faulty and $x_{2,5}$ is faulty, or $x_{1,3}$ is working, $x_{3,5}$ is faulty and $x_{2,5}$ is faulty. The resulting expression is $p_{1,2}p_{2,4}p_{4,6}\left[q_{5,6} + p_{5,6}q_{1,3}q_{2,5} + p_{5,6}p_{1,3}q_{3,5}q_{2,5}\right]$. The remaining terms in Equation 4.9 are similarly calculated and the sum of all 13 terms yields the required path reliability, R_{N_1,N_6}. ∎

The alert reader would have noticed the similarity between the calculation of the path reliability and the computation of the availability for a given set of read and write quorums in a distributed system with data replication that has been presented in Section 3.3. Here too, we have a number of components (links), each of which can be up or down and we need to calculate the probability that certain combinations of such components are up. In the last example we had nine links and we can enumerate all 2^9 states and calculate the probability of each state by multiplying nine factors of the form $p_{i,j}$ or $q_{i,j}$. We then add up the probabilities of all the states in which a path from node N_1 to node N_6 exists and thereby obtain the path reliability R_{N_1,N_6}.

4.3 Fault-Tolerant Routing

The objective of a fault-tolerant routing strategy is to get a message from source to destination despite a subset of the network being faulty. The basic idea is simple: if no shortest or most convenient path is available because of link or node failures, reroute the message through other paths to its destination.

The implementation of fault tolerance depends on the nature of the routing algorithm. In this section, we will focus on *unicast* routing in distributed computing. In a unicast, a message is sent from a source to just one destination. The problem of *multicast*, in which copies of a message are sent to a number of nodes, is an extension of the unicast problem.

Routing algorithms can be either centralized or distributed. Centralized routing involves having a central controller in the network, which is aware of the current network state (which links or nodes are up and which are down; which links are heavily congested) and lays out for each message the path it must take. A variation on this is to have the source act as the controller for that message and specify its route. In distributed routing, there is no central controller: the message is passed from node to node, and each intermediate node decides which node to send it to next.

The route can be chosen either uniquely or adaptively. In the former approach, just one path can be taken for each source–destination pair. For instance, in a rectangular mesh, the message can move in two dimensions: horizontal and vertical. The rule may be that the message has to move along the horizontal dimension until it is in the same column as the destination node, whereupon (if it is not already at the destination) it turns and moves vertically to reach the destination. In an adaptive approach, the path can be varied in response to network conditions. For instance, if a particular link is congested, the routing policy may avoid using it if at all possible.

Implementing fault tolerance in centralized routing is not difficult. A centralized router that knows the state of each link can use graph-theoretic algorithms to determine one or more paths that may exist from source to destination. Out of these, some secondary considerations (such as load balancing or number of hops) can be used to select the path to be followed.

In the rest of this section, we present routing approaches for two of the structures we have encountered before: the n-dimensional hypercube and the rectangular mesh.

4.3.1 Hypercube Fault-Tolerant Routing

Although the hypercube network can tolerate link failures, we still must modify the routing algorithm so that it continues to successfully route messages in injured hypercubes, i.e., hypercubes with some faulty nodes or links. The basic idea is to list the dimensions along which the message must travel and then traverse them one by one. As edges are traversed, they are crossed off the list. If, because of a link or a node failure, the desired link is not available, then another edge in the list, if any, is chosen for traversal. If no such edges are available (the message arrives at some node to find that all dimensions on its list are down), it backtracks to the previous node and tries again.

Before writing out the algorithm, we introduce some notation. Let TD denote the list of dimensions that the message has already traveled on, in the order in which they have been traversed. TD^R is the list TD reversed. $\bigoplus_{i=1}^{k}$ denotes the XOR operation carried out k times, sequentially. For example, $\bigoplus_{i=1}^{3} a_1 a_2 a_3$ means $(a_1 \oplus a_2) \oplus a_3$. If D is the destination and S the source, let $d = D \oplus S$, where $\oplus$ is a bitwise XOR operation on D and S. In general, $x \oplus y$ is called the relative address of node x with respect to node y. Let $SR(A)$ be the set of relative addresses reachable by traversing each of the dimensions listed in A, in that order. For example, if we travel along dimensions $1, 3, 2$ in a four-dimensional hypercube, the set of relative addresses reachable by this travel would be: $0010, 1010, 1110$. Denote by e_n^i the n-bit vector consisting of a 1 in the ith-bit position and 0 everywhere else, for example, $e_3^1 = 010$.

Messages are assumed to consist of (a) d: the list of dimensions that must be traversed from S to D, (b) the data being transmitted (the "payload"), and (c) TD: the list of dimensions taken so far.

By TRANSMIT(j) we mean "send the message ($d \oplus e^j$, payload, $TD \odot j$) along the jth-dimensional link from the present node," where $\odot$ denotes the "append" operation (e.g., $TD \odot x$ means "append x to the list TD").

If $(d == 0 \cdots 0)$
   Accept message and Exit algorithm // Final destination has been reached.
else
   for $j = 0$ to $(n-1)$ step 1 do {
      if $((d_j == 1)$ && (jth dimension link from this node is nonfaulty)
         && $(e_n^j \notin SR(TD^R))$ { // Message gets one step closer to its destination.
         TRANSMIT(j)
         Exit algorithm
      }
   }
end if
// If we are not done at this point, it means there is no way of getting one
// step closer to the destination from this node: we need to take a detour.
if (there is a non-faulty link not in $SR(TD^R)$) // there is a link not yet attempted.
   Let h be one such link
else {
   Define $g = \max\{m : \bigoplus_{i=1}^{m} e^{TD^R(i)} == 0 \cdots 0\}$
   if (g==number of elements in $SR(TD)$) {
      Give up // Network is disconnected and no path exists to destination.
      Exit algorithm
   }
   else
      h = element $(g+1)$ in TD^R // Prepare to backtrack.
   end if
   TRANSMIT(h)
end

FIGURE 4.15 **Algorithm for routing in hypercubes.**

The algorithm is shown in Figure 4.15. When node V receives a message, the algorithm checks to see if V is its intended destination. If so, it accepts the message, and the message's journey is over. If V was not the intended final destination, the algorithm checks if the message can be forwarded so that it is one hop (or, equivalently, one dimension) closer to its destination. If this is possible, the message is forwarded along the chosen link. If not, we need to take a detour. To take a detour, we see if there is a link that this message has not yet traversed from V. If so, we send it along such a link (any such link will do: we are trying to move the message to some other node closer to the destination). If the message has traversed every such link, we need to backtrack and send the message back to the node from which V originally received it. If V happens to be the source node itself, then it means that the hypercube is disconnected and there is no path from the source to the destination.

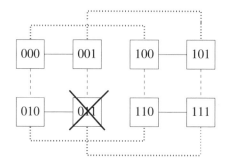

FIGURE 4.16   Routing in an injured hypercube.

■ **EXAMPLE**

We are given an H_3 with faulty node 011 (see Figure 4.16). Suppose node $S = 000$ wants to send a message to $D = 111$. At 000, $d = 111$, so it sends the message out on dimension-0, to node 001. At node 001, $d = 110$ and $TD = (0)$. This node attempts to send it out on its dimension-1 edge. However, because node 011 is down, it cannot do so. Since bit 2 of d is also 1, it checks and finds that the dimension-2 edge to 101 is available. The message is now sent to 101, from which it makes its way to 111. What if both 011 and 101 had been down? We invite the reader to solve this problem. ■

How can we be confident that this algorithm will, in fact, find a way of getting the message to its destination (so long as a source-to-destination path exists)? The answer is that this algorithm implements a depth-first search strategy for graphs, and such strategies have been shown to be effective in finding a path if one exists.

4.3.2 Origin-Based Routing in the Mesh

The depth-first strategy described above has the advantage of not requiring any advance information about which nodes are faulty: it uses backtracking if it arrives at a dead-end. In this section, we describe a different approach, in which we assume that the faulty regions are known in advance. With this information available, no backtracking is necessary.

The topology we consider is a two-dimensional rectangular $N \times N$ mesh with at most $N - 1$ failures. The procedure can be extended to meshes of dimension three or higher, and to meshes with more than $N - 1$ failures. It is assumed that all faulty regions are square. If they are not, additional nodes are declared to have *pseudo faults* and are treated for routing purposes as if they were faulty, so that the regions do become square. Figure 4.17 provides an example. Each node knows the

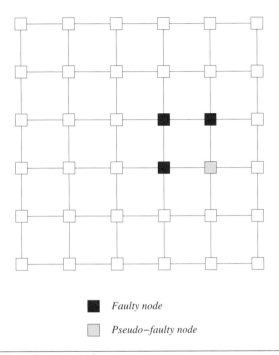

■ *Faulty node*

□ *Pseudo–faulty node*

FIGURE 4.17   Faulty regions must be square.

distance along each direction (east, west, north, and south) to the nearest faulty region in that direction.

The idea of origin-based routing is to define one node as the origin. By restricting ourselves to the case in which there are no more than $N-1$ failures in the mesh, we can ensure that the origin is chosen so that its row and column do not have any faulty nodes. Suppose we want to send a message from node S to node D. The path from S to D is divided into an IN-path, consisting of edges that take the message closer to the origin, and an OUT-path, which takes the message farther away from the origin, ultimately reaching the destination. Here, distance is measured in terms of the number of hops along the shortest path. In degenerate cases, either the IN or the OUT path sets can be empty.

Key to the functioning of the algorithm is the notion of an *outbox* associated with the destination node, D. The outbox is the smallest rectangular region that contains within it both the origin and the destination. See Figure 4.18 for an example.

Next, we need to define *safe nodes*. A node V is safe with respect to destination D and some set of faulty nodes, $\mathcal{F}$, if both the following conditions are met:

■ Node V is in the outbox for D.

■ Given the faulty set $\mathcal{F}$, if neither V nor D is faulty, there exists a fault-free OUT-path from V to D.

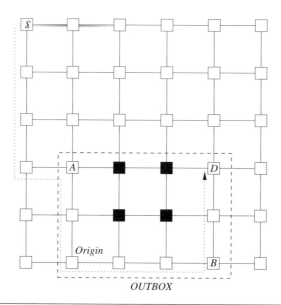

FIGURE 4.18 **Example of an outbox.**

Finally, we introduce the notion of a *diagonal band*. Denote by (x_A, y_A) the Cartesian coordinates of node A, then the diagonal band for a destination node D is the set of all nodes V in the outbox for D satisfying the condition that $x_V - y_V = x_D - y_D + e$, where $e \in \{-1, 0, 1\}$.

For example, $(x_D, y_D) = (3, 2)$ in Figure 4.18 and $x_D - y_D = 3 - 2 = 1$. Thus, any node V within the outbox of D such that $x_V - y_V \in \{0, 1, 2\}$ is in its diagonal band.

It is relatively easy to show by induction that the nodes of a diagonal band for destination D are safe nodes with respect to D. That is, once we get to a safe node, there exists an OUT-path from that node to D. Each step along an OUT-path increases the distance of the message to the origin: the message cannot therefore be traveling forever in circles.

The routing algorithm consists of three phases.

Phase 1. The message is routed on an IN path until it reaches the outbox. At the end of phase 1, suppose the message is in node U.

Phase 2. Compute the distance from U to the nearest safe node in each direction, and compare this to the distance to the nearest faulty region in that direction. If the safe node is closer than the fault, route to the safe node. Otherwise, continue to route on the IN links.

Phase 3. Once the message is at a safe node U, if that node has a safe, non-faulty neighbor V that is closer to the destination, send it to V. Otherwise, U must be on the edge of a faulty region. In such a case, move the message along the edge of the faulty region toward the destination D, and turn toward the diagonal band when it arrives at the corner of the faulty square.

As an example, return to Figure 4.18 and consider routing a message from node S at the northwest end of the network to D. The message first moves along the IN links, getting ever closer to the origin. It enters the outbox at node A. Since there is a failure directly east of A, it continues on the IN links until it reaches the origin. Then it continues, skirting the edge of the faulty region until it reaches node B. At this point, it recognizes the existence of a safe node immediately to the north and sends the message through this node to the destination.

For the case in which there are more than $N - 1$ failures in the mesh, we refer the reader to the Further Reading section for pointers to the literature.

4.4 Further Reading

Graph-theoretic connectivity is described in textbooks on graph theory. See, for example, [9,15]. An MS thesis [36] provides more up-to-date information on the use of connectivity in the study of network reliability. The notion of persistence was introduced in [8].

Several variations on the connectivity measure have been proposed. *Conditional connectivity* has been defined in [16] as follows: the node (link) conditional connectivity with respect to any network property P is the smallest number of nodes (links) which must be removed from the network so that it is disconnected *and* every component that is left has the property P. An example for the property P is: "the component has at most k nodes." A variation on this connectivity measure was presented in [19].

Another measure, called *network resilience* was introduced in [27]. Network resilience is defined with respect to some given probability threshold, p. Let $P(i)$ denote the probability that the network is disconnected exactly after the ith-node failure (but not before that) and assume that nodes fail according to some given probability law. Then, the network resilience is the maximum v such that

$$\sum_{i=1}^{v} P(i) \leqslant p$$

A third measure, call *toughness* was introduced in [11]. Toughness focuses on the number of components a network can be broken down into after a certain number of node failures. A network is said to have toughness t if the failure of any set of k of its nodes results in at most $\max\{1, k/t\}$ components. The greater the toughness, the fewer the components into which the graph splinters. Some related graph-theoretical work has been reported in [6]. A recent review of various measures of robustness and resilience of networks appears in [20].

The extra-stage network was described in [1]. The dependability analysis of the multistage and the extra-stage networks appears in [21–23]. Other fault-tolerant multistage networks are described in [2]. The bandwidth of multistage and crossbar networks was investigated in [29]. The dependability of meshes was investigated extensively with a study appearing in [26]. Interstitial redundancy for meshes was introduced in [33]. Several measures for hypercube reliability have been proposed and calculated. For a good summary, see [34]. The Cube-Connected Cycles network was introduced in [31] and a routing algorithm for it was developed in [25] where an expression for the diameter is also presented. Several proposals for modifying this network to increase its reliability exist, e.g., [4,35]. Loop topologies have been studied extensively. The analysis which we present in this chapter is based on [32]. A more recent paper citing many past publications is [30]. Path (or terminal) reliability is studied in [17]. A good source for network topologies in general is [13].

Fault-tolerant routing for hypercubes is presented in [7,10]. Such routing relies on a depth-first strategy: see any standard book on algorithms, e.g., [3,12]. The origin-based scheme for routing in meshes was introduced in [24]. The treatment there is more general, including the case in which there are N or more failures in the mesh.

4.5   **Exercises**

1. The node (link) connectivity of a graph is the minimum number of node-disjoint (link-disjoint) paths between any pair of nodes. Show that the node connectivity of a graph can be no greater than its link connectivity, and that neither the node nor the link connectivity can exceed the minimum node-degree of the graph (the degree of a node is the number of edges incident on it). In particular, show that for a graph with ℓ links and n nodes, the minimum node-degree can never exceed $\lfloor 2\ell/n \rfloor$.

2. In this problem, we will study the resilience of a number of networks using simulation (If you are unfamiliar with simulation, it may be helpful to skim through Chapter 10 on simulation techniques). Assume that nodes fail with probability q_c and individual links with probability q_ℓ. All failures are independent of one another, and a node failure takes with it all the links that are incident on it. Vary q_c and q_ℓ between 0.01 and 0.25, and find the probability that the network is disconnected. Do this for each of the following networks:

   a. $n \times n$ rectangular mesh, for $n = 10, 20, 30, 40$.

   b. $n \times n$ interstitial mesh with $(1, 4)$ interstitial redundancy, for $n = 10, 20, 30, 40$.

   c. n-dimensional hypercube, for $n = 3, 4, 6, 8, 10, 12$.

3. For the networks listed above, find the diameter stability vector, **DS**.

4. Consider a 2^k-input butterfly network, in which the input and output feed the same nodes (see the left subfigure of Figure 4.4). Write a simulation program to find the probability that the network is disconnected (even if we allow

multiple passes through it by routing through intermediate nodes to get to the ultimate destination), for $k = 4$ and 5, varying the probability of a switchbox failure from $q_s = 0.01$ to $q_s = 0.25$. Assume that if a switchbox fails, it acts as an open circuit.

5. Consider an 8×8 butterfly network. Suppose that each processor generates a new request every cycle. This request is independent of whether or not its previous request was satisfied, and is directed to memory module 0 with probability $1/2$ and to memory module i with probability $1/14$, for $i \in \{1, 2, \ldots, 7\}$. Obtain the bandwidth of this network.

6. We showed how to obtain the probability, for a multistage network, that a given processor is unable to connect to *any* memory. In our analysis, only link failures were considered. Extend the analysis to include switchbox failures, that occur with probability q_s. Assume that link and switchbox failures are all mutually independent of one another.

7. In a 4×4 multistage butterfly network, p_ℓ is the probability that a link is fault-free. Write expressions for the bandwidth BW, connectability Q, and the expected number of accessible processors. Assume that a processor generates memory requests with probability p_r. Assume that switchboxes do not fail.

8. Prove that the extra-stage butterfly network can tolerate the failure of up to one switchbox and still retain connectivity from any input to any output. (Assume that if the failed switchbox is either in the extra or the output stages, its bypass multiplexer is still functional.)

9. Compare the reliability of an $N \times M$ interstitial mesh (with M and N both even numbers) to that of a regular $N \times M$ mesh, given that each node has a reliability $R(t)$ and links are fault-free. For what values of $R(t)$ will the interstitial mesh have a higher reliability?

10. Derive an approximate expression for the reliability of a square $(4, 4)$ interstitial redundancy array with 16 primary nodes and 9 spares. Denote the reliability of a node by R and assume that the links are fault-free.

11. A 3×3 crossbar has been augmented by adding a row and a column, and input demultiplexers and output multiplexers. Assume that a switchbox can fail with probability q_s and when it fails all the incident links are disconnected. Also assume that all links are fault-free but multiplexers and demultiplexers can fail with probability q_m. Write expressions for the reliability of the original 3×3 crossbar and for the fault-tolerant crossbar. (For the purposes of this question, the reliability of the fault-tolerant crossbar is the probability that there is a functioning 3×3 crossbar embedded within the 4×4 system.) Will the fault-tolerant crossbar always have a higher reliability than the original 3×3 crossbar?

12. Show that the three cases enumerated in connection with the derivation of the hypercube network reliability (Section 4.2.4) are mutually exclusive. Further, show that H_n is connected under each of these cases. Assume that $q_c = 0$, i.e., that the nodes do not fail.

13. Obtain by simulation the network reliability of H_n for $n = 5, 6, 7$. Assume that $q_c = 0$. Compare this result in each instance with the lower bound that we derived.

14. The links in an H_3 hypercube are directed from the node with the lower index to the node with the higher index. Calculate the path reliability for the source node 0 and the destination node 7. Denote by $p_{i,j}$ the probability that the link from node i to node j is operational and assume that all nodes are fault-free.

15. All the links in a given 3×3 torus network are directed as shown in the diagram below. Calculate the terminal reliability for the source node 1 and the destination node 0. Denote by $p_{i,j}$ the probability that the link from node i to node j is operational and assume that all nodes are fault-free.

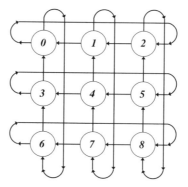

16. Generate random graphs in the following way. Start with n nodes; the probability that there is a (bidirectional) link connecting nodes i and j is p_e. Vary p_e between 0.2 to 0.8 in steps of 0.1, and answer the following for each value of p_e.

    a. What fraction of these networks are connected?

    b. Within the subset of connected networks, if links can fail with probability q_ℓ and nodes never fail, what is the diameter stability vector, **DS**, of the graph? Vary q_ℓ between 0.01 and 0.25.

17. In this question, you will use simulation to study the performance of the hypercube routing algorithm studied in Section 4.3.1. (If you are unfamiliar with simulation, it may be helpful to skim through Chapter 10 on simulation techniques.) Assume that links fail with probability q_ℓ and that nodes never fail. Generate message source and destination pairs at random; for each such source and destination between which a path exists, determine the ratio of the shortest distance between them and the distance of the path that is actually discovered by the routing algorithm. Plot this number for hypercubes of dimension $4, 6, 8, 10, 12$ as a function of q_ℓ, where q_ℓ varies from 0.01 to 0.25.

References

[1]   G. B. Adams III and H. J. Siegel, "The Extra Stage Cube: A Fault-Tolerant Interconnection Network for Supersystems," *IEEE Transactions on Computers*, Vol. C-31, pp. 443–454, May 1982.

[2]   G. B. Adams III, D. P. Agrawal, and H. J. Siegel, "Fault-Tolerant Multi-Stage Interconnection Networks," *IEEE Computer*, Vol. 28, pp. 14–27, June 1987.

[3]   A. V. Aho, J. E. Hopcroft, and J. D. Ullman, *The Design and Analysis of Computer Algorithms*, Addison-Wesley, 1974.

[4]   P. Banerjee, "The Cubical Ring Connected Cycles: A Fault Tolerant Parallel Computation Network," *IEEE Transactions on Computers*, Vol. 37, pp. 632–636, May 1988.

[5]   D. Bauer, E. Schmeichel, and H. J. Veldman, "Progress on Tough Graphs: Another Four Years," in Y. Alavi and A. J. Schwenk (Eds.), *Graph Theory, Combinatorics, and Applications—Seventh Quadrennial International Conference on the Theory and Application of Graphs*, pp. 19–34, 1995.

[6]   D. Bauer, H. J. Broersma, and E. Schmeichel, "More Progress on Tough Graphs: The Y2K Report," *Memorandum 1536*, Faculty of Mathematical Sciences, University of Twente, 2000.

[7]   D. M. Blough and N. Bagherzadeh, "Near-Optimal Message Routing and Broadcasting in Faulty Hypercubes," *International Journal of Parallel Programming*, Vol. 19, pp. 405–423, October 1990.

[8]   F. T. Boesch, F. Harary, and J. A. Kabell, "Graphs as Models of Communication Network Vulnerability," *Networks*, Vol. 11, pp. 57–63, 1981.

[9]   B. Bollobas, *Modern Graph Theory*, Springer-Verlag, 1998.

[10] M.-S. Chen and K. G. Shin, "Depth-First Search Approach for Fault-Tolerant Routing in Hypercube Multicomputers," *IEEE Transactions on Parallel and Distributed Systems*, Vol. 1, pp. 152–159, April 1990.

[11] V. Chvatal, "Tough Graphs and Hamiltonian Circuits," *Discrete Mathematics*, Vol. 2, pp. 215–228, 1973.

[12] T. H. Cormen, C. E. Leiserson, R. L. Rivest, and C. Stein, *Introduction to Algorithms*, MIT Press, 2001.

[13] W. J. Dally and B. Towles, *Principles and Practices of Interconnection Networks*, Morgan-Kaufman, 2004.

[14] J. Duato, S. Yalamanchili, and L. Ni, *Interconnection Networks: An Engineering Approach*, Morgan-Kaufman, 2003.

[15] J. L. Gross and J. Yellen (Eds.), *Handbook of Graph Theory*, CRC Press, 2003.

[16] F. Harary, "Conditional Connectivity," *Networks*, Vol. 13, pp. 346–357, 1983.

[17] S. Hariri and C. S. Raghavendra, "SYREL: A Symbolic Reliability Algorithm Based on Path and Cutset Methods," *IEEE Transactions on Computers*, Vol. C-36, pp. 1224–1232, October 1987.

[18] P. Jalote, *Fault Tolerance in Distributed Systems*, Prentice Hall, 1994.

[19] S. Latifi, M. Hegde, and M. Naraghi-Pour, "Conditional Connectivity Measures for Large Multicomputer Systems," *IEEE Transactions on Computers*, Vol. 43, pp. 218–222, February 1994.

[20] G. W. Klau and R. Weiskircher, "Robustness and Resilience," in U. Brandes and T. Erlebach (Eds.), *Network Analysis: Methodological Foundations,* Lecture Notes in Computer Science, Vol. 3418, pp. 417–437, Springer-Verlag, 2005.

[21] I. Koren and Z. Koren, "On the Bandwidth of a Multistage Network in the Presence of Faulty Components," *Eighth International Conference on Distributed Computing Systems,* pp. 26–32, June 1988.

[22] I. Koren and Z. Koren, "On Gracefully Degrading Multi-Processors with Multi-Stage Interconnection Networks," *IEEE Transactions on Reliability,* Special Issue on "Reliability of Parallel and Distributed Computing Networks," Vol. 38, pp. 82–89, April 1989.

[23] V. P. Kumar and A. L. Reibman, "Failure Dependent Performance Analysis of a Fault-Tolerant Multistage Interconnection Network," *IEEE Transactions on Computers,* Vol. 38, pp. 1703–1713, December 1989.

[24] R. Libeskind-Hadas and E. Brandt, "Origin-Based Fault-Tolerant Routing in the Mesh," *IEEE Symposium on High Performance Computer Architecture,* pp. 102–111, 1995.

[25] D. S. Meliksetian and C. Y. R. Chen, "Optimal Routing Algorithm and the Diameter of the Cube-Connected Cycles," *IEEE Transactions on Parallel and Distributed Systems,* Vol. 4, pp. 1172–1178, October 1993.

[26] P. Mohapatra and C. R. Das, "On Dependability Evaluation of Mesh-Connected Processors," *IEEE Transactions on Computers,* Vol. 44, pp. 1073–1084, September 1995.

[27] W. Najjar and J.-L. Gaudiot, "Network Resilience: A Measure of Network Fault Tolerance," *IEEE Transactions on Computers,* Vol. 39, pp. 174–181, February 1990.

[28] K. Padmanabhan and D. H. Lawrie, "Performance Analysis of Redundant-Path Networks for Multiprocessor Systems," *ACM Transactions on Computer Systems,* Vol. 3, pp. 117–144, May 1985.

[29] J. H. Patel, "Performance of Processor–Memory Interconnections for Multiprocessors," *IEEE Transactions on Computers,* Vol. C-30, pp. 771–780, October 1981.

[30] J. M. Peha and F. A. Tobagi, "Analyzing the Fault Tolerance of Double-Loop Networks," *IEEE/ACM Transactions on Networking,* Vol. 2, pp. 363–373, August 1994.

[31] F. P. Preparata and J. Vuillemin, "The Cube-Connected Cycles: A Versatile Network for Parallel Computation," *Communications of the ACM,* Vol. 24, pp. 300–309, May 1981.

[32] C. S. Raghavendra, M. Gerla, and A. Avizienis, "Reliable Loop Topologies for Large Local Computer Networks," *IEEE Transactions on Computers,* Vol. C-34, pp. 46–55, January 1985.

[33] A. D. Singh, "Interstitial Redundancy: A New Fault-Tolerance Scheme for Large-Scale VLSI Processor Arrays," *IEEE Transactions on Computers,* Vol. 37, pp. 1398–1410, November 1988.

[34] S. Soh, S. Rai, and J. L. Trahan, "Improved Lower Bounds on the Reliability of Hypercube Architectures," *IEEE Transactions on Parallel and Distributed Systems,* Vol. 5, pp. 364–378, April 1994.

[35] N.-F. Tzeng and P. Chuang, "A Pairwise Substitutional Fault Tolerance Technique for the Cube-Connected Cycles Architecture," *IEEE Transactions on Parallel and Distributed Systems,* Vol. 5, pp. 433–439, April 1994.

[36] G. E. Weichenberg, *High Reliability Architectures for Networks Under Stress,* MS thesis, MIT, 2003.

[37] B. Zhao, J. Kubiatowicz, and A. D. Joseph, "Tapestry: A Resilient Global-Scale Overlay for Service Deployment," *IEEE Journal on Selected Areas in Communications,* Vol. 22, pp. 41–53, January 2004.

Software Fault Tolerance

Much has been written about why software is so defect prone and about why the problem of designing and writing software is so intrinsically difficult. Researchers recognize both the *essential* and *accidental* difficulties of producing correct software. Essential difficulties arise from the inherent challenge of understanding a complex application and operating environment, and from having to construct a structure comprising an extremely large number of states, with very complex state-transition rules. Further, software is subject to frequent modifications, as new features are added to adapt to changing application needs. In addition, as hardware and operating system platforms change with time, the software has to adjust appropriately. Finally, software is often used to paper over incompatibilities between interacting system components.

Accidental difficulties in producing good software arise from the fact that people make mistakes in even relatively simple tasks. Translating the detailed design into correctly working code may not require such advanced skills as creating a correct design in the first place but is also mistake prone.

A great deal of work has gone into techniques to reduce the defect rate of modern software. These techniques rely on extensive procedures to test software programs for correctness and completeness. Testing, however, can never conclusively verify the correctness of an arbitrary program. This can only be approached through a formal mathematical proof. Constructing such formal proofs is currently the subject of much active research; however, the state of the art at the present time is rather primitive, and formal program proving is applicable only to small pieces of software. As a result, it is a reasonable assumption that any large piece of software that is currently in use contains defects.

Consequently, after doing everything possible to reduce the error rate of individual programs, we have to turn to fault-tolerance techniques to mitigate the impact of software defects (bugs). These techniques are the subject of this chapter.

5.1 Acceptance Tests

As with hardware systems, an important step in any attempt to tolerate faults is to detect them. A common way to detect software defects is through acceptance tests. These are used in wrappers and in recovery blocks, both of which are important software fault-tolerance mechanisms and will be discussed later.

If your thermometer were to read $-40\,°C$ on a sweltering midsummer day, you would suspect it was malfunctioning. This is an example of an *acceptance test*. An acceptance test is essentially a check of reasonableness. Most acceptance tests fall into one of the following categories.

Timing Checks. One of the simplest checks is timing. If we have a rough idea of how long the code should run, a watchdog timer can be set appropriately. When the timer goes off, the system can assume that a failure has occurred (either a hardware failure or something in the software that caused the node to "hang"). The timing check can be used in parallel with other acceptance tests.

Verification of Output. In some cases, the acceptance test is suggested naturally from the problem itself. That is, the nature of the problem is such that although the problem itself is difficult to solve, it is much easier to check that the answer is correct and it is also less likely that the check itself will be incorrect. To take a human analogy, solving a jigsaw puzzle can take a long time; checking to see that the puzzle has been correctly put together is trivial and takes just a glance.

Examples of such problems are calculating the square root (square the result to check if you get the original number back), the factorization of large numbers (multiply the factors together), the solution of equations (substitute the alleged solution into the original equations), and sorting. Note that in sorting, it is not enough merely to check that the numbers are sorted: we have also to verify that all the numbers at the input are included in the output.

Sometimes, to save time, we will restrict ourselves to probabilistic checks. These do not guarantee that all erroneous outputs will be caught even if the checks are executed perfectly, but have the advantage of requiring less time. One example of such a check for the correctness of matrix multiplication is as follows.

Suppose we multiply two $n \times n$ integer matrices A and B to produce C. To check the result without repeating the matrix multiplication, we may select at random an $n \times 1$ vector of integers, R, and carry out the operations $M_1 = A \times (B \times R)$ and $M_2 = C \times R$. If $M_1 \neq M_2$, then we know that an error has occurred. If $M_1 = M_2$, that still does not *prove* that the original result C was correct; however, it is very improbable that the random vector R was selected such that $M_1 = M_2$ even if $A \times B \neq C$. To further reduce this probability, we may select another $n \times 1$ vector and repeat the check. The complexity of this test is $O(mn^2)$ where m is the number of vectors selected.

Range Checks. In other cases, we do not have such convenient and obvious approaches to checking the correctness of the output. In such situations, range checks can be used. That is, we use our knowledge of the application to set acceptable bounds for the output: if it falls outside these bounds, it is declared to be erroneous. Such bounds may be either preset or some simple function of the inputs. If the latter, the function has to be simple enough to implement that the probability of the acceptance test software itself being faulty is sufficiently low.

For example, consider a remote-sensing satellite that takes thermal imagery of the earth. We could obviously set bounds on the temperature range and regard any output outside these bounds as indicating an error. Furthermore, we could use spatial correlations, which means looking for excessive differences between the temperatures in adjacent areas and flagging an error if the differences cannot be explained by physical features (such as volcanoes).

When setting the bounds on acceptance tests, we have to balance two parameters: *sensitivity* and *specificity*. We have encountered these quantities before in Chapter 2: recall that sensitivity is the probability that the acceptance test catches an erroneous output. To be more exact, it is the conditional probability that the test declares an error, given the output is erroneous. Specificity, in contrast, is the conditional probability that, given that the acceptance test declares an error, it is indeed an error and not a correct output that happens to fall outside the test bounds. A closely related parameter is the probability of *false alarm*, which is the conditional probability that the test declares as erroneous an output that is actually correct.

An increase in sensitivity can be achieved by narrowing the bounds. Unfortunately, this would at the same time decrease the specificity and increase the probability of false alarms. In an absurdly extreme case, we could narrow the acceptance range to zero, so that every output flags an error! In such a case the sensitivity would be 100%, but the probability of a false alarm would be high because every output, correct or not, is sure to be declared erroneous. The specificity in such a case would be low—equal to the underlying error rate. Clearly, such an acceptance test is useless.

5.2 Single-Version Fault Tolerance

In this section, we consider ways by which individual pieces of software can be made more robust. We start by looking at *wrappers*, which are robustness-enhancing interfaces for software modules. Then, we discuss software rejuvenation, and finally, we describe the use of data diversity.

5.2.1 Wrappers

As its name implies, a wrapper is a piece of software that encapsulates the given program when it is being executed (see Figure 5.1). We can wrap almost any level

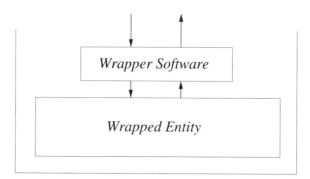

FIGURE 5.1 A wrapper.

of software: examples include application software, middleware, and even an operating system kernel. Inputs from the outside world to the wrapped entity are intercepted by the wrapper, which decides whether to pass them on or to signal an exception to the system. Similarly, outputs from the wrapped software are also filtered by the wrapper.

Wrappers became popular when people started using Commercial Off-the-Shelf (COTS) software components for high-reliability applications. COTS components are written for general-purpose applications, for which errors are an annoyance but not a calamity. Before such components can be used in applications requiring high reliability, they need to be embedded in some environment that reduces their error rate. This environment (the wrapper) has to head off inputs to the software that are either outside the specified range or are known to cause errors; similarly, the wrapper passes the output through a suitable acceptance test before releasing it. If the output fails the acceptance test, this fact must be conveyed to the system, which then decides on an appropriate course of action.

Wrappers are specific to the wrapped entity and the system. Here are some examples of their use.

(1) Dealing with Buffer Overflow. The C programming language does not perform range checking for arrays, which can cause either accidental or maliciously intended damage. Writing a large string into a small buffer causes buffer overflow; since no range checking is performed, a region of memory outside the buffer is overwritten. For example, consider the *strcpy()* function in C, which copies strings from one place to another. If one executes the call *strcpy(str1, str2)*, where *str1* is a buffer of size 5 and *str2* is a string of length 25, the resulting buffer overflow would overwrite a region of memory outside the *str1* buffer. Such overflows have been exploited by hackers to cause harm.

A wrapper can check to ensure that such overflows do not happen, for example, by checking that the buffer is large enough for the designated string to be copied.

Violating this rule prevents the *strcpy*() function from being called; instead, the wrapper returns an error or raises an exception.

(2) Checking the Correctness of the Scheduler. Consider a wrapper around the task scheduler in a fault-tolerant, real-time system. Unlike general-purpose operating systems, such schedulers do not generally use round-robin scheduling. One real-time scheduling algorithm is *Earliest Deadline First* (EDF), in which, as the term implies, the system executes the task with the earliest deadline among all the tasks that are ready to run. This is subject to constraints on preemptibility, because some tasks may not be preemptible in certain parts of their executions.

Such a scheduler can be wrapped by having the wrapper verify that the scheduling algorithm is being correctly executed, so that the scheduler always selects the ready task with the earliest deadline and that any arriving task with an earlier deadline preempts the executing task (assuming the latter is preemptible). To do its job, the wrapper obviously needs information about which tasks are ready to run and their deadlines and about whether the currently executing task is preemptible. To obtain this information, it may be necessary to get the vendor of the scheduler software to provide a suitable interface.

(3) Using Software with Known Bugs. Suppose we are using a software module with known bugs. That is, we have found, either through intensive testing or through field reports, that the software fails for a certain set of inputs, S. Suppose, further, that the software vendor has not (yet) put out a version that corrects these bugs. Then, we can implement a wrapper that intercepts the inputs to that software and checks to see if those inputs are in the set S. If not, it forwards them to the software module for execution; if yes, it returns a suitable exception to the system. Alternatively, the wrapper can redirect the input to some alternative, custom written, code that handles inputs in S.

(4) Using a Wrapper to Check for Correct Output. Such a wrapper includes an acceptance test through which every output is filtered. If the output passes the test, it is forwarded outside. If not, an exception is raised, and the system has to deal with a suspicious output.

Our ability to successfully wrap a piece of software depends on several factors:

1. *Quality of the Acceptance Tests.* This is application dependent and has a direct impact on the ability of the wrapper to stop erroneous outputs.

2. *Availability of Necessary Information from the Wrapped Component.* Often, the wrapped component is a "black box" and all we can observe about its behavior is the output produced in response to a given input; in such cases, the wrapper will be somewhat limited. For example, our scheduler wrapper would be impossible to implement without information about the deadlines of the tasks waiting to run. Ideally, we would like complete access to the source code; where this is impossible for commercial or other reasons, we would like to have the

vendors themselves provide well-defined interfaces by which the wrapper can obtain relevant information from the wrapped software.

3. *Extent to Which the Wrapped Software Module Has Been Tested.* Extensively testing software allows us to identify regions of the input space for which the software fails, and reduces the probability of contaminating the system with incorrect output.

5.2.2 Software Rejuvenation

When your personal computer hangs, the obvious reaction is to reboot it. This is an example of *software rejuvenation.*

As a process executes, it may keep acquiring memory and file locks without properly releasing them. Also, its data tend to get corrupted as uncorrected errors accumulate. The process may also consume (without releasing) threads and semaphores. If this goes on indefinitely, the process can become faulty and stop executing. To head this off, we can proactively halt the process, clean up its internal state, and then restart it. This is called software rejuvenation.

Rejuvenation Level

One can rejuvenate at either the application or at the processor level. Rejuvenation at the application level consists of suspending an individual application, cleaning up its state by garbage collection, reinitialization of data structures, etc., and then restarting it. Rejuvenation at the processor level consists of rebooting the processor and affects all applications running on that processor. If we have a processor cluster, it is beneficial to stagger such rejuvenations so that no more than a small fraction of the processors are under rejuvenation at any one time. Selecting the appropriate level consists of determining at what level the resources have degraded or become exhausted.

Timing of Rejuvenation

Software rejuvenation can be based on either time or prediction.

Time-based rejuvenation consists of rejuvenating at constant intervals. To determine the optimal inter-rejuvenation period, we must balance the benefits against the cost. Let us construct a simple mathematical model to do this. We use the following notation:

$\tilde{N}(t)$ Expected number of errors over an interval of length t
(without rejuvenation)

C_e Cost of each error

C_r Cost of each rejuvenation
P Inter-rejuvenation period

By adding up the costs due to rejuvenation and to errors, we obtain the overall expected cost of rejuvenation over a period P, denoted by $C_{\text{rejuv}}(P)$:

$$C_{\text{rejuv}}(P) = \tilde{N}(P)C_e + C_r$$

The cost per unit time, $C_{\text{rate}}(P)$, is then given by

$$C_{\text{rate}}(P) = \frac{C_{\text{rejuv}}(P)}{P} = \frac{\tilde{N}(P)C_e + C_r}{P} \tag{5.1}$$

To get some insight into this expression, let us study three cases for $\tilde{N}(P)$. First, consider what happens if the software has a constant error rate λ throughout its execution, which implies that $\tilde{N}(P) = \lambda P$. Substituting this into Equation 5.1, we have $C_{\text{rate}}(P) = \lambda C_e + C_r/P$. It is easy to see that to minimize $C_{\text{rate}}(P)$, we must set $P = \infty$. This implies that if the error rate is constant, software rejuvenation should not be applied at all. Rejuvenation is useful only to head off a potential increased error rate as the software executes.

Next, consider $\tilde{N}(P) = \lambda P^2$. From Equation 5.1, we obtain $C_{\text{rate}}(P) = \lambda P C_e + C_r/P$. To minimize this quantity, we find P such that $dC_{\text{rate}}(P)/dP = 0$ (and $d^2 C_{\text{rate}}(P)/dP^2 > 0$). Differentiating, we find the optimal value of the rejuvenation period, denoted by P^*, to be $P^* = \sqrt{\frac{C_r}{\lambda C_e}}$.

The third case is a generalization of the above: $\tilde{N}(P) = \lambda P^n$, $n > 1$. From Equation 5.1, we have $C_{\text{rate}}(P) = \lambda P^{n-1} C_e + C_r/P$. Using elementary calculus, as before, we find the optimal value of the rejuvenation period to be

$$P^* = \left(\frac{C_r}{(n-1)\lambda C_e} \right)^{1/n}$$

Figure 5.2 shows how the optimal rejuvenation period varies as a function of C_r/C_e and n for the model described above.

To set the period P appropriately, we need to know the values of the parameters C_r/C_e and $\tilde{N}(t)$. These can be obtained experimentally by running simulations on the software, or alternatively, the system could be made adaptive, with some default initial values being chosen to begin with. Over time, as we gather statistics reflecting the failure characteristics of the software, the rejuvenation period can be adjusted appropriately.

Prediction-based rejuvenation involves monitoring the system characteristics (amount of memory allocated, number of file locks held, and so on), and predicting when the system will fail. For example, if a process is consuming memory at a certain rate, the system can estimate when it will run out of memory. Rejuvenation then takes place just before the predicted crash.

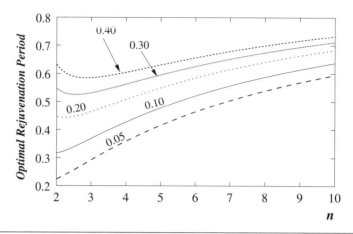

FIGURE 5.2   Optimal rejuvenation period. $\lambda = 1$; time units are arbitrary; curve labels indicate C_r/C_e.

The software that implements prediction-based rejuvenation must have access to enough state information to make such predictions. If it comes as part of the operating system, such information is easy to collect. If it is a package that runs atop the operating system with no special privileges, it will be constrained to using whatever interfaces are provided by the operating system to collect status information. For example, the Linux system provides the following utilities:

- *vmstat* provides information about processor utilization, memory and paging activity, traps, and I/O.

- *iostat* outputs the percentage CPU utilization at the user and system levels, as well as a report on the usage of each I/O device.

- *netstat* indicates network connections, routing tables, and a table of all the network interfaces.

- *nfsstat* provides information about network file server kernel statistics.

Once the appropriate status information has been collected, trends can be identified and a prediction made as to when these trends will cause errors to occur. For example, if we are tracking the allocation of memory to a process, we might do a least-squares fit of a polynomial to the memory allocations over some window of the recent past.

The simplest such fit is a straight line, or a polynomial of degree one, $f(t) = mt + c$. More complex ones may involve a higher-degree polynomial, say of degree n. Suppose the selected window of the recent past consist of k time instances $t_1 < t_2 < \cdots < t_k$, where t_k is the most recent one. Given the measurements $\mu(t_1), \mu(t_2), \ldots, \mu(t_k)$, where $\mu(t_i)$ is the allocated memory at time t_i, we seek to find the coefficients of the polynomial

$$f(t) = m_n t^n + m_{n-1} t^{n-1} + \cdots + m_1 t + m_0$$

so as to minimize the quantity

$$\sum_{i=1}^{k} \left[\mu(t_i) - f(t_i) \right]^2$$

This polynomial can then be used to extrapolate into the future and predict when the process will run out of memory.

In the standard least-squares fit, each observed point $\mu(t_i)$ has the same weight in determining the fit. A variation of this procedure is the *weighted* least-squares fit, in which we seek to minimize the weighted sum of the squares. In our memory allocation example, we would choose weights $w_1, w_2, \ldots, w_k$ and then determine the coefficients of $f(t)$ such that the quantity

$$\sum_{i=1}^{k} w_i \left[\mu(t_i) - f(t_i) \right]^2$$

is minimized. Having weights allows us to give greater emphasis to certain points. For example, if we use $w_1 < w_2 < \cdots < w_k$, recent data will influence the fit more than older data.

The above curve-fitting approaches are all vulnerable to the impact of a few outlying points (points that are unusually high or low), which can have a distorting effect on the fit. Techniques are available to make the fit more robust by reducing the impact of such points; see the Further Reading section for a pointer to more information.

Combined Approach. The two approaches described above can be combined by rejuvenating at either the scheduled P or at the time when the next error is predicted to happen, whichever comes first.

5.2.3 Data Diversity

The input space of a program is the space spanned by all possible inputs. This space can be divided into *failure* and *nonfailure* regions. The program fails if and only if an input from the failure region is applied. Data diversity may help in producing acceptable results even when the input is in a faulty region.

Failure regions come in every shape and size. Input spaces typically have a large number of dimensions, but we can visualize them only in the unrealistically simple case of a two-dimensional input space. Figure 5.3 shows two arbitrarily drawn failure regions. In both cases, the failure region occupies the same fraction of the input area, but in Figure 5.3a it consists of a number of relatively small islands, whereas in Figure 5.3b it consists of a single large, contiguous, area. In both

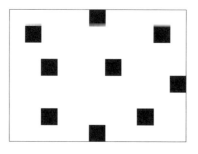

(a) Small, scattered failure regions   *(b) Large, contiguous failure region*

FIGURE 5.3   Failure regions.

cases, the software will fail for the same fraction of all possible inputs. The crucial difference is that in Figure 5.3a, a small perturbation of the inputs is sufficient to move them out of a failure region to a nonfailure region.

Failure regions such as in Figure 5.3a suggest a possible fault-tolerance approach: consider perturbing the input slightly and hope that if the original input falls in a failure region, the perturbed input will fall in a nonfailure region. This general approach is called *data diversity*. How it is actually implemented depends on the error-detection mechanism. If only one copy of the software is executed at any one time and an acceptance test is used to detect errors, then we can recompute with perturbed inputs and recheck the resulting output. If massive redundancy is used, we may apply slightly different input sets to different versions of the program and vote on their output (see Section 5.3).

Perturbation of the input data can be done either explicitly or implicitly. Explicit perturbation consists of adding a small deviation term to a selected subset of the inputs. Implicit perturbation involves gathering inputs to the program in such a way that we can expect them to be slightly different. For example, suppose we have software controlling an industrial process whose inputs are the pressure and temperature of a refrigeration equipment. Every second, these parameters (p_i, t_i) are measured and then input to the controller. Now, from physical considerations, we can expect that the pressure measured in sample i is not much different from that in sample $i - 1$. Implicit perturbation in this context may consist of using (p_{i-1}, t_i) as an input alternative to (p_i, t_i). With luck, if (p_i, t_i) is in a failure region, (p_{i-1}, t_i) will not be, thus providing some resilience. Whether or not this is acceptable obviously depends on the dynamics of the application and the sampling rate. If, as is often the case, we sample at a higher rate than is absolutely necessary, this approach is likely to be useful.

Another approach is to reorder the inputs. A somewhat contrived example is the program that adds a set of three input floating-point numbers, a, b, c. If the inputs are in the order a, b, c, then it first computes $a + b$ and then adds c to this partial sum. Consider the case $a = 2.2E + 20$, $b = 5$, $c = -2.2E + 20$. Depending on the precision used (e.g., if the significant [mantissa] field of the floating-point number has room for fewer than 20 decimal digits, which is about 66 bits) it is possible that $a + b$ as calculated will be $2.2E + 20$, so that the final result will be $a + b + c = 0$, which is incorrect. Now, change the order of the inputs; let it be a, c, b. Then, $a + c = 0$, so that $a + c + b = 5$.

There is one important difference between the two examples we have seen. Although in both cases we are reexpressing the inputs, the refrigeration controller was an example of *inexact reexpression*, whereas the example of calculating $a + b + c$ is an instance of *exact reexpression*. In the first example, the software is attempting to compute some function, $f(p, t)$, of the pressure and temperature, yet for inputs (p, t) falling in a failure region, the actual output of the software will not equal $f(p, t)$; we are also likely to have $f(p_i, t_i) \neq f(p_{i-1}, t_i)$. In the second example, that of calculating $a + b + c$, we should in theory have $a + b + c = a + c + b$, and it is only the limitations of the implementation (in this case the limited precision provided by floating-point arithmetic) that cause an error on this sequence a, b, c of inputs.

When exact reexpression is used, the associated output can be used as is (as long as it passes the acceptance test or the vote on the multiple versions of the program). If we have inexact reexpression, the output will not be exactly what was meant to be computed. Depending on the application and the amount of perturbation, we may or may not attempt to correct for the perturbation before using the output. If the application is somewhat robust, we may use the raw output as a somewhat degraded, but still acceptable, alternative to the desired output; if it is not, we must correct for the perturbation.

One way to correct the output for the perturbation is to use the Taylor expansion. Recall that for one variable (assuming that the function is differentiable to any degree) the Taylor expansion of $f(t)$ around the point t_0 is

$$f(t) = f(t_0) + \sum_{n=1}^{\infty} \frac{(t - t_0)^n f^{(n)}(t_0)}{n!}$$

where $f^{(n)}(t_0)$ is the value at $t = t_0$ of the nth derivative of $f(t)$ with respect to t.

In other cases, we may not have the desired function in analytic form and must use other approaches to correct the output.

5.2.4 Software Implemented Hardware Fault Tolerance (SIHFT)

Data diversity can be combined with time redundancy to construct techniques for Software Implemented Hardware Fault Tolerance (SIHFT) with the goal of detecting hardware faults. A SIHFT technique can provide an inexpensive alternative to hardware and/or information redundancy techniques and can be especially attractive when using COTS microprocessors which typically do not support error detection.

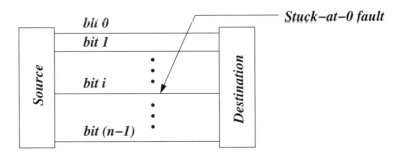

FIGURE 5.4   An n-bit bus with a permanent stuck-at-0 fault.

Suppose the program has all integer variables and constants. It can be transformed to a new program in which all variables and constants are multiplied by a constant k (called the *diversity factor*), and whose final results are expected to be k times the results of the original program. When both the original and the transformed programs are executed on the same hardware (i.e., using time redundancy), the results of these two programs will be affected by hardware faults in different ways, depending on the value of k. By checking whether the results of the transformed program are k times the results produced by the original program, hardware faults can be detected.

How do we select a suitable value of k? The selected value should result in a high probability of detecting a fault, yet it should be small enough so as not cause an overflow or underflow which may prevent us from correctly comparing the outputs of the two programs. Furthermore, if the original program includes logic operations such as bit-wise XOR or AND, we should restrict ourselves to values that are of the form $k = 2^\ell$, with an integer ℓ, since in this case multiplication by k becomes a simple shift operation.

■ E X A M P L E

Consider an n-bit bus shown in Figure 5.4 and suppose that bit i of the bus has a permanent stuck-at-0 fault. If the data sent over the bus has its ith bit equal to 1, the stuck-at fault will result in erroneous data being received at the destination. If a transformed program with $k = 2$ is executed on the same hardware, the ith bit of the data will now use line $(i + 1)$ of the bus and will not be affected by the fault. The executions of the two programs will yield different results, indicating the presence of a fault.

Obviously, the stuck-at-0 fault will not be detected if both bits i and $(i - 1)$ of the data that is forwarded on the bus are 0. Assuming that all 2^n possible values on the n-bit bus are equally likely, this event will occur with probability 0.25. If, however, the transformed program uses $k = -1$ (meaning that every variable and constant in the program undergoes a two's complement opera-

```
i = 0;
x = 3;
y = 1;
while (i < 5) {
    y = y * (x + i);
    i = i + 2;
}
z = y;
```

(a) The original program

```
i = 0;
x = 6;
y = 2;
while (i < 10) {
    y = y * (x + i)/2;
    i = i + 4;
}
z := y;
```

(b) The transformed program

FIGURE 5.5   An example of a program transformation for $k = 2$.

tion), almost all 0s in the original program will turn into 1s in the transformed program, greatly reducing the probability of an undetected fault. ■

The risk of overflow while executing the transformed program exists even for small values of k. In particular, even $k = -1$ can generate an overflow if the original variable assumed the value of the largest negative integer number that can be represented using the two's complement scheme (for a 32-bit integer this is -2^{31}). Thus, the transformed program should take appropriate precautions, for example, by scaling up the type of integer used for that variable. Range analysis can be performed to determine which variables must be scaled up to avoid overflows.

The actual transformation of the program, given the value of k, is quite straightforward and can be easily automated. The example in Figure 5.5 shows the transformation for $k = 2$. Note that the result of the multiplication in the transformed program must be divided by k to ensure proper scaling of the variable y.

If floating-point variables are used in the program, some of the simple choices for k considered above are no longer adequate. For example, for $k = -1$, only the sign bit of the transformed variable will change (assuming the IEEE standard representation of floating-point numbers is followed; see the Further Reading section). Even selecting $k = 2^\ell$ for an integer ℓ is inappropriate, since multiplying by such a k will only affect the exponent field. The significand field will remain intact, and any error in it will not be detected. Both the significand field and the exponent field must, therefore, be multiplied, possibly by two different values of k.

To select value(s) of k for a given program such that the SIHFT technique will provide a high coverage (detect a large fraction of the hardware faults) we can carry out experimental studies by injecting faults into a simulation of the hardware (see Chapter 10 for a discussion of fault injection) and determine the fault-detecting capability for each candidate value of k.

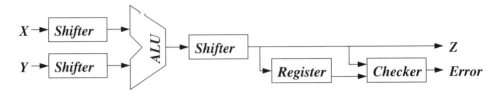

FIGURE 5.6   Example of the use of recomputing with shifted operands.

Recomputing with Shifted Operands (RESO)

The Recomputing with Shifted Operands (RESO) approach is similar to SIHFT, with the main difference being that the hardware is modified to support fault detection. In this approach, each unit that executes either an arithmetic or a logic operation is modified so that it first executes the operation on the original operands and then re-executes the same operation on transformed operands. The same issues that had to be resolved for the SIHFT technique exist for the RESO technique as well. Here, too, the transformations of the operands are limited to simple shifts which correspond to k being of the form $k = 2^\ell$ with ℓ an integer. Avoiding an overflow when executing the transformed computation is easier for RESO than for SIHFT, since the datapath of the modified hardware unit can be extended to include some extra bits. and thus avoid overflow. Figure 5.6 shows an ALU (Arithmetic and Logic Unit capable of executing addition, subtraction, and bit-wise logic operations) that has been modified to support the RESO technique. In the first step, the two original operands X and Y are, for example, added without being shifted, and the result Z stored in the register. In the next step, the two operands are shifted by ℓ bit positions and then added. The result of this second addition is then shifted by the same number of bit positions, but in the opposite direction, and then compared with the contents of the register, using the checker circuit.

5.3   *N*-Version Programming

In this approach to software fault tolerance, N independent teams of programmers develop software to the same specifications. These N versions of software are then run in parallel, and their output is voted on. The hope is that if the programs are developed independently, it is very unlikely that they will fail on the same inputs. Indeed, if the bugs are assumed to be statistically independent and each has the same probability, q, of occurring, then the probability of software failure of an N-version program can be computed in a way similar to that of an NMR cluster (see Chapter 2). That is, the probability of no more than m defective versions out of N versions, under the defect/bug independence assumption, is

$$p_{\text{ind}}(N, m, q) = \sum_{i=0}^{m} \binom{N}{i} q^i (1 - q)^{N-i}$$

N-version programming is far from trivial to implement. We start our discussion by showing how difficult it can be to even arrive at a consensus among *correctly* functioning versions.

5.3.1 Consistent Comparison Problem

Consider N independently written software versions, $V_1, \ldots, V_N$, for some application. Suppose the overall structure of each version involves computing some quantity, x, and comparing it with a constant, c. Let x_i denote the value of x as computed by version V_i. The comparison with c is said to be *consistent* if either $x_i \geqslant c$ for all $i = 1, \ldots, N$, or $x_i < c$ for all $i = 1, \ldots, N$.

Consider an application such that

```
if (f(p,t)<c)
    take action A1
else
    take action A2
end if
```

The job of each version is to output the action to be taken. In such a case, we clearly want all functional versions to be consistent in their comparisons.

Since the versions are written independently and may actually use different algorithms to compute the function $f(p,t)$, we expect that their respective calculations may yield values for $f(p,t)$ that differ slightly. To take a concrete example, let $c = 1.0000$ and $N = 3$. Suppose the versions V_1, V_2, and V_3 output values $0.9999, 0.9998$, and 1.0001, respectively. Then, $x_1 < c, x_2 < c$ but $x_3 > c$: the comparisons are not consistent. As a result, V_1 and V_2 will order action $A1$ to be taken and V_3 will order action $A2$, *even though all three versions are functioning correctly*.

Such inconsistent comparisons can occur even if the precision is so high that the version outputs deviate by very little from one another: there is no way to guarantee a general solution to the consistent comparison problem. We can establish this by showing that any algorithm which guarantees that any two *n*-bit integers which differ by less than 2^k will be mapped to the same *m*-bit output (where $m + k \leqslant n$), must be the trivial algorithm that maps every input to the same number. Suppose we have such an algorithm: we start the proof with $k = 1$. 0 and 1 differ by less than 2^k, so the algorithm will map both of them to the same number, say α. Similarly, 1 and 2 differ by less than 2^k, so they will also be mapped to α. Proceeding in this way, we can easily show that $3, 4, \ldots$ will all be mapped by this algorithm to α, which means that this must be the trivial algorithm that maps all integers to the same number, α.

The above discussion assumes that it is integers that are being compared; however, it is easy to prove that a similar result holds for real numbers of finite precision that differ even slightly from one another.

This problem may arise whenever the versions compare a variable with a given threshold. Given that the software may involve a large number of such comparisons, the potential exists for each version to produce distinct, unequal results, even if no errors have occurred so long as even minor differences exist in the values being calculated. Such differences cannot usually be removed, because each version may use a different algorithm and in any case is programmed independently.

Why is this a problem? After all, if nonfailing versions can differ in their output, it is reasonable to suppose that the output of any of them would be acceptable to the application. Although this is true, the system has no means to determine whether the outputs are in disagreement because they are erroneous or because of the consistent comparison problem. Note that it is possible for the nonfailing versions to disagree due to this problem while multiple failed versions produce identical wrong outputs (due to a common bug). The system would then most likely select the wrong output.

One can, in principle, bypass the consistent comparison problem completely, by having the versions decide on a consensus value of the variable before carrying out the comparison. That is, before checking if some variable $x > c$, the versions run an algorithm to agree on which value of x to use. However, this would add the requirement that, where there are multiple comparisons, the order of comparisons be specified. Restricting the implementation of the versions in this way can reduce version diversity, thus increasing the potential for correlated errors. Also, if the number of such comparisons is large, a significant degradation of performance could occur because a large number of synchronization points would be created. Versions that arrive at the comparison points early would have to wait for the slower ones to catch up.

Another approach that has been suggested is to use confidence signals. While carrying out the "$x > c$?" comparison, each version should consider the difference $|x - c|$. If $|x - c| < \delta$ for some prespecified δ, the version announces that it has low confidence in its output (because there is the potential for it to disagree with the other versions). The function that votes on the version outputs could then ignore the low-confidence versions or give them a lower weight. Unfortunately, if one functional version has $|x - c| < \delta$, chances are quite high that this will also be true of other functional versions, whose outputs will also be devalued by the voter. In addition, it raises the possibility of an incorrect result that is far from c, outvoting multiple correct results, which are (correctly) close to c.

The frequency with which the consistent comparison problem arises and the length of time for which it lasts depend on the nature of the application. In applications where historical state information is not used (e.g., if the calculation depends only on the latest input values and is not a function of past values), the consistent comparison problem may occur infrequently and go away fairly quickly.

5.3.2 Version Independence

Correlated errors between versions can increase the overall error probability by orders of magnitude. For example, consider the case $N = 3$, which can tolerate up to one failed version for any input. Suppose that the probability that a version produces an incorrect output is $q = 10^{-4}$. That is, on the average, each of these versions produces an incorrect output once every 10,000 runs. If the versions are stochastically independent, then the error probability of the three-version system is

$$q^3 + 3q^2(1 - q) \approx 3 \times 10^{-8}$$

Now, suppose stochastic independence does not hold and that there is one defect mode which is common to two of the three versions and is exercised on the average once every million runs (that is, about one in every 100 bugs of a version is due to a common mistake). Every time this bug is exercised, the system will fail. The error probability of the three-version system now increases to over 10^{-6}, which is more than 30 times the error probability of the uncorrelated system.

Let us explore the issue of correlation a little further. Quite often, the input space (the space of all possible input patterns) can be subdivided into regions according to the probability that an input from that region will cause a version to fail. Thus, for example, if there is some numerical instability in a given subset of the input space, the error rate for that subspace may be greater than the average error rate over the entire space of inputs. Suppose that versions are stochastically independent *in each subspace*, that is,

$$\text{Prob}\{V_1, V_2 \text{ both fail} | \text{input is from subspace } S_i\}$$
$$= \text{Prob}\{V_1 \text{ fails} | \text{input is from } S_i\} \cdot \text{Prob}\{V_2 \text{ fails} | \text{input is from } S_i\}$$

According to the total probability formula, the unconditional probability of failure of an individual version is

$$\text{Prob}\{V_j \text{ fails}\}$$
$$= \sum_i \text{Prob}\{V_j \text{ fails} | \text{input is from } S_i\} \cdot \text{Prob}\{\text{Input is from } S_i\} \quad (j = 1, 2)$$

The unconditional probability that both V_1 and V_2 will fail is

$$\text{Prob}\{V_1, V_2 \text{ both fail}\}$$
$$= \sum_i \text{Prob}\{V_1 \text{ fails} | S_i\} \cdot \text{Prob}\{V_2 \text{ fails} | S_i\} \cdot \text{Prob}\{\text{Input is from } S_i\}$$

Let us consider two numerical examples. For ease of exposition, we will assume the input space consists of only two subspaces S_1 and S_2, and that the probability of the input being from S_1 or S_2 is 0.5.

■ E X A M P L E

The conditional failure probabilities are as follows:

Version	S_1	S_2
V_1	0.010	0.001
V_2	0.020	0.003

The unconditional failure probabilities for the two versions are

$$\text{Prob}\{V_1 \text{ fails}\} = 0.01 \times 0.5 + 0.001 \times 0.5 = 0.0055$$

$$\text{Prob}\{V_2 \text{ fails}\} = 0.02 \times 0.5 + 0.003 \times 0.5 = 0.0115$$

If the two versions were stochastically independent, the probability of both failing for the same input would be

$$\text{Prob}\{V_1 \text{ fails}\} \cdot \text{Prob}\{V_2 \text{ fails}\} = 0.0055 \times 0.0115 = 6.33 \times 10^{-5}$$

The actual joint failure probability, however, is somewhat greater:

$$P(V_1, V_2 \text{ both fail}) = 0.01 \times 0.02 \times 0.5 + 0.001 \times 0.003 \times 0.5 = 1.02 \times 10^{-4}$$

The reason is that the two versions' failure propensities are positively correlated: they are both much more prone to failure in S_1 than in S_2. ■

■ E X A M P L E

The failure probabilities are as follows:

Version	S_1	S_2
V_1	0.010	0.001
V_2	0.003	0.020

The unconditional failure probabilities of the individual versions are identical to those in the previous example. However, the joint failure probability is now

$$\text{Prob}\{V_1, V_2 \text{ both fail}\} = 0.01 \times 0.003 \times 0.5 + 0.001 \times 0.02 \times 0.5 = 2.5 \times 10^{-5}$$

This is about a five-fold decrease from the corresponding number in the previous example, and less than half of what it would have been if the versions had been stochastically independent.

The reason is that now the propensities to failure of the two versions are negatively correlated: V_1 is better in S_1 than in S_2, whereas the opposite is true for V_2. Intuitively, V_1 and V_2 make up for each other's deficiencies. ■

Ideally, we would therefore like the multiple versions to be negatively corre- lated; realistically, we expect most correlations to be positive because the ver- sions are ultimately all addressing the same problem. In any event, the focus in *N*-version programming has historically been on making the versions as stochas- tically independent as possible, rather than on making them negatively correlated.

The stochastic independence of versions can be compromised by a number of factors.

- **Common Specifications.** If programmers work off the same specification, errors in these specifications will propagate to the software.

- **Intrinsic Difficulty of the Problem.** The algorithms being programmed may be far more difficult to implement in one subset of the input space than in others. Such a correlation in difficulty can translate into multiple versions having defects that are triggered by the same input sets.

- **Common Algorithms.** Even if the implementation of the algorithm is cor- rect, the algorithm itself may contain instabilities in certain regions of the input space. If the different versions are implementing the same algorithm, then these instabilities will be replicated across the versions.

- **Cultural Factors.** Programmers who are trained to think in similar ways can make similar (or the same) mistakes quite independently. Furthermore, such correlation can result in ambiguous specifications being interpreted in the same erroneous way.

- **Common Software and Hardware Platforms.** The operating environment comprises the processors on which the software versions are executed and the operating system. If we use the same hardware and operating system, faults/defects within these can trigger a correlated failure. Strictly speaking, this would not constitute a correlated *application software* failure; however, from the user's point of view, this would still be a failure. Common compil- ers can also cause correlated failures.

Independence among the versions can be gained by either *incidental diversity* or *forced diversity*. Incidental diversity is the by-product of forcing the developers of different modules to work independently of one another. Teams working on differ- ent modules are forbidden to directly communicate with one another. Questions regarding ambiguities in the specifications or any other issue have to be addressed to some central authority, which makes any necessary corrections and updates all the teams. Inspection of the software must be carefully coordinated so that the in- spectors of one version do not directly or indirectly leak information about another version.

Forced diversity is a more proactive approach and forces each development team to follow some approach that is believed to increase the chances of diversity. Here are some of the ways in which this can be forced.

Use Diverse Specifications. Several researchers have remarked that the majority of software bugs can be traced to the requirements specification. Some even claim that two-thirds of all bugs can be laid at the door of faulty specifications! This is one important motivation for using diverse specifications. That is, rather than working on a common specification, diversity can begin at the specification stage. The specifications may be expressed in different formalisms. The hope is that specification errors will not coincide across versions, and each specification version will trigger a different implementation error profile. It is beginning to be accepted that the specifications impact how one thinks about a problem: the *same* problem, if specified differently, may well pose a different level of difficulty to the implementor.

We may also decide to make the various versions have differing capabilities. For example, in a three-version system, one of the versions may be more rudimentary than the other two, providing a less accurate—but still acceptable—output. The hope is that the implementation of a simpler algorithm will be less error-prone and more robust (experience less numerical instability). In most cases, the two other versions will run correctly. In the (hopefully rare) instances when they do not, the third version can save the system (or at least help determine which of the two disagreeing other versions is correct). If the third version is very simple, then formal methods may be considered to actually *prove* that it is correct. A similar approach of using a simpler version is often used in recovery blocks, which are discussed in Section 5.4.

Use Diverse Programming Languages. Anyone experienced in programming knows that the programming language can significantly impact the quality of the software that is produced. For example, we would expect a program written in assembly language to be more bug-prone than is one in a higher-level language. The nature of the bugs can also be different. In our discussion of wrappers (in Section 5.2.1), we saw that it is possible to get programs written in C to overflow their allocated memory. Such bugs would be impossible in a language that strictly manages memory. Errors arising from an incorrect use of pointers, not uncommon in C programs, will not occur in Fortran, which has no pointers.

Diverse programming languages may have diverse libraries and compilers, which the user hopes will have uncorrelated (or, even better, negatively correlated) bugs.

Certain programming languages may be more attuned to a given problem than others. For example, many would claim that Lisp is a more natural language in which to code some artificial intelligence (AI) algorithms than are C or Fortran. In other words, Lisp's expressive power is more congruent to some AI problems than that of C or Fortran. In such a case, an interesting problem arises. Should all versions use the language that is well attuned to the problem or should we force some versions to be written in other languages that are less suited to the application? If all the versions are written in the most suitable language, we can expect that their individual error rate will be lower; on the other hand, the different versions may experience correlated errors. If they are written in diverse languages, the individual error rates of the versions written in the "poorer" languages may be greater, but the *overall* error rate of the *N*-version system may be lower if these bugs do not give rise to as many correlated errors. A similar comment applies to the use of diversity in other dimensions, such as development environments or tools. This trade-off is difficult to resolve without extensive—and expensive—experimental work.

Use Diverse Development Tools and Compilers. This may make possible "notational diversity" and thereby reduce the extent of positive correlation between bugs. Since tools can themselves be faulty, using diverse tools for different versions may allow for greater reliability. A similar remark applies to compilers.

Use Cognitively Diverse Teams. By *cognitive diversity*, we mean diversity in the way that people reason and approach problems. If teams are constituted to ensure that different teams have different approaches to reasoning, this can *potentially* give rise to software that has fewer correlated bugs. At the moment, however, procedures to ensure such cognitive diversity are not available.

Other Issues in *N*-Version Programming

Back-to-Back Testing. Having multiple versions that solve the same problem gives us the opportunity to test them back to back. The testing process consists of comparing their outputs for the same input, which helps identify noncoincident bugs.

In addition to comparing the overall outputs, designers have the option of comparing corresponding intermediate variables. Figure 5.7 shows an idealized example. We have three versions: *V*1, *V*2, *V*3. In addition to their final outputs, the designers have identified two points during their execution when corresponding variables are generated. These can be compared to provide additional back-to-back checks.

Using intermediate variables can provide increased observability into the behavior of the programs, and may identify defects that are not easily observable at the outputs. However, defining such variables constrains the developers to producing these variables and may reduce program diversity.

Using Diverse Hardware and Operating Systems. The output of the system depends on the interaction between the application software and its platform, mainly comprising the operating system and the processor. Both processors and operating systems are notorious for the bugs they contain. It is, therefore, a good idea to com-

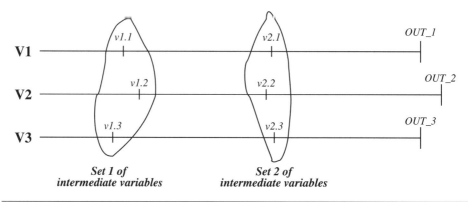

FIGURE 5.7   Example of intermediate variables in back-to-back testing.

plement software design diversity with hardware and operating system diversity, by running each version on a different processor type and operating system.

Cost of N-Version Programming. Software is expensive to develop, and creating N versions rather than one is more expensive still. Very little information is publicly available about the cost of developing N versions: for a pointer to a case study, see the Further Reading section. According to that study, the overhead of developing an additional version varies from 25% to 134% of the single-version cost. This is an extremely wide range!

A first-order estimate is that developing N versions is N times as expensive as developing a single version. However, some parts of the development process may be common. For instance, if all versions work off the same specifications, only one set of specifications needs to be developed. On the other hand, the management of an N-version project imposes overheads not found in traditional software development. Still, costs can be kept under control by carefully identifying the most critical portions of the code and only developing N versions for these.

Producing a Single Good Version Versus Many Versions. Given a total time budget, consider two choices: (a) develop a single version (over which we lavish the entire allocated time), and (b) develop N versions. Unfortunately, software reliability modeling is not yet sufficiently advanced for us to make an effective estimate of which would be better and under what circumstances.

Experimental Results. A few experimental studies have been carried out into the effectiveness of N-version programming. Published results are generally only available for work carried out in universities, and it is not clear how the results obtained by using student programmers would change if professional and experienced programmers were used.

One typical study was conducted at the University of Virginia and the University of California at Irvine. The study had a total of 27 students write code for an anti-missile application. The students ranged from some with no prior industrial experience to others with over 10 years. All versions were written in Pascal and run on a Prime machine at the University of Virginia and a DEC VAX 11/750 at the University of California at Irvine. A total of 93 correlated bugs were identified by standard statistical hypothesis-testing methods: if the versions had been stochastically independent, we would have expected no more than about five. Interestingly, no correlation was observed between the quality of the programs produced and the experience of the programmer. A similar conclusion—that versions were not stochastically independent—was drawn from another experiment, conducted under NASA auspices, by North Carolina State University, the University of California at Santa Barbara, the University of Virginia, and the University of Illinois.

5.4   Recovery Block Approach

Similarly to N-version programming, the recovery block approach also uses multiple versions of software. The difference is that in the latter, only one version runs at any one time. If this version should be declared as failing, execution is switched to a backup.

5.4.1 Basic Principles

Figure 5.8 illustrates a simple implementation of this method. There is a primary version and three secondary versions in this example. Only the primary is initially executed. When it completes execution, it passes along its output to an acceptance test, which checks to see if the output is reasonable. If it is, then the output is accepted by the system. If not, then the system state is rolled back to the point at which the primary started computation, and secondary 1 is invoked. If this succeeds (the output passes the acceptance test), the computation is over. Otherwise, we roll the system back to the beginning of the computation, and then invoke secondary 2. We keep going until either the outcome passes an acceptance test or we run out of secondaries. In the latter case, the recovery block procedure will have failed, and the system must take whatever corrective action is needed in response (e.g., the system may be put in a "safe" state, such as a reactor being shut down).

The success of the recovery block approach depends on: (a) the extent to which the primary and various secondaries fail on the same inputs (correlated bugs), and (b) the quality of the acceptance test. These clearly vary from one application to the next.

5.4.2 Success Probability Calculation

Let us set up a simple mathematical model for the success probability of the recovery block approach, under the assumption that the different versions fail independently of one another. We can use this model to determine which parameters most affect the software failure probability. We use the following notation:

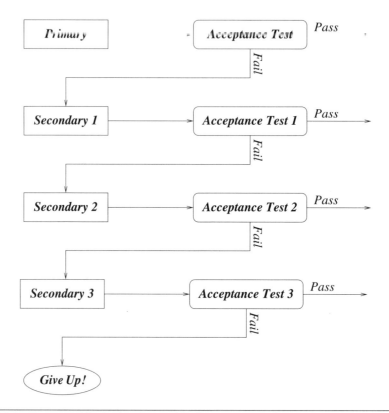

FIGURE 5.8 Recovery block structure with three secondaries.

E the event that the output of a version is erroneous
T the event that the test reports that the output is wrong
f the failure probability of a version
s the test sensitivity
σ the test specificity
n the number of available software versions (primary plus secondaries)

Thus,

$$f = P\{E\}, \qquad s = P\{T|E\}, \qquad \sigma = P\{E|T\}$$

For the scheme to succeed, it must succeed at some stage i, $1 \leqslant i \leqslant n$. This will happen if the test fails stages $1, \ldots, i-1$ (causing the scheme to go to the next version), and at stage i the version's output is correct and it passes the test. We now have

$$\text{Prob\{Success in stage } i\} = \left[P\{T\}\right]^{i-1} P\{\bar{E} \cap \bar{T}\}$$

$$\text{Prob\{Scheme is successful\}} = \sum_{i=1}^{n} [P\{T\}]^{i-1} P\{\bar{E} \cap \bar{T}\} \tag{5.2}$$

$$P\{E \cap T\} = P\{T|E\}P\{E\} = sf$$

$$P\{T\} = \frac{P\{E \cap T\}}{P\{E|T\}} = \frac{sf}{\sigma}$$

$$P\{\bar{E}|T\} = 1 - P\{E|T\} = 1 - \sigma$$

$$P\{\bar{E} \cap T\} = P\{\bar{E}|T\}P\{T\} = (1 - \sigma)\frac{sf}{\sigma} \tag{5.3}$$

$$P\{\bar{E}\} = 1 - P\{E\} = 1 - f$$

$$P\{\bar{E} \cap \bar{T}\} = P\{\bar{E}\} - P\{\bar{E} \cap T\} = (1 - f) - (1 - \sigma)\frac{sf}{\sigma} \tag{5.4}$$

Substituting Equations 5.3 and 5.4 into Equation 5.2 yields

$$\text{Prob\{Scheme is successful\}} = \sum_{i=1}^{n} \left[\frac{sf}{\sigma}\right]^{i-1} \left[(1 - f) - (1 - \sigma)\frac{sf}{\sigma}\right]$$

$$= \frac{1 - \left(\frac{sf}{\sigma}\right)^n}{1 - \frac{sf}{\sigma}} \left[(1 - f) - (1 - \sigma)\frac{sf}{\sigma}\right] \tag{5.5}$$

Equation 5.5 can be examined to determine the effect of the various parameters on the success probability of the scheme. One such analysis is shown in Figure 5.9 for a recovery block structure with one primary and two secondaries ($n = 3$) and two values of the acceptance test sensitivity and specificity, namely, 0.95 and 0.85. For these parameter values, the test sensitivity has a greater impact on the success probability than its specificity.

5.4.3 Distributed Recovery Blocks

The structure of the *distributed recovery block* is shown in Figure 5.10, where we consider the special case with just one secondary version. The two nodes carry identical copies of the primary and secondary. Node 1 executes the primary, while, in parallel, node 2 executes the secondary. If node 1 fails the acceptance test, the output of node 2 is used (provided that it passes the acceptance test). The output of node 2 can also be used if there is a watchdog timer and node 1 fails to produce an output within a prespecified time.

Once the primary copy fails, the roles of the primary and secondary copies are reversed. Node 2 continues to execute its copy, which is now treated as the primary. The execution by node 1 of what was previously the primary copy is used

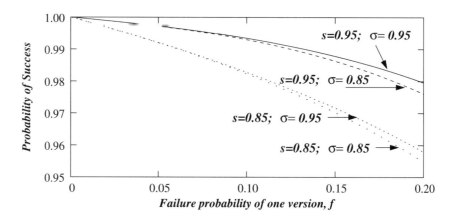

FIGURE 5.9   **Success probability of the recovery block structure for** $n = 3$ **and two values of the acceptance test sensitivity** s **and specificity** σ.

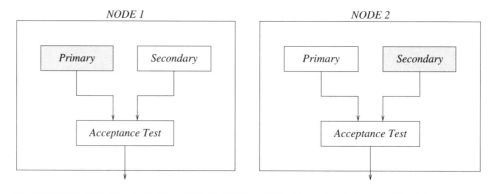

FIGURE 5.10   **Distributed recovery block structure.**

as a backup. This continues until the execution by node 2 is flagged as erroneous, in which case the system toggles back to using the execution by node 2 as a backup.

Because the secondary is executed in parallel with the primary, we do not have to wait for the system to be rolled back and the secondary to be executed: the execution is overlapped with that of the primary. This saves time, and is useful when the application is a real-time system with tight task deadlines.

Our example has included just two versions; the scheme can obviously be extended to an arbitrary number of versions. If we have n versions (primary plus $n - 1$ secondaries), we will run all n in parallel, one on each processor.

5.5   Preconditions, Postconditions, and Assertions

Preconditions, postconditions, and assertions are forms of acceptance tests that are widely used in software engineering to improve software reliability. The *precondition* of a method (or function, or subroutine, depending on the programming language) is a logical condition that must be true when that method is called. For example, if we are operating in the domain of real numbers and invoke a method to calculate the square root of a number, an obvious precondition is that this number must be non-negative.

A *postcondition* associated with a method invocation is a condition that must be true when we return from a method. For example, if a natural logarithm method was called with input X, and the method returns Y, we must have $e^Y = X$ (within the limits of the level of precision being used).

Preconditions and postconditions are often interpreted in contractual terms. The function invoking a method agrees to ensure that the preconditions are met for that method: if they are not, there is no guarantee that the invoked method will return the correct result. In return, the method agrees to ensure that the postconditions are satisfied upon returning from it.

Assertions are a generalization of preconditions and postconditions. An assertion tests for a condition that must be true at the point at which that assertion is made. For example, we know that the total node degree of an undirected graph must be an even number (since each edge is incident on exactly two nodes). So, we can assert at the point of computation of this quantity that it must be even. If it turns out not to be so, an error has occurred; the response to the failure of an assertion is usually to notify the user or carry out some other appropriate action.

Preconditions, postconditions, and assertions are used to catch errors before they propagate too far. The programmer has the opportunity to provide for corrective action to be taken if these conditions are violated.

5.6   Exception-Handling

An *exception* is raised to indicate that something has happened during execution that needs attention, e.g., an assertion has been violated due to either hardware or software failure. When an exception is raised, control is generally transferred to a corresponding *exception-handler*, which is a routine that takes the appropriate action. For example, if we have an arithmetic overflow when executing the operation $y = a * b$, then the result as computed will not be correct. This fact can be signaled as an exception, and the system must react appropriately.

Effective exception-handling can make a significant contribution to system fault tolerance. For this reason, a substantial fraction of the code in many current programs is devoted to exception-handling. Throughout this discussion, we will assume that an exception is triggered in some routine that is invoked by some other routine or by an operator external to the system.

Exceptions can be used to deal with (a) domain or range error, (b) an out-of-the-ordinary event (not failure) that needs special attention, or (c) a timing failure.

Domain and Range Errors

A domain error happens when an illegal input is used. For example, if X and Y are defined as real numbers and the operation $X = \sqrt{Y}$ is attempted with $Y = -1$, a domain error will have occurred, the value of Y being illegal. On the other hand, if X and Y are complex numbers, this operation will be perfectly legal.

A range error occurs when the program produces an output or carries out an operation that is seen to be incorrect in some way. Examples include the following:

- Reading from a file, and encountering an end-of-file while we should still be reading data.

- Producing a result that violates an acceptance test embedded within the program.

- Trying to print a line that is too long.

- Generating an arithmetic overflow or underflow.

Out-of-the-Ordinary Events

Exceptions can be used to ensure special handling of rare, but perfectly normal, events. For example, if we are reading a list of items from a file and the routine has just read the last item, it may trigger an exception to notify the invoker that this was the last item and that nothing further is available to be read.

Timing Failures

In real-time applications, tasks have deadlines associated with them. Missing a deadline can trigger an exception. The exception-handler then decides what to do in response: for instance, it may switch to a backup routine.

5.6.1 Requirements from Exception-Handlers

What do we look for in an exception-handling system? First, it should be easy to program and use. It should be modular and thus easily separable from the rest of the software. It should certainly not be mixed in with the other lines of code in a routine: that would obscure the purpose of the code and render it hard to understand, debug, and modify.

Second, exception-handling should not impose a substantial overhead on the normal functioning of the system. We expect exceptions to be, as the term suggests, invoked only in exceptional circumstances: most of the time they will not be raised. The well-known engineering principle that the common case must be made fast requires that the exception-handling system not inflict too much of a burden in the usual case when no exceptional conditions exist.

Third, exception-handling must not compromise the system state. That is, we must be careful not to render the system state inconsistent during exception-handling. This is especially important in the exception-resume approach, which we discuss in the next section.

5.6.2 Basics of Exceptions and Exception-Handling

When an exception occurs, it is said to be *thrown, raised,* or *signaled.* Some authors distinguish between the raising and the signaling of an exception: the former is when the exception notification is to the module within which it occurred; the latter when this notification propagates to another module.

Internal and External Exceptions

Exceptions can be either *internal* or *external.* An internal exception is one which is handled within the very same module in which it is raised. An external exception, on the other hand, *propagates* elsewhere. For example, if a module is called in a way that violates the specifications of its interface, an interface exception is generated, which has to be dealt with outside the called module.

Propagation of Exceptions

Figure 5.11 provides an example of exception-propagation. Here, module A calls module B, which executes normally until it encounters exception c. B does not have the handler for this exception, so it propagates the exception back to its calling module, A, which executes the appropriate handler. If no handler can be found, the execution is terminated.

Automatically propagating exceptions can violate the principle of information hiding. Information hiding involves the separation of the interface definition of a routine (method, function, subroutine) from the way it is actually designed and implemented. The interface is public information; in contrast, the caller of the routine does not need to know the details of the design and implementation of every routine being called. Not only does this reduce the burden on the caller, it also makes it possible to improve the implementation without any changes having to be propagated to outside the routine.

The invoker (the calling routine) is at a different level of abstraction from the invoked routine. In the example just considered, suppose that some variable X in the invoked routine violated its range constraint. This variable may not even be visible to the invoker.

To get around this problem, we may replace automatic propagation with explicit propagation, in which the propagated information is modified to be consonant with scope rules. For example, if the variable X is invisible to the invoker, it may be told that there was a violation of a range constraint within the invoked routine. It will then have to make the best use it can of this information.

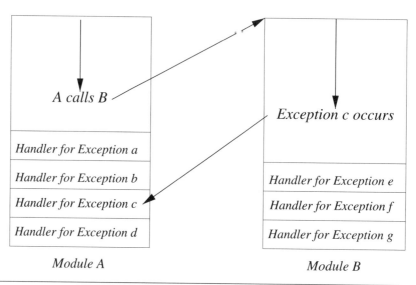

FIGURE 5.11   Example of exception-propagation.

Exception-Terminate and Exception-Resume

Exceptions may be classified into the *exception-terminate* (ET) and *exception-resume* (ER) categories. If an ET is generated while executing some module M, then execution of M is terminated, the appropriate exception-handler is executed, and control is returned to the routine which called module M. However, if an ER is generated, the exception-handling routine attempts to patch up the problem and returns control to M, which resumes execution.

Exception-terminates are much simpler to handle than are exception-resumes. Suppose, for example, that module A calls module B. While executing, module B encounters an exception. If the exception-terminate approach is taken, B will restore its state to what it was at its invocation, signal the exception, and terminate. Control is handed back to A. A thus has to deal only with the following two possibilities: either B executes without exceptions and returns a result, or B encounters an exception and terminates *with its state unchanged from before it was called.*

By contrast, if the exception-resume approach is taken, B will suspend execution and control is transferred to the appropriate exception-handler. After the handler finishes its task, it has the option of returning control to B, which can then resume. Alternatively, the handler could send control elsewhere (it depends on the semantics of the handler). Following this, control returns to A. Thus, when A gets back control after a call to B, we have the following three possibilities. The first is an exception-free execution of B, which poses no difficulties. The second is that an exception was encountered, which was dealt with by the exception-handler, after which control was returned to B, which resumes and finishes execution. The third possibility is that the exception-handler transfers control elsewhere in an attempt to handle the exception. After all this, control is handed back to *A*, possibly with *B* being in an inconsistent state. This third possibility requires that the programmer who wrote *A* knows the semantics of the exception-handler, which may not be realistic.

After the exception has been handled and control has been returned to the invoking routine, several options are available, based on what kind of exception occurred.

- **Domain Error.** We may choose to re-invoke, with corrected operands. If this is not possible, the entire computation may have to be abandoned.

- **Range Error.** There are cases in which some acceptable value may be substituted for the incorrect one which triggered the exception, and the execution resumed. For example, if we have an underflow, we may choose to replace that result by 0 and carry on. If we have additional versions of the software, we may invoke alternatives. Or we may just retry the whole operation, hoping that it arose from some transient failure which has since gone away, or from some combination of concurrent events that is unlikely to recur.

- **Out-of-the-Ordinary Events.** These must be identified by the programmer and handled on a case-by-case basis.

- **Timing Failures.** If the routine is iterative, we may simply use the latest value. For example, if the invoked routine was searching for the optimum value of some function, we may decide to use the best one it has found so far. Alternatively, we may switch to another version of the software (if available) and hope that it will not suffer from the same problem. If we are using the software in a real-time system that is controlling some physical device (e.g., a valve), we may leave the setting unchanged or switch to a safety position.

It is important to stress that many exceptions can only be properly dealt with in context: it is the context that determines what the appropriate response should be. For example, suppose we encounter an arithmetic overflow. In some applications, it may be perfectly acceptable to set the result to ∞ and carry on. In others, it may not, and may require a far more involved response.

5.6.3 Language Support

Older programming languages generally have very little built-in exception handling support. By contrast, more recent languages such as C++ and Java have extensive exception-handling support. For example, in Java, the user can specify exceptions that are *thrown* if certain conditions occur (such as the temperature of a nuclear reactor exceeding a prespecified limit). Such exceptions must be *caught* by an exception-handling routine, which deals with them appropriately (by raising an alarm or printing some output).

5.7   Software Reliability Models

As opposed to the well-established analytical models of hardware reliability, the area of modeling error rates and software reliability is relatively young and often controversial. There are many models in the literature, which sometimes give rise to contradictory results. Our inability to accurately predict the reliability of software is a matter of great concern, since software is often the major cause of system unreliability.

In this section, we briefly describe three models which are a sampling of the software reliability models available. Unfortunately, there is not yet enough evidence to determine which model would be best for what type of software. Models are useful in providing general guidance as to what the software *quality* is; they should not be used as the ultimate word on the actual numerical reliability of any piece of software.

In what follows we distinguish between a *defect* (or a bug) which exists in the software when it is written and an *error* which is a deviation of the program operation from its exact requirements (as the result of a defect) and occurs only when the program is running (or is being tested). Once an error occurs, the bug causing it can be corrected; however, other bugs may still remain. An accepted definition of software reliability is *the probability of error-free operation of a computer program in a specified environment for a specified time*. To calculate this probability, the notion of *software error rate* must be introduced. Software reliability models attempt to predict this error rate as a function of the number of bugs in the software, and their purpose is to determine the length of testing (and subsequent correcting) required until the predicted future error rate of the software goes below some predetermined threshold (and the software can be released).

All three models described next have in common the following assumptions: The software has initially some unknown number of bugs. It is tested for a period of time, during which time some of the bugs cause errors. Whenever an error occurs, the bug causing it is fixed (fixing time is negligible) without causing any additional bugs, thus reducing the number of existing bugs by one. The models differ in their modeling of $\lambda(t)$, the software error rate at time t, and consequently, in the software reliability prediction.

5.7.1 Jelinski–Moranda Model

This model assumes that at time 0 the software has a fixed (and finite) number $N(0)$ of bugs, out of which $N(t)$ bugs remain at time t. The error process is a non-homogeneous Poisson process, i.e., a Poisson process with a rate $\lambda(t)$ that may vary with time. The error rate $\lambda(t)$ at time t is assumed to be proportional to $N(t)$,

$$\lambda(t) = cN(t) \quad \text{(for some constant } c\text{)}$$

Note that $\lambda(t)$ in this model is a step function; it has an initial value of $\lambda_0 = \lambda(0) = cN(0)$, decreases by c whenever an error occurs and the bug that caused it is corrected, and is constant between errors. The (testing, not including fixing) time between consecutive errors (say i and $i + 1$) is exponentially distributed with parameter $\lambda(t)$, where t is the time of the ith error. The reliability at time t, or the probability of a error-free operation during $[0, t]$ is therefore

$$R(t) = e^{-\lambda_0 t} \tag{5.6}$$

Given an error occurred at time τ, the conditional future reliability, or the conditional probability that the following interval of length t, namely $[\tau, \tau + t]$ will be error-free is

$$R(t|\tau) = e^{-\lambda(\tau)t} \tag{5.7}$$

As the software runs for longer and longer, more bugs are caught and purged from the system, and so the error rate declines and the future reliability increases.

The obvious objection to this model is that it assumes that all bugs contribute equally to the error rate, as expressed by the constant of proportionality c. Actually, not all bugs are created equal: some of them are exercised more often than others. Indeed, the more troublesome bugs are those that are not exercised often: these are extremely difficult to catch during testing.

5.7.2 Littlewood–Verrall Model

Similarly to the first model, this model assumes a fixed and finite number, $N(0)$, of initial bugs, out of which $N(t)$ remain at time t. The difference is that this model considers $M(t)$—the number of bugs discovered and corrected during $[0, t]$—rather than $N(t)$ $(M(t) = N(0) - N(t))$.

The errors occur according to a nonhomogeneous Poisson process with rate $\lambda(t)$, but $\lambda(t)$, rather than being deterministic, is considered a random variable with a Gamma density function. The Gamma density function has two parameters α and ψ, where the parameter ψ is a monotonically increasing function of $M(t)$

$$f_{\lambda(t)}(\ell) = \frac{[\psi(M(t))]^\alpha \ell^{\alpha-1} e^{-\psi(M(t))\ell}}{\Gamma(\alpha)} \tag{5.8}$$

where $\Gamma(x) = \int_0^\infty e^{-y} y^{x-1} \, dy$ is the Gamma function (defined in Section 2.2).

The Gamma density function was chosen for practical reasons. It lends itself to analysis, and its two parameters provide a wide range of differently shaped density functions, making it both mathematically tractable and flexible. The expected value of the Gamma density function in Equation 5.8 is $\frac{\alpha}{\psi(M(t))}$, so that the predicted error rate will decrease and the reliability will increase as the software is run for longer periods of time and more bugs are discovered.

Calculating the reliability requires some integrations, which we omit: see the Further Reading section for a pointer to the analysis. After such analysis, we obtain the following expressions for the software reliability:

$$R(t) = \left(1 + \frac{t}{\psi(0)}\right)^{-\alpha} \tag{5.9}$$

and

$$R(t|\tau) = \left(1 + \frac{t}{\psi(M(\tau))}\right)^{-\alpha} \tag{5.10}$$

5.7.3 Musa–Okumoto Model

This model assumes an infinite (or at least very large) number of initial bugs in the software, and similarly to the previous model, uses $M(t)$—the number of bugs discovered and corrected during time $[0, t]$. We use the following notation:

λ_0 the error rate at time 0
c a constant of proportionality
$\mu(t)$ the expected number of errors experienced during $[0, t]$ ($\mu(t) = E(M(t))$)

Under this model, the error rate after testing for a length of time t is given by

$$\lambda(t) = \lambda_0 e^{-c\mu(t)}$$

The intuitive basis for this model is that, when testing first starts, the "easiest" bugs are caught quite quickly. After these have been eliminated, the bugs that still remain are more difficult to catch, either because they are harder to exercise or because their effects get masked by subsequent computations. As a result, the rate at which an as-yet-undiscovered bug causes errors drops exponentially as testing proceeds.

From the definition of $\lambda(t)$ and $\mu(t)$, we have

$$\frac{d\mu(t)}{dt} = \lambda(t) = \lambda_0 e^{-c\mu(t)}$$

The solution of this differential equation is

$$\mu(t) = \frac{\ln(\lambda_0 ct + 1)}{c}$$

and

$$\lambda(t) = \frac{\lambda_0}{\lambda_0 ct + 1}$$

The reliability $R(t)$ can now be calculated as

$$R(t) = e^{-\int_0^t \lambda(z)\,dz} = e^{-\mu(t)} = (1 + \lambda_0 ct)^{-\frac{1}{c}}$$

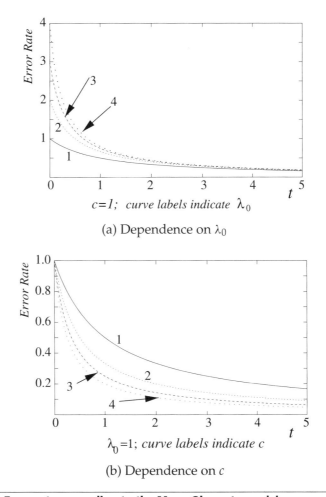

(a) Dependence on λ_0

(b) Dependence on c

FIGURE 5.12   Error rates according to the Musa–Okumoto model.

and the conditional reliability $R(t|\tau)$ is

$$R(t|\tau) = e^{-\int_\tau^{\tau+t} \lambda(z)\,dz} = e^{-(\mu(\tau+t)-\mu(\tau))} = \left(1 + \frac{\lambda_0 ct}{1 + \lambda_0 c\tau}\right)^{-\frac{1}{c}}$$

In Figure 5.12, we show how the error rate varies with time for the Musa–Okumoto model. Note the very slow decay of the error rate. To get the error rate of software down to a sufficiently low point (following this model) clearly requires a significant amount of testing.

5.7.4 Model Selection and Parameter Estimation

The literature on software error models is vast and varied. In the previous section, we have only outlined a very small subset of the existing models. Anyone planning to use one of these models has two problems. First, which of the many available models would be appropriate? Second, how are the model parameters to be estimated?

Selecting the appropriate model is not easy. The American Institute of Aeronautics and Astronautics (AIAA) recommends using one of the following four models, three of which we covered in this chapter: the Jelinski–Moranda, Littlewood–Verrall, Musa–Okumoto, and Schneidewind models. However, as mentioned earlier, no comprehensive and openly accessible body of experimental data is available to guide the user. This is in sharp contrast to hardware reliability modeling, where a systematic data collection effort formed the basis for much of the theory. Software reliability models are based on plausibility arguments. The best that one can suggest is to study the error rate as a function of testing and guess which model it follows. For example, if the error rate seems to exhibit an exponential dependence on the testing time, then we may consider using the Musa–Okumoto model. Once a suitable model is selected, the parameters can be estimated by using the Maximum Likelihood method, which is outlined in Chapter 10. Chapter 10 also outlines the difficulty in accurately predicting the reliability of a highly reliable system (whether due to hardware failures or to software errors).

5.8 Fault-Tolerant Remote Procedure Calls

A Remote Procedure Call (RPC) is a mechanism by which one process can call another process executing on some other processor. RPCs are widely used in distributed computing.

We will describe next two ways of making RPCs fault tolerant: both are based on replication and bear similarities to the problem of managing replicated data (see Section 3.3). Throughout, we will assume that processes are fail-stop.

5.8.1 Primary-Backup Approach

Each process is implemented as primary and backup processes, running on separate nodes. RPCs are sent to both copies, but normally only the primary executes them. If the primary should fail, the secondary is activated and completes the execution.

The actual implementation of this approach depends on whether the RPCs are *retryable* or *nonretryable*. A retryable RPC is one which can be executed multiple times without violating correctness. One example is the reading of some database. A nonretryable RPC should be completed exactly once. For example, incrementing somebody's bank balance is a nonretryable operation.

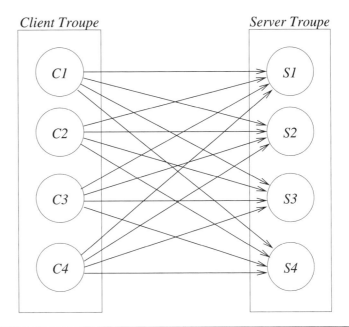

FIGURE 5.13 Example of a circus.

If the system is running only retryable operations, then implementation of the primary-backup approach is quite straightforward. On the other hand, if non-retryable operations may be involved, it is important to ensure that these be completed exactly once, even if multiple processes are used for fault tolerance. This can be done by the primary process checkpointing its operations on the backup. Should the primary fail while executing the RPC, the backup can pick up from the last checkpoint (see Chapter 6).

5.8.2 The Circus Approach

The *circus* approach also involves the replication of processes. Client and server processes are each replicated. Continuing the circus metaphor, these replicated sets are called *troupes*.

This system is best described through an example. Figure 5.13 shows four replicates of a client process, making identical calls to four replicates of a server process. Each call has a *sequence number* associated with it, that uniquely identifies it.

A server waits until it has received identical calls from each of the four client copies, or the waiting times out, before executing the RPC. The results are then sent back to each of the clients. These replies are also marked by a sequence number to uniquely identify them.

A client may wait until receiving identical replies from each of the server copies before accepting the input (subject to a timeout to prevent it from waiting forever for a failed server process). Alternatively, it could simply take the first reply it gets and ignore the rest.

An additional complication must be taken care of: it is possible for multiple client troupes to be sending concurrent calls to the same server troupe. In such a case, each member of the server troupe must, to ensure correct functioning, serve the calls in exactly the same order.

There are two ways of ensuring that this order is preserved, called the *optimistic* and *pessimistic* approaches. In the optimistic approach, we make no special attempt to ensure preservation of the order. Instead, we let everything run freely and then check to see if they preserved order. If so, we accept the outputs, otherwise, we abort the operations and try again. This approach will perform very poorly if ordering is frequently not preserved.

The pessimistic approach, on the other hand, has built-in mechanisms which ensure that order is preserved.

Let us now present a simple optimistic scheme. Each member of the server troupe receives requests from one or more client troupes. When a member completes processing and is ready to commit, it sends a *ready_to_commit* message to each element of the client troupe. It then waits until *every* member of the client troupe acknowledges this call, before proceeding to commit. On the client side, a similar procedure is followed: the client waits until it has received the *ready_to_commit* message from every member of the server troupe, before acknowledging the call. Once the server receives an acknowledgment from each member of the client troupe, it commits.

This approach ensures correct functioning by forcing deadlock if the serial order is violated. For example, let C_1 and C_2 be two client troupes making concurrent RPCs ρ_1 and ρ_2 to a server troupe consisting of servers S_1 and S_2. Let us see what happens if S_1 tries to commit ρ_1 first and then ρ_2, while S_2 works in the opposite order.

Once S_1 is ready to commit ρ_1, it sends a *ready_to_commit* message to each member of C_1, and waits to receive an acknowledgment from each of them. Similarly, S_2 gets ready to commit ρ_2, and sends a *ready_to_commit* message to each member of C_2. Now, members of each client troupe will wait until hearing a *ready_to_commit* from both S_1 and S_2. Since members of C_1 will not hear from S_2 and members of C_2 will not hear from S_1, there is a deadlock. Algorithms exist to detect such deadlocks in distributed systems. Once the deadlock is detected, the operations can be aborted before being committed, and then retried.

5.9   Further Reading

An excellent introduction to the intrinsic difficulties of making software run correctly can be found in [7,8]. A contrary view, arguing that complexity can be successfully encapsulated in software modules to render it invisible to users of those modules (human or software routines that call these modules) is presented in [12].

[28] is regarded as a classic in the field of software safety. Other excellent, general, references for software fault tolerance are [20,43].

Wrappers are motivated in [46]. Systematic design procedures for wrappers are discussed in [38,39]. In [41], the authors describe how to wrap a kernel. In [15], wrappers are used to prevent heap-smashing attacks. Finally, [19] describes the wrapping of Windows NT software.

Software rejuvenation has a long history. People were rebooting their computers when they failed or hung long before it was called rejuvenation. However, its formal use to enhance software reliability is fairly new. A good introduction can be found in [17,21]. The use of software rejuvenation, including a tool to implement it, is described in [10]. A method by which to estimate the rate of software aging (and hence to determine when to rejuvenate) is provided in [18]. The application of rejuvenation to cluster systems, including a discussion of the relative merits of time-based and prediction-based approaches, can be found in [44], and the smoothing approach they use for prediction was proposed in [11].

Data diversity is described in some detail in [1] where experimental results are provided of a radar tracking application. A good reference to SIHFT techniques which also includes a detailed overview of related schemes appears in [36]. The IEEE floating-point number representation and the precision of floating-point operations are discussed in many books, e.g., [25]. The RESO technique is described in [37].

A good introduction to N-version programming can be found in [3]. A design paradigm is provided in [2]. The observation that requirements specifications are the cause of most software bugs is stated in multiple places, for example, see [5,28, 45].

A survey of modeling software design diversity can be found in [32]. This chapter draws on the foundational work of the authors of [14]. An excellent description of the ways by which forced diversity among versions can be obtained can be found in [29]. An experiment in design diversity is described in [6]. Experiments to determine if the versions are stochastically independent or not have not been without some controversy: see [26] regarding some early experiments in this field. A recent study of the impact of specification language diversity on the diversity of the resulting software was published in [49]. An investigation into whether the results from different inspectors of software are independent of one another appears in [34].

The cost of creating multiple versions has not been systematically surveyed: an interesting initial study appears in [24].

An introduction to exceptions and exception-handling can be found in [13], and a useful survey can be found in [9]. A discussion of the comparative merits of exception-terminate and exception-resume is in [33]. The exception-handling mechanism in individual languages is generally treated in some detail in their language manuals and books: for example, see [4]. Exception-handling in object-oriented systems is surveyed in [16] and in real-time software in [27]. A good outline of issues in distributed systems can be found in [48].

oriented systems is surveyed in [16] and in real-time software in [27]. A good outline of issues in distributed systems can be found in [49].

There is a substantial literature on software reliability models (also called software reliability growth models). A useful survey can be found in [48]. A recent paper which uses a Bayesian approach is [41]. The three models discussed in this chapter have been presented in [23,30,31,35].

A good discussion of fault-tolerant remote procedure calls can be found in [22].

5.10 Exercises

1. Join $N - 1$ other people ($N = 3, 4, 5$ are probably the best choices) to carry out an experiment in writing N-version programs. Write software to solve a set of differential equations, using the Runge–Kutta method. Programs for doing so are widely available and can be used to check the correctness of each version produced. Pick one of these, and compare the output of each version against this reference program for a large number of test cases. Identify the number of bugs in each version and the extent to which they are correlated.

2. The correct output, z, of some system has as its probability density function the truncated exponential function (assume L is some positive constant):

$$f(z) = \begin{cases} \dfrac{\mu e^{-\mu z}}{1 - e^{-\mu L}} & \text{if } 0 \leqslant z \leqslant L \\ 0 & \text{otherwise} \end{cases}$$

    If the program fails, it may output any value over the interval $[0, L]$ with equal probability. The probability that the program fails on some input is q.

    The penalty for putting out an incorrect value is π_{bad}; the penalty for not producing any output at all is π_{stop}.

    We want to set up an acceptance test in the form of a range check, which rejects outputs outside the range $[0, \alpha]$. Compute the value of α for which the expected total penalty is minimized.

3. In this problem, we will use simulation to study the performance of a bug removal process after an initial debugging (see Chapter 10).

    Assume you have a program that has N possible inputs. There are b bugs in the program, and bug i is activated whenever any input in the set F_i is applied. It is not required that $F_i \cap F_j = \emptyset$, and so the bug sets may overlap. That is, the same input may trigger multiple bugs. If F_i has k elements in it, the elements of F_i are obtained by randomly drawing k different elements from the set of possible inputs.

    Assume that you have a test procedure that applies inputs to the program. These inputs are randomly chosen from among the ones that have not been applied so far. Also assume that when an input is applied which triggers one or more bugs, those bugs are immediately removed from the program.

Plot the number of software bugs remaining in the program as a function of the number of inputs applied. Use the following parameters in your simulation:

i. $N = 10^8$, and the number of elements in F_i is uniformly distributed over the set $\{1, 2, \ldots, n\}$.

    a. The total number of bugs is $b = 1000$. $n = 50$ and a total of 10^6 randomly chosen test inputs are applied.

    b. Repeat (a) for $n = 75$.

    c. Repeat (a) for $n = 100$.

ii. $N = 10^8$; and the number of elements in F_i has the following probability mass function:

$$\text{Prob}\{F_i \text{ has } k \text{ elements}\} = \frac{p(1-p)^{k-1}}{1-(1-p)^n}, \quad \text{where } k = 1, \ldots, n$$

Apply 10^6 randomly chosen test vectors in all. As before, assume there are $b = 1000$ software bugs.

    a. $n = 50$, $p = 0.1$.

    b. $n = 75$, $p = 0.1$.

    c. $n = 100$, $p = 0.1$.

    d. Repeat (a) to (c) for $p = 0.2$.

    e. Repeat (a) to (c) for $p = 0.3$.

Discuss your results.

4. In this problem, we will use Bayes' law to provide some indication of whether bugs still remain in the system after a certain amount of testing. Suppose you are given that the probability of uncovering a bug (given that at least one exists) after t seconds of testing is $1 - e^{-\mu t}$. Your belief at the beginning of testing is that the probability of having at least one bug is q. (Equivalently, you think that the probability that the program was completely bug-free is $p = 1 - q$.) After t seconds of testing, you fail to find any bugs at all. Bayes' law gives us a concrete way in which to use this information to refine your estimate of the chance that the software is bug-free: find the probability that the software is actually bug-free, *given that you have observed no bugs at all, despite t seconds of testing.*

Let us use the following notation:

■ *A* is the event that the software is actually bug-free.

■ *B* is the event that no bugs were caught despite *t* seconds of testing.

a. Show that

$$\text{Prob}\{A|B\} = \frac{p}{p + qe^{-\mu t}}$$

b. Fix $p = 0.1$, and plot curves of $\text{Prob}\{A|B\}$ against t for the following parameter values: $\mu = 0.001, 0.01, 0.1, 0 \leqslant t \leqslant 10{,}000$.

c. Fix $\mu = 0.01$ and plot curves of $\text{Prob}\{A|B\}$ against t for the following parameter values: $p = 0.1, 0.3, 0.5$.

d. What conclusions do you draw from your plots in (b) and (c) above?

5. Based on the expressions for sensitivity and specificity presented in Section 5.4, derive an expression for the probability of a false alarm (in a single stage).

6. In the context of the SIHFT technique, the term *data integrity* has been defined as the probability that the original and the transformed programs will not both generate identical incorrect results. Show that if the only faults possible are single stuck-at faults in a bus (see Figure 5.4) and k is either -1 or 2^{ℓ} with ℓ an integer, then the data integrity is equal to 1. Give an example when the data integrity will be smaller than 1. (Hint: Consider ripple-carry addition with $k = -1$.)

7. Compare the use of the *AN* code (see Chapter 3) to the RESO technique. Consider the types of faults that can be detected and the overheads involved in both cases.

References

[1] P. E. Ammann and J. C. Knight, "Data Diversity: an Approach to Software Fault Tolerance," *IEEE Transactions on Computers*, Vol. 37, pp. 418–425, April 1988.

[2] A. Avizienis, "The Methodology of *N*-Version Programming," in M. Liu (Ed.), *Software Fault Tolerance*, pp. 23–46, Wiley, 1995.

[3] A. Avizienis and J. Kelly, "Fault Tolerance by Design Diversity: Concepts and Experiments," *IEEE Computer*, Vol. 17, pp. 67–80, August 1984.

[4] J. G. P. Barnes, *Programming in ADA*, Addison-Wesley, 1994.

[5] J. P. Bowen and V. Stavridou, "Safety-Critical Systems, Formal Methods and Standards," *IEE/BCS Software Engineering Journal*, Vol. 8, pp. 189–209, July 1993.

[6] S. Brilliant, J. C. Knight, and N. G. Leveson, "Analysis of Faults in an *N*-Version Software Experiment," *IEEE Transactions on Software Engineering*, Vol. 16, pp. 238–247, February 1990.

[7] F. P. Brooks, Jr., "No Silver Bullet—Essence and Accidents of Software Engineering," *IEEE Computer*, Vol. 20, pp. 10–19, April 1987.

[8] F. P. Brooks, Jr., *The Mythical Man-Month: Essays on Software Engineering*, Addison-Wesley, 1995.

[9] A. Burns and A. Wellings, *Real-Time Systems and Programming Languages*, Addison-Wesley Longman, 1997.

[10] V. Castelli, R. E. Harper, P. Heidelberger, S. W. Hunter, K. S. Trivedi, K. Vaidyanathan, and W. P. Zeggert, "Proactive Management of Software Aging," *IBM Journal of Research and Development*, Vol. 45, pp. 311–332, March 2001.

[11] W. S. Cleveland, "Robust Locally Weighted Regression and Smoothing Scatterplots," *Journal of the American Statistical Association*, Vol. 74, pp. 829–836, December 1979.

[12] B. Cox, "No Silver Bullet Revisited," *American Programmer*, Vol. 8, November 1995. Available at: http://www.virtualschool.edu/cox/pub/NoSilverBulletRevisted/.

[13] F. Cristian, "Exception Handling and Tolerance of Software Faults," in M. Liu (Ed.), *Software Fault Tolerance*, pp. 81–107, Wiley, 1995.

[14] D. E. Eckhardt and L. D. Lee, "A Theoretical Basis for the Analysis of Multiversion Software," *IEEE Transactions on Software Engineering*, Vol. SE-11, pp. 1511–1517, December 1985.

[15] C. Fetzer and Z. Xiao, "Detecting Heap Smashing Attacks through Fault Containment Wrappers," *20th Symposium on Reliable Distributed Systems*, pp. 80–89, 2001.

[16] A. F. Garcia, C. M. F. Rubira, A. Romanovsky, and J. Xu, "A Comparative Study of Exception Handling Mechanisms for Building Dependable Object Oriented Software," *Journal of Systems and Software*, Vol. 59, pp. 197–222, 2001.

[17] S. Garg, Y. Huang, C. Kintala, and K. S. Trivedi, "Minimizing Completion Time of a Program by Checkpointing and Rejuvenation," *ACM SIGMetrics*, pp. 252–261, 1996.

[18] S. Garg, A. van Moorsell, K. Vaidyanathan, and K. Trivedi, "A Methodology for Detection and Elimination of Software Aging," *Ninth International Symposium on Software Reliability Engineering*, pp. 282–292, 1998.

[19] A. K. Ghosh, M. Schmid, and F. Hill, "Wrapping Windows NT Software for Robustness," *Fault-Tolerant Computing Symposium, FTCS-29*, pp. 344–347, 1999.

[20] R. Gilreath, P. Porter, and C. Nagy, "Advanced Software Fault Tolerance Strategies for Mission Critical Spacecraft Applications," *Task 3 Interim Report*, NASA Ames Research Center, 1999.

[21] Y. Huang, C. Kintala, N. Kolettis, and N. D. Fulton, "Software Rejuvenation: Analysis, Module and Applications," *Fault Tolerant Computing Symposium, FTCS-25*, pp. 381–390, 1995.

[22] P. Jalote, *Fault Tolerance in Distributed Systems*, Prentice Hall, 1994.

[23] Z. Jelinski and P. Moranda, "Software Reliability Research," in W. Freiberger (Ed.), *Statistical Computer Performance Evaluation*, pp. 465–484, Academic Press, 1972.

[24] K. Kanoun, "Cost of Software Diversity: An Empirical Evaluation," *International Symposium on Software Reliability*, pp. 242–247, 1999.

[25] I. Koren, *Computer Arithmetic Algorithms*, A.K. Peters, 2001.

[26] J. C. Knight and N. G. Leveson, "A Reply to the Criticisms of the Knight and Leveson Experiment," *ACM SIGSoft Software Engineering Notes*, Vol. 15, pp. 24–35, January 1990.

[27] J. Lang and D. B. Stewart, "A Study of the Applicability of Existing Exception-Handling Techniques to Component-Based Real-Time Software Technology," *ACM Transactions on Programming Languages and Systems*, Vol. 20, pp. 274–301, March 1998.

[28] N. G. Leveson, "Software Safety: Why, What, and How," *ACM Computing Surveys*, Vol. 18, pp. 34–46, February 1991.

[29] B. Littlewood and L. Strigini, "A Discussion of Practices for Enhancing Diversity in Software Designs," *DISPO Technical Report LS_DI_TR-04_v1_1d*, November 2000.

[30] B. Littlewood and J. L. Verrall, "A Bayesian Reliability Growth Model for Computer Software," *Applied Statistics*, Vol. 22, pp. 332–346, 1973.

[31] B. Littlewood and J. L. Verrall, "A Bayesian Reliability Model with a Stochastically Monotone Failure Rate," *IEEE Transactions on Reliability*, Vol. R-23, pp. 108–114, June 1974.

[32] B. Littlewood, P. Popov, and L. Strigini, "Modeling Software Design Diversity—A Review," *ACM Computing Surveys*, Vol. 33, pp. 177–208, June 2001.

[33] B. Liskov and A. Snyder, "Exception Handling in CLU," *IEEE Transactions on Software Engineering*, Vol. SE-5, pp. 546–558, June 1979.

[34] J. Miller, "On the Independence of Software Inspectors," *Journal of Systems and Software*, Vol. 60, pp. 5–10, January 2002.

[35] J. D. Musa and K. Okumoto, "A Logarithmic Poisson Execution Time Model for Software Reliability Measurement," *Seventh International Conference on Software Engineering (ICSE'84)*, pp. 230–238, 1984.

[36] N. Oh, S. Mitra, and E.J. McCluskey, "ED4I: Error Detection by Diverse Data and Duplicated Instructions," *IEEE Transactions on Computers*, Vol. 51, pp. 180–199, February 2002.

[37] J. H. Patel and L. Y. Fung, "Concurrent Error Detection in ALU's by Recomputing with Shifted Operands," *IEEE Transactions on Computers*, Vol. C-31, pp. 589–595, July 1982.

[38] P. Popov, S. Riddle, A. Romanovsky, and L. Strigini, "On Systematic Design of Protectors for Employing OTS Items," *27th EuroMicro Conference*, pp. 22–29, 2001.

[39] P. Popov, L. Strigini, S. Riddle, and A. Romanovsky, "Protective Wrapping of OTS Components," *4th ICSE Workshop on Component-Based Software Engineering: Component Certification and System Prediction*, 2001. Available at: http://www.sei.cmu.edu/pacc/CBSE4_papers/Popov+-CBSE4-11.pdf.

[40] N. E. Rallis and Z. F. Lansdowne, "Reliability Estimation for a Software System with Sequential Independent Reviews," *IEEE Transactions on Software Engineering*, Vol. 27, pp. 1057–1061, December 2001.

[41] F. Salles, M. Rodrigues, J.-C. Fabre, and J. Arlat, "Metakernels and Fault Containment Wrappers," *IEEE Fault-Tolerant Computing Symposium, FTCS-29*, pp. 22–29, 1999.

[42] S. M. Sutton, Jr., "Preconditions, Postconditions, and Provisional Execution in Software Processes," *CMPSCI Technical Report 95-77*, Department of Computer Science, University of Massachusetts at Amherst, 1995.

[43] W. Torres-Pomales, "Software Fault-Tolerance: A Tutorial," *NASA Technical Memorandum TM-2000-210616*, 2000. Available at: http://hdl.handle.net/2002/12633.

[44] K. Vaidyanathan, R. E. Harper, S. W. Hunter, and K. S. Trivedi, "Analysis and Implementation of Software Rejuvenation in Cluster Systems," *ACM SIGMetrics*, pp. 62–71, June 2001.

[45] A. Villemeur, *Reliability, Availability, Maintainability and Safety Assessment*, Wiley, 1991.

[46] J. Voas and J. Payne, "COTS Software Failures: Can Anything be done?" Available at: http://citeseer.nj.nec.com/7769.html.

[47] D. Wallace and C. Coleman, "Application and Improvement of Software Reliability Models," *Report of Task 323-08*, NASA Software Assurance Technology Center, 2001.

[48] J. Xu, A. Romanovsky, and B. Randell, "Concurrent Exception Handling and Resolution in Distributed Object Systems," *IEEE Transactions on Parallel and Distributed Systems*, Vol. 11, pp. 1019–1032, October 2000.

[49] C. S. Yoo and P. H. Seong, "Experimental Analysis of Specification Language Diversity Impact of NPP Software Diversity," *Journal of Systems and Software*, Vol. 62, pp. 111–122, May 2002.

Checkpointing

Computers today are thousands of times faster than they were just a few decades ago. Despite this, many important applications take days or more of computer time. Indeed, as computing speeds increase, computational problems that were previously dismissed as intractable become practical. Here are some applications that take a very long time to execute, even on today's fastest computers.

1. *Fluid-Flow Simulation.* Many important physics applications require the simulation of fluid flows. These are notoriously complex, consisting of large assemblages of three-dimensional cells interacting with one another. Examples include weather and climate modeling.

2. *Optimization.* Optimally deploying resources is often very complex. For example, airlines must schedule the movement of aircraft and their crews so that the correct combination of crews and aircraft are available, with all the regulatory constraints (such as flight crew rest hours, aircraft maintenance, and the aircraft types that individual pilots are certified for) satisfied.

3. *Astronomy.* N-body simulations that account for the mutual gravitational interactions of N bodies, the formation of stars during the merger of galaxies, the dynamics of galactic cluster formation and the hydrodynamic modeling of the universe are problems that can require huge amounts of time on even the fastest computers.

4. *Biochemistry.* The study of protein folding holds the potential for tailoring treatments to an individual patient's genetic makeup and disease. This problem is sufficiently complex to require petaflops of computing power.

When a program takes very long to execute, the probability of failure during execution, as well as the cost of such a failure, become significant.

To illustrate this problem, we introduce the following analytical model, which we will use throughout this chapter. Consider a program that takes T time units to execute if no failures occur during its execution. Suppose the system suffers transient failures according to a Poisson process with a rate of λ failures per time unit. Here, to simplify the derivation, we assume that transients are point failures, i.e., they induce an error in the system and then go away. All the computation done by the program prior to the error is lost; the system takes negligible time to recover from the failure. Some of these simplifying assumptions are removed in Section 6.3.

Let E be the expected execution time, including any computational work lost to failure. To calculate E, we follow standard conditioning arguments. We list all the possible cases, systematically work through each one, weigh each case with its probability of occurrence, and sum them all up to get the overall expected execution time.

It is convenient to break the problem down into two cases. Either (Case 1) there are no failures during the execution or (Case 2) there is at least one. If there are no failures during execution, the execution time is (by definition) T. The probability of no failures happening over an interval of duration T is $e^{-\lambda T}$, so the contribution of Case 1 to the average execution time is $Te^{-\lambda T}$.

If failure does occur, things get a bit more complicated. Suppose that the first failure to hit the execution occurs τ time units into the execution time T. Then, we have lost these τ units of work and will have to start all over again. In such an event, the expected execution time will be $\tau + E$. The probability that the first failure falls in the infinitesimal interval $[\tau, \tau + d\tau]$ is given by $\lambda e^{-\lambda \tau}\, d\tau$.

τ may be anywhere in the range $[0, T]$. We remove the conditioning on τ to obtain the contribution of Case 2 to the average execution time:

$$\int_{\tau=0}^{T} (\tau + E)\lambda e^{-\lambda \tau}\, d\tau = \frac{1}{\lambda} + E - e^{-\lambda T}\left\{ \frac{1}{\lambda} + T + E \right\}$$

Adding the contributions of Cases 1 and 2, we have

$$E = Te^{-\lambda T} + \frac{1}{\lambda} + E - e^{-\lambda T}\left\{ \frac{1}{\lambda} + T + E \right\} \tag{6.1}$$

Solving this equation for E, we obtain the (surprisingly simple) expression:

$$E = \frac{e^{\lambda T} - 1}{\lambda}. \tag{6.2}$$

We can see that the average execution time E is very sensitive to T; indeed, it increases exponentially with T. The penalty imposed by the failure process can be measured by $E - T$ (the extra time wasted due to failures). When normalizing $E - T$ by the failure-free execution time T, we obtain η, a dimensionless metric of this penalty:

$$\eta = \frac{E - T}{T} = \frac{E}{T} - 1 = \frac{e^{\lambda T} - 1}{\lambda T} - 1 \tag{6.3}$$

Note that η depends only on the product λT, the number of failures expected to strike the processor over the duration of an execution.

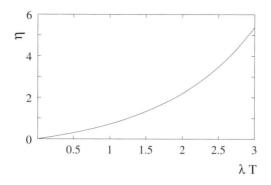

FIGURE 6.1 η **as a function of the expected number of failures.**

Figure 6.1 plots η as a function of λT, showing that η starts quite small, but then goes up rapidly.

6.1   What Is Checkpointing?

Let us start with an example to which almost everyone who has balanced a checkbook can relate. We have a long list of numbers to add up using a hand calculator. As we do the addition, we record on a slip of paper the partial sum so far for, say, every five additions. Suppose we hit the Clear button by mistake after adding up the first seven numbers. To recover, all we need to do is to add to the partial sum recorded after five additions, the sixth and seventh terms (see Figure 6.2). We have been saved the labor of redoing all six additions: only two need to be done to recover. This is the principle of checkpointing: the partial sums are *checkpoints*.

In general, a *checkpoint* is a snapshot of the entire state of the process at the moment it was taken. It represents all the information that we would need to restart the process from that point. We record the checkpoint on *stable storage*, i.e., storage in whose reliability we have sufficient confidence. Disks are the most commonly used medium of stable storage: they can hold data even if the power supply is interrupted (so long as there is no physical damage to the disk surface), and enormous quantities of data can be stored very cheaply. This is important because a checkpoint can be very large: tens or hundreds of megabytes (or more) is not uncommon.

Occasionally, standard memory (RAM) that is rendered (relatively) nonvolatile by the use of a battery backup is also used as stable storage. When choosing a stable storage medium, it is important to keep in mind that nothing is perfectly reliable. When we use a particular device as stable storage, we are making the judgment that its reliability is sufficiently high for the application at hand.

Two more terms are worth defining at this point. Taking a checkpoint increases the application execution time: this increase is defined as the *checkpoint overhead*.

Item number	Amount	Checkpoint
1	23.51	
2	414.78	
3	147.20	
4	110.00	
5	326.68	1022.17
6	50.00	
7	215.00	
8	348.96	
9	3.89	
10	4.55	1644.57
11	725.95	

FIGURE 6.2   Example of checkpointing.

Checkpoint latency is the time needed to save the checkpoint. In a very simple system, the overhead and latency are identical. However, in systems that permit some part of the checkpointing operation to be overlapped with application execution, the latency may be substantially greater than the overhead. For example, suppose a process checkpoints by writing its state into an internal buffer. Having done so, the CPU continues executing the process, while another unit handles writing out the checkpoint from the buffer to disk. Once this is done, the checkpoint has been stored and is available for use in the event of failure.

The checkpointing latency obviously depends on the checkpoint size. This can vary from program to program, as well as with time, during the execution of a single program. For example, consider the following contrived piece of C code:

```
for (i = 0; i < 1000000; i++)
    if (f(i) < min) {min = f(i); imin = i;}
for (i = 0; i < 100; i++) {
    for (j = 0; j < 100; j++) {
        c[i][j]+ = i*j/ min;
    }
}
```

This program fragment consists of two easily distinguishable portions. In the first, we compute the smallest value of $f(i)$ for $0 \leqslant i < 1,000,000$, where $f()$ is some function specified in the program. In the second portion, we do a matrix multiplication followed by a division.

A checkpoint taken when the program is executing the first portion need not be large. In fact, all we need to record are the program counter and the variables *min* and *imin*. (The system will usually record all the registers, but most of them will not actually be relevant here). A checkpoint taken when the second portion is being executed must include the array $c[i][j]$ as it has been computed so far.

The size of the checkpoint is therefore program-dependent. It may be as small as a few kilobytes or as large as several gigabytes.

6.1.1 Why Is Checkpointing Nontrivial?

From the preceding discussion, the reader may be wondering why checkpointing merits a full chapter in this book. Surely the concept as outlined above is quite trivial. Unfortunately, in checkpointing (as in so much else), the devil is in the detail. Here are some of the issues that arise:

1. At what level (user or kernel) should we checkpoint: what are the pros and cons of each level? How transparent to the user should the checkpointing process be?

2. How many checkpoints should we have?

3. At which points during the execution of a program should we checkpoint?

4. How can we reduce checkpointing overhead?

5. How do we checkpoint distributed systems in which there may or may not be a central controller, and in which messages pass between individual processes?

In addition to these issues, there is the question of how to restart the computation at a different node if that becomes necessary. A program does not exist in isolation: it interacts with libraries and the operating system. Its page tables may need to be adjusted to reflect any required changes to the virtual-to-physical address translation. In other words, we have to be careful to ensure, when restarting on processor B a task checkpointed on processor A, that the execution environment of B is sufficiently aligned with that of A to allow this restart to proceed correctly.

Furthermore, program interactions with the outside world should be carefully considered because some of them cannot be undone. For example, if the system has printed something, it cannot unprint it. A missile, once launched, cannot be unlaunched. Such outputs must therefore not be delivered before the system is certain that it will not have to undo them.

6.2 Checkpoint Level

Checkpointing can be done at the kernel, application, or the user level.

■ Kernel-Level Checkpointing. If checkpointing procedures are included in the kernel, checkpointing is transparent to the user and generally no changes are required to programs to render them checkpointable. When the system restarts after failure, the kernel is responsible for managing the recovery operation.

   In a sense, every modern operating system takes checkpoints. When a process is preempted, the system records the process state, so that execution can resume from the interrupted point without loss of computational work. However, most operating systems provide little or no checkpointing explicitly for fault tolerance.

■ User-Level Checkpointing. In this approach, a user-level library is provided to do the checkpointing. To checkpoint, application programs are linked to this library. As with kernel-level checkpointing, this approach generally requires no changes to the application code; however, explicit linking is required with the user-level library. The user-level library also manages recovery from failure.

■ Application-Level Checkpointing. Here, the application is responsible for carrying out all the checkpointing functions. Code for checkpointing and managing recovery from failure must therefore be written into the application. This approach provides the user with the greatest control over the checkpointing process but is expensive to implement and debug.

Note that the information available to each level may be different. For example, if the process consists of multiple threads, the kernel is generally not aware of them: threads are a level of detail invisible at the kernel level. Similarly, the user and application levels do not have access to information held at the kernel level. Nor can they ask, upon recovery, that a recovering process be assigned a particular process identifying number. As a result, a single program could have multiple process identifiers over the course of its life. This may or may not be a problem, depending on the application. Similarly, the user and application levels may not be allowed to checkpoint parts of the file system: in such cases, we may have to store the names and pointers to the appropriate files instead.

6.3   Optimal Checkpointing— An Analytical Model

We next provide a model which quantifies the impact of latency and overhead on the optimal placement of checkpoints. We have already mentioned that in a modern system, the checkpointing overhead may be much smaller than the checkpointing latency. Briefly, the overhead is that part of the checkpointing activity that

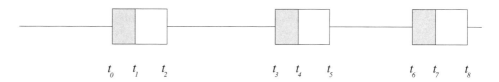

FIGURE 6.3 Checkpointing latency and overhead (squares represent latency and the shaded portions represent overhead).

is not hidden from the application; it is the part that is not done in parallel with the application execution. Intuitively, it should be clear that the checkpointing overhead has a much greater impact on performance than the latency.

Let us begin by introducing some notation, with the aid of Figure 6.3. Denoting the latency by T_{lt}, it is the time interval between when the checkpointing operation starts (e.g., t_0 in the figure) and when it ends (t_2 in the figure). To simplify the expressions below, we assume that this time interval is of a fixed size; in other words, $T_{lt} = t_2 - t_0 = t_5 - t_3 = t_8 - t_6$. The three checkpoints that are shown in Figure 6.3 represent the state of the system at t_0, t_3, and t_6, respectively. The overhead, denoted by T_{ov}, is that part of the T_{lt} interval during which the application is blocked from executing due to the checkpointing process. Here too, for simplicity, we assume that this is a fixed-size interval and in the figure, $T_{ov} = t_1 - t_0 = t_4 - t_3 = t_7 - t_6$.

If a failure occurs some time during the latency interval T_{lt}, we assume that the checkpoint being taken is useless and that the system must roll back to the previous checkpoint. For example, if a failure occurs anytime in the interval $[t_3, t_5]$ in Figure 6.3, we have to roll back to the preceding checkpoint that contains the state of the process at time t_0.

In the previous simpler model, we assumed that recovery from failure was instantaneous. Here, we make the more realistic assumption that the recovery time has an average of T_r. That is, if a transient failure hits a process at time τ, the process becomes active again only at an expected time of $\tau + T_r$. This recovery time includes the time spent in a faulty state plus the time it takes to recover to a functional state (e.g., the time it takes to complete rebooting the processor).

Let us consider the interval of time between when the ith checkpoint has been completed (and is ready to be used, if necessary) and when the $i + 1$st checkpoint is complete, and denote its expected value by E_{int}. Let T_{ex} be the amount of time spent executing the application over this period. That is, if N checkpoints are placed uniformly through the program's execution time T, then $T_{ex} = T/(N + 1)$. Thus, if E_{int} is unaffected by failure, it will be equal to $T_{ex} + T_{ov}$.

What happens if there is a failure τ units into the interval $T_{ex} + T_{ov}$? First, we lose all the work that was done after the preceding checkpoint was taken. That work is the union of (a) the useful work done during the latency period, which is equal to $T_{lt} - T_{ov}$, and (b) the work done since the interval began. The lost work is thus given by $\tau + T_{lt} - T_{ov}$.

Second, it takes an average time of T_r units to recover from this failure and restart computations. Hence, the total amount of extra time due to a failure that occurs τ time units into the interval is $\tau + T_{lt} - T_{ov} + T_r$.

6.3.1 Time Between Checkpoints— A First-Order Approximation

In the first-order approximation, we assume that at most one failure strikes the system between successive checkpoints. To calculate the expected time between two successive checkpoints, we follow the same conditioning strategy as before: we look at two cases, find the contribution of each case to the expected time, and add up the weighted contributions.

Case 1 involves no failure between successive checkpoints. Since the intercheckpoint interval is $T_{ex} + T_{ov}$, the probability of Case 1 is $e^{-\lambda(T_{ex}+T_{ov})}$ and the contribution of Case 1 to the expected interval length is

$$(T_{ex} + T_{ov})e^{-\lambda(T_{ex}+T_{ov})}$$

Case 2 involves one failure during the intercheckpoint interval: this happens with a probability that can be approximated by $1 - e^{-\lambda(T_{ex}+T_{ov})}$. This is actually the probability of *at least* one failure over an interval of length $T_{ex} + T_{ov}$, but if we assume that fault arrivals follow a Poisson process, then the probability of experiencing n failures over the interval $T_{ex} + T_{ov}$ drops very rapidly with n when $\lambda(T_{ex} + T_{ov}) \ll 1$ (as is usually the case). We therefore assume that the probability of more than one failure between checkpoints is negligible. The amount of additional time taken due to the failure is $\tau + T_r + T_{lt} - T_{ov}$; the average value of τ is $(T_{ex} + T_{ov})/2$. Hence, the expected amount of *additional* time is $(T_{ex} + T_{ov})/2 + T_r + T_{lt} - T_{ov}$. This time period is spent on top of the basic time needed for execution and checkpointing $T_{ex} + T_{ov}$, and thus the total expected contribution of Case 2 is approximately

$$\left(1 - e^{-\lambda(T_{ex}+T_{ov})}\right)\left\{T_{ex} + T_{ov} + \frac{T_{ex} + T_{ov}}{2} + T_r + T_{lt} - T_{ov}\right\}$$

$$= \left(1 - e^{-\lambda(T_{ex}+T_{ov})}\right)\left\{\frac{3T_{ex}}{2} + \frac{T_{ov}}{2} + T_r + T_{lt}\right\}$$

Adding up the contributions of Cases 1 and 2, we obtain the expected length of the intercheckpoint interval, E_{int}:

$$E_{int} \approx \frac{3}{2}T_{ex} + \frac{T_{ov}}{2} + T_r + T_{lt} - \left(\frac{T_{ex}}{2} + T_r + T_{lt} - \frac{T_{ov}}{2}\right)e^{-\lambda(T_{ex}+T_{ov})} \tag{6.4}$$

Now, consider the sensitivity of E_{int} to T_{ov} and T_{lt}. From Equation 6.4, we have

$$\frac{\mathrm{d}E_{\text{int}}}{\mathrm{d}T_{\text{ov}}} \approx \frac{1}{2} + \left[\frac{1}{2} + \lambda\left(\frac{T_{\text{ex}} - T_{\text{ov}}}{2} + T_r + T_{\text{lt}}\right)\right]\mathrm{e}^{-\lambda(T_{\text{ex}}+T_{\text{ov}})} \qquad (6.5)$$

$$\frac{\mathrm{d}E_{\text{int}}}{\mathrm{d}T_{\text{lt}}} \approx 1 - \mathrm{e}^{-\lambda(T_{\text{ex}}+T_{\text{ov}})} \qquad (6.6)$$

From these equations, we can see that

$$\frac{\mathrm{d}E_{\text{int}}}{\mathrm{d}T_{\text{ov}}} \gg \frac{\mathrm{d}E_{\text{int}}}{\mathrm{d}T_{\text{lt}}}$$

when $\lambda(T_{\text{ex}} + T_{\text{ov}}) \ll 1$.

This confirms our intuition that the sensitivity of the expected intercheckpoint interval to the overhead, T_{ov}, is much greater than its sensitivity to the latency, T_{lt}. Therefore, we should do whatever we can to keep T_{ov} low, even if we have to pay for it by increasing T_{lt} substantially.

6.3.2 Optimal Checkpoint Placement

The above analysis focused on calculating the expected length of the intercheckpoint interval, E_{int}, given a specific number, N, of equally spaced checkpoints, such that we execute the program for $T_{\text{ex}} = T/(N + 1)$ time units between any two consecutive checkpoints (where T is the execution time of the program, not including checkpointing and recovery from failures.) One of the main problems of checkpointing is the need to decide on the value of T_{ex} or, in other words, determine how many checkpoints to schedule during the execution of a long program.

The problem of determining the optimal number of checkpoints is known as the *checkpoint placement problem* and its objective is to select N (or equivalently, T_{ex}) so as to minimize the expected total execution time of the program or equivalently, to minimize the figure of merit

$$\eta = \frac{E_{\text{int}}}{T_{\text{ex}}} - 1$$

We show next how to determine the optimal value of T_{ex} for the simple model described above. Simplifying Equation 6.4 by using the first-order approximation

$$\mathrm{e}^{-\lambda(T_{\text{ex}}+T_{\text{ov}})} \approx 1 - \lambda(T_{\text{ex}} + T_{\text{ov}})$$

we obtain

$$\eta = \frac{\frac{3}{2}T_{en} + \frac{T_{ov}}{2} + T_r + T_{lt} - \left(\frac{T_{ex}}{2} + T_r + T_{lt} - \frac{T_{ov}}{2}\right)(1 - \lambda(T_{ex} + T_{ov}))}{T_{ex}} \quad 1$$

$$= \frac{(T_{ex} + T_{ov})\left[1 + \lambda\left(\frac{T_{ex}}{2} + T_r + T_{lt} - \frac{T_{ov}}{2}\right)\right]}{T_{ex}} - 1 \tag{6.7}$$

To select T_{ex} so as to minimize η, we differentiate Equation 6.7 with respect to T_{ex} and equate the derivative to zero, yielding

$$T_{ex}^{opt} = \sqrt{\frac{2T_{ov}}{\lambda} + 2T_{ov}\left(T_r + T_{lt} - \frac{T_{ov}}{2}\right)} \tag{6.8}$$

Based on the value of T_{ex}^{opt}, we can calculate the number of checkpoints to minimize η

$$N_{opt} = \frac{T}{T_{ex}^{opt}} - 1$$

Keep in mind that the above result is correct only for the simplified model with at most one failure during the intercheckpoint interval. We relax this assumption in the next section, where a more accurate model is presented.

The alert reader may have been somewhat surprised by the appearance of T_r in the above expression for N_{opt}. T_r is the cost of recovering from a failure and, intuitively, is not expected to affect the optimal number of checkpoints. Indeed, T_r disappears from the expression for N_{opt} in the more exact model, as we will see below. In the Exercises, we invite the reader to find an intuitive reason for the presence of T_r in the expression for N_{opt} for the approximate model.

Note that we arrived at this result while deciding to place the checkpoints uniformly along the time axis. Is uniform placement optimal? If the checkpointing cost is the same, irrespective of when the checkpoint is taken, the answer is "yes." If the checkpoint size—and hence the checkpoint cost—varies greatly from one part of the execution to the other, the answer is often "no," and depends on the extent to which the checkpoint size varies.

6.3.3 Time Between Checkpoints— A More Accurate Model

To relax the assumption that there is at most one failure in an intercheckpoint interval, we go back to the conditioning on the time of the first failure but now deal more accurately with Case 2. As before, Case 1 in which there are no failures between successive checkpoints contributes

$$(T_{ex} + T_{ov})e^{-\lambda(T_{ex}+T_{ov})}$$

to the average intercheckpoint time E_{int}.

In Case 2, suppose a failure occurred at time τ ($\tau < T_{\mathrm{ex}} + T_{\mathrm{ov}}$), an event that has a probability of $\lambda e^{-\lambda \tau}\, d\tau$. The amount of time wasted due to the failure is $\tau + T_r + T_{\mathrm{lt}} - T_{\mathrm{ov}}$, after which the computation will resume and will take an added average time of E_{int}. The contribution of Case 2 is therefore

$$\int_{\tau=0}^{T_{\mathrm{ex}}+T_{\mathrm{ov}}} (\tau + T_r + T_{\mathrm{lt}} - T_{\mathrm{ov}} + E_{\mathrm{int}})\lambda e^{-\lambda \tau}\, d\tau$$

$$= E_{\mathrm{int}} + T_r + T_{\mathrm{lt}} - T_{\mathrm{ov}} + \frac{1}{\lambda} - \left(T_{\mathrm{ex}} + T_r + T_{\mathrm{lt}} + \frac{1}{\lambda} + E_{\mathrm{int}} \right) e^{-\lambda(T_{\mathrm{ex}}+T_{\mathrm{ov}})}$$

Adding the two cases results in the following equation for E_{int}

$$E_{\mathrm{int}} = (T_{\mathrm{ex}} + T_{\mathrm{ov}})e^{-\lambda(T_{\mathrm{ex}}+T_{\mathrm{ov}})} + E_{\mathrm{int}} + T_r + T_{\mathrm{lt}} - T_{\mathrm{ov}} + \frac{1}{\lambda}$$

$$- \left(T_{\mathrm{ex}} + T_r + T_{\mathrm{lt}} + \frac{1}{\lambda} + E_{\mathrm{int}} \right) e^{-\lambda(T_{\mathrm{ex}}+T_{\mathrm{ov}})}$$

whose solution is

$$E_{\mathrm{int}} = \left(T_r + T_{\mathrm{lt}} - T_{\mathrm{ov}} + \frac{1}{\lambda} \right) (e^{\lambda(T_{\mathrm{ex}}+T_{\mathrm{ov}})} - 1) \tag{6.9}$$

Since T_{ov} appears in the exponent in Equation 6.9, E_{int} is more sensitive to T_{ov} than to T_{lt}.

Consider again the figure of merit,

$$\eta = \frac{E_{\mathrm{int}}}{T_{\mathrm{ex}}} - 1$$

that should be minimized to ensure that the normalized cost of checkpointing is minimal.

Suppose we look for a T_{ex} that minimizes η: this is obviously the value of T_{ex} for which $\partial \eta / \partial T_{\mathrm{ex}} = 0$ and $\partial^2 \eta / \partial T_{\mathrm{ex}}^2 > 0$. It is easy to show that the optimal value of T_{ex} is one that satisfies the equation

$$e^{\lambda(T_{\mathrm{ex}}+T_{\mathrm{ov}})} = \frac{1}{1 - \lambda T_{\mathrm{ex}}} \tag{6.10}$$

Thus, the optimal value, $T_{\mathrm{ex}}^{\mathrm{opt}}$, does not depend on the latency T_{lt} or the recovery time T_r, just the overhead, T_{ov}. Once the value of $T_{\mathrm{ex}}^{\mathrm{opt}}$ is known, we can calculate the corresponding optimal number of checkpoints: $N_{\mathrm{opt}} = \frac{T}{T_{\mathrm{ex}}^{\mathrm{opt}}} - 1$.

In sequential checkpointing, the application cannot be executed in parallel with the checkpointing. We therefore have $T_{\mathrm{lt}} = T_{\mathrm{ov}}$, and the overhead ratio becomes

$$\eta = \frac{(T_r + \frac{1}{\lambda})(e^{\lambda(T_\text{ex}+T_\text{ov})} - 1)}{T_\text{ex}} - 1 \qquad (6.11)$$

which reduces to the expression in Equation 6.3 when $T_r = T_\text{ov} = 0$.

6.3.4 Reducing Overhead

Buffering

The most obvious way to reduce checkpointing overhead is to use a buffer. The system writes the checkpoint into a part of its main memory and then returns to executing the application. Direct memory access (DMA) is then used to copy the checkpoint from main memory to disk. DMA in most modern machines only requires CPU involvement at the beginning and at the end of the operation.

A refinement of this approach is called *copy-on-write* buffering. The idea is that if large portions of the process state have remained unchanged since the last checkpoint, it is a waste of time to copy the unchanged pages to disk all over again. Avoiding the recopying of the unaltered pages is facilitated by exploiting the memory protection bits provided by most memory systems. Briefly, each page of the physical main memory is provided with protection bits that can indicate whether the page is read–write, read-only, or inaccessible. To implement copy-on-write buffering, the protection bits of the pages belonging to the process are all set to read-only when the checkpoint is taken. The application continues running while the checkpointed pages are transferred to disk. Should the application attempt to update a page, an access violation is triggered. The system is then supposed to respond by buffering the appropriate page, following which the permission on that page can be set to read–write. The buffered page is, in due course, copied to disk. (Clearly, the user-specified status of a page has to be saved elsewhere, to prevent a read-only or inaccessible page being written into).

The advantage of copy-on-write over simple buffering is that if the process does not update the main memory pages too often, most of the work involved in copying the pages to a buffer area can be avoided. This is an example of *incremental checkpointing*, which consists of simply recording the changes in the process state since the previous checkpoint was taken. If these changes are few, the size of the incremental checkpoints will be quite small, and much less will have to be saved per checkpoint.

The obvious drawback of incremental checkpointing is that the process of recovery is more complicated. It is no longer a matter of simply loading the latest checkpoint and resuming computation from there; one has to build the system state by examining a succession of incremental checkpoints.

Memory Exclusion

Another approach to lowering the checkpointing overhead attempts to reduce the amount of information that must be stored upon a checkpoint. There are two types of variables that are unnecessary to record in a checkpoint: those that have not been updated since the last checkpoint, and those that are "dead." A dead variable is one whose present value will never again be used by the program. There are two kinds of dead variables: those that will never again be referenced by the program, and those for which the next access will be a write. The challenge is to accurately identify such variables.

The address space of a process has four segments: code, global data, heap, and stack. Finding some dead variables in the code and stack is not difficult. Because self-modifying code is no longer used, we can regard the code segment in memory as read-only, which need not be checkpointed. The stack segment is equally simple: the contents of addresses held in locations below the stack pointer are obviously dead. (The virtual address space usually has the stack segment at the top, growing downward: locations below the stack pointer represent memory not currently being used by the stack.) As far as the heap segment is concerned, many languages allow the programmer to explicitly allocate and deallocate memory (e.g., the *malloc*() and *free*() calls in C). The contents of the free list are dead by definition. Finally, some user-level checkpointing packages (e.g., *libckpt*) provide the programmer with procedure calls (such as *checkpoint_here*()) that specify regions of the memory that should be excluded from, or included in, future checkpoints.

6.3.5 Reducing Latency

Checkpoint compression has been suggested as one way to reduce latency. The smaller the checkpoint, the less that has to be written onto disk. How much, if anything, is gained through compression depends on

- The extent of the compression. This is application dependent: in some cases, the compression reduces checkpoint size by over 50%; in others, it barely makes a difference.

- The work required to execute the compression algorithm. This usually has to be done by the CPU and thus contributes to the checkpointing overhead.

In simple sequential checkpointing, where the CPU does not execute until the checkpoint has been committed to disk, compression is beneficial whenever the reduction in disk write time more than compensates for the execution time of the compression algorithm. In more efficient systems, where $T_{ov} < T_{lt}$, the usefulness of this approach is questionable and must be carefully assessed before being used.

Another way of reducing latency is the incremental checkpointing technique mentioned earlier.

6.4   Cache-Aided Rollback Error Recovery (CARER)

Reducing checkpointing overhead allows us to increase the checkpointing frequency, thereby reducing the penalty of a rollback upon failure. The Cache-Aided Rollback Error Recovery (CARER) approach is a scheme that seeks to reduce the time required to take a checkpoint by marking the process footprint in main memory and the cache as parts of the checkpointed state. This, of course, assumes that the memory and cache are far less prone to failure than is the processor itself, and are therefore reliable enough to store checkpoints. If not, the probability of the checkpoint itself being corrupted will be unacceptably high and the CARER approach cannot be used.

The checkpoint consists of the processes' footprint in main memory, together with any lines of the cache which may be marked as being part of the checkpoint. This approach requires a hardware modification to be made to the system, in the form of an extra checkpoint bit associated with each cache line. When this bit is 1, it indicates the corresponding line is *unmodifiable*, which means that the line is part of the latest checkpoint, and so the processor may not update any word in that line without being forced to take a checkpoint immediately after that update. If the bit is 0, the processor is free to modify the word.

Because all of the process footprint in the main memory and the marked lines in the cache do double duty as both memory and part of the checkpoint, we have less freedom in deciding when checkpoints have to be taken. The general rule is that a checkpoint is forced whenever the system needs to update anything in a cache line whose checkpoint bit is 1, or in the main memory. If a checkpoint is not taken at such a time, then, upon a fault occurring afterward, the system will rollback to the old values of the processor registers, but to modified contents of the memory and/or cache. The above implies that checkpoints are also forced when an external interrupt occurs or an I/O instruction is executed (since either could update the memory). To summarize, we are forced to take a checkpoint every time one of the following happens:

- A cache line marked *unmodifiable* is to be updated.

- The main memory is to be updated.

- An I/O instruction is executed or an external interrupt occurs.

Taking a checkpoint involves (a) saving the processor registers in memory, and (b) setting to 1 the checkpoint bit associated with each valid cache line. By definition, therefore, a line in the cache whose checkpoint bit is 1 was last modified before the latest checkpoint was taken.

As a result, the checkpoint consists of the footprint of the process in the main memory, together with all the cache lines that are marked unmodifiable and the register copies. Rolling back to the previous checkpoint is now very simple: just restore the registers from their copies in memory and mark as invalid all the lines in the cache whose checkpoint bit is 0.

This approach is not without its costs. The hardware of the cache has to be modified to introduce the checkpoint bit, and every write-back of any cache line into main memory involves taking a checkpoint.

6.5 Checkpointing in Distributed Systems

A distributed system consists of a set of processors and their associated memories, connected by means of an interconnection network (see Chapter 4). Each processor usually has local disks, and there can also be a network file system equally accessible to all the processors.

Logically, we will consider a distributed system to consist of a number of *processes* connected together by means of directional *channels*. Channels can be thought of as point-to-point connections from one process to another. Unless otherwise specified, we will assume that each channel is error-free and delivers all messages in the order in which it received them.

We start by providing some details about the system model underlying the analysis that follows.

The state of a process has the obvious meaning: the state of the channel at any time t is the set of messages carried by this channel up to time t (together with the order in which they were received). The state of the distributed system is the aggregate of the states of the individual processes and of the channels.

The state of a distributed system is said to be *consistent* if, for every message delivery recorded in the state, there is a corresponding message-sending event. A state that violated this constraint would, in effect, be saying that we have a message delivered that had not yet been sent. This violates causality, and such a message is called an *orphan*. Note that the converse need not be the case; it is perfectly consistent to have the system state reflect the sending of a message but not its receipt.

Figure 6.4 provides an illustration. Here, we have two processes, P and Q, each of which has two checkpoints (CP_1, CP_2, and CQ_1, CQ_2, respectively), taken over the duration shown here. Message m is sent by P to Q.

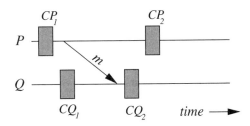

FIGURE 6.4   Consistent and inconsistent states.

The following sets of checkpoints represent a consistent system state:

- $\{CP_1, CQ_1\}$: Neither checkpoint has any information about m.

- $\{CP_2, CQ_1\}$: CP_2 records that m was sent; CQ_1 has no record of receiving m.

- $\{CP_2, CQ_2\}$: CP_2 records that m was sent; CQ_2 records that it was received.

In contrast, the set $\{CP_1, CQ_2\}$ does *not* represent a consistent system state. CP_1 has no record of m being sent, whereas CQ_2 records that m was received. m is therefore an orphan message in this set of checkpoints.

A set of checkpoints that represents a consistent system state is said to form a *recovery line*. We can roll the system back to any available recovery line and restart from there:

- $\{CP_1, CQ_1\}$: Rolling back P to CP_1 undoes the sending of m and rolling back Q to CQ_1 means that Q does not have any record of having received m. Thus, restarting from these checkpoints, P will again send out m, which Q will receive in due course.

- $\{CP_2, CQ_1\}$: Rolling back P to CP_2 means that it will not retransmit m; however, rolling back Q to CQ_1 means that now Q has no record of ever having received m. In this case, the system managing the recovery has to be able to play back m to Q. This can be done by using the checkpoint of P or by having a separate message log, recording everything received by Q. We will discuss message logs later.

- $\{CP_2, CQ_2\}$: The checkpoints record the sending, and receipt, of m.

Sometimes, checkpoints may be placed in such a way that they will never form part of a recovery line. Figure 6.5 provides such an example. CQ_2 records the receipt of m_1, but not the sending of m_2. $\{CP_1, CQ_2\}$ cannot be consistent (since otherwise m_1 would become an orphan); similarly $\{CP_2, CQ_2\}$ cannot be consistent (since otherwise m_2 would become an orphan).

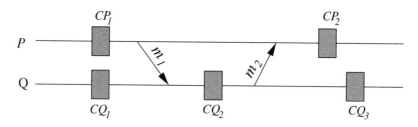

FIGURE 6.5 CQ_2 **is a useless checkpoint.**

6.5.1 The Domino Effect and Livelock

If we do not coordinate checkpoints either directly (through message passing) or indirectly (by using synchronized clocks), a single failure could cause a sequence of rollbacks that send every process back to its starting point. This is called the *domino effect*.

In Figure 6.6, we have a distributed system consisting of two processors, P and Q, sending messages to each other. The checkpoints are positioned as shown. When P suffers a transient failure, it rolls back to checkpoint CP_3. However, because it sent out a message, m_6, after CP_3 was taken, Q has to roll back to before it received this message (otherwise Q would have recorded a message that was officially never sent: an *orphan* message). Consequently, Q must roll back to CQ_2. But this will trigger a rollback of P to CP_2 because Q sent a message, m_5, to P, and P has to move back to a state in which it never received this message. This continues until all of the processes have rolled back to their starting positions. This sequence of rollbacks is an example of the domino effect.

It is the interaction between the processes in the form of messages being passed between them that gives rise to the domino effect. The problem arises when we insist on the checkpoints forming a consistent distributed state, at which no orphan messages exist. There is a somewhat weaker problem that arises when messages are lost due to rollback, illustrated in Figure 6.7. Suppose Q rolls back to CQ_1 after receiving message m from P. When it does so (unless inter-processor messages are stored somewhere safe), all activity associated with having received that message is lost. If P does not roll back to CP_2, then the situation is as if P had sent a message which was never received by Q. This is not as severe a problem as orphan

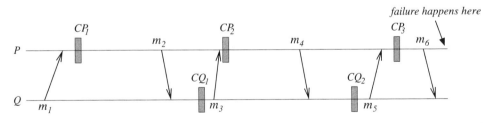

FIGURE 6.6 Example of the domino effect.

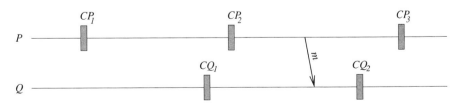

FIGURE 6.7 Example of a lost message.

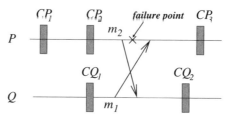

FIGURE 6.8   Example of livelock.

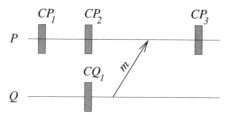

FIGURE 6.9   P taking CP_3 forces Q to checkpoint.

messages because lost messages do not violate causality. They can be treated as any messages that may be lost due to network problems, for example, by retransmission. Note, however, that if Q had sent an acknowledgment of that message to P before rolling back, then that acknowledgment would be an orphan message unless P rolls back to CP_2.

There is another problem that can arise in distributed checkpointed systems: that of *livelock*. Consider the situation shown in Figure 6.8. Q sends P a message m_1, and P sends Q message m_2. Then, P fails at the point shown, *before receiving m_1*. To prevent m_2 from being orphaned, Q must roll back to CQ_1. In the meantime, P recovers, rolls back to CP_2, sends another copy of m_2, and then receives the copy of m_1 that was sent before all the rollbacks began. However, because Q has rolled back, this copy of m_1 is now orphaned, and so P has to repeat its rollback. This in turn, orphans the second copy of m_2 as well, forcing Q to also repeat its rollback. This dance of the rollbacks may continue indefinitely unless there is some outside intervention.

6.5.2 A Coordinated Checkpointing Algorithm

We have seen that if checkpointing is uncoordinated, distributed systems can suffer the domino effect or livelock. In this section, we outline one approach to checkpoint coordination.

Consider Figure 6.9 and suppose that P wants to establish a checkpoint at CP_3. This checkpoint will record, among other things, that message m was received from Q. As a result, to prevent this message from ever being orphaned, Q must checkpoint as well. That is, if we want to prevent m from ever becoming an orphan message, the fact that P establishes a checkpoint at CP_3 forces Q to take a checkpoint to record the fact that m was sent.

Let us now describe an algorithm that carries out such coordinated checkpointing. There are two types of checkpoints in this algorithm, *tentative* and *permanent*. When a process P wants to take a checkpoint, it records its current state in a tentative checkpoint. P then sends a message to all other processes from whom it received a message since taking its last checkpoint. Call this set $\hat{P}$. This message tells each process Q the last message, m_{qp}, that P received from it before the tentative checkpoint was taken. If sending message m_{qp} has not been recorded in a checkpoint by Q, then to prevent m_{qp} from being orphaned, Q will be asked to take a tentative checkpoint recording the sending of m_{qp}. If all the processes in $\hat{P}$ that need to, confirm taking a checkpoint as requested, then all the tentative checkpoints can be converted to permanent checkpoints. If, for some reason, one or more members of $\hat{P}$ are not able to checkpoint as requested, P and all other members of $\hat{P}$ abandon their tentative checkpoints, instead of making them permanent.

Note that this process can set off a chain reaction of checkpoints. If P initiates a round of checkpointing among processes in $\hat{P}$, each member of $\hat{P}$ can itself potentially spawn a set of checkpoints among processes within its corresponding set.

6.5.3 Time-Based Synchronization

Orphan messages cannot happen if each process checkpoints at exactly the same global time. However, this is practically impossible because clock skews and message communication times cannot be reduced to zero. Time-based synchronization can still be used to facilitate checkpointing: we just have to take account of nonzero clock skews in doing so.

In time-based synchronization, we checkpoint the processes at previously agreed times. For example, we may ask each process to checkpoint when its local clock reads a multiple of 100 seconds. By itself, such a procedure is not enough to avoid orphan messages (see Figure 6.10). Here, each process is checkpointing at

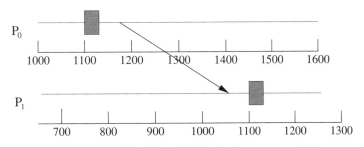

FIGURE 6.10   Creation of an orphan message in time-based synchronization.

time 1100 (where time is read off the local clock). Unfortunately, the skew between the two clocks is such that process P_0 checkpoints much earlier (in real time) than does process P_1. As a result, P_0 sends out a message to P_1 after its checkpoint, which is received by P_1 before its checkpoint. This message is a potential orphan.

If clock skews can be bounded, it is easy to prevent such orphan messages from being generated. Suppose the maximum skew between any two clocks in the distributed system is δ, and each process is asked to checkpoint when its local clock reads τ. Following this checkpoint, a process P_0 should not send out messages to any process P_1 until it is certain that P_1's local clock reads later than τ. Because the skews are upper-bounded by δ, this means that P_0 should remain silent over the duration $[\tau, \tau + \delta]$ (as measured by P_0's local clock).

We can shorten this interval of silence if there is a lower bound on the inter-process message delivery time. If this time is ϵ, then it is clearly enough for process P_0 to remain silent over the duration $[\tau, \tau + \delta - \epsilon]$ to prevent the formation of orphan messages. (If $\epsilon > \delta$, this interval is of zero length, and there is no need for such an interval of silence.)

Yet another variation is for a process that receives a message to not include it in its checkpoint and not act upon it if the message could possibly become an orphan. Suppose message m is received by process P_1 when its clock reads t. Message m must have been sent (by, say, process P_0) no later than ϵ units earlier, before P_1's clock reads $t - \epsilon$. Because the clock skew is upper-bounded by δ, at this time, P_0's clock should have read at most $t - \epsilon + \delta$. If $t - \epsilon + \delta < \tau$, then the sending of this message would have been recorded in P_0's checkpoint, and as a result, the message cannot be an orphan. Hence, if message m is received by P_1 when its clock reads at least $\tau - \delta + \epsilon$, it cannot be an orphan. Thus, another way to avoid orphan messages is for a receiving process not to act upon any message received in a window of time $[\tau - \delta + \epsilon, \tau]$ (neither use it nor include it in its checkpoint at time τ) until after taking its own checkpoint at time τ (time as told by the receiving process's local clock).

6.5.4 Diskless Checkpointing

Main memory is volatile and is, by itself, often unsuitable as a medium in which to store a checkpoint. However, with extra processors, we can borrow some techniques from RAID (see Section 3.2) to permit checkpointing in main memory. By avoiding disk writes, checkpointing can be made much faster. Diskless checkpointing is probably best used as one level in a two-level checkpointing scheme which is mentioned in the Further Reading section.

Diskless checkpointing is implemented by having redundant processors using RAID-like techniques to deal with failure. For example, suppose we have a distributed system consisting of six executing, and one extra, processors. Each executing processor stores its checkpoint in its own memory; the extra processor stores in its memory the parity of these checkpoints. Thus, if any one of the executing

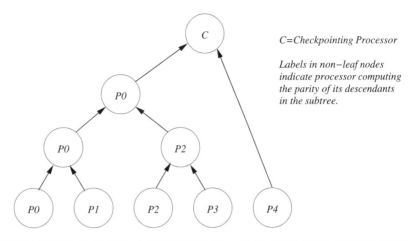

C=Checkpointing Processor

Labels in non−leaf nodes indicate processor computing the parity of its descendants in the subtree.

FIGURE 6.11   Distributing the parity computations.

processors were to fail, its checkpoint can be reconstructed from the remaining five checkpoints plus the parity checkpoint.

We can similarly use other levels of RAID as analogs. For example, RAID level 1 involves disk mirroring. By analogy, we can mirror the checkpoints; in other words, hold in two separate main memory modules identical copies of each checkpoint. Such a system can obviously withstand up to one failure.

In such systems, the interprocessor network must have enough bandwidth to cope with the sending of checkpoints. Also, hotspots can develop that will slow down the whole system. For example, suppose we have several executing and one checkpointing processors. If all the executing processors send their checkpoints to the checkpointing processor to have the parity calculated, the result will be a potentially debilitating hotspot. We can alleviate the problem by distributing the parity computations as shown in Figure 6.11.

6.5.5 Message Logging

Recovery consists of rolling back to the latest checkpointing and taking up the computation from that point. In a distributed system, however, to continue the computation beyond the latest checkpoint, the recovering process may require all the messages it received since that checkpoint, played back in the same order as it originally got them. If coordinated checkpointing is used, each process can be rolled back to its latest checkpoint and restarted: those messages will automatically be resent during the re-execution. However, if we want to avoid the overhead of coordination and decide to let processes checkpoint independently of one another, logging messages into stable storage is an option.

We will consider two approaches to message logging: *pessimistic* and *optimistic*. Pessimistic message logging ensures that rollback will not spread to other processes, if a process fails, no other process will need to be rolled back to ensure consistency. In contrast, in optimistic logging, we may have a situation in which a process failure can trigger the rollback of other processes as well.

Throughout this section, we will assume that to recover a process, it is sufficient to roll it back to some checkpoint and then replay to it the messages it received since that point, in the order in which they were originally received.

Pessimistic Message Logging

Several pessimistic message logging algorithms exist. Perhaps the simplest is for the receiver of a message to stop whatever it is doing when it receives a message, log the message onto stable storage, and then resume execution. Recovering a process from failure is extremely simple: just roll it back to its latest checkpoint and play back to it the messages it received since that checkpoint, in the right order. No orphan messages will exist in the sense that every message will have been either received before the latest checkpoint or explicitly saved in the message log. As a result, rolling back one process will not trigger the rollback of any other process.

The requirement that a process must log messages into its stable storage (as opposed to a volatile storage) can impose a significant overhead. If we are designing the system to be able to withstand at most one isolated failure at any one time, then the above-mentioned basic algorithm is overkill, and *sender-based message logging* can be used instead.

As its name implies, the sender of a message records it in a log. To save time, this log is stored initially in a high-speed buffer; when required, the log can be read to replay the message. This scheme is implemented as follows. Each process has a send-counter and a receive-counter, which increments every time the process sends or receives a message, respectively. Each message has a Send Sequence Number (SSN), which is the value of the send-counter at the node when it is transmitted. When a process receives a message, it allocates it a Receive Sequence Number (RSN), which is the value of the receive-counter (at the receiver end) when it was received. The receiver also sends out an acknowledgment to the sender, including the RSN it has allocated to the message. Upon receiving this acknowledgment, the sender acknowledges the acknowledgment in a message to the receiver. Between the time that the receiver receives the message and sends its acknowledgment, and when it receives the sender's acknowledgment of its own acknowledgment, the receiver is forbidden to send any messages to any other processes. This, as we shall see, is essential to maintaining correct functioning upon recovery.

A message is said to be *fully logged* when the sending node knows both its SSN and its RSN; it is *partially logged* when the sending node does not yet know its RSN.

When a process rolls back and restarts computation from the latest checkpoint, it sends out to the other processes a message listing the SSN of their latest message that it recorded in its checkpoint. When this message is received by a process, it knows which messages are to be retransmitted, and does so.

The recovering process now has to use these messages in the same order as they were used before it failed. This is easy to do for fully logged messages, because their RSNs are available, and they can be sorted by this number. The only remaining problem is the partially logged messages, whose RSNs are not available. Partially logged messages are those that were sent out, but whose acknowledgment was never received by the sender. This could be either because the receiver failed before the message could be delivered to it or because it failed after receiving the message but before it could send out the acknowledgment. However, recall that the receiver is forbidden to send out messages of its own to other processes between receiving the message and sending out its acknowledgment. As a result, receiving the partially logged messages in a different order the second time cannot affect any other process in the system, and correctness is preserved. This approach is only guaranteed to work if there is at most one failed node at any time.

Optimistic Message Logging

Optimistic message logging has a lower overhead than pessimistic logging; however, recovery from failure is much more complex. At the moment, optimistic logging is probably not much more than of theoretical interest, and so we only provide here a brief outline of the technique.

When messages are received, they are written into a high-speed volatile buffer. Then, at a suitable time, the buffer is copied into stable storage. Process execution is not disrupted, and so the logging overhead is very low. The problem is that upon failure, the contents of the buffer can be lost. This can lead to multiple processes having to be rolled back. For this method to work we need a scheme to compute the recovery line. See the Further Reading section for a pointer to such a scheme.

Staggered Checkpointing

Many checkpointing algorithms can result in a large number of processes taking checkpoints at nearly the same time. If they are all writing to a shared stable storage, such as a set of disks equally available to all processes through a network, this surge can lead to congestion at the disks or network or both. To avoid this problem, we can take one of the following two approaches.

The first is to write the checkpoint into a local buffer and then stagger the *writes* of this buffer into stable storage. This assumes that we have a buffer of sufficiently large capacity.

The second approach is to try staggering the checkpoints in time. Staggering can be done as follows. Ensure that, at any time, at most one process is taking its checkpoint. These checkpoints may not be consistent, meaning that there may well be orphan messages in the system. To avoid this, have a coordinating phase in which each process logs in stable storage all messages it sent out since its previous checkpoint. The message-logging phase of the processes will overlap in time; however, if the volume of messages sent is smaller than the size of the individual checkpoints, the disk system and the network will see a much reduced surge.

If a process fails, it can be restarted after rolling it back to its last checkpoint. All the messages that are stored in the message log can be played back to it. As a result, the process can be recovered up to the point just before τ, the time when it first received a message that was not logged. It is as if a checkpoint was taken just prior to τ; we call this combination of checkpoint and message log a *logical* checkpoint. The staggered checkpointing algorithm guarantees that all the logical checkpoints form a consistent recovery line.

Let us now state in a more precise manner the algorithm for a distributed system consisting of the n processors $P_0, P_1, \ldots, P_{n-1}$. The algorithm consists of two phases: a checkpointing and a message-logging phase. The first phase is as follows:

> /* Checkpointing Phase */
> for $(i = 0; i <= n - 1; i++)\{$
> P_i takes a checkpoint.
> P_i sends a message to $P_{(i+1) \bmod n}$, ordering the
>   latter to take a checkpoint.
> }

The second phase begins at the end of the above loop when P_0 gets a message from P_{n-1} ordering P_0 to take a checkpoint: this is the cue for P_0 not to take another checkpoint but to initiate the second phase. It does this by sending out a *marker* message on each of its outgoing channels. When a process P_i receives a marker message, it does the following:

> /* Message Logging Phase */
> if (*no previous marker message was received in this round by P_i*)
>   then {P_i sends a marker message on each of its outgoing channels.
> P_i logs all messages received by it after the preceding
>   checkpoint and before the marker was received.
> }
> else
> P_i updates its message log by adding all the messages received by
>   it since the last message log and before the marker was received.
> end if.

Consider the system shown in Figure 6.12a. It consists of three processes, P_0, P_1, and P_2, each of which can communicate with the others. Process P_0 acts as the checkpointing coordinator; it starts the first phase of the algorithm by taking a checkpoint and sending out a *take_checkpoint* order to P_1 to do so. P_1 sends such an order to P_2 after taking its own checkpoint. P_2 sends a *take_checkpoint* order back to P_0. When P_0 receives this *take_checkpoint* order, it knows the first phase has completed: each of the processes has taken a checkpoint and the second phase of the algorithm can begin. P_0 sends a *message_log* order on each of its outgoing

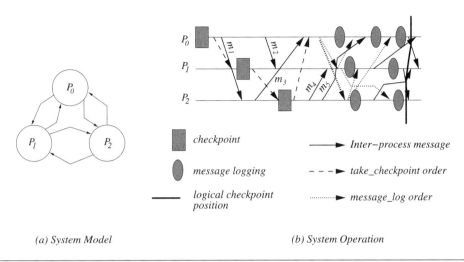

(a) System Model   *(b) System Operation*

FIGURE 6.12   Example for staggered checkpointing.

channels, to P_1 and P_2, asking them to log onto stable storage the (application) messages they received since they recorded the checkpoint. P_1 does so; P_2 has no such message to log. In each case, they send out similar *message_log* orders. When, for example, P_0 receives such an order from P_1, it checks if it has received any messages between the last time it logged messages and when it received this order, and discovers that it has nothing to log. A little time later, it receives such an order from P_2: it responds to this by logging m_5.

Each time such a message is received, the process logs the messages; if it is the first time such a *message_log* order is received by it, the process sends out marker messages on each of its outgoing channels.

We are proceeding on the assumption that given the checkpoint and the messages received, a process can be recovered. Hence, each process can be recovered up to the point when it receives a message that is not logged (this is the logical checkpoint position indicated in Figure 6.12b).

Note that in this algorithm, we may have orphan messages with respect to the physical checkpoints that are taken in the first phase. However, orphan messages will not exist with respect to the latest (in time) logical checkpoints that can be generated using the physical checkpoint and the message log.

6.6   Checkpointing in Shared-Memory Systems

We now describe a variant of the CARER scheme for shared-memory, bus-based multiprocessors, in which each processor has its own private cache. This scheme involves changing the algorithm used to maintain cache coherence among the multiple caches in a multiprocessor. In this variant, in place of the single bit that marked a line as unmodifiable, we have a multi-bit identifier: we associate a checkpoint identifier C_{id} with each cache line. A checkpoint counter, C_{count}, keeps track of the current checkpoint number. To take a checkpoint, we increment this counter. Thus, any line that was modified before this instant will have a C_{id} field which is smaller than the value of the counter. Whenever a line is updated, we set $C_{id} = C_{count}$. If a line has been modified since being brought into the cache and $C_{id} < C_{count}$, this line is part of the checkpoint state, and is therefore *unmodifiable*. Any *writes* into such a line must wait until the line is first written into the main memory.

If the counter has k bits, it rolls over to 0 after reaching $2^k - 1$. When it reaches $2^k - 1$ and a checkpoint is to be taken, each modified line has its C_{id} set to 0.

6.6.1 Bus-Based Coherence Protocol

Let us first consider a cache coherence algorithm without checkpointing. We will then see how it can be modified to take account of checkpointing.

The algorithm is for bus-based multiprocessors: all the traffic between caches and memory must travel on this bus. This means that all the caches can watch the traffic on the bus.

A cache line can be in one of the following states: *invalid*, *shared unmodified*, *exclusive modified*, and *exclusive unmodified*. *Exclusive* means that this is the only valid copy in any of the caches; *modified* means that the line has been modified since it was brought into the cache from the main memory. Figure 6.13 shows the state diagram associated with this algorithm. If the line is in *shared unmodified* state and the processor wishes to update it, it moves into the *exclusive modified* state. (All other caches holding the same line must invalidate their copies, since these

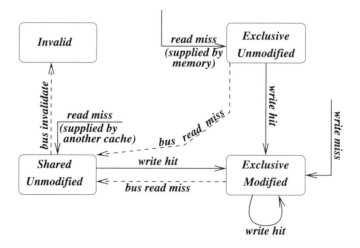

FIGURE 6.13   Original bus-based cache coherence algorithm.

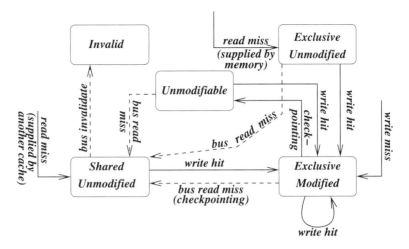

FIGURE 6.14   Bus-based cache coherence and checkpointing algorithm.

are no longer current.) When in the *exclusive modified* or *exclusive unmodified* states, another cache puts out a read request on the bus, this cache must service that request (since it holds the only current copy of that line). As a by-product of this action, the memory is also updated if necessary. After doing so, the state moves from *exclusive modified* to *shared unmodified*. A write miss is handled by considering it to be a read miss followed by a write hit. Hence, when there is a write miss, the line is brought into the cache and its state becomes *exclusive modified*, because it is modified upon the write and this cache holds the only current copy of that line. The other transitions are reasoned similarly.

How can we modify this protocol to account for checkpointing? The original *exclusive modified* state now splits into two: *exclusive modified* and *unmodifiable*. The state diagram for this algorithm is shown in Figure 6.14. When a line becomes part of the checkpoint, it is marked *unmodifiable* to keep it stable. Before this line can be changed, it must first be copied to memory so that it will be retained for use in the event of a rollback.

6.6.2 Directory-Based Protocol

In this approach to cache coherence, a directory is maintained centrally, which records the status of each line. We can regard this directory as being controlled by some shared-memory controller. This controller handles all read and write misses and all other operations that change line state. For example, if a line is in the *exclusive unmodified* state and the cache holding that line wants to modify it, it notifies the controller of its intention. The controller can then change the state to *exclusive modified*. It is then a simple matter to implement this checkpointing scheme atop such a protocol.

6.7   Checkpointing in Real-Time Systems

A real-time system is characterized by the need to meet deadlines. In *hard* real-time systems, missing a deadline can be very costly; process control is one such example. In *soft* real-time systems, on the other hand, missed deadlines may lower the quality of service provided but are not catastrophic. Most multimedia systems are soft real-time systems. However, it is ultimately the application that determines whether the system is hard or soft. A multimedia system that is used for the remote control of a vehicle is a hard real-time system; the more common case in which it is used to watch movies over the Internet is soft real-time.

The performance of a real-time system is related to the probability that the system will meet all its critical deadlines. Therefore, the goal of checkpointing in a real-time system is to maximize this probability and not to minimize the mean execution time. Indeed, checkpointing in a real-time system may well *increase* the average execution time: this is a price worth paying if the probability of missing a deadline decreases sufficiently.

We present next an analytical model similar to the one presented in Section 6.3, but one that calculates the *density function* of the execution time of a task instead of the *average* execution time. We place a checkpoint after every T_{ex} units of useful work; each checkpoint takes T_{ov} units in overhead. We are assuming here that checkpoint latency and overhead are identical: the system is so simple that the CPU has no other unit to which to delegate the checkpointing task. Transient faults occur at a constant rate λ. When a transient failure hits the processor, it goes down for time T_r (including rebooting if necessary).

Let $f_{int}(t)$ be the probability density function of the time taken between successive initiations of checkpoints. There are two cases. In *Case 1*, there is no failure over the interval $T_{ex} + T_{ov}$; in *Case 2*, there is at least one failure.

If Case 1 occurs (which it does with probability $e^{-\lambda(T_{ex}+T_{ov})}$), the interval between checkpoint initiations will be $T_{ex} + T_{ov}$. In Case 2, the time will be greater than $T_{ex} + T_{ov}$. To analyze Case 2, let us condition on the epoch of the first failure. Suppose the first failure hits τ time units into the interval. Then, we lose all τ time units of computation. Further, we take T_r time units to recover. Hence, $\tau + T_r$ time units later, the processor is ready to restart execution of this interval. Following such a restart, the density function of the rest of the execution of this interval will be identical to the unconditional density function. Therefore, the conditional density function of the execution time, conditioned on the first failure happening τ time units into the interval, is $f_{int}(t - [\tau + T_r])$. The probability of the first failure happening in the interval $[\tau, \tau + d\tau]$ is $\lambda e^{-\lambda\tau}\, d\tau$. Thus,

$$f_{int}(t) = \int_{\tau=0}^{T_{ex}+T_{ov}} \lambda e^{-\lambda\tau} f_{int}\big(t - [\tau + T_r]\big)\, d\tau \quad \text{if } t > T_{ex} + T_{ov} + T_r \qquad \textbf{(6.12)}$$

Clearly, the execution time can never be less than $T_{\text{ex}} + T_{\text{ov}}$, nor can it fall in the interval $(T_{\text{ex}} + T_{\text{ov}}, T_{\text{ex}} + T_{\text{ov}} + T_r)$ because a failure takes time T_r to recover from. Further, it will be exactly equal to $T_{\text{ex}} + T_{\text{ov}}$ in the (common) case that there is no failure. This is represented by a Dirac delta function at that point of magnitude $e^{-\lambda(T_{\text{ex}}+T_{\text{ov}})}$. (For those unfamiliar with the term, a Dirac delta function, $\delta(t)$, has the property that for any density function $f(t)$ and some constant a, $\int_{-\infty}^{\infty} f(t)\delta(t-a)\,dt = f(a)$. It is an impulse function).

To summarize, we can now write the density function as

$$f_{\text{int}}(t)$$
$$= \begin{cases} e^{-\lambda(T_{\text{ex}}+T_{\text{ov}})}\delta\big(t - [T_{\text{ex}} + T_{\text{ov}}]\big) & \text{if } t = T_{\text{ex}} + T_{\text{ov}} \\ 0 & \text{if } t \neq T_{\text{ex}} + T_{\text{ov}} \text{ and } t \leqslant T_{\text{ex}} + T_{\text{ov}} + T_r \\ \int_{\tau=0}^{T_{\text{ex}}+T_{\text{ov}}} \lambda e^{-\lambda\tau} f_{\text{int}}\big(t - [\tau + T_r]\big)\,d\tau & \text{if } t > T_{\text{ex}} + T_{\text{ov}} + T_r \end{cases}$$

$$\textbf{(6.13)}$$

Such an equation can be solved numerically.

If we take N checkpoints, the density function of the overall execution time is the $(N+1)$-fold convolution of the density function per intercheckpoint interval: $f_{\text{exec}}(t) = f_{\text{int}}^{*(N+1)}(t)$. The average time taken is calculated as shown in Section 6.3.1. If the real-time deadline is t_d, the probability of missing it is given by

$$p_{\text{miss}} = \int_{t=t_d}^{\infty} f_{\text{exec}}(t)\,dt$$

To demonstrate the tradeoff, let us consider a specific numerical example. Let $T = 0.15$ time units and $\lambda = 10^{-3}$ per time unit. The recovery time is $T_r = 0.1$ unit. In Figure 6.15, the probability of missing a deadline is plotted for two cases: $T_{\text{ov}} = 0.015$ and $T_{\text{ov}} = 0.025$. Table 6-1 shows the average execution time as a function of the number of checkpoints. For the parameters used, the expected execution time actually worsens as we increase the number of checkpoints: this is to be expected because the probability of failure during execution is less than 1%. However, when we focus on the probability of missing a deadline, the situation is more complicated (see Figure 6.15). For tight deadlines, when there is little available slack, increasing the number of checkpoints can make things worse. When deadlines are further into the future, thereby making more slack available, a greater number of checkpoints improves matters. For example, for a deadline of 0.5 and $T_{\text{ov}} = 0.015$, using six checkpoints is significantly better than using three. By contrast, for a deadline of 0.3, having three checkpoints is better than six. In every case, the deadline-missing probabilities are small; however, there are real-time applications where such probabilities have to be very low indeed.

The reader should compare the results for $T_{\text{ov}} = 0.025$ with those for $T_{\text{ov}} = 0.015$ and obtain an intuitive explanation for the differences seen.

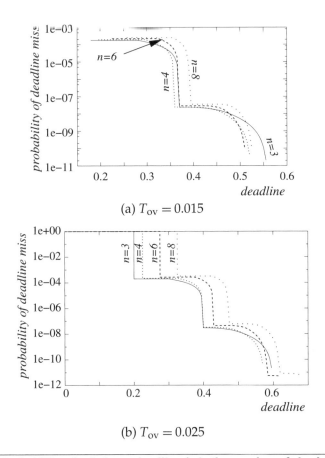

(a) $T_{ov} = 0.015$

(b) $T_{ov} = 0.025$

FIGURE 6.15   **Probability of missing a deadline (n is the number of checkpoints).**

TABLE 6-1 ■ Average execution time for different numbers of checkpoints, n		
Number of checkpoints, n	$T_{ov} = 0.015$	$T_{ov} = 0.025$
1	0.180	0.200
2	0.195	0.225
3	0.210	0.250
4	0.225	0.275
5	0.240	0.300
6	0.255	0.325
7	0.270	0.350
8	0.285	0.375

6.8   Other Uses of Checkpointing

Fault tolerance is but one application of checkpoints. Here, briefly, are two others.

- **Process Migration.** Since a checkpoint represents a process state, migrating a process from one processor to another simply involves moving the checkpoint, after which computation can resume on the new processor. The nature of the checkpoint determines whether the new processor must be of the same kind and run the same operating system as the old one.

  Process migration can be used to recover from permanent or intermittent faults. Another use is in load balancing, to achieve overall better utilization of a distributed system by ensuring that the computational load is appropriately shared among the processors.

- **Debugging.** Checkpointing can be used to provide the programmer with snapshots of the program state at discrete epochs. Such snapshots can be extremely useful to study the change of variable values over time and to get a deeper understanding of program behavior.

6.9   Further Reading

A good discussion of the various levels at which checkpointing can be done appears in [21]. The distinction between checkpointing latency and overhead, and the greater impact of overhead, was pointed out in [31]. Copy-on-write for faster checkpointing is discussed in [17] and memory exclusion in [23]. A study of the feasibility of incremental checkpointing for scientific applications can be found in [25].

Checkpoint placement for general-purpose systems has a large literature associated with it: some examples are [6,9,15,26,36,37]. An early performance model for checkpointing is presented in [28]. CARER is described in [2,11]. A more recent work on using caches in checkpointing can be found in [29].

There is an excellent survey of distributed checkpointing issues with a comprehensive bibliography in [8]. A slightly more theoretical treatment can be found in [4]. Two widely cited early works in checkpointing in distributed systems are the algorithms which appeared in [5] and in [14] (described in Section 6.5.2). The staggered checkpointing algorithm is presented in [32]. A good reference for the use of synchronized clocks to avoid explicit coordination during checkpointing is [19].

Diskless checkpointing using approaches similar to that in RAID is discussed in detail in [20,22]. Two-level recovery is considered in [30]. This paper contains a detailed performance model of a two-level recovery scheme.

There is a substantial literature on message logging, including optimistic and pessimistic algorithms [3,8], sender-based message logging [12], optimistic recovery schemes [13,27,33] and the drawbacks of optimistic algorithms [10].

When discussing message logging, we assumed that process recovery would follow if we rolled back the affected process to a checkpoint and then replayed the messages that it received beyond that point. This is not always true: it is possible for the process to take a different execution path if something in the operating environment is different (e.g., the amount of available swap space in the processor is different). For a discussion on this, see [7].

The bus-based coherence protocol is covered in [35].

Checkpointing in real-time systems is discussed in [16,26]. Checkpointing for mobile computers is a topic of growing interest, given the proliferation of mobile applications. For some algorithms, see [1,18,24]. Other applications of checkpointing (besides fault tolerance) are discussed in [34].

6.10 Exercises

1. In Section 6.3.1, we derived an approximation for the expected time between checkpoints as a function of the checkpoint parameters.

   a. Calculate the optimum number of checkpoints, and plot the approximate total expected execution time as a function of T_{ov}. Assume that $T = 1$, $T_{lt} = T_{ov}$ and $\lambda = 10^{-5}$. Vary T_{ov} from 0.01 to 0.2.

   b. Plot the approximate total expected execution time as a function of λ. Fix $T = 1$, $T_{ov} = 0.1$, and vary λ from 10^{-7} to 10^{-1}.

2. In Section 6.3.1, we derived an expression for N_{opt}, the optimal number of checkpoints. We noted that this term includes T_r, the recovery time per failure. In particular, N_{opt} tends to decrease as T_r increases.

   Explain why the assumption that there can be no more than one failure in any intercheckpoint interval contributes to the presence of T_r in this expression.

3. You have a task with execution time T. You take N checkpoints, equally spaced through the lifetime of that task. The overhead for each checkpoint is T_{ov} and $T_{lt} = T_{ov}$. Given that during execution, the task is affected by a total of k point failures (i.e., failures from which the processor recovers in negligible time), answer the following questions.

a. What is the maximum execution time of the task?

b. Find N such that this maximum execution time is minimized. It is fine to get a non-integer answer (say x): in practice, this will mean that you will pick the better of $\lfloor x \rfloor$ and $\lceil x \rceil$.

4. Solve Equation 6.10 numerically, and compare the calculated T_{ex}^{opt} to the value obtained in Equation 6.8 for the simpler model. Assume $T_r = 0$ and $T_{lt} = T_{ov} = 0.1$. Vary λ from 10^{-7} to 10^{-2}. $T = 1$.

5. In this problem, we will look at checkpointing for real-time systems. You have a task with an execution time of T and a deadline of D. N checkpoints are placed equidistantly through the lifetime of the task. The overhead for each checkpoint is T_{ov}. Point transient failures occur at a constant rate λ.

   a. Derive a first-order model for the probability of missing a deadline, by conditioning on the number of failures over $[0, T + NT_{ov}]$. Start by calculating the probability of missing a deadline if there is exactly one failure over $[0, T + NT_{ov}]$. Then, find lower and upper bounds for the probability of missing a deadline if there is more than one failure over $[0, T + NT_{ov}]$. Use the total probability formula to derive expressions for lower and upper bounds of this probability.

   b. Plot the upper bound of the deadline-missing probability as a function of N, where N varies from 0 to $\min(20, \lfloor (P - T)/T_{ov} \rfloor)$.

   b1. Set $\lambda = 10^{-5}$, $P = 1.0$, $T_{ov} = 0.05$, and plot curves for the following values of T: $0.5, 0.6, 0.7$.

   b2. Set $\lambda = 10^{-5}$, $P = 1.0$, $T = 0.6$, and plot curves for the following values of T_{ov}: $0.01, 0.05, 0.09$.

   b3. Set $P = 1.0$, $T = 0.6$, $T_{ov} = 0.05$, and plot curves for the following values of λ: $10^{-3}, 10^{-5}, 10^{-7}$.

6. In this problem, we will study what happens if the checkpoint overheads are not constant over time but vary. That is, there are times when the size of the process state is small and others when they are substantial. Suppose you are given this information, namely, you have a function, $T_{ov}(t)$, which is the checkpointing overhead t seconds into the task execution.

   a. Devise an algorithm to place checkpoints in such a way that the expected overall overhead is approximately minimized. (You may want to consult reference works on optimization for this). You can assume that if the execution time is T and failure occurs at constant rate λ, $\lambda T \ll 1$.

   b. Let $T_{ov}(t) = 10 + \sin(t)$. For $T = 1000$ and failure rate $\lambda = 10^{-5}$, run your algorithm to place the checkpoints appropriately.

7. Identify all the consistent recovery lines in the following execution of two concurrent processes:

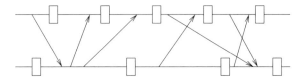

8. Suppose you are designing a checkpointing scheme for a distributed system specified to be single-fault tolerant. That is, the system need only guarantee successful recovery from any one failure: a second failure before the system has recovered from the first one is assumed to be of negligible probability. You decide to take checkpoints and carry out message-logging. Show that it is sufficient for each processor to simply record the messages it sends out in its volatile memory. (By volatile memory, we mean memory that will lose its contents in the event of a failure).

9. We have seen that checkpointing distributed systems is quite complex and that uncoordinated checkpointing can give rise to a domino effect. In this problem, we will run a simulation to get a sense of how likely it is that a domino effect will happen.

You have N processors, each of which has its own clock. A processor checkpoints when its clock reads nT for $n = 1, 2, \ldots$. Each processor has its own clock. If t is the time told by a perfect clock, the time told by any of these clocks is given by $t + \epsilon$, where ϵ is uniformly distributed over the range $[-\Delta, \Delta]$. The clocks are therefore synchronized with a maximum skew between any two clocks of 2Δ.

The messages sent out by the processors can be modeled as follows. Each processor generates messages according to a Poisson process with rate μ; any message can be to any of the $N - 1$ other processors with equal probability.

Failures strike processors according to a Poisson process with rate λ, and processors fail independently of one another.

Write a simulation to evaluate the probability that the domino effect happens in this system. (If you are not familiar with how to write such simulations, look in Chapter 10.) Study the impact of varying N, Δ, λ, and μ. Comment on your results.

References

[1] A. Acharya and B. R. Badrinath, "Checkpointing Distributed Applications on Mobile Computers," *International Conference on Parallel and Distributed Information Systems*, pp. 73–80, September 1994.

[2] R. E. Ahmed, R. C. Frazier, and P. N. Marinos, "Cache-Aided Rollback Error Recovery (CARER) Algorithms for Shared-Memory Multiprocessor Systems," *Fault-Tolerant Computing Symposium*, pp. 82–88, 1990.

[3] L. Alvisi and K. Marzullo, "Message Logging: Pessimistic, Optimistic, Causal, and Optimal," *IEEE Transactions on Software Engineering*, Vol. 24, pp. 149–159, February 1998.

[4] O. Babaoglu and K. Marzullo, "Consistent Global States of Distributed Systems: Fundamental Concepts and Mechanisms," in S. Mullender (Ed.), *Distributed Systems*, pp. 55–96, ACM Press, 1993.

[5] K. M. Chandy and L. Lamport, "Distributed Snapshots: Determining Global States of Distributed Systems," *ACM Transactions on Computing Systems*, Vol. 3, pp. 63–75, August 1985.

[6] K. M. Chandy, J. C. Browne, C. W. Dissly, and W. R. Uhrig, "Analytic Models for Rollback and Recovery Strategies in Data Base Systems," *IEEE Transactions on Software Engineering*, Vol. SE-1, pp. 100–110, March 1975.

[7] E. Cohen, Y.-M. Wang, and G. Suri, "When Piecewise Determinism Is Almost True," *Pacific Rim Symposium on Fault-Tolerant Systems*, pp. 66–71, 1995.

[8] E. N. Elnozahy, L. Alvisi, Y. M. Wang, and D. B. Johnson, "A Survey of Rollback-Recovery Protocols in Message-Passing Systems," *ACM Computing Surveys*, Vol. 34, pp. 375–408, September 2002.

[9] E. Gelenbe, "On the Optimum Checkpoint Interval," *Journal of the ACM*, Vol. 26, pp. 259–270, April 1979.

[10] Y. Huang and Y. M. Wang, "Why Optimistic Message Logging Has Not Been Used in Telecommunications Systems," *Fault-Tolerant Computing Symposium*, pp. 459–463, 1995.

[11] D. B. Hunt and P. N. Marinos, "A General Purpose Cache-Aided Rollback Error Recovery (CARER) Technique," *Fault-Tolerant Computing Symposium*, pp. 170–175, 1987.

[12] D. B. Johnson and W. Zwaenepoel, "Sender-Based Message Logging," *Fault-Tolerant Computing Symposium*, pp. 14–19, July 1987.

[13] D. B. Johnson and W. Zwaenepoel, "Recovery in Distributed Systems Using Optimistic Message Logging and Checkpointing," *ACM Symposium on Principles of Distributed Computing*, pp. 171–181, August 1988.

[14] R. Koo and S. Toueg, "Checkpointing and Rollback Recovery for Distributed Systems," *IEEE Transactions on Software Engineering*, Vol. 13, pp. 23–31, January 1987.

[15] I. Koren, Z. Koren, and S. Y. H. Su, "Analysis of a Class of Recovery Procedures," *IEEE Transactions on Computers*, Vol. C-35, pp. 703–712, August 1986.

[16] C. M. Krishna, K. G. Shin, and Y.-H. Lee, "Optimization Criteria for Checkpointing," *Communications of the ACM*, Vol. 27, pp. 1008–1012, October 1984.

[17] K. Li, J. F. Naughton, and J. S. Plank, "Low-latency, Concurrent Checkpointing for Parallel Programs," *IEEE Transactions on Parallel and Distributed Systems*, Vol. 5, pp. 874–879, August 1994.

[18] N. Neves and W. K. Fuchs, "Adaptive Recovery for Mobile Environments," *Communications of the ACM*, Vol. 40, pp. 68–74, January 1997.

[19] N. Neves and W. K. Fuchs, "Coordinated Checkpointing without Direct Coordination," *IEEE International Computer Performance & Dependability Symposium*, pp. 23–31, September 1998.

[20] J. S. Plank, "Improving the Performance of Coordinated Networks of Workstations Using RAID Techniques," *IEEE Symposium on Reliable Distributed Systems*, pp. 76–85, 1996.

[21] J. S. Plank, "An Overview of Checkpointing in Uniprocessor and Distributed Systems, Focusing on Implementation and Performance," *Technical Report* UT-CS-97-372, University of Tennessee, 1997.

[22] J. S. Plank, K. Li, and M. A. Puening, "Diskless Checkpointing," *IEEE Transactions on Parallel and Distributed Systems*, Vol. 9, pp. 972–986, October 1998.

[23] J. S. Plank, Y. Chen, K. Li, M. Beck, and G. Kingsley, "Memory Exclusion: Optimizing the Performance of Checkpointing Systems," *Software—Practice and Experience*, Vol. 29, pp. 125–142, 1999. Available at: http://www.cs.utk.edu/~plank/plank/papers/CS-96-335.html.

[24] D. K. Pradhan, P. Krishna, and N. H. Vaidya, "Recovery in Mobile Applications: Design and Tradeoff Analysis," *Fault-Tolerant Computing Symposium*, pp. 16–25, June 1996.

[25] J. C. Sancho, F. Pertini, G. Johnson, J. Fernandez, and E. Frachtenberg, "On the Feasibility of Incremental Checkpointing for Scientific Computing," *Parallel and Distributed Processing Symposium* (IPDPS), pp. 58–67, 2004.

[26] K. G. Shin, T.-H. Lin, and Y.-H. Lee, "Optimal Checkpointing of Real-Time Tasks," *IEEE Transactions on Computers*, Vol. 36, pp. 1328–1341, November 1987.

[27] R. B. Strom and S. Yemeni, "Optimistic Recovery in Distributed Systems," *ACM Transactions on Computer Systems*, Vol. 3, pp. 204–226, April 1985.

[28] A. N. Tantawi and M. Ruschitzka, "Performance Analysis of Checkpointing Strategies," *ACM Transactions on Computing Systems*, Vol. 2, pp. 123–144, May 1984.

[29] R. Teodorescu, J. Nakano, and J. Torrellas, "SWICH: A Prototype for Efficient Cache-Level Checkpointing and Rollback," *IEEE Micro,* Vol. 26, pp. 28–40, September 2006.

[30] N. H. Vaidya, "A Case for Two-Level Distributed Recovery Schemes," *ACM SIGMetrics Conference on Measurement and Modeling of Computer Systems*, pp. 64–73, May 1995.

[31] N. H. Vaidya, "Impact of Checkpoint Latency on Overhead Ratio of a Checkpointing Scheme," *IEEE Transactions on Computers*, Vol. 46, pp. 942–947, August 1997.

[32] N. H. Vaidya, "Staggered Consistent Checkpointing," *IEEE Transactions on Parallel and Distributed Systems*, Vol. 10, pp. 694–702, July 1999.

[33] Y.-M. Wang and W. K. Fuchs, "Optimistic Message Logging for Independent Checkpointing in Message Passing Systems," *Symposium on Reliable Distributed Systems*, pp. 147–154, October 1992.

[34] Y.-M. Wang, Y. Huang, K.-P. Vo, P.-Y. Chung, and C. Kintala, "Checkpointing and Its Applications," *Fault-Tolerant Computing Symposium*, pp. 22–31, June 1995.

[35] K.-L. Wu, W. K. Fuchs, and J. H. Patel, "Error Recovery in Shared Memory Multiprocessors Using Private Caches," *IEEE Transactions on Parallel and Distributed Systems*, Vol. 1, pp. 231–240, April 1990.

[36] J. W. Young, "A First Order Approximation to the Optimum Checkpoint Interval," *Communications of the ACM*, Vol. 17, pp. 530–531, September 1974.

[37] A. Ziv and J. Bruck, "An Online Algorithm for Checkpoint Placement," *IEEE Transactions on Computers*, Vol. 46, pp. 976–985, September 1997.

7

Case Studies

The purpose of this chapter is to illustrate the practical use of methods described previously in the book, by highlighting the fault-tolerance aspects of six different computer systems that have various fault-tolerance techniques implemented in their design. We do not aim at providing a comprehensive, low-level description; for that, the interested reader should consult the references mentioned in the Further Reading section.

7.1 NonStop Systems

Several generations of NonStop systems have been developed since 1976, by Tandem Computers (since acquired by Hewlett Packard). The main use for these fault-tolerant systems has been in online transaction processing, where a reliable response to inquiries in real time must be guaranteed. The fault-tolerance features implemented in these systems have evolved through several generations, taking advantage of better technologies and newer approaches to fault tolerance. In this section we present the main (although not all) fault-tolerance aspects of the Non-Stop designs.

7.1.1 Architecture

The NonStop systems have followed four key design principles, listed below.

- *Modularity.* The hardware and software are constructed of modules of fine granularity. These modules constitute units of failure, diagnosis, service, and repair. Keeping the modules as decoupled as possible reduces the probability that a fault in one module will affect the operation of another.

- *Fail-Fast Operation.* A fail fast module either works properly or stops. Thus, each module is self-checking and stops upon detecting a failure. Hardware checks (through error-detecting codes; see Chapter 3) and software consistency tests (see Chapter 5) support fail-fast operation.

- *Single Failure Tolerance.* When a single module (hardware or software) fails, another module immediately takes over. For processors, this means that a second processor is available. For storage modules, it means that the module and the path to it are duplicated.

- *Online Maintenance.* Hardware and software modules can be diagnosed, disconnected for repair and then reconnected, without disrupting the entire system's operation.

We next discuss briefly the original architecture of the NonStop systems, focusing on the fault-tolerance features. In the next two sections, the maintenance aids and software support for fault tolerance are presented. Finally, we describe the modifications which have been made to the original architecture.

Although there have been several generations of NonStop systems, many of the underlying principles remain the same and are illustrated in Figure 7.1. The system consists of clusters of computers, in which a cluster may include up to 16 processors. Each custom-designed processor has a CPU, a local memory containing its own copy of the operating system, a bus control unit, and an I/O channel. The CPU differs from standard designs in its extensive error detection capabilities to support the fail-fast mode of operation. Error detection on the datapath is accomplished through parity checking and prediction, whereas the control part is checked using parity, detection of illegal states, and specially designed self-checking logic (the description of which is beyond the scope of this book, but a pointer to the literature is provided in the Further Reading section). In addition, the design includes several serial-scan shift registers, allowing fast testing to isolate faults in field-replaceable units.

The memory is protected with a Hamming code capable of single-error correction and double-error detection (see Section 3.1). The address is protected with a single-error-detection parity code.

The cache has been designed to perform retries to take care of transient faults. There is also a spare memory module that can be switched in if permanent failures occur. The cache supports a write-through policy, guaranteeing the existence of a valid copy of the data in the main memory. A parity error in the cache will force a cache miss followed by refetching of the data from the main memory.

Parity checking is not limited to memory units but is also used internally in the processor. All units that do not modify the data, such as buses and registers, propagate the parity bits. Other units that alter the data, such as arithmetic units and counters, require special circuits that predict the parity bits based on the data and parity inputs. The predicted parity bits can then be compared to the parity bits generated out of the produced outputs, and any mismatch between the two will raise a parity error indication. This technique is discussed in Chapter 9 and is very suitable to adders. Extending it to multipliers would result in a very complicated circuit, and consequently, a different technique to detect faults in the multiplier has been followed. After each multiply operation, a second multiplication is performed with the two operands exchanged and one of them shifted prior to the operation. Since the correlation between the results of the two multiplications is trivial, a simple circuit can detect faults in the multiply operation. Note that even a permanent fault will be detected because the same multiplication is not repeated. This error detection scheme is similar to the recomputation with shifted operands technique for detecting faults in arithmetic operations (see Section 5.2.4).

Note the absence of a shared memory in Figure 7.1. A shared memory can simplify the communication among processors but may become a single point of failure. The 16 (or fewer) processors operate independently and asynchronously and communicate with each other through messages sent over the dual Dynabuses. The Dynabus interface is designed such that a single processor failure will not disable both buses. Similar duplication is also followed in the I/O systems, in which a group of disks is controlled by dual-ported controllers which are connected to I/O buses from two different processors. One of the two ports is designated as the primary. If the processor (or its associated I/O bus) that is connected to the primary port fails, the controller switches to the secondary/backup port. With dual-ported controllers and dual-ported I/O devices, four separate paths run to each device. All data transfers are parity-checked, and a watchdog timer detects if a controller stops responding or if a nonexistent controller was addressed.

The above design allows the system to continue its operation despite the failure of any single module. To further support this goal, the power, cabling and packaging were also carefully designed. Parts of the system are redundantly powered from two different power supplies, allowing them to tolerate a power supply failure. In addition, battery backups are provided so that the system state can be preserved in case of a power failure.

The controllers have a fail-fast requirement similar to the processors. This is achieved through the use of dual lock-stepped microprocessors (executing the same instructions in a fully synchronized manner) with comparison circuits to detect errors in their operation, and self-checking logic to detect errors in the remaining circuitry within the controller. The two independent ports within the controller are implemented using physically separated circuits to prevent a fault in one from affecting the other.

The system supports disk mirroring (see Section 3.2), which, when used, provides eight paths for data read and write operations. Disk mirroring is further discussed in Section 7.1.3. The disk data is protected by end-to-end checksums (see Section 3.1). For each data block, the processor calculates a checksum and appends it to the data written to the disk. This checksum is verified by the processor when the data block is read from the disk. The checksum is used for error detection, whereas the disk mirroring is used for data recovery.

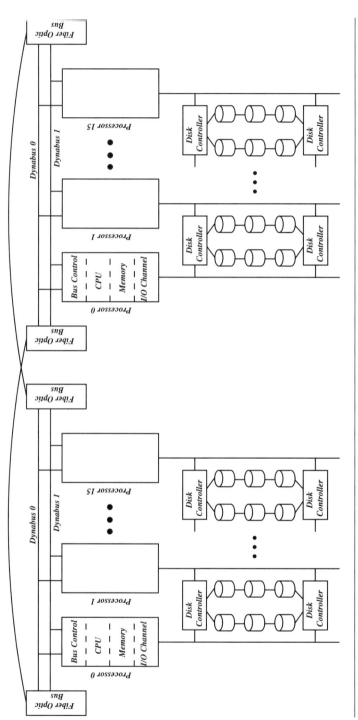

FIGURE 7.1   Original NonStop system architecture.

7.1.2 Maintenance and Repair Aids

Special effort has been made to automatically detect errors, analyze them, and report the analysis to remote support centers, and then track related repair actions. The system includes a maintenance and diagnostic processor which communicates with all the processors in the system and with a remote service center. This maintenance processor collects failure related information and allows engineers at the remote center to run diagnostic tests. It is also capable of reconfiguring the system in response to detected faults.

Internally, each computing processor module has a diagnostic unit which monitors the status of the computing processor and the associated logic, including the memory, the Dynabus interface, and the I/O channel. It reports to the central maintenance processor any errors that are detected. In addition, the diagnostic unit, upon a request received from the remote service center (through the central maintenance processor), can force the computing processor to run in a single-step mode and collect diagnostic information obtained through the scan paths. It can also generate pseudo-random tests and run them on the different components of the computing processor module.

The central maintenance processor is capable of some automatic fault diagnosis through the use of a knowledge database that includes a large number of known error values. It also controls and monitors a large number of sensors for power supply voltages, intake and outlet air temperatures, and fan rotation.

7.1.3 Software

As should be clear by now, the amount of hardware redundancy in the original NonStop system was quite limited, and massive redundancy schemes, such as triple modular redundancy, were avoided. Almost all redundant hardware modules that do exist (such as redundant communication buses) contribute to the performance of the fault-free system. Most of the burden of the system fault-tolerance is borne by the operating system (OS) software. The OS detects failures of processors or I/O channels and performs the necessary recovery. It manages the process pairs that constitute the primary fault-tolerance scheme used in Non-Stop. A process pair includes a primary process and a passive backup process that is ready to become active when the primary process fails. When a new process starts, the OS generates a clone of this process on another processor. This backup process goes immediately into a passive mode and waits for messages from either its corresponding primary or the OS. At certain points during the execution of the primary process, checkpoints are taken (see Chapter 6), and a checkpointing message containing the process state is sent by the primary to the backup. The process state of the backup is updated by the OS, whereas the backup process itself remains passive. If the primary process fails, the OS orders the backup to start execution from the last checkpoint.

Processors continuously check on each other's health through sending "I am alive" messages once every second to all other processors (over the two inter-processor buses) and to themselves (to verify that the bus send and receive circuits are working). Every two seconds, each processor checks whether it has received at least one "I am alive" message from every other processor. If such a message is missing, the corresponding processor is declared faulty and all outstanding communications with it are canceled. All processors operate as independent entities, and no master processor exists that could become a single point of failure.

An important component of the OS is the disk access process, which provides reliable access to the data on the disks despite any failure in a processor, channel, controller, or the disk module itself. This process is also implemented as a (primary/backup) process pair, and it manages a pair of mirrored disks that are connected through two controllers and two I/O channels providing eight possible paths to the data. As was indicated in Section 3.2, mirrored disks provide better performance through shorter read times (by preferring the disk with the shorter seek time) and support of multiple read operations. Disk write operations are more expensive, but not necessarily much slower, since the two writes are done in parallel.

Because transaction processing has been the main market for the NonStop systems, special care has been taken to ensure reliable transactions. A Transaction Monitoring Module (of the OS) controls all the steps from the beginning of the transaction to its completion, going through multiple database accesses and multiple file updates on several disks. This module guarantees that each transaction will have the standard so-called *ACID* properties required of databases:

- *Atomic.* Either all, or none, of the database updates are executed.

- *Consistent.* Every successful transaction preserves the consistency of the database.

- *Isolated.* All events within a transaction are isolated from other transactions which may execute concurrently to allow any failing transaction to be reset.

- *Durable.* Once a transaction commits, its results survive any failure.

Any failure during the execution of a transaction will result in an abort-transaction step, which will undo all database updates.

Most of the above techniques focus on tolerating hardware failures. To deal with software failures, numerous consistency checks are included in every software module, and upon the detection of a problem, the processor is halted, resulting in the backup process being initiated. These consistency checks stop the process when a system data structure becomes contaminated, reducing considerably the chances of a database contamination. They also make system software errors very visible, allowing their correction, thus resulting in high-quality software.

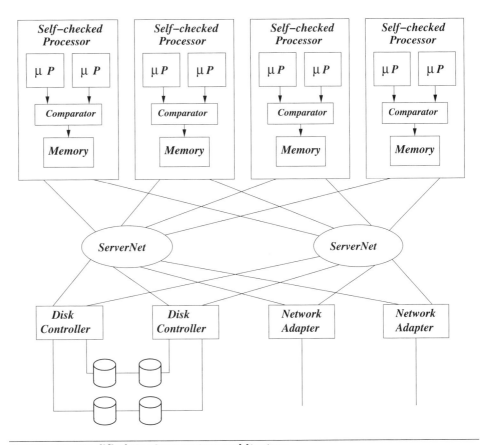

FIGURE 7.2   Modified NonStop system architecture.

7.1.4 Modifications to the NonStop Architecture

Numerous modifications have been integrated into the hardware and software design of the NonStop systems as they evolved over time. We describe in what follows only the most significant ones.

The original NonStop architecture relied heavily on custom-designed processors with extensive use of self-checking techniques to allow processors to follow the fast-fail design principle. With the rapid increase in the cost of designing and fabricating custom processors, the original approach was no longer economically viable, and the architecture was modified to use commercial microprocessors. Such microprocessors do not support the level of self-checking that is required for the fast-fail operation, and consequently, the design was changed to a scheme based on tight lock-stepping of pairs of microprocessors as shown in Figure 7.2. A memory operation will not be executed unless the two separate requests are identical; if they are not, the self-checked processor will stop executing its task.

Another significant modification to the architecture is the replacement of the I/O channels and the interprocessor communication links (through the Dynabuses; see Figure 7.1) by a high-bandwidth, packet-switched network called *ServerNet*, shown in Figure 7.2. As the figure shows, this network is comprised of two independent fabrics so that a single failure can disrupt the operation of at most one fabric. Both fabrics are used by all the processors: each processor decides independently which fabric to use for a given message.

The ServerNet provides not only high bandwidth and low latency but also better support for detection and isolation of errors. Each packet transferred through the network is protected with a Cyclic Redundancy Check (CRC; see Section 3.1). Every router that forwards the packet checks the CRC and appends either a "This packet is bad" or "This packet is good" flag to the packet, allowing easy isolation of link failures.

Current trends in commercial microprocessors are such that achieving self-checking through lock-step operation will no longer be viable: guaranteeing that two microprocessors will execute a task in a fully synchronous manner is becoming very difficult, if not impractical. The reasons for this include (1) the fact that certain functional units within microprocessors use multiple clocks and asynchronous interfaces; (2) the need to deal with soft errors (which become more likely as VLSI feature sizes become smaller) leads to low-level fix-up routines that may be executed on one microprocessor and not the other, and (3) the use of variable frequencies by power/temperature management techniques. Moreover, most future high-end microprocessors will have multiple processor cores running multiple tasks. A failure in one processor running a single task in a lock-stepped mode will disrupt the operation of multiple processors—an undesirable event.

To address the above, the NonStop system architecture has been further modified, moving from tight lock-step to loose lock-step operation. Instead of comparing the outputs of the individual processors every memory operation, only the outputs of I/O operations are compared. As a result, variations due to soft-error corrections, cache retries, and the like, are more likely to be tolerated and not result in mismatches. Furthermore, the modified NonStop architecture also allows triple modular redundancy (TMR; see Chapter 2) configurations. The standard NonStop configuration of dual redundancy can only detect errors, whereas the TMR configuration allows uninterrupted operation even after a failure or a mismatch due to asynchronous executions of the copies of the same task. An additional benefit of the TMR configuration is that it is capable of protecting applications that do not follow the recommended implementation as primary/backup process pairs.

7.2   Stratus Systems

The Stratus fault tolerant system has quite a few similarities to the NonStop system described above. Every unit in both systems is replicated (at least once) to avoid single points of failure. This includes the processors, memory units, I/O controllers, disk and communication controllers, buses, and power supplies. The main

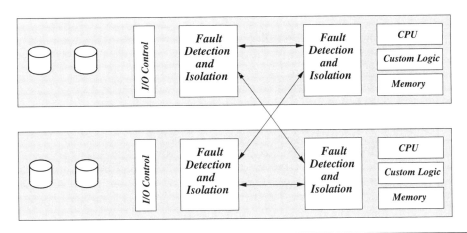

FIGURE 7.3   A single pair in a Stratus system.

difference between the two types of system is that the NonStop fault-tolerance approach focuses mainly on the software, whereas the Stratus design achieves its fault tolerance mainly through hardware redundancy. As a result, off-the-shelf software need not be modified to consist of primary/backup process pairs before running it on a Stratus server.

Stratus systems use the pair-and-spare principle described in Section 2.3.6, in which each pair consists of two processors operating in lock-step mode. The architecture of a single pair is shown in Figure 7.3. Upon a mismatch between the two CPUs, the pair will declare itself faulty and will no longer be involved in producing results. The second pair will continue to execute the application.

As discussed in the previous section, modern off-the-shelf microprocessors have asynchronous behavior. For this reason, enforcing a tight lock-step operation that requires a match for every memory operation would drastically decrease performance. Consequently, in more recent designs of Stratus servers (as shown in Figure 7.3), only the I/O outputs from the motherboards are compared and a mismatch will signal an error. A motherboard consists of a standard microprocessor, a standard memory unit and a custom unit that contains the I/O interface and interrupt logic.

Similarly to NonStop systems, current Stratus systems can be configured to use TMR structures with voting to detect or mask failures. If such a TMR configuration suffers a processor or memory failure, it can be reconfigured to a duplex until the failed unit has been repaired or replaced.

Unlike NonStop systems, the memory unit is also duplicated allowing the contents of the main memory to be preserved through most system crashes. The I/O and disks are duplicated as well, with redundant paths connecting individual I/O controllers and disks to the processors. The disk systems use disk mirroring (see Section 3.2). A disk utility checks for bad blocks on the disks and repairs them by copying from the other disk.

The processors, memories, and I/O units have hardware error-checking and the error signals that they generate are used by the system software which includes extensive detection and recovery capabilities for both transient and permanent faults. Hardware components judged to have failed permanently are removed, and the provided redundancy ensures that in most cases the system can continue to function despite the removal of the failed component. A component that was hit by a transient fault but has since recovered is restarted and rejoins the system.

Device drivers, which cause a significant fraction of operating system crashes, are hardened to reduce their failure rate. Such hardening takes the form of (a) reducing the chances that a device will malfunction, (b) promptly detecting the malfunctioning of a device, and (c) dealing with any such malfunctioning locally as much as possible to contain its effects and prevent it from propagating to the operating system.

I/O device malfunctioning probability can be reduced, for example, by running sanity checks on the input, thus protecting the device from an obviously bad input. Prompt detection can be carried out by using timeouts to detect device hangs and to check the value returned by the device for obvious errors. In some cases, it may be possible—when the device is otherwise idle—to make it carry out some test actions.

Upon a system crash, an automatic reboot is carried out. One of the CPUs is kept offline in order to dump its memory to disk: such a dump can be analyzed to diagnose the cause of the failure. Once this dump has been completed, the offline CPU can be resynchronized with its functioning counterpart(s) and rejoin the system. If the reboot is unsuccessful, the system is powered down and then powered up again, followed by another reboot attempt.

Every fault detected by the system is reported to a remote Stratus support center, allowing service engineers to continuously monitor the system and, if necessary, troubleshoot and resolve problems online. If permanent faults are detected, hot-swappable replacement parts are automatically ordered and shipped to the customer.

7.3   Cassini Command and Data Subsystem

The Cassini spacecraft was designed to explore Saturn and its satellites. Launched in 1997, it reached Saturn in 2004 and is scheduled to continue its mission through 2008. The activity level was relatively low until the spacecraft reached Saturn; since then, it has launched the Huygens probe to study the satellite Titan, and has carried out detailed studies of Saturn, its rings, and several of its satellites.

The spacecraft has three mission modes: *normal*, which takes up most of the mission; *mission-critical*, which occurs during three critical stages of the mission: launch, Saturn orbit insertion, and Titan probe relay; and *safing*, in which the satellite has suffered a fault and has to be placed in a configuration that is safe and appropriate for manual intervention from Earth.

The Command and Data Subsystem (CDS) issues commands to the other subsystems and controls the buffering and formatting of data for sending back to Earth. In particular, it has the following functions:

- *Communications.* Management of commands from the ground and of telemetry to send data from the spacecraft to Earth. Also, communication with the spacecraft's engineering and science subsystems (such as the Attitude and Articulation Control [AACS] and the Radio Frequency [RFS] subsystems).

- *Command Sequencing.* Storing and playing out command sequences to manage given activities such as launch and Saturn orbit insertion.

- *Time Keeping.* Maintaining the spacecraft time reference, to coordinate activity and facilitate synchronization.

- *Data Handling.* Buffering data as needed if the data collection rate is greater than the downlink transmission rate.

- *Temperature Control.* Monitoring and managing spacecraft temperatures.

- *Fault Protection.* Running algorithms which react to faults detected either outside or in the CDS.

Because the spacecraft is meant to operate for about 11 years without any chance of hardware replacement or repair, the CDS must be fault tolerant. Such fault tolerance is provided by a dual-redundant system.

Figure 7.4 provides a block diagram of the CDS. The heart of the CDS is a pair of flight computers, each with very limited memory: 512 KWords of RAM and 8 KWords of PROM. For storage of data meant for transmission to Earth, there are two solid-state recorders, each of 2 GBit capacity. Each flight computer is connected to both recorders. Communication is by means of a dual-redundant 1553B bus. The 1553B bus was introduced in the 1970s and consists of the cable (plus couplers and connectors), a bus controller that manages transmissions on the bus (all traffic on the bus either originates with the bus controller or is in response to a bus controller command), and a remote terminal at each flight computer, to allow it to communicate with the other computer. Sensors connected to the bus provide the flight computers with state information, such as temperature, pressure, and voltage levels. One flight computer is the primary at any given time; the other is a backup. The bus controller of the backup computer is inhibited; that of the primary is the only one that is active.

The CDS was designed under the assumption that the system will never have to cope with multiple faults at any given time. Apart from a specified set of failures, the system is supposed to be protected against any single failure. The exception set includes stuck bits in the interface circuitry that take the CDS to an uncommanded state, design faults, and the issuing of wrong commands from Earth.

Errors are classified according to the location of the corresponding fault (central vs. peripheral), their impact (noninterfering vs. interfering), and their duration

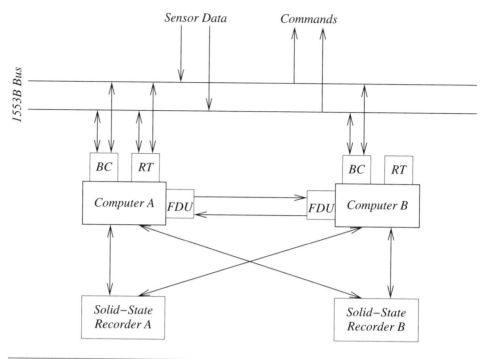

FIGURE 7.4   Cassini CDS block diagram.

(transient vs. permanent). Central faults are those that occur in one of the flight computers; faults occurring in other units, such as the solid-state recorders, bus, or the sensor units, are classified as peripheral.

Noninterfering faults are, as the term implies, faults that do not affect any service that is necessary to the current mission phase. For some such faults, it is sufficient to log them for future analysis; for others, some corrective action may need to be taken. Interfering faults are those that affect a service that is important to the current mission phase. Transient faults can be allowed to die away, and then the system is restored to health; permanent faults require either automatic switching to a redundant entity or placing the spacecraft in a safe mode and awaiting instructions from ground control. As a general rule, if a fault can be handled by ground control, it is so handled: the philosophy is to carry out autonomous recovery only if ground-based intervention is not practical.

If the CDS itself fails for a substantial period of time, this is detected by the AACS which places the spacecraft in a default "safe mode" to wait for the CDS to recover. The AACS also has the ability to recognize some obviously unsafe operating configurations, and can reject orders to configure the system in an unsafe way.

7.4 IBM G5

The IBM G5 processor makes extensive use of fault-tolerance techniques to recover from transient faults that constitute the majority of hardware faults (see Chapter 1). Fault tolerance is provided for the processor, memory, and I/O systems. In the processor and I/O systems, this takes the form of physical replication; in memory, extensive use is made of error detection and correction codes of the type described in Section 3.1. In addition, extensive hardware support is provided for rollback recovery from transient failures (see Chapter 6).

Traditional redundancy methods are used to implement fault tolerance in the I/O subsystem. There are multiple paths from the processor to the I/O devices: these can be dynamically switched as necessary to route around faults. Inline error checking is provided, and the channel adapters are designed to prevent interface errors from propagating into the system.

The G5 processor pipeline includes an I-unit, which is responsible for fetching instructions, decoding them, generating any necessary addresses, and placing pending instructions in an instruction queue. There is an E-unit, which executes the instructions and updates the machine state. Both the I- and E-units are duplicated: they work in lock-step, which allows the results of their activity to be compared. A successful comparison indicates that all is well; a divergence between the two instances indicates an error.

In addition, the processor has an R-unit, which consists of 128 32-bit and 128 64-bit registers. The R-unit is used to store the checkpointed machine state to facilitate rollback recovery: this includes general-purpose, status word, and control registers. The R-unit registers are protected by an error-correcting code (ECC), and the R-unit is updated whenever the duplicate E-units generate identical results.

The processor has an ECC-protected store buffer, into which pending stores can be written. When a store instruction commits, the relevant store buffer entry can be written into cache.

All writes to the L1 cache are also written through to the L2 cache; as a result, there is always a backup copy of the L1 contents. The L2 cache and the main memory, as well as the buses connecting the processor to the L2 cache and the L2 cache to main memory, are protected using ECC (a $(72, 64)$ SEC/DED Hamming code; see Section 3.1), whereas errors in L1 are detected using parity. When an L2 line is detected as erroneous, it is invalidated in cache. If this line is dirty (i.e., was modified since being brought in from main memory), the line is corrected if possible and the updated line is stored in the main memory. If it is not possible to correct the error, the line is invalidated in cache and steps are taken to prevent the propagation of the erroneous data.

Special logic detects the same failures happening repeatedly in the same storage location in the L2 cache. Such repeated identical failures are taken to indicate a permanent fault; the affected cache line is then retired from use.

The data in the main memory are protected by the same $(72, 64)$ SEC/DED code, and the address bus is protected using parity bits, one parity bit for every 24 bits.

Memory *scrubbing* is used to prevent transient memory errors from accumulating. Memory scrubbing consists of regularly reading the memory, word by word, and correcting any bit errors encountered. This way, memory errors are corrected before they accumulate and their number exceeds the correction capabilities of the SEC/DED code. Spare DRAM is also provided, which can be switched in to replace a malfunctioning memory chip.

G5 systems have a variety of responses to errors. Localized data errors in the registers or the L2 cache can be corrected by means of an ECC. Errors in the L1 cache are detected by means of parity and corrected by using the corresponding copy in the L2 cache. If a processor operation results in an erroneous output (detected by disagreeing outputs from the duplicated I or E-units), the system retries the instruction in the hope that the error was caused by a transient fault. Such a retry is started by freezing the checkpointed state: updates to the R-unit are not permitted. Pending write-throughs to the L2 cache from instructions that have already been checkpointed are completed. The checkpointed state held in the R-unit is loaded into the appropriate machine registers and the machine is restarted from the checkpointed state. Note that this is not a system checkpointing process (which, upon a failure, re-executes a large section of the application) of the type that has been described in Chapter 6. Instead, it is a hardware-controlled process for *instruction retry* and is transparent even to the operating system.

There may be instances in which recovery fails. For example, a permanent fault that results in repeated errors may occur. In such an event, the checkpoint data are transferred to a spare processor (if available) and execution continues on that processor.

Unless the system runs out of spares to deal with permanent failures or the checkpointed data are found to have been corrupted, a failure and the subsequent recovery will be transparent to the operating system and the application: the recovery process is generally handled rapidly in hardware.

7.5   IBM Sysplex

The IBM Sysplex is a multinode system that offers some fault-tolerance protection for enterprise applications. The system is configured as shown in Figure 7.5. A number of computing nodes (up to 32) are interconnected; each node is either a single- or multiple-processor entity. The system includes a global timer, which provides a common time reference to unambiguously order the events across nodes. A storage director connects this cluster of processors to shared storage, in the form of multiple disk systems. This storage is equally shared: every node has access to any part of it. Connection between the computing nodes and the storage devices is made fault tolerant through redundant connections. The storage itself can be made sufficiently reliable through coding or replication. The existence of truly shared disk storage makes it possible for applications running on one node to be easily restarted on another.

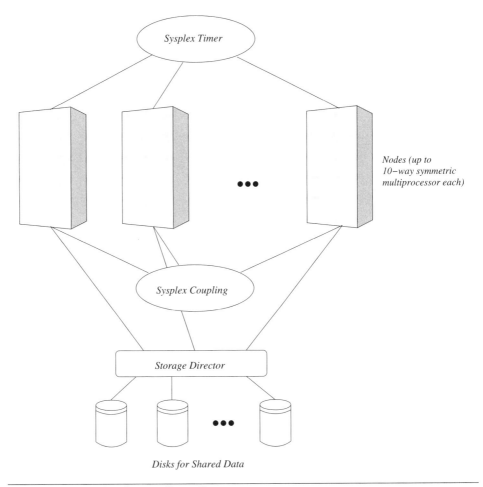

FIGURE 7.5   IBM Sysplex configuration.

Processes indicate, through a registration service, whether a restart may be required. When a process is completed, it deregisters itself, to indicate that it will no longer require restart.

When the system detects a node failure, it must (i) try to restart that node and (ii) restart the applications that were running on that node. Failure detection is through a heartbeat mechanism: the nodes periodically emit heartbeats or "I am alive" messages. If a sufficiently long sequence of heartbeat messages is missed from a node, it is declared to have failed. False alarms can arise because it is possible under some circumstances for functional nodes to miss sending out heartbeats at the right time. The heartbeat mechanism must therefore be carefully tuned to balance the need to catch failures against the need to keep the false alarm rate sufficiently low.

When a node failure is detected, the Automatic Restart Manager (ARM) takes charge of restarting the affected tasks. The ARM has access to the global system state: it is aware of the loading of each node and can carry out load balancing while in the process of migrating affected tasks to other nodes. The ARM is also aware of task affinity groups, which are tasks that must be assigned together to the same node (e.g., because they have a heavy amount of intercommunication), and of any sequencing constraints (e.g., that task P should be restarted only after task Q has done so). Also provided are the maximum number of restart attempts, both on the original node and on other nodes, as well as the amount of memory required.

When restarting tasks on other nodes, care has to be taken that the supposedly failed node is really down. This is necessary to avoid the possibility of two copies of the same task—the original and restarted versions—both being active. Such duplicates may be no more than a harmless waste of computational resources in some applications; in other cases, however, duplication may result in erroneous results (e.g., incorrect updates may occur in databases). Similarly, care must be taken when a node's access to the global shared state is lost, to ensure that erroneous events do not occur. For example, if node x loses access to the global state and decides to recover application α, it may well be that some other node y is restarting α as well, thus resulting in two copies of α. Sysplex deals with such problems by disallowing restarts on nodes which have lost access to the global state. To implement such a policy, an array of system sequence numbers, SysSeqNum(), is used. The system sequence number associated with a node is incremented every time access to global shared state is lost and then re-established. Every process, P, on a given node x is labeled with the value of SysSeqNum(x) at the time it registers for the restart service (notifies the system that it should be restarted if there is a failure). Should access to the shared state now be lost and then be restored, process P's sequence number will no longer equal the latest value of SysSeqNum(x). P will now be de-registered from the recovery service.

ARM also provides support for hot-standby mode. In such a mode, there are primary and secondary servers for a given application: if the primary fails, the output of the secondary can be used. The switchover from primary to secondary is much faster than when hot-standby is not used.

7.6 Itanium

The Intel Itanium processor is a 64-bit design, meant for use in high-end server and similar applications. It is an Explicitly Parallel Instruction Computer (EPIC) capable of executing up to six instructions per cycle, which are bundled by the compiler so that data dependencies are avoided. It has several built-in features for fault tolerance to enhance availability.

The Itanium makes extensive use of parity and error-correcting coding in its data buses (where a single-bit error can be corrected), and in its three levels of cache. There are separate data (L1D) and instruction (L1I) caches at the L1 level while L2 and L3 are unified caches.

L1I and L1D (both the tag and data arrays) are protected by error-detecting parity. When an error is detected, the entire cache is invalidated. L1D has byte-wise parity to facilitate load/store operations of granularity finer than a word. Since faults tend to be spatially correlated (meaning that if a particular location is suffering a transient fault, it is more likely that physically neighboring locations will be affected as well), bits from adjacent cache lines are physically interleaved on silicon. This reduces the probability of a (potentially undetectable) multiple-bit error in a given cache line.

The L2 cache has its data array protected by error-correcting codes (a (72,64) SEC/DED Hamming code) and its tag array by error-detecting parity (one parity bit for no more than 24 bits). Errors correctable by coding are usually automatically corrected; other (more wide-ranging) responses are outlined below.

Both the tag and data arrays of L3 are protected by similar error-correcting codes. Single-bit data errors are silently corrected when the data are written back. Upon a tag array error, all four ways of the relevant entry in the tag array are scrubbed.

When an error in any level of the cache is detected, the system corrects it if possible, sends out a "corrected machine check interrupt" to indicate that such a correction has occurred, and resumes its normal operation. An exception to this is when an error is "promoted," as is described later.

Suppose the error is not hardware-correctable. If it requires hardware error containment to prevent it from spreading, a bus reset is carried out. A bus reset clears all pending memory and bus transactions and all the internal state machines. All architectural state is preserved (meaning that the register files, caches and TLBs [Translation Lookaside Buffers] are not cleared).

If hardware error containment is not required, a Machine Check Abort (MCA) is signaled. An MCA may be either local or global. If local, it is restricted to the processor or thread encountering the error: information about this is not sent out to any other processors in the system. In contrast, all the processors will be notified of a global MCA.

Error handling is done layer by layer. We have already seen that the hardware will correct such errors as it can. Above the hardware layer are the Processor Abstraction (PAL) and the System Abstraction (SAL) layers, whose job it is to hide lower-level implementation levels concerning, respectively, the processor and the system external to the processor (such as the memory or the chipset) from higher-level entities (such as the operating system). Error handling is attempted by these layers in turn. If either layer can successfully handle the error, error handling can end there once information about the error has been sent to the operating system. If neither of these abstraction layers can deal with the error, the operating system gets into the act. For example, if an individual process is identified as the error source, the operating system can abort it.

There are instances in which the error is impossible to successfully handle at any level. In such an instance, a reboot and I/O reinitialization may be necessary.

Such a reboot may be local to an individual processor or involve the entire system, depending on the nature of the error.

In some cases, an error may be "promoted," and a higher-level response than is strictly necessary may be employed. For example, suppose the processor is being used in a duplex or some other redundant architecture in which multiple processors are executing the same code, off identical inputs, and to the beat of a synchronized clock. The cycle-by-cycle output of the redundant processors can then be compared in order to detect faults. In such a setup, taking a processor out of lock-step to carry out a hardware error correction may not be the most appropriate thing to do: instead, it may be best to signal a global MCA and let some higher-scope entity handle the problem.

When erroneous data are detected (but not corrected), the usual response is to reboot the entire system (or at least the affected node if the system has multiple processors). The Itanium offers a more focused approach. Erroneous data are marked as such (something that is called *data poisoning*), and any process that tries to use such data is aborted. The effect of erroneous data is therefore less pronounced, especially if used by only a small number of processes. Data poisoning is carried out at the L2 cache level, and the rules for implementing it are as follows:

- Any store to a poisoned cache line is ignored.

- If a poisoned line is removed from the cache (to make room for a new line), it is written back to main memory and a flag is raised at that location, to indicate that the contents are poisoned.

- Any process that attempts to fetch a poisoned line triggers an MCA.

As mentioned before, once an error has been detected, information about it is passed on to the operating system. This can be done through an interrupt. Alternatively, the operating system may choose to mask out such interrupts and, from time to time, poll lower layers for this information. Such information can be used to better manage the system. For example, if a particular page frame in main memory is observed to suffer from a high error rate, the operating system could decide to stop mapping anything into it.

Due to the extensive set of fault-tolerance mechanisms implemented in the Itanium (compared to most other commercial microprocessors), it has been selected as a building block in several fault-tolerant multiprocessors, including the most recent designs of the NonStop systems.

7.7   Further Reading

Most books on fault tolerance include descriptions of existing fault-tolerant systems, for example [12,18,20]. Further details on the original Tandem systems can be found at [2,14,24]. The more recent design of the NonStop system is described in [4]. Self-checking logic which is used in the design of some nonstop processors is described in [13]. Design of self-checking checkers is presented in [1]. The shifted operands technique for detecting errors in arithmetic units appears in [17,22].

The Stratus systems are described in white papers published by Stratus Technologies and available at www.stratus.com/whitep/index.htm. Hardening drivers to make them more resilient is discussed in [8].

The Cassini spacecraft CDS is described in [7]; information about the Cassini AACS can be found in [6].

The main source for the IBM G5 processor is the 1999 September/November special issue of the IBM *Journal of Research and Development*. An overview of the fault-tolerance techniques used in G5 is provided in [23]. Another good introduction can be found in [21]. The G5 cache and the I/O system are described in [25] and [9], respectively.

The main reference for the IBM S/390 Sysplex is the Volume 36, No. 2, issue of the *IBM Systems Journal*, for an overview, see [16], and for a description of high-availability, see [5]. A very informative comparison of the IBM and HP/Tandem NonStop designs is included in [3].

Information about the Intel Itanium processor is widely available. Excellent introductions can be found in the September/October 2000 issue of *IEEE Micro*, which contains several relevant papers, and in [15]. Another good source is the Intel Corporation website, especially [10,11]. The Itanium has been used in several designs of fault-tolerant systems including IBM, NEC, Fujitsu and Hewlett-Packard's NonStop [4,19].

References

[1] M. J. Ashjaee and S. M. Reddy, "On-Totally Self-Checking Checkers for Separable Codes," *IEEE Transactions on Computers*, Vol. C-26, pp. 737–744, August 1977.

[2] W. Bartlett and B. Ball, "Tandems Approach to Fault Tolerance," *Tandem Systems Review*, Vol. 8, pp. 84–95, February 1988.

[3] W. Bartlett and L. Spainhower, "Commercial Fault Tolerance: A Tale of Two Systems," *IEEE Transactions on Dependable and Secure Computing*, Vol. 1, pp. 87–96, January 2004.

[4] D. Bernick, B. Bruckert, P. Del-Vigna, D. Garcia, R. Jardine, J. Klecka, and J. Smullen, "NonStop Advanced Architecture," *Dependable Systems and Networks Symposium (DSN'05)*, pp. 12–21, 2005.

[5] N. S. Bowen, J. Antognini, R. D. Regan, and N. C. Matsakis, "Availability in Parallel Systems: Automatic Process Restart," *IBM Systems Journal*, Vol. 36, pp. 284–300, 1997. Available at: www.research.ibm.com/journal/sj/362/antognini.html.

[6] G. M. Brown, D. E. Bernard, and R. D. Rasmussen, "Attitude and Articulation Control for the Cassini Spacecraft: A Fault Tolerance Overview," *14th Annual Digital Avionics Systems Conference*, pp. 184–192, 1995.

[7] T. K. Brown and J. A. Donaldson, "Fault Protection Design for the Command and Data Subsystem on the Cassini Spacecraft," *13th Annual Digital Avionics Systems Conference*, pp. 408–413, 1994.

[8] S. Graham, "Writing Drivers for Reliability, Robustness Fault Tolerant Systems," *Microsoft Windows Hardware Engineering Conference*, April 2002. Available at: www.stratus.com/resources/pdf/drivers.pdf.

[9] T. A. Gregg, "S/390 CMOS Server I/O: The Continuing Evolution," *IBM Journal of Research and Development*, Vol. 41, pp. 449–462, July/September 1997.

[10] Intel Corporation, "Intel Itanium Processor Family Error Handling Guide," Document 249278-003. Available at: www.intel.com/design/itanium/downloads/24927802.pdf.

[11] Intel Corporation, "Intel Itanium2 Processor." Available at: www.intel.com/design/itanium2/documentation.htm.

[12] B. W. Johnson, *Design and Analysis of Fault-Tolerant Digital Systems,* Addison-Wesley, 1989.

[13] P. K. Lala, *Self-Checking and Fault-Tolerant Digital Design,* Morgan Kaufmann, 2000.

[14] I. Lee and R. K. Iyer, "Software Dependability in the Tandem Guardian System," *IEEE Transactions on Software Engineering,* Vol. 8, pp. 455–467, May 1995.

[15] T. Luck, "Machine Check Recovery for Linux on Itanium Processors," *Linux Symposium*, pp. 313–319, July 2003.

[16] J. M. Nick, B. B. Moore, J.-Y. Chung, and N. S. Bowen, "S/390 Cluster Technology: Parallel Sysplex," *IBM Systems Journal*, Vol. 36, pp. 172–201, 1997. Available at: www.research.ibm.com/journal/sj/362/nick.html.

[17] J. H. Patel and L. Y. Fung, "Concurrent Error Detection in ALUs by Recomputing with Shifted Operands," *IEEE Transactions on Computers,* Vol. 31, pp. 589–595, July 1982.

[18] D. K. Pradhan (Ed.), *Fault Tolerant Computer System Design,* Prentice Hall, 1996.

[19] Y. Shibata, "Fujitsu's Chipset Development for High-Performance, High-Reliability Mission-Critical IA Servers PRIMEQUEST," *Fujitsu Science and Technology Journal,* Vol. 41, pp. 291–297, October 2005. Available at: www.fujitsu.com/downloads/MAG/vol41-3/paper03.pdf.

[20] D. P. Siewiorek and R. S. Swarz, *Reliable Computer Systems: Design and Evaluation,* A.K. Peters, 1998.

[21] T. J. Slegel, R. M. Averill III, M. A. Check, B. C. Giamei, B. W. Krumm, C. A. Krygowski, W. H. Li, J. S. Liptay, J. D. MacDougall, T. J. McPherson, J. A. Navarro, E. M. Schwarz, K. Shum, and C. F. Webb, "IBM's S/390 G5 Microprocessor Design," *IEEE Micro*, pp. 12–23, March/April 1999.

[22] G. S. Sohi, M. Franklin, and K. K. Saluja, "A Study of Time-redundant Fault-tolerance Techniques for High Performance Pipelined Computers," *Fault-Tolerant Computing Symposium*, pp. 436–443, 1989.

[23] L. Spainhower and T. A. Gregg, "IBM S/390 Parallel Enterprise Server G5 Fault Tolerance: A Historical Perspective," *IBM Journal of Research and Development*, Vol. 43, pp. 863–873, September/November 1999.

[24] Tandem Technical Reports. Available at: http://www.hpl.hp.com/techreports/tandem/.

[25] P. R. Turgeon, P. Mak, M. A. Blake, C. B. Ford III, P. J. Meaney, R. Seigler, and W. W. Shen, "The S/390 G5/G6 Binodal Cache," *IBM Journal of Research and Development*, Vol. 43, pp. 661–670, September/November 1999.

Defect Tolerance in VLSI Circuits

With the continuing increase in the total number of devices in VLSI circuits (e.g., microprocessors) and in the density of these devices (due to the reduction in their size) has come an increasing need for defect tolerance. Some of the millions of submicron devices that are included in a VLSI chip are bound to have imperfections resulting in yield-reducing manufacturing defects, where yield is defined as the percentage of operational chips out of the total number fabricated.

Consequently, increasing attention is being paid to the development and use of defect-tolerance techniques for yield enhancement, to complement existing efforts at the manufacturing stage. Design-stage yield enhancement techniques are aimed at making the integrated circuit *defect tolerant*, or less sensitive to manufacturing defects, and include incorporating redundancy into the design, modifying the circuit floorplan, and modifying its layout. We concentrate in this chapter on the first two, which are directly related to the focus of this book.

Adding redundant components to the circuit can help in tolerating manufacturing defects and thus increase the yield. However, too much redundancy may reduce the yield since a larger-area circuit is expected to have a larger number of defects. Moreover, the increased area of the individual chip will result in a reduction in the number of chips that can fit in a fixed-area wafer. Successful designs of defect-tolerant chips must therefore rely on accurate yield projections to determine the optimal amount of redundancy to be added. We discuss several statistical yield prediction models and their application to defect-tolerant designs. Then, various yield enhancement techniques are described and their use illustrated.

8.1   Manufacturing Defects and Circuit Faults

Manufacturing defects can be roughly classified into global defects (or gross area defects) and spot defects. Global defects are relatively large-scale defects, such as scratches from wafer mishandling, large-area defects from mask misalignment, and over- and under-etching. Spot defects are random local and small defects from materials used in the process and from environmental causes, mostly the result of undesired chemical and airborne particles deposited on the chip during the various steps of the process.

Both defect types contribute to yield loss. In mature, well-controlled fabrication lines, gross-area defects can be minimized and almost eliminated. Controlling random spot defects is considerably more difficult, and the yield loss due to spot defects is typically much greater than the yield loss due to global defects. This is especially true for large-area integrated circuits, since the frequency of global defects is almost independent of the die size, whereas the expected number of spot defects increases with the chip area. Consequently, spot defects are of greater significance when yield projection and enhancement are concerned and are therefore the focus of this chapter.

Spot defects can be divided into several types according to their location and to the potential harm they may cause. Some cause missing patterns which may result in open circuits, whereas others cause extra patterns that may result in short circuits. These defects can be further classified into intralayer and interlayer defects. Intralayer defects occur as a result of particles deposited during the lithographic processes and are also known as photolithographic defects. Examples of these are missing metal, diffusion or polysilicon, and extra metal, diffusion or polysilicon. Also included are defects in the silicon substrate, such as contamination in the deposition processes. Interlayer defects include missing material in the vias between two metal layers or between a metal layer and polysilicon, and extra material between the substrate and metal (or diffusion or polysilicon) or between two separate metal layers. These interlayer defects occur as a result of local contamination, because of, for example, dust particles.

Not all spot defects result in structural faults such as line breaks or short circuits. Whether or not a defect will cause a fault depends on its location, size, and the layout and density of the circuit (see Figure 8.1). For a defect to cause a fault, it has to be large enough to connect two disjoint conductors or to disconnect a continuous pattern. Out of the three circular missing-material defects appearing in the layout of metal conductors in Figure 8.1, the two top ones will not disconnect any conductor, whereas the bottom defect will result in an open-circuit fault.

We make, therefore, the distinction between physical *defects* and circuit *faults*. A defect is any imperfection on the wafer, but only those defects that actually affect the circuit operation are called faults: these are the only ones causing yield losses. Thus, for the purpose of yield estimation, the distribution of faults, rather than that of defects, is of interest.

Some random defects that do not cause structural faults (also termed functional faults) may still result in parametric faults; that is, the electrical parameters of some devices may be outside their desired range, affecting the performance of the circuit. For example, although a missing-material photolithographic defect may be too small to disconnect a transistor, it may still affect its performance. Parametric

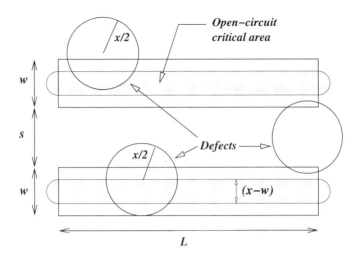

FIGURE 8.1 The critical area for missing-metal defects of diameter x. I. Koren and Z. Koren, "Defect Tolerant VLSI Circuits: Techniques and Yield Analysis," Proceedings of the IEEE © 1998 IEEE.

faults may also be the result of global defects that cause variations in process parameters. This chapter does not deal with parametric faults and concentrates instead on functional faults, against which fault-tolerance techniques can be used.

8.2 Probability of Failure and Critical Area

We next describe how the fraction of manufacturing defects that result in functional faults can be calculated. This fraction, also called the *probability of failure* (POF), depends on a number of factors: the type of the defect, its size (the greater the defect size, the greater the probability that it will cause a fault), its location, and circuit geometry. A commonly adopted simplifying assumption is that a defect is circular with a random diameter x (as shown in Figure 8.1). Accordingly, we denote by $\theta_i(x)$ the probability that a defect of type i and diameter x will cause a fault, and by θ_i the average POF for type i defects. Once $\theta_i(x)$ is calculated, θ_i can be obtained by averaging over all defect diameters x. Experimental data lead to the conclusion that the diameter x of a defect has a probability density function, $f_d(x)$, given by

$$f_d(x) = \begin{cases} kx^{-p} & \text{if } x_0 \leqslant x \leqslant x_M \\ 0 & \text{otherwise} \end{cases} \tag{8.1}$$

where $k = (p-1)x_0^{p-1}x_M^{p-1}/(x_M^{p-1} - x_0^{p-1})$ is a normalizing constant, x_0 is the resolution limit of the lithography process, and x_M is the maximum defect size. The values of p and x_M can be determined empirically and may depend on the defect type. Typically, p ranges in value between 2 and 3.5. θ_i can now be calculated as

$$\theta_i = \int_{x_0}^{x_M} \theta_i(x) f_d(x)\, dx \tag{8.2}$$

Analogously, we define the *critical area*, $A_i^{(c)}(x)$, for defects of type i and diameter x as the area in which the center of a defect of type i and diameter x must fall in order to cause a circuit failure, and by $A_i^{(c)}$ the average over all defect diameters x of these areas. $A_i^{(c)}$ is called the critical area for defects of type i, and can be calculated as

$$A_i^{(c)} = \int_{x_0}^{x_M} A_i^{(c)}(x) f_d(x)\, dx \tag{8.3}$$

Assuming that given a defect, its center is uniformly distributed over the chip area, and denoting the chip area by A_{chip}, we obtain

$$\theta_i(x) = \frac{A_i^{(c)}(x)}{A_{\text{chip}}} \tag{8.4}$$

and consequently, from Equations 8.2 and 8.3,

$$\theta_i = \frac{A_i^{(c)}}{A_{\text{chip}}} \tag{8.5}$$

Since the POF and the critical area are related through Equation 8.5, any one of them can be calculated first. There are several methods of calculating these parameters. Some methods are geometry based, and they calculate $A_i^{(c)}(x)$ first, others are Monte Carlo-type methods, where $\theta_i(x)$ is calculated first.

We illustrate the geometrical method for calculating critical areas through the VLSI layout in Figure 8.1, which shows two horizontal conductors. The critical area for a missing-material defect of size x in a conductor of length L and width w is the size of the shaded area in Figure 8.1, given by

$$A_{\text{miss}}^{(c)}(x) = \begin{cases} 0 & \text{if } x < w \\ (x - w)L + \frac{1}{2}(x - w)\sqrt{x^2 - w^2} & \text{if } x \geqslant w \end{cases} \tag{8.6}$$

The critical area is a quadratic function of the defect diameter, but for $L \gg w$, the quadratic term becomes negligible. Thus, for long conductors we can use just the linear term. An analogous expression for $A_{\text{extra}}^{(c)}(x)$ for extra-material defects in a rectangular area of width s between two adjacent conductors can be obtained by replacing w by s in Equation 8.6.

Other regular shapes can be similarly analyzed, and expressions for their critical area can be derived. Common VLSI layouts consist of many shapes in different sizes and orientations, and it is very difficult to derive the exact expression for the critical area of all but very simple and regular layouts. Therefore, other techniques have been developed, including several more efficient geometrical methods and Monte Carlo simulation methods. One geometrical method is the polygon expansion technique, in which adjacent polygons are expanded by $x/2$ and the intersection of the expanded polygons is the critical area for short-circuit faults of diameter x.

In the Monte Carlo approach, simulated circles representing defects of different sizes are "placed" at random locations of the layout. For each such "defect," the circuit of the "defective" IC is extracted and compared with the defect-free circuit to determine whether the defect has resulted in a circuit fault. The POF, $\theta_i(x)$, is calculated for defects of type i and diameter x, as the fraction of such defects that would have resulted in a fault. It is then averaged using Equation 8.2 to produce θ_i, and $A_i^{(c)} = \theta_i A_{\text{chip}}$. An added benefit of the Monte Carlo method is that the circuit fault resulting from a given defect is precisely identified. However, the Monte Carlo approach has traditionally been very time consuming. Only recently have more efficient implementations been developed, allowing this method to be used for large ICs.

Once $A_i^{(c)}$ (or θ_i) has been calculated for every defect type i, it can be used as follows. Let d_i denote the average number of defects of type i per unit area; then the average number of manufacturing *defects* of type i on the chip is $A_{\text{chip}}d_i$. The average number on the chip of circuit *faults* of type i can now be expressed as $\theta_i A_{\text{chip}}d_i = A_i^{(c)}d_i$.

In the rest of this chapter, we will assume that the defect densities are given and the critical areas are calculated. Thus, the average number of faults on the chip, denoted by λ, can be obtained using

$$\lambda = \sum_i A_i^{(c)}d_i = \sum_i \theta_i A_{\text{chip}}d_i \tag{8.7}$$

where the sum is taken over all possible defect types on the chip.

8.3 Basic Yield Models

To project the yield of a given chip design, we can construct an analytical probability model that describes the expected spatial distribution of manufacturing defects and, consequently, of the resulting circuit faults that eventually cause yield loss. The amount of detail needed regarding this distribution differs between chips that have some incorporated defect tolerance and those which do not. In case of a chip with no defect tolerance, its projected yield is equal to the probability of no faults occurring anywhere on the chip. Denoting by X the number of faults on the chip, the chip yield, denoted by Y_{chip}, is given by

$$Y_{\text{chip}} = \text{Prob}\{X = 0\} \tag{8.8}$$

If the chip has some redundant components, projecting its yield requires a more intricate model that provides information regarding the distribution of faults over partial areas of the chip, as well as possible correlations among faults occurring in different subareas. In this section we describe statistical yield models for chips without redundancy; in Section 8.4, we generalize these models for predicting the effects of redundancy on the yield.

8.3.1 The Poisson and Compound Poisson Yield Models

The most common statistical yield models appearing in the literature are the Poisson model and its derivative, the Compound Poisson model. Although other models have been suggested, we will concentrate here on this family of distributions, due to the ease of calculation when using them and the documented good fit of these distributions to empirical yield data.

Let λ denote the average number of faults occurring on the chip; in other words, the expected value of the random variable X. Assuming that the chip area is divided into a very large number, n, of small statistically independent subareas, each with a probability λ/n of having a fault in it, we get the following Binomial probability for the number of faults on the chip:

$$\text{Prob}\{X = k\} = \text{Prob}\{k \text{ faults occur on chip}\}$$

$$= \binom{n}{k}\left(\frac{\lambda}{n}\right)^k\left(1 - \frac{\lambda}{n}\right)^{n-k} \tag{8.9}$$

Letting $n \to \infty$ in Equation 8.9 results in the Poisson distribution

$$\text{Prob}\{X = k\} = \text{Prob}\{k \text{ faults occur on chip}\} = \frac{e^{-\lambda}\lambda^k}{k!} \tag{8.10}$$

and the chip yield is equal to

$$Y_{\text{chip}} = \text{Prob}\{X = 0\} = e^{-\lambda} \tag{8.11}$$

Note that we use here the *spatial* (area dependent) Poisson distribution rather than the Poisson process in time discussed in Chapter 2.

It has been known since the beginning of integrated circuit manufacturing that Equation 8.11 is too pessimistic and leads to predicted chip yields that are too low when extrapolated from the yield of smaller chips or single circuits. It later became clear that the lower-predicted yield was caused by the fact that defects, and consequently faults, do not occur independently in the different regions of the chip but rather tend to cluster more than is predicted by the Poisson distribution. Figure 8.2 demonstrates how increased clustering of faults can increase the yield.

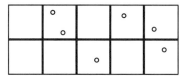 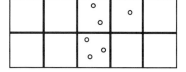

(a) Non-clustered faults, $Y_{\text{chip}} = 0.5$ (b) Clustered faults, $Y_{\text{chip}} = 0.7$

FIGURE 8.2   Effect of clustering on chip yield. I. Koren and Z. Koren, "Defect Tolerant VLSI Circuits: Techniques and Yield Analysis," Proceedings of the IEEE © 1998 IEEE.

The same number of faults occur in both wafers, but the wafer on the right has a higher yield due to the tighter clustering.

Clustering of faults implies that the assumption that subareas on the chip are statistically independent, which led to Equation 8.9 and consequently to Equations 8.10 and 8.11, is an oversimplification. Several modifications to Equation 8.10 have been proposed to account for fault clustering. The most commonly used modification is obtained by considering the parameter λ in Equation 8.10 as a random variable rather than a constant. The resulting *Compound Poisson distribution* produces a distribution of faults in which the different subareas on the chip are correlated and which has a more pronounced clustering than that generated by the pure Poisson distribution.

Let us now demonstrate this compounding procedure. Let λ be the expected value of a random variable L with values ℓ and a density function $f_L(\ell)$, where $f_L(\ell)d\ell$ denotes the probability that the chip fault average lies between ℓ and $\ell + d\ell$. Averaging (or compounding) Equation 8.10 with respect to this density function results in

$$\text{Prob}\{X = k\} = \int_0^\infty \frac{e^{-\ell}\ell^k}{k!} f_L(\ell)\, d\ell \tag{8.12}$$

and the chip yield is

$$Y_{\text{chip}} = \text{Prob}\{X = 0\} = \int_0^\infty e^{-\ell} f_L(\ell)\, d\ell \tag{8.13}$$

The function $f_L(\ell)$ in this expression is known as the *compounder* or *mixing function*. Any compounder must satisfy the conditions

$$\int_0^\infty f_L(\ell)\, d\ell = 1, \qquad E(L) = \int_0^\infty \ell f_L(\ell)\, d\ell = \lambda$$

The most commonly used mixing function is the Gamma density function with the two parameters α and $\frac{\alpha}{\lambda}$

$$f_L(\ell) = \frac{\alpha^\alpha}{\lambda^\alpha \Gamma(\alpha)} \ell^{\alpha-1} e^{-\frac{\alpha}{\lambda}\ell} \tag{8.14}$$

where $\Gamma(y) = \int_0^\infty e^{-u} u^{y-1} \, du$ (see Section 2.2). Evaluating the integral in Equation 8.12 with respect to Equation 8.14 results in the widely used *Negative Binomial* yield formula

$$\text{Prob}\{X = k\} = \frac{\Gamma(\alpha + k)}{k! \Gamma(\alpha)} \frac{\left(\frac{\lambda}{\alpha}\right)^k}{\left(1 + \frac{\lambda}{\alpha}\right)^{\alpha + k}} \tag{8.15}$$

and

$$Y_{\text{chip}} = \text{Prob}\{X = 0\} = \left(1 + \frac{\lambda}{\alpha}\right)^{-\alpha} \tag{8.16}$$

This last model is also called *the large-area clustering* Negative Binomial model. It implies that the whole chip constitutes one unit and that subareas within the same chip are correlated with regard to faults. The Negative Binomial yield model has two parameters and is therefore flexible and easy to fit to actual data. The parameter λ is the average number of faults per chip, whereas the parameter α is a measure of the amount of fault clustering. Smaller values of α indicate increased clustering. Actual values for α typically range between 0.3 and 5. When $\alpha \to \infty$, Expression 8.16 becomes equal to Equation 8.11, which represents the yield under the Poisson distribution, characterized by a total absence of clustering. (Note that the Poisson distribution does not *guarantee* that the defects will be randomly spread out: all it says is that there is no inherent clustering. Clusters of defects can still form by chance in individual instances.)

8.3.2 Variations on the Simple Yield Models

The large-area clustering compound Poisson model described above makes two crucial assumptions: the fault clusters are large compared with the size of the chip, and they are of uniform size. In some cases, it is clear from observing the defect maps of manufactured wafers that the faults can be divided into two classes—heavily clustered and less heavily clustered (see Figure 8.3)—and clearly originate from two sources: systematic and random. In these cases, a simple yield model as described above will not be able to successfully describe the fault distribution. This inadequacy will be more noticeable when attempting to evaluate the yield of chips with redundancy. One way to deal with this is to include in the model a gross yield factor Y_0 that denotes the probability that the chip is *not* hit by a gross defect. Gross defects are usually the result of systematic processing problems that affect whole wafers or parts of wafers. They may be caused by misalignment, over- or under-etching or out-of-spec semiconductor parameters such as threshold voltage. It has been shown that even fault clusters with very high fault densities can be modeled by Y_0. If the Negative Binomial yield model is used, then introducing a gross yield factor Y_0 results in

$$Y_{\text{chip}} = Y_0 \left(1 + \frac{\lambda}{\alpha}\right)^{-\alpha} \tag{8.17}$$

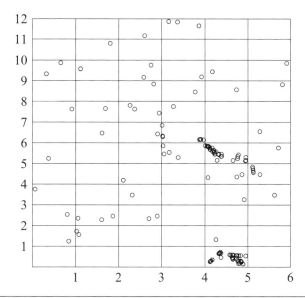

FIGURE 8.3 A wafer defect map. I. Koren and Z. Koren, "Defect Tolerant VLSI Circuits: Techniques and Yield Analysis," Proceedings of the IEEE © 1998 IEEE.

As chips become larger, this approach becomes less practical since very few faults will hit the entire chip. Instead, two fault distributions, each with a different set of parameters, may be combined. X, the total number of faults on the chip, can be viewed as $X = X_1 + X_2$, where X_1 and X_2 are statistically independent random variables, denoting the number of faults of type 1 and of type 2, respectively, on the chip. The probability function of X can be derived from

$$\text{Prob}\{X = k\} = \sum_{j=0}^{k} \text{Prob}\{X_1 = j\} \cdot \text{Prob}\{X_2 = k - j\} \tag{8.18}$$

and

$$Y_{\text{chip}} = \text{Prob}\{X = 0\} = \text{Prob}\{X_1 = 0\} \cdot \text{Prob}\{X_2 = 0\} \tag{8.19}$$

If X_1 and X_2 are modeled by a Negative Binomial distribution with parameters λ_1, α_1, and λ_2, α_2, respectively, then

$$Y_{\text{chip}} = \left(1 + \frac{\lambda_1}{\alpha_1}\right)^{-\alpha_1} \left(1 + \frac{\lambda_2}{\alpha_2}\right)^{-\alpha_2} \tag{8.20}$$

Another variation on the simple fault distributions may occur in very large chips, in which the fault clusters appear to be of uniform size but are much smaller than the chip area. In this case, instead of viewing the chip as one entity for statistical purposes, it can be viewed as consisting of statistically independent regions called *blocks*. The number of faults in each block has a Negative Binomial distribution, and the faults within the area of the block are uniformly distributed. The large-area Negative Binomial distribution is a special case in which the whole chip constitutes one block. Another special case is the small-area Negative Binomial distribution, which describes very small independent fault clusters. Mathematically, the medium-area Negative Binomial distribution can be obtained, similarly to the large-area case, as a Compound Poisson distribution, where the integration in Equation 8.12 is performed independently over the different regions of the chip. Let the chip consist of B blocks with an average of ℓ faults. Each block will have an average of ℓ/B faults, and according to the Poisson distribution, the chip yield will be

$$Y_{\text{chip}} = e^{-\ell} = \left(e^{-\ell/B}\right)^{B} \tag{8.21}$$

where $e^{-\ell/B}$ is the yield of one block.

When each factor in Equation 8.21 is compounded separately with respect to Equation 8.14, the result is

$$Y_{\text{chip}} = \left[\left(1 + \frac{\lambda/B}{\alpha}\right)^{-\alpha}\right]^{B} = \left(1 + \frac{\lambda}{B\alpha}\right)^{-B\alpha} \tag{8.22}$$

It is also possible that each region on the chip has a different sensitivity to defects, and thus, block i has the parameters λ_i, α_i, resulting in

$$Y_{\text{chip}} = \prod_{i=1}^{B}\left(1 + \frac{\lambda_i}{\alpha_i}\right)^{-\alpha_i} \tag{8.23}$$

It is important to note that the differences among the various models described in this section become more noticeable when they are used to project the yield of chips with built-in redundancy.

To estimate the parameters of a yield model, the "window method" is regularly used in the industry. Wafer maps that show the location of functioning and failing chips are analyzed using overlays with grids or windows. These windows contain some adjacent chip multiples (e.g., 1, 2, and 4), and the yield for each such multiple is calculated. Values for the parameters Y_0, λ, and α are then determined by means of curve fitting.

8.4   Yield Enhancement Through Redundancy

In this section we describe several techniques to incorporate redundancy in the design of VLSI circuits to increase the yield. We start by analyzing the yield enhancement due to redundancy, and then present schemes to introduce redundancy into memory and logic designs.

8.4.1 Yield Projection for Chips with Redundancy

In many integrated circuit chips, identical blocks of circuits are often replicated. In memory chips, these are blocks of memory cells, which are also known as *sub-arrays*. In digital chips they are referred to as *macros*. We will use the term *modules* to include both these designations.

In very large chips, if the whole chip is required to be fault-free, the yield will be very low. The yield can be increased by adding a few spare modules to the design and accepting those chips that have the required number of fault-free modules. However, adding redundant modules increases the chip area and reduces the number of chips that will fit into the wafer area. Consequently, a better measure for evaluating the benefit of redundancy is the *effective yield*, defined as

$$Y_{\text{chip}}^{\text{eff}} = Y_{\text{chip}} \frac{\text{Area of chip without redundancy}}{\text{Area of chip with redundancy}} \tag{8.24}$$

The maximum value of $Y_{\text{chip}}^{\text{eff}}$ determines the optimal amount of redundancy to be incorporated into the chip.

The yield of a chip with redundancy is the probability that it has enough fault-free modules for proper operation. To calculate this probability, a much more detailed statistical model than described earlier is needed, a model that specifies the fault distribution for any subarea of the chip, as well as the correlations among the different subareas of the chip.

Chips with One Type of Modules

For simplicity, let us first deal with projecting the yield of chips whose only circuitry is N identical modules, out of which R are spares and at least $M = N - R$ must be fault-free for proper operation. Define the following probability

$$F_{i,N} = \text{Prob}\{\text{Exactly } i \text{ out of the } N \text{ modules are fault-free}\}.$$

Then the yield of the chip is given by

$$Y_{\text{chip}} = \sum_{i=M}^{N} F_{i,N} \tag{8.25}$$

Using the spatial Poisson distribution implies that the average number of faults per module, denoted by λ_m, is $\lambda_m = \lambda/N$. In addition, when using the Poisson model, the faults in any distinct subareas are statistically independent, and thus,

$$F_{i,N} = \binom{N}{i} \left(e^{-\lambda_m} \right)^i \left(1 - e^{-\lambda_m} \right)^{N-i}$$

$$= \binom{N}{i} \left(e^{-\lambda/N} \right)^i \left(1 - e^{-\lambda/N} \right)^{N-i} \tag{8.26}$$

and the yield of the chip is

$$Y_{chip} = \sum_{i=M}^{N} \binom{N}{i} (e^{-\lambda/N})^i (1 - e^{-\lambda/N})^{N-i} \tag{8.27}$$

Unfortunately, although the Poisson distribution is mathematically convenient, it does not match actual defect and fault data. If any of the Compound Poisson distributions is to be used, then the different modules on the chip are not statistically independent but rather correlated with respect to the number of faults. A simple formula such as Equation 8.27, which uses the Binomial distribution, is therefore not appropriate. Several approaches can be followed to calculate the yield in this case, all leading to the same final expression.

The first approach applies only to the Compound Poisson models, and is based on compounding the expression in Equation 8.26 over λ_m (as shown in Section 8.3). Replacing λ/N by ℓ, expanding $(1 - e^{-\ell})^{N-i}$ into the binomial series $\sum_{k=0}^{N-i}(-1)^k \binom{N-i}{k}(e^{-\ell})^k$ and substituting into Equation 8.26 results in

$$F_{i,N} = \binom{N}{i} \sum_{k=0}^{N-i} (-1)^k \binom{N-i}{k} (e^{-\ell})^{i+k} \tag{8.28}$$

By compounding Equation 8.28 with a density function $f_L(\ell)$, we obtain

$$F_{i,N} = \binom{N}{i} \sum_{k=0}^{N-i} (-1)^k \binom{N-i}{k} \int_0^\infty e^{-(i+k)\ell} f_L(\ell)\, d\ell$$

Defining $y_n = \int_0^\infty e^{-n\ell} f_L(\ell)\, d\ell$ (y_n is the probability that a *given* subset of n modules is fault-free, according to the Compound Poisson model) results in

$$F_{i,N} = \binom{N}{i} \sum_{k=0}^{N-i} (-1)^k \binom{N-i}{k} y_{i+k} \tag{8.29}$$

and the yield of the chip is equal to

$$Y_{chip} = \sum_{i=M}^{N} \sum_{k=0}^{N-i} (-1)^k \binom{N}{i} \binom{N-i}{k} y_{i+k} \tag{8.30}$$

The Poisson model can be obtained as a special case by substituting

$$y_{i+k} = e^{-(i+k)\lambda/N},$$

whereas for the Negative Binomial model

$$y_{i+k} = \left(1 + \frac{(i+k)\lambda}{N\alpha}\right)^{-\alpha} \tag{8.31}$$

The yield of the chip under this model is

$$Y_{\text{chip}} = \sum_{i=M}^{N} \sum_{k=0}^{N-i} (-1)^k \binom{N}{i} \binom{N-i}{k} \left(1 + \frac{(i+k)\lambda}{N\alpha}\right)^{-\alpha} \tag{8.32}$$

The approach described above to calculating the chip yield applies only to the Compound Poisson models. A more general approach involves using the Inclusion and Exclusion formula in order to calculate the probability $F_{i,N}$ and results in:

$$F_{i,N} = \binom{N}{i} \sum_{k=0}^{N-i} (-1)^k \binom{N-i}{k} y_{i+k} \tag{8.33}$$

which is the same expression as in Equation 8.29 which leads to Equation 8.30.

Since Equation 8.30 can be obtained from the basic Inclusion and Exclusion formula, it is quite general and applies to a larger family of distributions than the Compound Poisson models. The only requirement for it to be applicable is that for a given n, any subset of n modules have the same probability of being fault-free, and no statistical independence among the modules is required.

As shown above, the yield for any Compound Poisson distribution (including the pure Poisson) can be obtained from Equation 8.30 by substituting the appropriate expression for y_n. If a gross yield factor Y_0 exists, it can be included in y_n. For the model in which the defects arise from two sources and the number of faults per chip, X, can be viewed as $X = X_1 + X_2$,

$$y_n = y_n^{(1)} y_n^{(2)}$$

where $y_n^{(j)}$ denotes the probability that a given subset of n modules has no type j faults ($j = 1, 2$). The calculation of y_n for the medium-size clustering Negative Binomial probability is slightly more complicated and a pointer to it is included in the Further Reading section.

More Complex Designs

The simple architecture analyzed in the preceding section is an idealization, because actual chips rarely consist entirely of identical circuit modules. The more general case is that of a chip with multiple types of modules, each with its own redundancy. In addition, all chips include support circuits which are shared by the replicated modules. The support circuitry almost never has any redundancy and, if damaged, renders the chip unusable. In what follows, expressions for the yield of chips with two different types of modules, as well as some support circuits, are presented. The extension to a larger number of module types is straightforward but cumbersome and is therefore not included.

Denote by N_j the number of type j modules, out of which K_j are spares. Each type j module occupies an area of size a_j on the chip ($j = 1, 2$). The area of the support circuitry is a_{ck} (ck stands for chip-kill, since any fault in the support circuitry is fatal for the chip). Clearly, $N_1 a_1 + N_2 a_2 + a_{ck} = A_{chip}$.

Since each circuit type has a different sensitivity to defects, it has a different fault density. Let λ_{m_1}, λ_{m_2}, and λ_{ck} denote the average number of faults per type 1 module, type 2 module, and the support circuitry, respectively. Denoting by F_{i_1, N_1, i_2, N_2} the probability that exactly i_1 type 1 modules, exactly i_2 type 2 modules, and all the support circuits are fault-free, the chip yield is given by

$$Y_{chip} = \sum_{i_1 = M_1}^{N_1} \sum_{i_2 = M_2}^{N_2} F_{i_1, N_1, i_2, N_2} \tag{8.34}$$

where $M_j = N_j - R_j$ ($j = 1, 2$). According to the Poisson distribution,

$$F_{i_1, N_1, i_2, N_2} = \binom{N_1}{i_1} \left(e^{-\lambda_{m_1}} \right)^{i_1} \left(1 - e^{-\lambda_{m_1}} \right)^{N_1 - i_1}$$

$$\times \binom{N_2}{i_2} \left(e^{-\lambda_{m_2}} \right)^{i_2} \left(1 - e^{-\lambda_{m_2}} \right)^{N_2 - i_2} e^{-\lambda_{ck}} \tag{8.35}$$

To get the expression for F_{i_1, N_1, i_2, N_2} under a general fault distribution, we need to use the two-dimensional Inclusion and Exclusion formula reulting in

$$F_{i_1, N_1, i_2, N_2} = \sum_{k_1 = 0}^{N_1 - i_1} \sum_{k_2 = 0}^{N_2 - i_2} (-1)^{k_1} (-1)^{k_2} \binom{N_1}{i_1} \binom{N_1 - i_1}{k_1} \binom{N_2}{i_2} \binom{N_2 - i_2}{k_2} y_{i_1 + k_1, i_2 + k_2} \tag{8.36}$$

where y_{n_1, n_2} is the probability that a given set of n_1 type 1 modules, a given set of n_2 type 2 modules, and the support circuitry are all fault-free. This probability can be calculated using any of the models described in Section 8.3 with λ replaced by $n_1 \lambda_{m_1} + n_2 \lambda_{m_2} + \lambda_{ck}$.

Two noted special cases are the Poisson distribution, for which

$$y_{n_1, n_2} = \left(e^{-\lambda_{m_1}} \right)^{n_1} \left(e^{-\lambda_{m_2}} \right)^{n_2} e^{-\lambda_{ck}} = e^{-(n_1 \lambda_{m_1} + n_2 \lambda_{m_2} + \lambda_{ck})} \tag{8.37}$$

and the large-area Negative Binomial distribution, for which

$$y_{n_1, n_2} = \left(1 + \frac{n_1 \lambda_{m_1} + n_2 \lambda_{m_2} + \lambda_{ck}}{\alpha} \right)^{-\alpha} \tag{8.38}$$

Some chips have a very complex redundancy scheme that does not conform to the simple M-of-N redundancy. For such chips, it is extremely difficult to develop closed-form yield expressions for any model with clustered faults. One possible solution is to use Monte Carlo simulation, in which faults are thrown at the wafer according to the underlying statistical model, and the percentage of operational chips is calculated. A much faster solution is to calculate the yield using the Poisson distribution, which is relatively easy (although complicated redundancy schemes may require some non-trivial combinatorial calculations). This yield is then compounded with respect to λ using an appropriate compounder. If the Poisson yield expression can be expanded into a power series in λ, analytical integration is possible. Otherwise, which is more likely, numerical integration has to be performed. This very powerful compounding procedure was employed to derive yield expressions for interconnection buses in VLSI chips, for partially good memory chips, and for hybrid redundancy designs of memory chips.

8.4.2 Memory Arrays with Redundancy

Defect-tolerance techniques have been successfully applied to many designs of memory arrays due to their high regularity, which greatly simplifies the task of incorporating redundancy into their design. A variety of defect-tolerance techniques have been exploited in memory designs, from the simple technique using spare rows and columns (also known as word lines and bit lines, respectively) through the use of error-correcting codes. These techniques have been successfully employed by many semiconductor manufacturers, resulting in significant yield improvements ranging from 30-fold increases in the yield of early prototypes to 1.5-fold or even 3-fold yield increases in mature processes.

The most common implementations of defect-tolerant memory arrays include redundant bit lines and word lines, as shown in Figure 8.4. The figure shows a memory array that was split into two subarrays (to avoid very long word and bit lines which may slow down the memory read and write operations) with spare rows and columns. A defective row, for example, or a row containing one or more defective memory cells can be disconnected by blowing a fusible link at the output of the corresponding decoder as shown in Figure 8.5. The disconnected row is then replaced by a spare row which has a programmable decoder with fusible links, allowing it to replace any defective row (see Figure 8.5).

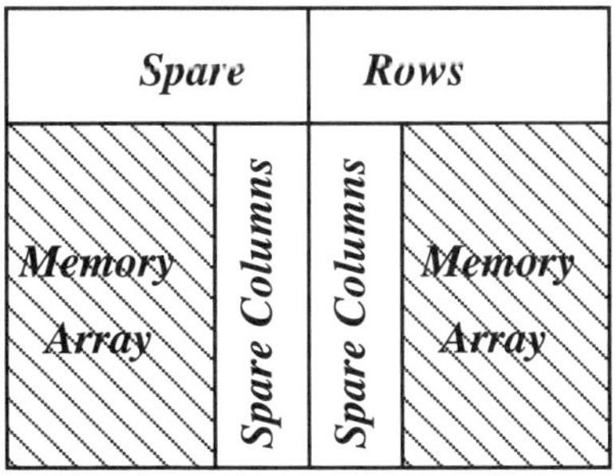

FIGURE 8.4   A memory array with spare rows and columns.

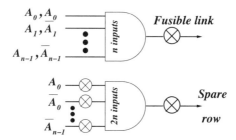

FIGURE 8.5   Standard and programmable decoders.

The first designs that included spare rows and columns relied on laser fuses that impose a relatively large area overhead and require the use of special laser equipment to disconnect faulty lines and connect spare lines in their place. In recent years, laser fuses have been replaced by CMOS fuses, which can be programmed internally with no need for external laser equipment. Since any defect that may occur in the internal programming circuit will constitute a chip-kill defect, several memory designers have incorporated error-correcting codes into these programming circuits to increase their reliability.

To determine which rows and columns should be disconnected and replaced by spare rows and columns, respectively, we first need to identify all the faulty memory cells. The memory must be thoroughly tested, and for each faulty cell, a decision has to be made as to whether the entire row or column should be disconnected. In recent memory chip designs, the identification of faulty cells is done internally using Built-In Self-Testing (BIST), thus avoiding the need for external testing equipment. In more advanced designs, the reconfiguration of the memory array based on the results of the testing is also performed internally. Implementing self-testing of the memory is quite straightforward and involves scanning sequentially all memory locations and writing and reading 0s and 1s into all the bits. The next step of determining how to assign spare rows and columns to replace all defective rows and columns is considerably more complicated because individual defective cells can be taken care of by either replacing the cell's row or the cell's column. An arbitrary assignment of spare rows and columns may lead to a situation where the available spares are insufficient, while a different assignment may allow the complete repair of the memory array.

To illustrate the complexity of this assignment problem, consider the 6×6 memory array with two spare rows (SR_0 and SR_1) and two spare columns (SC_0 and SC_1), shown in Figure 8.6. The array has 7 of its 36 cells defective, and we need to decide which rows and columns to disconnect and replace by spares to obtain a fully operational 6×6 array. Suppose we use a simple *Row First* assignment algorithm that calls for using all the available spare rows first and then the spare columns. For the array in Figure 8.6, we will first replace rows R_0 and R_1 by the two spare rows and be left with four defective cells. Because only two spare columns

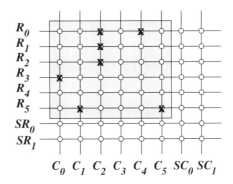

FIGURE 8.6 A 6 × 6 memory array with two spare rows, two spare columns, and seven defective cells (marked by x).

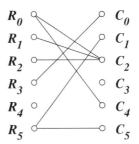

FIGURE 8.7 The bipartite graph corresponding to the memory array in Figure 8.6.

exist, the memory array is not repaired. As we will see below, a different assignment can repair the array using the available spare rows and columns.

To devise a better algorithm for determining which rows and columns should be switched out and replaced by spares, we can use the bipartite graph shown in Figure 8.7. This graph contains two sets of vertices corresponding to the rows (R_0 through R_5) and columns (C_0 through C_5) of the memory array and has an edge connecting R_i to C_j if the cell at the intersection of row R_i and column C_j is defective. Thus, to determine the smallest number of rows and columns that must be disconnected (and replaced by spares), we need to select the smallest number of vertices in Figure 8.7 required to cover all the edges (for each edge at least one of the two incident nodes must be selected). For the simple example in Figure 8.7, it is easy to see that we should select C_2 and R_5 to be replaced by a spare column and row, respectively, and then select one out of C_0 and R_3 and, similarly, one out of C_4 and R_0.

This problem is known as bipartite graph edge covering and has been shown to be NP-complete. Therefore, there is currently no algorithm of polynomial complexity to solve the spare rows and columns assignment problem. We could restrict our designs to have, for example, spare rows only, which would considerably reduce the complexity of this problem. If only spare rows are available, we must replace every row with one or more defective cells by a spare row if one exists. This, however, is not a practical solution for two reasons. First, if two (or more) defects happen in a single column, we will need to use two (or more) spare rows instead of a single spare column (see for example, column C_2 in Figure 8.6), which would significantly increase the required number of spare rows. Second, a reasonably common defect in memory arrays is a completely defective column (or row), which would be uncorrectable if no spare columns (or rows) are provided.

As a result, many heuristics for the assignment of spare rows and columns have been developed and implemented. These heuristics rely on the fact that it is not necessary to find the minimum number of rows and columns that should be replaced by spares, but only to find a feasible solution for repairing the array with the given number of spares.

A simple assignment algorithm consists of two steps. The first identifies which rows (and columns) must be selected for replacement. A *must-repair* row is a row that contains a number of defective cells that is greater than the number of currently available spare columns. *Must-repair* columns are defined similarly. For example, column C_2 in Figure 8.6 is a must-repair column because it contains three defective cells, whereas only two spare rows are available. Once such must-repair rows and columns are replaced by spares, the number of available spares is reduced and other rows and columns may become must-repair. For example, after identifying C_2 as a must-repair column and replacing it by, say SC_0, we are left with a single spare column, making row R_5 a must-repair row. This process is continued until no new must-repair rows and columns can be identified, yielding an array with sparse defects.

Although the first step of identifying must-repair rows and columns is reasonably simple, the second step is complicated. Fortunately, to achieve high performance, the size of memory arrays that have their own spare rows and columns is kept reasonably small (about 1 Mbit or less) and as a result, only a few defects remain to be taken care of in the second step of the algorithm. Consequently, even a very simple heuristic such as the above-mentioned *row-first* will work properly in most cases. In the example in Figure 8.6, after replacing the must-repair column C_2 and the must-repair row R_5, we will replace R_0 by the remaining spare row and then replace C_0 by the remaining spare column. A simple modification to the row-first algorithm that can improve its success rate is to first replace rows and columns with multiple defective cells and only then address the rows and columns which have a single defective cell.

Even the yield of memory chips that use redundant rows and columns cannot be expected to reach 100%, especially during the early phases of manufacturing when the defect density is still high. Consequently, several manufacturers package and sell partially good chips instead of discarding them. Partially good chips are chips that have some but not all of their cell arrays operational, even after using all the redundant lines.

The embedding of large memory arrays in VLSI chips is becoming very common with the most well-known example of large cache units in microprocessors. These large embedded memory arrays are designed with more aggressive design rules compared with the remaining logic units and, consequently, tend to be more prone to defects. As a result, most manufacturers of microprocessors include some form of redundancy in the cache designs, especially in the second level cache units, which normally have a larger size than the first level of caches. The incorporated redundancy can be in the form of spare rows, spare columns or spare subarrays.

Advanced Redundancy Techniques

The conventional redundancy technique (using spare rows and columns) can be enhanced, for example, by using an error-correcting code (ECC). Such an approach has been applied in the design of a 16-Mb DRAM chip. This chip includes four independent subarrays with 16 redundant bit lines and 24 redundant word lines per subarray. In addition, for every 128 data bits, nine check bits were added to allow the correction of any single-bit error within these 137 bits (this is a (137,9) SEC/DED Hamming code; see Section 3.1). To reduce the probability of two or more faulty bits in the same word (e.g., due to clustered faults), every eight adjacent bits in the subarray were assigned to eight separate words. It was found that the benefit of the combined strategy for yield enhancement was greater than the sum of the expected benefits of the two individual techniques. The reason is that the ECC technique is very effective against individual cell failures, whereas redundant rows and columns are very effective against several defective cells within the same row or column, as well as against completely defective rows and columns. As mentioned in Chapter 3, the ECC technique is commonly used in large memory systems to protect against intermittent faults occurring while the memory is in operation, in order to increase its reliability. The reliability improvement due to the use of ECC was shown to be only slightly affected by the use of the check bits to correct defective memory cells.

Increases in the size of memory chips in the last several years made it necessary to partition the memory array into several subarrays in order to decrease the current and reduce the access time by shortening the length of the bit and word lines. Using the conventional redundancy method implied that each subarray has its own spare rows and columns, leading to situations in which one subarray had an insufficient number of spare lines to handle local faults and other subarrays still had some unused spares. One obvious approach to resolve this problem is to turn some of the local redundant lines into global redundant lines, allowing for a more efficient use of the spares at the cost of higher silicon area overhead due to the larger number of required programmable fuses.

Several other approaches for more efficient redundancy schemes have been developed. One such approach was followed in the design of a 1-Gb DRAM. This design used fewer redundant lines than the traditional technique, and the redundant lines were kept local. For added defect-tolerance, each subarray of size 256 Mb (a quarter of the chip) was fabricated in such a way that it could become part of

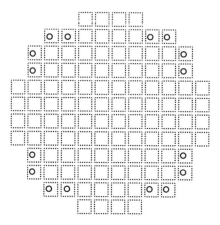

FIGURE 8.8   An 8″ wafer containing 112 256-MByte subarrays. (The 16 subarrays marked with a circle would not be fabricated in an ordinary design.)

up to four different memory ICs. The resulting wafer shown in Figure 8.8 includes 112 such subarrays out of which 16 (marked by a circle in the figure) would not be fabricated in an ordinary design in which the chip boundaries are fixed.

To allow this flexibility in determining the chip boundaries, the area of the subarray had to be increased by 2%, but in order to keep the overall area of the subarray identical to that in the conventional design, row redundancy was eliminated, thus compensating for this increase. Column redundancy was still implemented.

Yield analysis of the design in Figure 8.8 shows that if the faults are almost evenly distributed and the Poisson distribution can be used, there is almost no advantage in using the new design compared to the conventional design with fixed chip boundaries and use of the conventional row and column redundancy technique. There is, however, a considerable increase in yield if the medium-area Negative Binomial distribution (described in Section 8.3.2) applies. The extent of the improvement in yield is very sensitive to the fabrication parameter values.

Another approach for incorporating defect-tolerance into memory ICs combines row and column redundancy with several redundant subarrays that are to replace those subarrays hit by chip-kill faults. Such an approach was followed by the designers of another 1-Gbit memory which includes eight mats of size 128 Mbit each and eight redundant blocks of size 1 Mbit each (see Figure 8.9). The redundant block consists of four basic 256-Kbit arrays and has an additional eight spare rows and four spare columns (see Figure 8.10), the purpose of which is to increase the probability that the redundant block itself is operational and can be used for replacing a block with chip-kill faults.

Every mat consists of 512 basic arrays of size 256 Kbit each and has 32 spare rows and 32 spare columns. However, these are not global spares. Four spare rows are allocated to a 16-Mbit portion of the mat and eight spare columns are allocated to a 32-Mbit portion of the mat.

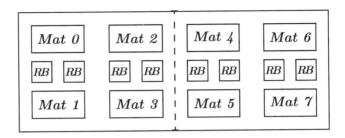

FIGURE 8.9 A 1-Gb chip with eight mats of size 128 Mbit each and eight redundant blocks (*RB*) of size 1 Mbit each. I. Koren and Z. Koren, "Defect Tolerant VLSI Circuits: Techniques and Yield Analysis," Proceedings of the IEEE © 1998 IEEE.

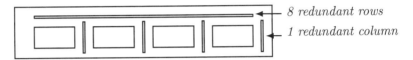

FIGURE 8.10 A redundant block including four 256-Kbit arrays, eight redundant rows, and four redundant columns. I. Koren and Z. Koren, "Defect Tolerant VLSI Circuits: Techniques and Yield Analysis," Proceedings of the IEEE © 1998 IEEE.

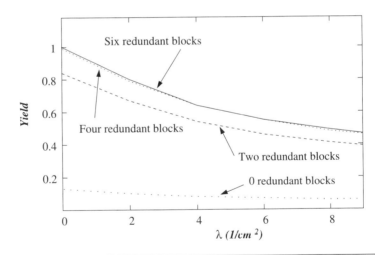

FIGURE 8.11 Yield as a function of λ for different numbers of redundant blocks per half chip (chip-kill probability $= 5 \times 10^{-4}$). I. Koren and Z. Koren, "Defect Tolerant VLSI Circuits: Techniques and Yield Analysis," Proceedings of the IEEE © 1998 IEEE.

The yield of this new design of a memory chip is compared to that of the traditional design with only row and column redundancy in Figure 8.11, demonstrating the benefits of some amount of block redundancy. The increase in yield is much greater than the 2% area increase required for the redundant blocks. It can also be shown that column redundancy is still beneficial even when redundant blocks are incorporated and that the optimal number of such redundant columns is independent of the number of spare blocks.

8.4.3 Logic Integrated Circuits with Redundancy

In contrast to memory arrays, very few logic ICs have been designed with any built-in redundancy. Some regularity in the design is necessary if a low overhead for redundancy inclusion is desired. For completely irregular designs, duplication and even triplication are currently the only available redundancy techniques, and these are often impractical due to their large overhead. Regular circuits such as Programmable Logic Arrays (PLAs) and arrays of identical computing elements require less redundancy, and various defect-tolerance techniques have been proposed (and some implemented) in order to enhance their yield. These techniques, however, require extra circuits such as spare product terms (for PLAs), reconfiguration switches, and additional input lines to allow the identification of faulty product terms. Unlike memory ICs in which all defective cells can be identified by applying external test patterns, the identification of defective elements in logic ICs (even for those with regular structure) is more complex and usually requires the addition of some built-in testing aids. Thus, testability must also be a factor in choosing defect-tolerant designs for logic ICs.

The situation becomes even more complex in random logic circuits such as microprocessors. When designing such circuits, it is necessary to partition the design into separate components, preferably with each having a regular structure. Then, different redundancy schemes can be applied to the different components, including the possibility of no defect-tolerance in components for which the cost of incorporating redundancy becomes prohibitive.

We describe next two examples of such designs: a defect-tolerant microprocessor and a wafer-scale design. These demonstrate the feasibility of incorporating defect tolerance for yield enhancement in the design of processors and prove that the use of defect tolerance is not limited to the highly regular memory arrays.

The Hyeti microprocessor is a 16-bit defect-tolerant microprocessor that was designed and fabricated to demonstrate the feasibility of a high-yield defect-tolerant microprocessor. This microprocessor may be used as the core of an application-specific microprocessor-based system that is integrated on a single chip. The large silicon area consumed by such a system would most certainly result in low yield, unless some defect tolerance in the form of redundancy were incorporated into the design.

The data path of the microprocessor contains several functional units such as registers, an arithmetic and logic unit (ALU), and bus circuitry. Almost all the units in the data path have circuits that are replicated 16 times, leading to the classic bit-slice organization. This regular organization was exploited for yield enhancement by providing a spare slice that can replace a defective slice. Not all the circuits in the data path, though, consist of completely identical subcircuits. The status reg-

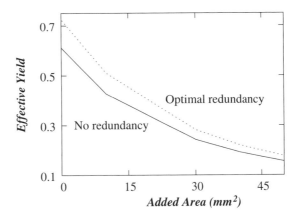

FIGURE 8.12   The effective yield as a function of the added area, without redundancy and with optimal redundancy, for the Negative Binomial distribution with $\lambda = 0.05/mm^2$ and $\alpha = 2$. I. Koren and Z. Koren, "Defect Tolerant VLSI Circuits: Techniques and Yield Analysis," Proceedings of the IEEE © 1998 IEEE.

ister, for example, has each bit associated with unique random logic and therefore has no added redundancy.

The control part has been designed as a hardwired control circuit that can be implemented using PLAs only. The regular structure of a PLA allows a straightforward incorporation of redundancy for yield enhancement through the addition of spare product terms. The design of the PLA has been modified to allow the identification of defective product terms.

Yield analysis of this microprocessor has shown that the optimal redundancy for the data path is a single 1-bit slice and the optimal redundancy for all the PLAs is one product term. A higher-than-optimal redundancy has, however, been implemented in many of these PLAs, because the floorplan of the control unit allows for the addition of a few extra product terms to the PLAs with no area penalty. A practical yield analysis should take into consideration the exact floorplan of the chip and allow the addition of a limited amount of redundancy beyond the optimal amount. Still, not all the available area should be used up for spares, since this will increase the switching area, which will, in turn, increase the chip-kill area. This greater chip-kill area can, at some point, offset the yield increase resulting from the added redundancy.

Figure 8.12 depicts the effective yield (see Equation 8.24) without redundancy in the microprocessor and with the optimal redundancy as a function of the area of the circuitry added to the microprocessor (which serves as a controller for that circuitry). The figure shows that an increase in yield of about 18% can be expected when the optimal amount of redundancy is incorporated in the design.

A second experiment with defect-tolerance in nonmemory designs is the 3-D Computer, an example of a wafer-scale design. The 3-D Computer is a cellular array processor implemented in wafer scale integration technology. The most unique feature of its implementation is its use of stacked wafers. The basic processing element is divided into five functional units, each of which is implemented on a different wafer. Thus, each wafer contains only one type of functional unit and includes spares for yield enhancement as explained below. Units in different wafers are connected vertically through microbridges between adjacent wafers to form a complete processing element. The first working prototype of the 3-D Computer was of size 32×32. The second prototype included 128×128 processing elements.

Defect tolerance in each wafer is achieved through an interstitial redundancy scheme (see Section 4.2.3) in which the spare units are uniformly distributed in the array and are connected to the primary units with local and short interconnects. In the 32×32 prototype, a $(1,1)$ redundancy scheme was used, and each primary unit had a separate spare unit. A $(2,4)$ scheme was used in the 128×128 prototype; each primary unit is connected to two spare units, and each spare unit is connected to four primary units, resulting in a redundancy of 50% rather than the 100% for the $(1,1)$ scheme. The $(2,4)$ interstitial redundancy scheme can be implemented in a variety of ways. The exact implementation in the 3-D Computer and its effect on the yield are further discussed in the next section.

Since it is highly unlikely that a fabricated wafer will be entirely fault-free, the yield of the processor would be zero if no redundancy were included. With the implemented redundancy, the observed yield of the 32×32 array after repair was 45%. For the 128×128 array, the $(1,1)$ redundancy scheme would have resulted in a very low yield (about 3%), due to the high probability of having faults in a primary unit and in its associated spare. The yield of the 128×128 array with the $(2,4)$ scheme was projected to be much higher.

8.4.4 Modifying the Floorplan

The floorplan of a chip is normally not expected to have an impact on its yield. This is true for chips that are small and have a fault distribution that can be accurately described by either the Poisson or the Compound Poisson yield models with large-area clustering (in which the size of the fault clusters is larger than the size of the chip).

The situation has changed with the introduction of integrated circuits with a total area of 2 cm^2 and up. Such chips usually consist of different component types, each with its own fault density, and have some incorporated redundancy. If chips with these attributes are hit by medium-sized fault clusters, then changes in the floorplan can affect their projected yield.

Consider the following example, depicted in Figure 8.13, of a chip consisting of four equal-area modules (functional units), M_1, M_2, M_3, and M_4. The chip has no incorporated redundancy, and all four modules are necessary for the proper operation of the chip.

Assuming that the defect clusters are medium-sized relative to the chip size and that the four modules have different sensitivities to defects, we use the medium-area Negative Binomial distribution (described in Section 8.3.2) for the spatial dis-

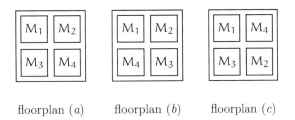

floorplan (a) floorplan (b) floorplan (c)

FIGURE 8.13 Three floorplans of a 2×2 array. I. Koren and Z. Koren, "Defect Tolerant VLSI Circuits: Techniques and Yield Analysis," Proceedings of the IEEE © 1998 IEEE.

tribution of faults, with parameters λ_i (for module M_i) and α (per block), and $\lambda_1 \leqslant \lambda_2 \leqslant \lambda_3 \leqslant \lambda_4$.

This chip has $4! = 24$ possible floorplans. Since rotation and reflection will not affect the yield, we are left with three distinct floorplans, shown in Figure 8.13. If small-area clustering (clusters smaller than or comparable to the size of a module) or large-area clustering (clusters larger than or equal to the chip area) is assumed, the projected yields of all possible floorplans will be the same. This is not the case, however, when medium-area clustering (with horizontal or vertical blocks of two modules) is assumed.

Assuming horizontal defect blocks of size two modules, the yields of floorplans (a), (b), and (c) are

$$Y(a) = Y(b) = \left(1 + (\lambda_1 + \lambda_2)/\alpha\right)^{-\alpha}\left(1 + (\lambda_3 + \lambda_4)/\alpha\right)^{-\alpha}$$

$$Y(c) = \left(1 + (\lambda_1 + \lambda_4)/\alpha\right)^{-\alpha}\left(1 + (\lambda_2 + \lambda_3)/\alpha\right)^{-\alpha} \qquad (8.39)$$

A simple calculation shows that under the condition $\lambda_1 \leqslant \lambda_2 \leqslant \lambda_3 \leqslant \lambda_4$, floorplans ($a$) and ($b$) have the higher yield. Similarly, for vertical defect blocks of size two modules,

$$Y(a) = Y(c) = \left(1 + (\lambda_1 + \lambda_3)/\alpha\right)^{-\alpha}\left(1 + (\lambda_2 + \lambda_4)/\alpha\right)^{-\alpha}$$

$$Y(b) = \left(1 + (\lambda_1 + \lambda_4)/\alpha\right)^{-\alpha}\left(1 + (\lambda_2 + \lambda_3)/\alpha\right)^{-\alpha} \qquad (8.40)$$

and floorplans (a) and (c) have the higher yield. Thus, floorplan (a) is the one which maximizes the chip yield for any cluster size. An intuitive explanation for the choice of (a) is that the less sensitive modules are placed together, increasing the chance that the chip will survive a cluster of defects.

If the previous chip is generalized to a 3×3 array (as depicted in Figure 8.14), and $\lambda_1 \leqslant \lambda_2 \leqslant \cdots \leqslant \lambda_9$, then, unfortunately, there is no one floorplan which is always the best and the optimal floorplan depends on the cluster size. However, the following generalizations can be made.

For all cluster sizes, the module with the highest fault density (M_9) should be placed in the center of the chip, and each row or column should be rearranged so that its most sensitive module is in its center (such as, for example, floorplan (b)

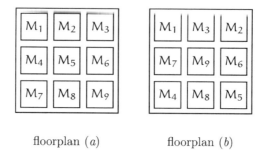

floorplan (a) floorplan (b)

FIGURE 8.14   Two floorplans of a 3×3 **array.** I. Koren and Z. Koren, "Defect Tolerant VLSI Circuits: Techniques and Yield Analysis," Proceedings of the IEEE © 1998 IEEE.

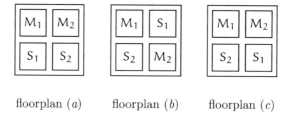

floorplan (a) floorplan (b) floorplan (c)

FIGURE 8.15   Three alternative floorplans for a chip with redundancy. I. Koren and Z. Koren, "Defect Tolerant VLSI Circuits: Techniques and Yield Analysis," Proceedings of the IEEE © 1998 IEEE.

in Figure 8.14). Note that we reached this conclusion without assuming that the boundaries of the chip are more prone to defects than its center. The intuitive explanation to this recommendation is that placing highly sensitive modules at the chip corners increases the probability that a single fault cluster will hit two or even four adjacent chips on the wafer. This is less likely to happen if the less sensitive modules are placed at the corners.

The next example is that of a chip with redundancy. The chip consists of four modules, M_1, S_1, M_2, and S_2, where S_1 is a spare for M_1 and S_2 is a spare for M_2. The three topologically distinct floorplans for this chip are shown in Figure 8.15. Let the number of faults have a medium-area Negative Binomial distribution with an average of λ_1 for M_1 and S_1, and λ_2 for M_2 and S_2, and a clustering parameter of α per block. Assuming that the defect clusters are horizontal and of size two modules each, the yields of the three floorplans are

$$
\begin{aligned}
Y(a) = Y(c) = {} & 2\left[1+(\lambda_1+\lambda_2)/\alpha\right]^{-\alpha} + 2\left[1+\lambda_1/\alpha\right]^{-\alpha}\left[1+\lambda_2/\alpha\right]^{-\alpha} \\
& - 2\left[1+(\lambda_1+\lambda_2)/\alpha\right]^{-\alpha}\left[1+\lambda_1/\alpha\right]^{-\alpha} \\
& - 2\left[1+(\lambda_1+\lambda_2)/\alpha\right]^{-\alpha}\left[1+\lambda_2/\alpha\right]^{-\alpha} + \left[1+(\lambda_1+\lambda_2)/\alpha\right]^{-2\alpha} \quad \textbf{(8.41)}
\end{aligned}
$$

$$
\begin{aligned}
Y(b) = {} & \left[2(1+\lambda_1/\alpha)^{-\alpha} - (1+2\lambda_1/\alpha)^{-\alpha}\right] \\
& \times \left[2(1+\lambda_2/\alpha)^{-\alpha} - (1+2\lambda_2/\alpha)^{-\alpha}\right] \quad \textbf{(8.42)}
\end{aligned}
$$

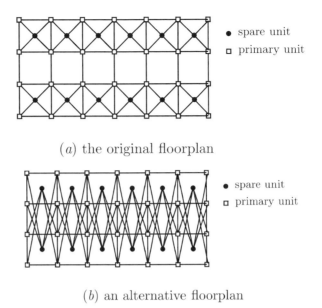

(*a*) the original floorplan

(*b*) an alternative floorplan

FIGURE 8.16   The original and alternative floorplans of a wafer in the 3-D Computer.
I. Koren and Z. Koren, "Defect Tolerant VLSI Circuits: Techniques and Yield Analysis," Proceedings of
the IEEE © 1998 IEEE.

It can be easily proved that for any values of λ_1 and λ_2, $Y(a) = Y(c) \geqslant Y(b)$.

If, however, the defect clusters are vertical and of size two modules, then clearly, $Y(a)$ is given by Equation 8.42 and $Y(b) = Y(c)$ and are given by Equation 8.41. In this case, $Y(b) = Y(c) \geqslant Y(a)$ for all values of λ_1 and λ_2. Floorplan (*c*) should therefore be preferred over floorplans (*a*) and (*b*). An intuitive justification for the choice of floorplan (*c*) is that it guarantees the separation between the primary modules and their spares for any size and shape of the defect clusters. This results in a higher yield, since it is less likely that the same cluster will hit both the module and its spare, thus killing the chip.

This last recommendation is exemplified by the design of the 3-D Computer, described in Subsection 8.4.3. The (2,4) structure that has been selected for implementation in the 3-D Computer is shown in Figure 8.16a.

This floorplan has every spare unit adjacent to the four primary units that it can replace. This layout has short interconnection links between the spare and any primary unit that it may replace, and as a result, the performance degradation upon a failure of a primary unit is minimal. However, the close proximity of the spare and primary units results in a low yield in the presence of clustered faults, since a single fault cluster may cover a primary unit and all of its spares.

Several alternative floorplans can be designed that place the spare farther apart from the primary units connected to it (as recommended above). One such floorplan is shown in Figure 8.16b. The projected yields of the 128×128 array using

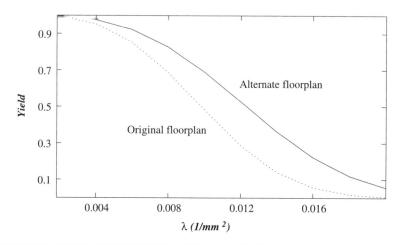

FIGURE 8.17   The yield of the original and alternate floorplans, depicted in Figure 8.16, as a function of λ **($\alpha = 2$).** I. Koren and Z. Koren, "Defect Tolerant VLSI Circuits: Techniques and Yield Analysis," Proceedings of the IEEE © 1998 IEEE.

the original floorplan (Figure 8.16a) or the alternative floorplan (Figure 8.16b) are shown in Figure 8.17. The yield has been calculated using the medium-area Negative Binomial distribution with a defect block size of two rows of primary units (see Figure 8.16a). Figure 8.17 clearly shows that the alternative floorplan, in which the spare unit is separated from the primary units that it can replace, has a higher projected yield.

8.5   Further Reading

Several books (e.g., [8–10]), an edited collection of articles [5], and journal survey papers (e.g., [18,23,32,34,35,50]) have been devoted to the topic of this chapter. More specifically, for a detailed description of how critical areas and POFs can be calculated; see Chapter 5 in [10] as well as [47,53]. Two geometrical methods different from those mentioned in this chapter are the virtual artwork technique [33] and the Voronoi diagram approach [39]. Parametric faults resulting from variations in process parameters are described in [7,45].

Triangular and exponential density functions have been proposed as compounders in [36] and [42], respectively. The more commonly used (as a mixing function) Gamma distribution has been suggested in [38] and [46]. The "window method" that is used to estimate the parameters of yield models is described in [23,38,40,42,48]. It has been extended in [26] to include estimation of the block size for the medium-area clustering yield model.

Designs of defect-tolerant memories are described in [12–14,51,55,56]. The use of ECC is presented in [12]; the flexible chip boundaries scheme appears in [51] and the memory design with redundant subarrays is described in [56]. Some of these designs have been analyzed in [15,17,49]. Many techniques for assigning spare rows and columns to defective rows and columns in memory arrays have been developed, see for example [1,2,29,43]. Defect-tolerance techniques for logic circuits have been proposed (and some implemented) in [3,21,22,25,30,31,37,54, 57]. The **Hyeti** microprocessor is described and analyzed in [31] and the 3-D Computer is presented in [57].

The designers of many modern microprocessors have incorporated redundancy into the design of the embedded cache units. To determine the type of redundancy to be employed in the cache units of the PowerPC microprocessors, row, column, and subarray redundancies were compared considering the area and performance penalties and the expected yield improvements [52]. Based on their analysis, the designers have decided to use row only redundancy for the level-1 cache unit and row and column redundancy for the level-2 cache unit.

Intel's Pentium Pro processor incorporates redundancy in its 512-KByte level-2 cache [11]. This cache unit consists of 72 subarrays of 64-K memory cells each, organized into four quadrants, and a single redundant subarray has been added to every quadrant. The reported increase in yield due to the added redundancy is 35%. This design includes a circuit for a BIST that identifies the faulty cells, and a flash memory circuit that is programmed to replace a defective subarray with a spare subarray.

The two 64-KBytes cache unit in Hewlett-Packard's PA7300LC microprocessor have been designed with redundant columns. Four spare columns are included in a spare block that can be used to replace a faulty four-column block using multiplexers that are controlled by programmable fuses. A BIST circuit is included to test the cache unit and identify the faulty block [28].

The spare rows and columns assignment algorithm used in the self-repair circuit for the embedded memory unit in an Alpha microprocessor is described in [1].

The effect of floorplanning on yield has been analyzed in [16,19].

8.6 Exercises

1. Derive an expression for the critical area $A_{miss}^{(c)}(u)$ for square $u \times u$ missing-material defects in a conductor of length L and width w. Assume that one side of the defect is always parallel to the conductor, and that $L \gg w$ so that the nonlinear edge effects can be ignored.

2. Use the polygon expansion technique to calculate approximately the critical area for circular short-circuit defects of diameter 3 for the 14×7 layout consist-

ing of two conductors shown below:

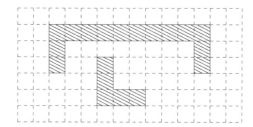

3. Find the average critical area $A^{(c)}_{\text{miss}}$ for circular missing-material defects in a single conductor of length L and width w using the defect size distribution in Equation 8.1 with $p = 3$. Assume that $L \gg w$ and ignore the nonlinear term in Equation 8.6.

4. **a.** Derive an expression for the critical area $A^{(c)}_{\text{miss}}(x)$ of a circular missing-material defect with diameter x in the case of two conductors of length L, width w and separation s (as shown in Figure 8.1). Ignore the nonlinear terms and note that the expression differs for the three cases: $x < w$; $w \leqslant x \leqslant 2w + s$; and $2w + s < x \leqslant x_M$.

   b. Find the average critical area $A^{(c)}_{\text{miss}}$ using the defect size distribution in Equation 8.1 with $p = 3$. For simplicity, assume $x_M = \infty$.

5. A chip with an area of 0.2 cm^2 (and no redundancy) is currently manufactured. This chip has a POF of $\theta = 0.6$ and an observed yield of $Y_1 = 0.87$. The manufacturer plans to fabricate a similar but larger chip, with an area of 0.3 cm^2, using the same wafer fabrication equipment. Assume that there is only one type of defects, and that the yield of both chips follows the Poisson model $Y = e^{-\theta A_{\text{chip}} d}$ with the same POF θ and the same defect density d.

   a. Calculate the defect density d and the projected yield Y_2 of the second chip.

   b. Let the area of the second chip be a variable A. Draw the graph of Y_2, the yield of the second chip, as a function of A (for A between 0 and 2).

6. A chip of area A_{chip} (without redundancy, and with one type of defects) is currently manufactured at a yield of $Y = 0.9$. The manufacturer is examining the possibility of designing and fabricating two larger chips with areas of $2A_{\text{chip}}$ and $4A_{\text{chip}}$. The designs and layouts of the new chips will be similar to those of the current chip (i.e., same θ), and the defect density d will remain the same.

   a. Calculate the expected yields of the two new chips assuming a Poisson model.

    b. Calculate the expected yields of the two new chips assuming a Negative Binomial model with $\alpha = 1.5$.

    c. Discuss the difference between the results of a and b.

7. For a chip without redundancy assume that X, the number of faults on the chip, follows a compound Poisson distribution.

    a. Use as a compounder the triangular density function

$$f_L(\ell) = \begin{cases} \frac{\ell}{\lambda^2} & 0 \leqslant \ell \leqslant \lambda \\ \frac{2\lambda - \ell}{\lambda^2} & \lambda \leqslant \ell \leqslant 2\lambda \end{cases}$$

and show that it results in the following expression for the chip yield:

$$Y_{\text{chip}} = \text{Prob}\{X = 0\} = \int_0^{2\lambda} e^{-\ell} f_L(\ell) \, d\ell = \left(\frac{1 - e^{-\lambda}}{\lambda}\right)^2 \qquad (8.43)$$

    b. Now use as a compounder the exponential density function

$$f_L(\ell) = \frac{e^{-\ell/\lambda}}{\lambda}$$

and show that it results in

$$Y_{\text{chip}} = \text{Prob}\{X = 0\} = \int_0^{\infty} e^{-\ell} f_L(\ell) \, d\ell = \frac{1}{1 + \lambda} \qquad (8.44)$$

    c. Compare the yield expressions in Equations 8.43 and 8.44 to those for the Poisson and Negative Binomial models (for chips without redundancy) by drawing the graph of the yield as a function of λ for $0.001 \leqslant \lambda \leqslant 1.5$. For the Negative Binomial model, use three values of α, namely, $\alpha = 0.25, 2$, and 5.

8. Why does the spare row in Figure 8.5 include a fusible link?

9. To a memory array with four rows and eight columns, a single spare row and two spare columns have been added. The testing of the memory array has identified four defective cells indicated by an x in the diagram below:

$$\begin{bmatrix} x & 0 & 0 & 0 & 0 & 0 & 0 & 0 \\ 0 & 0 & 0 & 0 & 0 & x & 0 & 0 \\ 0 & 0 & 0 & 0 & 0 & 0 & 0 & 0 \\ 0 & x & 0 & 0 & 0 & x & 0 & 0 \end{bmatrix}$$

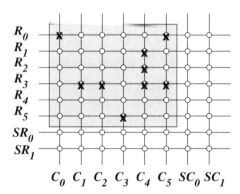

FIGURE 8.18   A 6×6 memory array with two spare rows, two spare columns, and nine defective cells (marked by an x).

a. List two ways to reconfigure the memory array, i.e., which rows and columns will be disconnected and replaced by spares.

b. Show a distribution of the four defective cells within the array for which the available spares will be insufficient. How many such distributions of four defective cells exist?

c. Given that there are four defective cells and that they are randomly distributed over the array, what is the probability of such an irreparable distribution?

10. A 6 × 6 memory array with two spare rows and two spare columns is shown in Figure 8.18. Show the corresponding bipartite graph, identify all the must-repair rows and columns, and select additional rows/columns to cover the remaining defective cells. Will the column-first (row-first) algorithm, if applied after replacing the must-repair rows (must-repair columns), be able to repair the memory array?

11. A chip consists of five modules, out of which four are needed for proper operation and one is a spare. Suppose the fabrication process has a fault density of 0.7 faults/cm², and the area of each module is 0.1 cm².

a. Calculate the expected yield of the chip using the Poisson model.

b. Calculate the expected yield of the chip using the Negative Binomial model with $\alpha = 1$.

c. For each of the two models in parts (a) and (b), is the addition of the spare module to the chip beneficial from the point of view of the effective yield?

d. Discuss the difference in the answer to (c) between the two models.

References

[1] D. K. Bhavsar, "An Algorithm for Row-Column Self-Repair of RAMs and Its Implementation in the Alpha 21264," *International Test Conference (ITC'99)*, pp. 311–318, 1999.

[2] D. Blough, "Performance Evaluation of a Reconfiguration Algorithm for Memory Arrays Containing Clustered Faults," *IEEE Transactions on Reliability*, Vol. 45, pp. 274–284, June 1996.

[3] A. Boubekeur, J.-L. Patry, G. Saucier, and J. Trilhe, "Configuring a Wafer Scale Two-Dimensional Array of Single-Bit Processors," *IEEE Computer*, Vol. 25, pp. 29–39, April 1992.

[4] V. K. R. Chiluvuri and I. Koren, "Layout Synthesis Techniques for Yield Enhancement," *IEEE Transactions on Semiconductor Manufacturing*, Vol. 8, Special Issue on Defect, Fault, and Yield Modeling, pp. 178–187, May 1995.

[5] B. Ciciani (Ed.), *Manufacturing Yield Evaluation of VLSI/WSI Systems*, IEEE Computer Society Press, 1998.

[6] J. A. Cunningham, "The Use and Evaluation of Yield Models in Integrated Circuit Manufacturing," *IEEE Transactions on Semiconductor Manufacturing*, Vol. 3, pp. 60–71, May 1990.

[7] S. W. Director, W. Maly, and A. J. Strojwas, *VLSI Design for Manufacturing: Yield Enhancement*, Kluwer Academic Publishers, 1990.

[8] A. V. Ferris-Prabhu, *Introduction to Semiconductor Device Yield Modeling*, Artech House, 1992.

[9] J. P. Gyvez, *Integrated Circuit Defect-Sensitivity: Theory and Computational Models*, Kluwer Academic Publishers, 1993.

[10] J. P. Gyvez (Ed.), *IC Manufacturability: The Art of Process and Design Integration*, IEEE Computer Society Press, 1998.

[11] C. W. Hampson, "Redundancy and High-Volume Manufacturing Methods," *Intel Technology Journal*, 4th Quarter, 1997. Available at: http://developer.intel.com/technology/itj/q41997/articles/art_4.htm.

[12] H. L. Kalter, C. H. Stapper, J. E. Barth, J. Dilorenzo, C. E. Drake, J. A. Fifield, G. A. Kelley, S. C. Lewis, W. B. Van Der Hoeven, and J. A. Yankosky, "A 50-ns 16 Mb DRAM with 10-ns Data Rate and On-Chip ECC," *IEEE Journal of Solid-State Circuits*, Vol. 25, pp. 1118–1128, October 1990.

[13] T. Kirihata, Y. Watanabe, H. Wong, and J. K. DeBrosse, "Fault-Tolerant Designs for 256 Mb DRAM," *IEEE Journal of Solid-State Circuits*, Vol. 31, pp. 558–566, April 1996.

[14] G. Kitsukawa, M. Horiguchi, Y. Kawajiri, and T. Kawahara, "256-Mb DRAM Circuit Technologies for File Applications," *IEEE Journal of Solid-State Circuits*, Vol. 28, pp. 1105–1110, November 1993.

[15] I. Koren and Z. Koren, "Yield Analysis of a Novel Scheme for Defect-Tolerant Memories," *IEEE International Conference on Innovative Systems in Silicon*, pp. 269–278, October 1996.

[16] Z. Koren and I. Koren, "On the Effect of Floorplanning on the Yield of Large Area Integrated Circuits," *IEEE Transactions on VLSI Systems*, Vol. 5, pp. 3–14, March 1997.

[17] I. Koren and Z. Koren, "Analysis of a Hybrid Defect-Tolerance Scheme for High-Density Memory ICs," *IEEE International Symposium on Defect and Fault Tolerance in VLSI Systems*, pp. 166–174, October 1997.

[18] I. Koren and Z. Koren, "Defect Tolerant VLSI Circuits: Techniques and Yield Analysis," *Proceedings of the IEEE*, Vol. 86, pp. 1817–1836, September 1998.

[19] I. Koren and Z. Koren, "Incorporating Yield Enhancement into the Floorplanning Process," *IEEE Transactions on Computers*, Special Issue on Defect Tolerance in Digital Systems, Vol. 49, pp. 532–541, June 2000.

[20] I. Koren, "The Effect of Scaling on the Yield of VLSI Circuits," *Yield Modelling and Defect Tolerance in VLSI*, in W. Moore, W. Maly, and A. Strojwas (Eds.), pp. 91–99, Adam Hilger, 1988.

[21] I. Koren and D. K. Pradhan, "Yield and Performance Enhancement through Redundancy in VLSI and WSI Multiprocessor Systems," *Proceedings of the IEEE*, Vol. 74, pp. 699–711, May 1986.

[22] I. Koren and D. K. Pradhan, "Modeling the Effect of Redundancy on Yield and Performance of VLSI Systems," *IEEE Transactions on Computers*, Vol. 36, pp. 344–355, March 1987.

[23] I. Koren and C. H. Stapper, "Yield Models for Defect Tolerant VLSI Circuits: A Review," *Defect and Fault Tolerance in VLSI Systems*, Vol. 1, I. Koren (Ed.), pp. 1–21, Plenum, 1989.

[24] I. Koren and A. D. Singh, "Fault Tolerance in VLSI Circuits," *IEEE Computer, Special Issue on Fault-Tolerant Systems*, Vol. 23, pp. 73–83, July 1990.

[25] I. Koren, Z. Koren, and D. K. Pradhan, "Designing Interconnection Buses in VLSI and WSI for Maximum Yield and Minimum Delay," *IEEE Journal of Solid-State Circuits*, Vol. 23, pp. 859–866, June 1988.

[26] I. Koren, Z. Koren, and C. H. Stapper, "A Unified Negative Binomial Distribution for Yield Analysis of Defect Tolerant Circuits," *IEEE Transactions on Computers*, Vol. 42, pp. 724–437, June 1993.

[27] I. Koren, Z. Koren, and C. H. Stapper, "A Statistical Study of Defect Maps of Large Area VLSI ICs," *IEEE Transactions on VLSI Systems*, Vol. 2, pp. 249–256, June 1994.

[28] D. Kubicek, T. Sullivan, A. Mehra, and J. McBride, "High-Performance Processor Design Guided by System Costs," *Hewlett-Packard Journal*, Vol. 48, Article 8, June 1997. Available at: http://www.hpl.hp.com/hpjournal/97jun/jun97a8.htm.

[29] S.-Y. Kuo and W. Fuchs, "Efficient Spare Allocation for Reconfigurable Arrays," *IEEE Design and Test*, Vol. 4, pp. 24–31, February 1987.

[30] S.-Y. Kuo and W. Kent Fuchs, "Fault Diagnosis and Spare Allocation for Yield Enhancement in Large Reconfigurable PLA's," *IEEE Transactions on Computers*, Vol. 41, pp. 221–226, February 1992.

[31] R. Leveugle, Z. Koren, I. Koren, G. Saucier, and N. Wehn, "The HYETI Defect Tolerant Microprocessor: A Practical Experiment and a Cost-Effectiveness Analysis," *IEEE Transactions on Computers*, Vol. 43, pp. 1398–1406, December 1994.

[32] W. Maly, "Computer-Aided Design for VLSI Circuit Manufacturability," *Proceedings of IEEE*, Vol. 78, pp. 356–392, February 1990.

[33] W. Maly, W. R. Moore, and A. Strojwas, "Yield Loss Mechanisms and Defect Tolerance," in W. R. Moore, W. Maly, and A. Strojwas (Eds.), *Yield Modelling and Defect Tolerance in VLSI*, pp. 3–30, Adam Hilger, 1988.

[34] T. L. Michalka, R. C. Varshney, and J. D. Meindl, "A Discussion of Yield Modeling with Defect Clustering, Circuit Repair, and Circuit Redundancy," *IEEE Transactions on Semiconductor Manufacturing*, Vol. 3, pp. 116–127, August 1990.

[35] W. R. Moore, "A Review of Fault-Tolerant Techniques for the Enhancement of Integrated Circuit Yield," *Proceedings of the IEEE*, Vol. 74, pp. 684–698, May 1986.

[36] B. T. Murphy, "Cost-Size Optima of Monolithic Integrated Circuits," *Proceedings of the IEEE*, Vol. 52, pp. 1537–1545, December 1964.

[37] R. Negrini, M. G. Sami, and R. Stefanelli, *Fault Tolerance Through Reconfiguration in VLSI and WSI arrays*, MIT Press, 1989.

[38] T. Okabe, M. Nagata, and S. Shimada, "Analysis of Yield of Integrated Circuits and a New Expression for the Yield," *Electric Engineering Japan*, Vol. 92, pp. 135–141, December 1972.

[39] E. Papadopoulou, "Critical Area Computation for Missing Material Defects in VLSI Circuits," *IEEE Transactions on CAD*, Vol. 20, pp. 503–528, May 2001.

[40] O. Paz and T. R. Lawson, Jr., "Modification of Poisson Statistics: Modeling Defects Induced by Diffusion," *IEEE Journal of Solid-State Circuits*, Vol. SC-12, pp. 540–546, October 1977.

[41] J. E. Price, "A New Look at Yield of Integrated Circuits," *Proceedings of the IEEE*, Vol. 58, pp. 1290–1291, August 1970.

[42] R. B. Seeds, "Yield, Economic, and Logistic Models for Complex Digital Arrays," *IEEE International Convention Record*, Part 6, pp. 61–66, 1967.

[43] A. Sehgal, A. Dubey, E. J. Marinissen, C. Wouters, H. Vranken, and K. Chakrabarty, "Redundancy Modelling and Array Yield Analysis for Repairable Embedded Memories," *IEE Proceedings—Computers and Digital Techniques*, Vol. 152, pp. 97–106, January 2005.

[44] A. D. Singh, "Interstitial Redundancy: An Area Efficient Fault Tolerance Scheme for Larger Area VLSI Processor Array," *IEEE Transactions on Computers*, Vol. 37, pp. 1398–1410, November 1988.

[45] R. Spence and R. S. Soin, *Tolerance Design of Electronic Circuits*, Addison-Wesley, 1988.

[46] C. H. Stapper, "Defect Density Distribution for LSI Yield Calculations," *IEEE Transactions Electron Devices*, Vol. ED-20, pp. 655–657, July 1973.

[47] C. H. Stapper, "Modeling of Defects in Integrated Circuit Photolithographic Patterns," *IBM Journal of Research and Development*, Vol. 28, pp. 461–474, July 1984.

[48] C. H. Stapper, "On Yield, Fault Distributions and Clustering of Particles," *IBM Journal of Research and Development*, Vol. 30, pp. 326–338, May 1986.

[49] C. H. Stapper, A. N. McLaren, and M. Dreckmann, "Yield Model for Productivity Optimization of VLSI Memory Chips with Redundancy and Partially Good Product," *IBM Journal of Research and Development*, Vol. 20, pp. 398–409, 1980.

[50] C. H. Stapper, F. M. Armstrong, and K. Saji, "Integrated Circuit Yield Statistics," *Proceedings of the IEEE*, Vol. 71, pp. 453–470, April 1983.

[51] T. Sugibayashi, I. Naritake, S. Utsugi, K. Shibahara, and R. Oikawa, "A 1-Gb DRAM for File Applications," *IEEE Journal of Solid-State Circuits*, Vol. 30, pp. 1277–1280, November 1995.

[52] T. Thomas and B. Anthony, "Area, Performance, and Yield Implications of Redundancy in On-Chip Caches," *IEEE International Conference on Computer Design*, pp. 291–292, October 1999.

[53] D. M. H. Walker, *Yield Simulation for Integrated Circuits*, Kluwer Academic Publishers, 1987.

[54] C. L. Wey, "On Yield Considerations for the Design of Redundant Programmable Logic Arrays," *IEEE Transactions on Computer-Aided Design*, Vol. CAD-7, pp. 528–535, April 1988.

[55] T. Yamagata, H. Sato, K. Fujita, Y. Nishimura, and K. Anami, "A Distributed Globally Replaceable Redundancy Scheme for Sub-Half-micron ULSI Memories and Beyond," *IEEE Journal of Solid-State Circuits*, Vol. 31, pp. 195–201, February 1996.

[56] J.-H. Yoo, C.-H. Kim, K.-C. Lee, and K.-H. Kyung, "A 32-Bank 1 Gb Self-Strobing Synchronous DRAM with 1 GB/s Bandwidth," *IEEE Journal of Solid-State Circuits*, Vol. 31, pp. 1635–1643, November 1996.

[57] M. W. Yung, M. J. Little, R. D. Etchells, and J. G. Nash, "Redundancy for Yield Enhancement in the 3D Computer," *Wafer Scale Integration Conference*, pp. 73–82, January 1989.

Fault Detection in Cryptographic Systems

Cryptographic algorithms are being applied in an increasing number of devices to satisfy their high security requirements. Many of these devices require high-speed operation and include specialized hardware encryption and/or decryption circuits for the selected cryptographic algorithm. A unique characteristic of these circuits is their very high sensitivity to faults. Unlike ordinary arithmetic/logic circuits such as adders and multipliers, even a single data bit fault in an encryption or decryption circuit will, in most cases, spread quickly and result in a totally scrambled output (an almost random pattern). There is, therefore, a need to prevent such faults or, at the minimum, be able to detect them.

There is another, even more compelling, reason for paying special attention to fault detection in cryptographic devices. The cryptographic algorithms (also called ciphers) that are being implemented are designed so that they are difficult to break. To obtain the secret key, which allows the decryption of encrypted information, an attacker must perform a prohibitively large number of experiments. However, it has been shown that by deliberately injecting faults into a cryptographic device and observing the corresponding outputs, the number of experiments needed to obtain the secret key can be drastically reduced. Thus, incorporating some form of fault detection into cryptographic devices is necessary for security purposes as well as for data integrity.

We start this chapter with a brief overview of two important classes of ciphers, namely, symmetric key and asymmetric (or public) key, and describe the fault injection attacks that can be mounted against them. We then present techniques that can be used to detect the injected faults in an attempt to foil the attacks.

9.1   Overview of Ciphers

Cryptographic algorithms use secret keys for encrypting the given data (known as *plaintext*) thus generating a *ciphertext*, and for decrypting the ciphertext to reconstruct the original plaintext. The keys used for the encryption and decryption steps can be either identical (or trivially related), leading to what are known as *symmetric key* ciphers, or different, leading to what are known as *asymmetric key* (or *public key*) ciphers. Symmetric key ciphers have simpler, and therefore faster, encryption and decryption processes compared with those of asymmetric key ciphers. The main weakness of symmetric key ciphers is the shared secret key, which may be subject to discovery by an adversary and must therefore be changed periodically. The generation of new keys, commonly carried out using a pseudo-random-number generator (see Section 10.4), must be very carefully executed because, unless properly initialized, such generators may result in easy to discover keys. The new keys must then be distributed securely, preferably by using a more secure (but also more computationally intensive) asymmetric key cipher.

9.1.1 Symmetric Key Ciphers

Symmetric key ciphers can be either *block ciphers*, which encrypt a block of a fixed number of plaintext bits at the same time, or *stream ciphers*, which encrypt 1 bit at a time. Block ciphers are more commonly used, and are therefore the focus of this chapter.

Some well-known block cyphers include the Data Encryption Standard (DES) and the more recent Advanced Encryption Standard (AES). DES uses 64-bit plaintext blocks and a 56-bit key, whereas AES uses 128-bit blocks and keys of size between 128 and 196 bits. Longer secret keys are obviously more secure, but the size of the data block also plays a role in the security of the cipher. For example, smaller blocks may allow frequency-based attacks, such as relying on the higher frequency of the letter "e" in English-language text.

Almost all symmetric key ciphers use the same key for encryption and for decryption. The process used for encryption must be reversible so that the reverse process followed during decryption can generate the original plaintext. The main objective of the encryption process is to scramble the plaintext as much as possible. This is done by repeating a computationally simple series of steps (called a *round*) several times to achieve the desired scrambling.

The DES cipher follows the approach ascribed to Feistel. The Feistel scheme divides the block of plaintext bits into two parts B_1 and B_2. B_1 is unchanged, whereas the bits in B_2 are added (using modulo-2 addition, which is the logical bit-wise Exclusive-OR (XOR) operation) to a one-way hash function $F(B_1, K)$, where K is the key. A hash function is a function that takes a long input string (in general, of any length) and produces a fixed-length output string. A function is called a one-way hash function if it is hard to reverse the process and find an input string that will generate a given output value. The two subblocks B_1 and $B_2 + F(B_1, K)$ are then swapped.

These operations constitute a round, and the round is repeated several times. Following a round, we end up with $B'_1 = B_2 + F(B_1, K)$ and $B'_2 = B_1$. A single round is not secure since the bits of B_1 are unchanged and were only moved, but repeating the round several times will considerably scramble the original plaintext.

The one-way hash function F may seem to prevent decryption. Still, by the end of the round, both B_1 and the key K are available and it is possible to recalculate $F(B_1, K)$ and thus obtain B_2. Therefore, all the rounds can be "undone" in reverse order to retrieve the plaintext.

DES has been the first official standard cipher for commercial purposes. It became a standard in 1976, and although there is currently a newer standard (AES established in 2002), the use of DES is still widespread either in its original form or in its more secure variation called Triple DES. Triple DES applies DES three times with different keys and offers as a result a higher level of security (one variation uses three different keys for a total of 168 bits instead of 56 bits, while another variation uses 112 bits).

The Feistel-function–based structure of DES is shown in Figure 9.1. It consists of 16 identical rounds similar to the one described above. Each round first uses a Feistel function (the F block in the figure), performs the modulo-2 addition (the $\oplus$ circle in the figure), and then swaps the two halves. In addition, DES includes an initial and final permutations (see Figure 9.1) that are inverses and cancel each other. These do not provide any additional scrambling and were included to simplify loading blocks of data in the original hardware implementation.

The 16 rounds use different 48-bit subkeys generated by a key schedule process shown in Figure 9.2. The original key has 64 bits, eight of which are parity bits, so the first step in the key schedule (the "*Permuted Choice 1*" in Figure 9.2) is to select 56 out of the 64 bits. The remaining 16 steps are similar: the 56 incoming bits are split into two 28-bit halves, and each half is rotated to the left by either one or two bits (specified for each step). Then, 24 bits from each half are selected by the "*Permuted Choice 2*" block to generate the 48-bit round subkey. As a result of the rotations, performed by the "$<<<$" block in the figure, a different set of bits is used in each subkey.

The particular Feistel (hash) function used in DES is shown in Figure 9.3. It consists of four steps:

1. *Expansion.* The 32 input bits are expanded to 48, using an expansion permutation that duplicates some of the bits.

2. *Adding a key.* The 48-bit result is added (addition modulo-2 which is a bit-wise XOR operation) to a 48-bit subkey generated by the key schedule process.

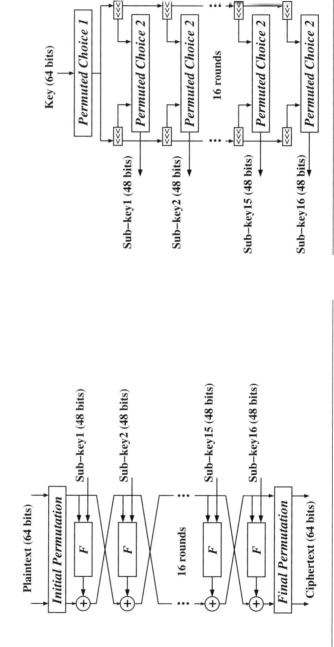

FIGURE 9.2   The key schedule process for DES.

FIGURE 9.1   The overall structure of the data encryption standard (DES).

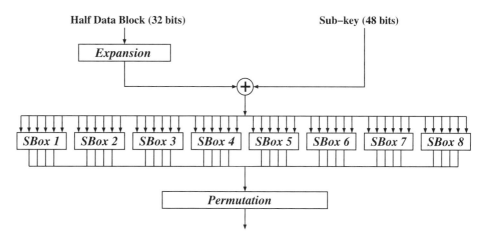

FIGURE 9.3   The Feistel function in DES.

3. *Substitution.* The 48-bit result of step 2 is divided into eight groups of 6 bits each, which are then processed by substitution boxes (called *SBoxes*). An SBox generates 4 bits according to a nonlinear transformation implemented as a lookup table.

4. *Permutation.* The 32 bits generated by the eight SBoxes undergo a permutation.

Two crucial properties that every good cipher must have are called *confusion* and *diffusion*. Confusion refers to establishing a complex relationship between the ciphertext and the key, and diffusion implies that any natural redundancy that exists in the plaintext (and can be exploited by an adversary) will dissipate in the ciphertext. In DES, most of the *confusion* is provided by the SBoxes, and the expansion and permutation provide the *diffusion*. If the confusion and diffusion are done correctly, a single bit change in the plaintext will cause every bit of the ciphertext to change with a probability of 0.5, independently of the others.

In 1999, a specially designed circuit was successful in breaking a DES key in less than 24 hours, demonstrating that the security provided by the 56-bit key is weak. Consequently, Triple DES has been declared as the preferred cipher and was itself later replaced in 2002 by AES, described next.

AES does not use a Feistel function; instead, it is based on substitutions and permutations, with most of its calculations being finite-field operations. AES uses blocks of 128-bit plaintext and three possible key sizes of 128, 192, or 256 bits. The 128-bit block is represented as a 4×4 array of bytes called the *state*, which is denoted by S with byte elements $s_{i,j}$ ($0 \leqslant i, j \leqslant 3$). The state S is modified during each encryption round, until the final ciphertext is produced. Each round of the encryption process consists of four steps (see Figure 9.4):

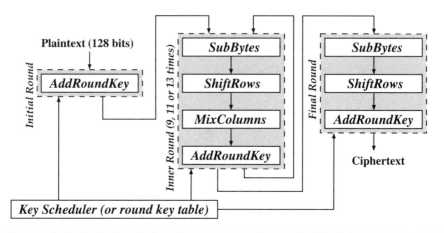

FIGURE 9.4   **The overall structure of the advanced encryption standard (AES).**

TABLE 9-1 ■ **The advanced encryption standard (AES) SBox: substitution values for the byte xy (in hexadecimal format)**

x	y 0	1	2	3	4	5	6	7	8	9	a	b	c	d	e	f
0	63	7c	77	7b	f2	6b	6f	c5	30	01	67	2b	fe	d7	ab	76
1	ca	82	c9	7d	fa	59	47	f0	ad	d4	a2	af	9c	a4	72	c0
2	b7	fd	93	26	36	3f	f7	cc	34	a5	e5	f1	71	d8	31	15
3	04	c7	23	c3	18	96	05	9a	07	12	80	e2	eb	27	b2	75
4	09	83	2c	1a	1b	6e	5a	a0	52	3b	d6	b3	29	e3	2f	84
5	53	d1	00	ed	20	fc	b1	5b	6a	cb	be	39	4a	4c	58	cf
6	d0	ef	aa	fb	43	4d	33	85	45	f9	02	7f	50	3c	9f	a8
7	51	a3	40	8f	92	9d	38	f5	bc	b6	da	21	10	ff	f3	d2
8	cd	0c	13	ec	5f	97	44	17	c4	a7	7e	3d	64	5d	19	73
9	60	81	4f	dc	22	2a	90	88	46	ee	b8	14	de	5e	0b	db
a	e0	32	3a	0a	49	06	24	5c	c2	d3	ac	62	91	95	e4	79
b	e7	c8	37	6d	8d	d5	4e	a9	6c	56	f4	ea	65	7a	ae	08
c	ba	78	25	2e	1c	a6	b4	c6	e8	dd	74	1f	4b	bd	8b	8a
d	70	3e	b5	66	48	03	f6	0e	61	35	57	b9	86	c1	1d	9e
e	e1	f8	98	11	69	d9	8e	94	9b	1e	87	e9	ce	55	28	df
f	8c	a1	89	0d	bf	e6	42	68	41	99	2d	0f	b0	54	bb	16

1. *SubBytes.* Each byte in the state matrix undergoes (independently of all other bytes) a nonlinear substitution of the form $T(s_{i,j}^{-1})$. Due to the complexity of this transformation, its 256 possible outcomes are (in almost all implementations of AES) precomputed and stored in an SBox lookup table. Unlike in DES, this is an 8- to 8-bit substitution (shown in Table 9-1) rather than a 6- to 4-bit one. The AES SBox has been designed to resist simple attacks.

2. *ShiftRows.* The bytes of the first, second, third, and fourth rows of the state matrix are rotated by 0, 1, 2, and 3 bytes, respectively. The state after this step is

$$S = \begin{bmatrix} s_{0,0} & s_{0,1} & s_{0,2} & s_{0,3} \\ s_{1,1} & s_{1,2} & s_{1,3} & s_{1,0} \\ s_{2,2} & s_{2,3} & s_{2,0} & s_{2,1} \\ s_{3,3} & s_{3,0} & s_{3,1} & s_{3,2} \end{bmatrix} \tag{9.1}$$

so that every column of the matrix is now composed of bytes from all columns of the input matrix.

3. *MixColumns.* The four bytes in each column are used to generate four new bytes through linear transformations, as follows ($j = 0, 1, 2, 3$)

$$s_{0,j} = (\alpha \otimes s_{0,j}) \oplus (\beta \otimes s_{1,j}) \oplus s_{2,j} \oplus s_{3,j}$$
$$s_{1,j} = s_{0,j} \oplus (\alpha \otimes s_{1,j}) \oplus (\beta \otimes s_{2,j}) \oplus s_{3,j}$$
$$s_{2,j} = s_{0,j} \oplus s_{1,j} \oplus (\alpha \otimes s_{2,j}) \oplus (\beta \otimes s_{3,j})$$
$$s_{3,j} = (\beta \otimes s_{0,j}) \oplus s_{1,j} \oplus s_{2,j} \oplus (\alpha \otimes s_{3,j}) \tag{9.2}$$

where $\alpha = x$ (or 02 in hexadecimal notation), $\beta = x + 1$ (or 03 in hexadecimal notation). $\otimes$ and $\oplus$ are the modulo-2 multiply and add operations, respectively, of the polynomial representations of the state bytes, and the α and β coefficients. These operations are performed modulo the irreducible generator polynomial of AES, which is $g(x) = x^8 + x^4 + x^3 + x + 1$. Polynomial presentations of binary numbers and operations modulo a given generator polynomial have been discussed in Section 3.1. The MixColumns step together with ShiftRows provide the required diffusion in the AES cipher.

4. *AddRoundKey.* The round subkey is added (modulo-2) to the state. As in DES, separate round subkeys are generated using a key schedule process.

All four steps are performed in nine out of the 10 rounds of a 128-bit key implementation, but in the 10th round, the MixColumns step is omitted. In addition, prior to the first round, the first subkey is added to the original plaintext (see Figure 9.4). The round subkeys are either generated on-the-fly following the key schedule process shown in Figure 9.5 or are taken out of a lookup table that is filled up every time a new key is established. The total number of rounds is increased to 12 and 14 for a 192-bit key and a 256-bit key AES, respectively.

■ EXAMPLE

A detailed example to illustrate the use of the AES algorithm (or for that matter, any other symmetric key cipher such as DES) for even the smallest sizes of its parameters (number of bits in the key and plaintext) will be tedious and not very illuminating. We present therefore only some of the key steps of the ex-

```
KeyExpansion(byte key[4 * Nk], word w[4 * (Nr + 1)], Nk)
begin
      word temp
      i = 0
      while (i < Nk)
            w[i] = word(key[4 * i], key[4 * i + 1], key[4 * i + 2], key[4 * i + 3])
            i = i + 1
      end while
      i = Nk
      while (i < 4 * (Nr + 1))
            temp = w[i − 1]
            if (i mod Nk = 0)
                  temp = SubWord(RotWord(temp)) xor Rcon[i/Nk]
            else if (Nk > 6 and i mod Nk = 4)
                  temp = SubWord(temp)
            end if
            w[i] = w[i − Nk] xor temp
            i = i + 1
      end while
end
```

FIGURE 9.5 The key schedule of AES ($Nr = 10, 12, 14$ **is the number of rounds,** $Nk = 4, 6, 8$ **is the number of 32-bit words in the plaintext, and** $Rcon$ **is an array of round constants,** $Rcon[j] = (x^{j-1}, 00, 00, 00)$**).**

$$\begin{bmatrix} 32 & 88 & 31 & e0 \\ 43 & 5a & 31 & 37 \\ f6 & 30 & 98 & 07 \\ a8 & 8d & a2 & 34 \end{bmatrix}$$

(a) Initial state matrix

$$\begin{bmatrix} 2b & 28 & ab & 09 \\ 7e & ae & f7 & cf \\ 15 & d2 & 15 & 4f \\ 16 & a6 & 88 & 3c \end{bmatrix}$$

(b) Key added in round 1

$$\begin{bmatrix} 19 & a0 & 9a & e9 \\ 3d & f4 & c6 & f8 \\ e3 & e2 & 8d & 48 \\ be & 2b & 2a & 08 \end{bmatrix}$$

(c) State matrix — end of round 1

$$\begin{bmatrix} d4 & e0 & b8 & 1e \\ 27 & bf & b4 & 41 \\ 11 & 98 & 5d & 52 \\ ae & f1 & e5 & 30 \end{bmatrix}$$

(d) After SubBytes

$$\begin{bmatrix} d4 & e0 & b8 & 1e \\ bf & b4 & 41 & 27 \\ 5d & 52 & 11 & 98 \\ 30 & ae & f1 & e5 \end{bmatrix}$$

(e) After ShiftRows

$$\begin{bmatrix} 04 & e0 & 48 & 28 \\ 66 & cb & f8 & 06 \\ 81 & 19 & d3 & 26 \\ e5 & 9a & 7a & 4c \end{bmatrix}$$

(f) After MixColumns

$$\begin{bmatrix} a0 & 88 & 23 & 2a \\ fa & 54 & a3 & 6c \\ fe & 2c & 39 & 76 \\ 17 & b1 & 39 & 05 \end{bmatrix}$$

(g) The key added in round 2

$$\begin{bmatrix} a4 & 68 & 6b & 02 \\ 9c & 9f & 5b & 6a \\ 7f & 35 & ea & 50 \\ f2 & 2b & 43 & 49 \end{bmatrix}$$

(h) State matrix — end of round 2

$$\begin{bmatrix} 39 & 02 & dc & 19 \\ 25 & dc & 11 & 6a \\ 84 & 09 & 85 & 0b \\ 1d & fb & 97 & 32 \end{bmatrix}$$

(i) State matrix — end of round 10

FIGURE 9.6   Example illustrating the AES algorithm.

ample that appears in full detail in the official AES document (see the Further Reading section).

Suppose the 128-bit plaintext is

$$32\,43\,f6\,a8\,88\,5a\,30\,8d\,31\,31\,98\,a2\,e0\,37\,07\,34$$

and the 128-bit key is

$$2b\,7e\,15\,16\,28\,ae\,d2\,a6\,ab\,f7\,15\,88\,09\,cf\,4f\,3c$$

Both have 32 hexadecimal digits and are shown in a matrix format in Figures 9.6a and b, respectively. The reader can verify that the byte-wise XOR operation of these two matrices yields the state matrix at the end of round 1, shown in Figure 9.6c.

The first step in round 2 is SubBytes and its results are shown in Figure 9.6d. For example, the first byte in the state matrix was $s_{0,0} = 19$, and based on the corresponding entry in Table 9-1, it is replaced by $d4$. The second step is ShiftRows, and Figure 9.6e shows the results of rotating the first, second, third, and fourth rows of the matrix by 0, 1, 2, and 3 bytes, respectively. The next step is MixColumns, and its results are shown in Figure 9.6f. For example, the first byte in the state matrix is calculated based on Equation 9.2 as follows:

$$s_{0,0} = (\alpha \otimes s_{0,0}) \oplus (\beta \otimes s_{1,0}) \oplus s_{2,0} \oplus s_{3,0}$$
$$= (02 \otimes d4) \oplus (03 \otimes bf) \oplus 5d \oplus 30 = 1b8 \oplus 1c1 \oplus 5d \oplus 30 = 04$$

Note that since the result is smaller than 100 (x^8 in polynomial notation), there is no need to further reduce it modulo-$g(x)$ (recall that $g(x) = x^8 + x^4 + x^3 + x + 1$ is the generator polynomial of AES).

The situation is different when calculating the second byte in the first column. Here,

$$s_{1,0} = s_{0,0} \oplus (\alpha \otimes s_{1,0}) \oplus (\beta \otimes s_{2,0}) \oplus s_{3,0}$$
$$= d4 \oplus (02 \otimes bf) \oplus (03 \otimes 5d) \oplus 30 = d4 \oplus 17e \oplus e7 \oplus 30 = 17d$$

This value must be reduced modulo-$g(x)$, and since

$$x^8 \bmod g(x) = x^4 + x^3 + x + 1$$

we obtain

$$17d \bmod g(x) = 7d \oplus \left(x^4 + x^3 + x + 1\right) = 7d \oplus 1b = 66$$

which is the final value of the second byte in the first column in Figure 9.6f.

We now need to calculate a new round key using the procedure in Figure 9.5. The original key is first rewritten as the following four words:

$$w[0] = 2b7e1516, \qquad w[1] = 28aed2a6$$
$$w[2] = abf71588, \qquad w[3] = 09cf4f3c$$

To calculate $w[4]$ (the first column in the key matrix for round 2), we start with

$$temp = w[i-1] = w[3] = 09cf4f3c$$

Then, we rotate this word by 1 byte obtaining $cf4f3c09$. Next, we substitute each of the 4 bytes using the SubBytes transformation in Table 9-1, yielding $8a84eb01$. We then perform a bit-wise XOR operation with

$$Rcon[1] = (x^{1-1}, 00, 00, 00) = 01000000$$

obtaining $8b84eb01$. Finally, we calculate

$$w[i] = w[i-4] \quad \text{xor} \quad temp = w[0] \quad \text{xor} \quad 8b84eb01$$
$$= 2b7e1516 \quad \text{xor} \quad 8b84eb01 = a0fafe17$$

This is the first column in the key matrix in Figure 9.6g. Adding the resulting key matrix to the state matrix, we obtain the new state matrix shown in Figure 9.6h. Continuing this process for the remaining rounds (recall that in the last round the MixColumns step is skipped) results in the ciphertext

$$39\,25\,84\,1d\,02\,dc\,09\,fb\,dc\,11\,85\,97\,19\,6a\,0b\,32$$

as shown in Figure 9.6i.

If a single bit is changed in the plaintext, for example, instead of

$$32\,43\,f6\,a8\,88\,5a\,30\,8d\,31\,31\,98\,a2\,e0\,37\,07\,34$$

we use

$$30\,43\,f6\,a8\,88\,5a\,30\,8d\,31\,31\,98\,a2\,e0\,37\,07\,34$$

a very different ciphertext is obtained:

$$c0\,06\,27\,d1\,8b\,d9\,e1\,19\,d5\,17\,6d\,bc\,ba\,73\,37\,c1$$

Similarly, if a single bit is changed in the key, for example, instead of

$$2b\,7e\,15\,16\,28\,ae\,d2\,a6\,ab\,f7\,15\,88\,09\,cf\,4f\,3c$$

we use

$$2a\,7e\,15\,16\,28\,ae\,d2\,a6\,ab\,f7\,15\,88\,09\,cf\,4f\,3c$$

the ciphertext produced is

$$c4\,61\,97\,9e\,e4\,4d\,e9\,7a\,ba\,52\,34\,8b\,39\,9d\,7f\,84$$

These two examples illustrate the fact that even a single-bit fault may result in a totally scrambled (almost random) output, demonstrating the significance of detecting such faults. ∎

9.1.2 Public Key Ciphers

Unlike symmetric key ciphers, asymmetric key ciphers (also known as public key ciphers) allow users to communicate securely without having access to a shared secret key. Public key ciphers are, however, considerably more computationally complex than symmetric key ciphers. Instead of a single key shared by the two entities communicating with each other, the sender and recipient each have two cryptographic keys called the public key and the private key. The private key is kept secret, and the public key may be widely distributed. In a way, one of the two keys can be used to "lock" a safe, whereas the other key is needed to unlock it. If a sender encrypts a message using the recipient's public key, only the recipient can decrypt it using the corresponding private key.

Another noteworthy application of public key ciphers is sender authentication: the sender encrypts a message with her own private key. By managing to decrypt the message using the sender's public key, the recipient is assured that the sender (and no one else) generated the message.

The best-known public key cipher is the RSA algorithm named after its three inventors Rivest, Shamir and Adleman, but other public key ciphers have been developed and are in use. Person *A* wishing to use the RSA cipher must first generate a secret private key and a public key. The latter will be distributed to everyone who may wish to communicate with her. The key generation process consists of the following steps:

1. Select two large prime numbers p and q, and calculate their product $N = pq$.

2. Select a small odd integer e that is relatively prime to

$$\phi(N) = (p - 1)(q - 1)$$

   Two numbers (not necessarily primes) are said to be relatively prime if their only common factor is 1. For example, 6 and 25 are relatively prime, although neither is a prime number.

3. Find the integer d that satisfies

$$de = 1 \bmod \phi(N)$$

   (d is often called the "inverse" of e).

The pair (e, N) constitutes the public key, and A should broadcast it to everyone who may wish to communicate with her. The pair (d, N) will serve as A's secret private key. The security provided by RSA depends on the difficulty of factoring the large integer N into its prime factors. Small integers can be factored in a reasonable amount of time, allowing the secret private key to be easily derived from the public key. To make the factoring time prohibitively large, each of the prime numbers p and q must have at least a hundred digits.

Given a message M that person B wishes to send to A, B will encrypt it using A's public key as

$$S = M^e \bmod N$$

Note that this encryption scheme makes it necessary to restrict the message M to

$$0 \leqslant M \leqslant N - 1$$

Upon receiving the encrypted message S, A will decrypt it using her private key by calculating

$$S^d \bmod N = M^{de} \bmod N$$

which can be shown to be equal to the original plaintext message M. The encryption and decryption of RSA messages thus entail exponentiations modulo-N.

Although there are techniques for reducing the complexity of such modular exponentiation (e.g., Montgomery reduction), the complexity of encryption and decryption for the RSA cipher is still considerably higher than that for symmetric key ciphers.

■ E X A M P L E

To illustrate the use of the RSA algorithm, consider the following simple example. Suppose we select the prime numbers $p = 7$ and $q = 11$, yielding $N = 77$ and $\phi(N) = 60$. We can then select $e = 7$, which is obviously relatively prime with respect to $\phi(N)$. The pair $(e,n) = (7,77)$ constitutes our public key. We search now for d that satisfies $7d = 1 \bmod 60$, and find $d = 43$ (since $7 \cdot 43 = 301 = 1 \bmod 60$). Suppose now that B wishes to send us the message $M = 9$. B encrypts it using the public key $(e,N) = (7,77)$, which we have given him, obtaining $9^7 \bmod 77 = 4782969 \bmod 77 = 37$. We receive 37 and decrypt it using our private key by calculating $37^{43} \bmod 77$, revealing the plaintext 9. ■

9.2   Security Attacks Through Fault Injection

The level of security provided by the different ciphers has not been proved in an absolute sense, and all ciphers rely on the difficulty of finding the secret key directly and having to resort to exhaustive searches which may take a prohibitive amount of time. However, attacks on cryptographic systems have been developed which take advantage of side-channel information. This is information that can be obtained from the physical implementation of a cipher rather than through exploitation of some weakness of the cipher itself. One example of such side-channel information is the time needed to perform an encryption (or decryption), which in certain implementations may depend on the bits of the key. This allows the attacker to narrow down the range of values which need to be attempted. Another example is the amount of power consumed in various steps of the encryption process: the power consumption profile of certain implementations may depend on whether the bits of the key are 0 or 1.

Schemes to protect cryptosystems against such attacks have been developed. For example, a random number of instructions that do not perform any useful calculation can be injected into the code, scrambling the relationship between the bits in the key and the total time needed to complete the encryption (or decryption). These randomly-injected instructions can also help protect against power measurements-based attacks. Other countermeasures that have been followed include designs that have a data-independent delay or use dual-rail logic that consumes the same power independently of whether a particular bit is 1 or 0. Most such techniques incur delay and/or power penalties.

An important type of side-channel attacks, which is of particular interest to us in this book, relies on the intentional injection of faults into a hardware implementation of a cipher. Such attacks proved to be both easy to apply and very efficient; an attacker can guess the secret key after a very small number of fault injection experiments. This has been shown to be true for many types of ciphers, both symmetric and asymmetric.

The different techniques for injecting intentional faults into a cryptographic device include varying the supply voltage (generating a *spike*), varying the clock frequency (generating a *glitch*), overheating the device, or, as is more commonly done, exposing the device to intense light using either a camera flash or a more precise laser (or X-ray) beam.

Injecting a fault through a voltage spike or a clock glitch is likely to render a complete byte (or even several bytes) faulty, whereas the more precise laser or X-ray beams may be successful in inducing a single-bit fault. Fault-based attacks have been developed for both cases, and since most of these attacks induce transient faults, they allow the attacker to repeat her attempts multiple times until sufficient information is collected for extracting the secret key and even use the device after breaking the cipher.

A practical issue that must be considered when mounting a fault-based attack is the need for precise timing of the fault injection. To achieve the desired effect, the fault must be injected during a particular step of the encryption or decryption algorithm. This turns out to be achievable in practice by analyzing the power and/or electromagnetic profile of the cryptographic device.

We next describe briefly possible fault attacks on symmetric and asymmetric key ciphers.

9.2.1 Fault Attacks on Symmetric Key Ciphers

Various fault injection based attacks on DES have been described, two of which are presented next.

TABLE 9-2 ■ Fault attack on data encryption standard (DES)

DES Key	Output
$K_0 = xx\ xx\ xx\ xx\ xx\ xx\ xx\ xx$	S_0
$K_1 = xx\ xx\ xx\ xx\ xx\ xx\ xx\ 00$	S_1
$K_2 = xx\ xx\ xx\ xx\ xx\ xx\ 00\ 00$	S_2
$K_3 = xx\ xx\ xx\ xx\ xx\ 00\ 00\ 00$	S_3
$K_4 = xx\ xx\ xx\ xx\ 00\ 00\ 00\ 00$	S_4
$K_5 = xx\ xx\ xx\ 00\ 00\ 00\ 00\ 00$	S_5
$K_6 = xx\ xx\ 00\ 00\ 00\ 00\ 00\ 00$	S_6
$K_7 = xx\ 00\ 00\ 00\ 00\ 00\ 00\ 00$	S_7

In cryptographic devices that use DES (e.g., smart cards), the secret key is often stored in an EEPROM and then transferred to the memory when a message needs to be encrypted or decrypted. If the attacker can reset an entire byte of the key (set the eight bits of that byte to zero) during its transfer from the EEPROM to the memory, he can figure out the secret key. The attack consists of eight steps as outlined in Table 9-2. In all of these experiments, known (to the attacker) plaintext messages are encrypted with a different number of bytes of the key being forced to 0 as shown in Table 9-2. Based on the ciphertext S_7, the attacker can derive the first byte of the secret key by trying out all possible values of the first byte until the value that would produce S_7 is found. Since in DES each byte of the key includes a parity bit, at most 128 values need to be checked rather than 256. In a similar manner, the second byte of the key can be found based on S_6. This procedure is continued until all eight bytes of the secret key are discovered.

A second fault-based attack relies on causing an instruction to fail (most commonly using clock glitches). For example, if the loop variable controlling the number of times the basic round is executed is corrupted and, as a result, only one or two rounds are executed, the task of finding the secret key is greatly simplified.

This type of attack can also be mounted against a device that uses AES and implements the cipher via software. Fault injection attacks on AES that focus, for example, on a byte of either the round subkey or on the state in the last round of the encryption have also been developed. Some of these attacks have been applied in practice to smart cards, yielding the secret key after fewer than 300 experiments. References to the descriptions of these attacks are provided in the Further Reading section.

9.2.2 Fault Attacks on Public (Asymmetric) Key Ciphers

Unlike symmetric key ciphers for which both encryption and decryption processes are vulnerable to security attacks, for a public key cipher, only the decryption process may be subject to attacks attempting to extract the secret private key. One easily understood fault attack on the RSA decryption process assumes that the attacker can flip a randomly selected single bit of the private key d. Given an encrypted message S and its corresponding plaintext M, both of which are known to the attacker, he flips a random bit of d. If the ith bit of d, d_i, is flipped to produce its complement $\bar{d}_i$, the decryption device will generate an erroneous plaintext $\widehat{M}$ instead of M. The ratio between these two is

$$\frac{\widehat{M}}{M} = \frac{S^{2^i \bar{d}_i}}{S^{2^i d_i}} \bmod N$$

If this ratio is equal to $S^{2^i} \bmod N$ for some i, the attacker can conclude that $d_i = 0$. A ratio of $\frac{1}{S^{2^i}} \bmod N$ for some i implies that $d_i = 1$. Repeating this process will eventually provide all the bits of the secret private key d.

In a similar way, the bits of d can be obtained by flipping a bit in the ciphertext S, and even by flipping two (or more) bits simultaneously. Showing this is left as an exercise for the reader. This type of attack can therefore, be successful even if the attacker is unable to precisely flip a single bit.

■ EXAMPLE

Let us use the example discussed in Section 9.1.2 with $(e, N) = (7, 77)$ as the public key and $d = 43$ (or in binary $d_5 d_4 d_3 d_2 d_1 d_0 = 101011$) as the private key. Suppose the decryption device receives the ciphertext 37 and produces the plaintext $M = 9$ if no fault is injected, and the erroneous text $\widehat{M} = 67$ if a single bit fault is injected into d. We now search for i such that $9 = (67 \cdot 37^{2^i}) \bmod 77$. It is easy to verify that among the possible values of i, $i = 3$ is the one because

$$\left(67 \cdot 37^8\right) \bmod 77 = (67 \cdot 53) \bmod 77 = 9$$

Consequently, we deduce that $d_3 = 1$. ■

9.3 Countermeasures

We presented above only a small sample out of the large number of possible fault-based attacks that can be mounted against cryptographic devices. Due to the relative ease of applying these attacks, it is obvious that proper countermeasures must be taken in order to keep the devices secure. Any such countermeasure must first detect the fault, and then prevent the attacker from observing the output of the device after the fault has been injected. Either the output could be blocked (by producing a constant value such as all zeroes) or a random result generated, mis-loading the attacker. Clearly, the original design of the device must be modified to include any such countermeasure.

Two approaches can be followed when modifying the design of a cryptographic device to protect it against fault injection–based attacks. One relies on duplicating the encryption or decryption process (using either hardware or time redundancy) and comparing the two results. This approach assumes that the injected faults are transient and will not manifest themselves in exactly the same time in the two calculations. This approach is easy to apply but may, in certain situations, impose an overhead too high to be practical. The second approach is based on error-detection codes (see Section 3.1) that usually require a smaller overhead compared with brute-force duplication, although possibly at the cost of a lower fault coverage. Thus, a trade-off between the fault coverage and the hardware and/or time overhead should be expected.

9.3.1 Spatial and Temporal Duplication

Applying duplication to the encryption (or decryption) procedure is quite straight-forward. Spatial duplication requires redundant hardware to allow independent calculations so that faults injected into one hardware unit do not affect (in the same way) the other unit(s). Temporal redundancy can be applied by reusing the same hardware unit or re-executing the same software program, assuming that the manifestation of the injected faults will change from one execution to the other. These schemes are similar to the conventional hardware and time redundancy techniques that are described in Chapter 2. The recalculation with shifted/modified operands techniques that have been described in Section 5.2.4 can be used here to prevent the possibility of both computations being affected by the injected fault in exactly the same way.

A different scheme for applying duplication relies on having a separate hardware unit or software program for executing the reverse procedure. For example, after completing the encryption, the decryption unit or program is applied to the ciphertext, and only if the result of the decryption is equal to the original plaintext is the ciphertext considered fault-free and is output.

The latter approach is costly if applied to an RSA decryption device. The decrypted result $\hat{M}$ obtained from the received encrypted message S is verified by calculating $\hat{S} = \hat{M}^e \bmod N$ and comparing $\hat{S}$ to S. This calculation is time-consuming if the public key e is very large.

9.3.2 Error-Detecting Codes

This section illustrates the use of error-detecting codes (EDCs) for detecting faults in the encryption process of symmetric key ciphers. Similar rules apply to using EDCs during the decryption and key schedule procedures, because these use the same basic mathematical operations as the encryption.

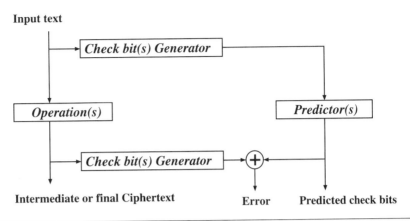

Input text

Check bit(s) Generator

Operation(s)

Predictor(s)

Check bit(s) Generator

Intermediate or final Ciphertext

Error

Predicted check bits

FIGURE 9.7 The general structure for detecting faults in encryption devices using error-detecting codes.

When using an EDC during the encryption process, check bits are first generated for the input plaintext, then for each operation(s) that the data bits undergo, the check bits of the expected result are predicted. Periodically, check bits for the actual result are generated and compared with the predicted check bits, and a fault is detected if the two sets do not match. The general approach is depicted in Figure 9.7. The validation checks can be scheduled at various granularities of the encryption, be it after every operation applied to the data, after each round, or only once at the end of the encryption process.

The first step, that of generating the check bits for the plaintext, is straightforward. The difficult part is devising the prediction rules for the new values of the check bits after each transformation that the data bits undergo during the encryption process. The complexity of these prediction rules, combined with the frequency at which the comparison is made, determines the overhead of applying the EDC, instead of duplication, as a protection against fault attacks.

Various EDCs have been proposed for symmetric and public-key ciphers, most of them being the traditional EDCs described in Chapter 3. In particular, parity-based EDCs were found to be effective for the DES and AES symmetric ciphers. Parity bits can be associated with entire 32-bit words, with individual bytes, or even with nibbles (sets of 4 bits), with each such scheme providing a different fault coverage and entailing a different overhead in terms of extra hardware and delay.

As an example, we illustrate the procedure for developing parity prediction rules when using a parity-based EDC for the AES cipher. Since most data transformations performed in the AES cipher operate on bytes, the natural choice is assigning a parity bit to each byte of the state. This will simplify the prediction rules and provide a high fault coverage. We discuss next the prediction rules for the four steps included in each round.

The prediction of the output parity bits for the ShiftRows transformation is straightforward: it is a rotated version of the input parity bits, following Equation 9.1.

Equally simple is the prediction of the output parity bits of the AddRoundKey step: it consists of adding modulo-2 the input parity matrix associated with the state to the parity matrix associated with the current round key.

The SubBytes step uses SBox lookup tables where each SBox is usually implemented as a 256×8 bits memory. The input to the SBox will already have an associated parity bit. To generate the outgoing parity, a parity bit can be stored with each data byte, increasing the number of bits in each location in the SBox to 9. To make sure that input parity errors are not discarded, we will have to check the parity of the input data and, if an error is detected, stop the encryption process. This would add hardware overhead (parity checkers for 16 bytes) and extra delay.

A better choice would be to propagate the input parity errors so that they can be detected later on. This can be achieved by including the incoming parity bit when addressing the SBox, thus further increasing the table size to 512×9. The entries that correspond to input bytes with correct parity will include the appropriate SubBytes transformation result, with a correct parity bit. The other entries will contain a deliberately incorrect result, such as an all-zeroes byte with an incorrect parity bit.

If fault attacks on the SBox address decoder can be expected, the above scheme is insufficient. In this case, we can add a small and separate table of size 256×1, which will include the predicted parity bit for the correct output byte. This separate table will only allow detection of a mismatch between the parity bit of the correct output byte and the parity bit of the incorrect (but with a valid parity) output byte. We can increase the detection capabilities of this scheme by adding one (or more) correct output data bits to each location in the small table, thus increasing its size. Comparing the output of this table to the appropriate output bits of the main SBox table allows the detection of most addressing circuitry faults.

The output parity bits of the MixColumns step are the most complex to predict. As the reader is requested to verify in the Exercises, the equations for predicting these parity bits are as follows:

$$p_{0,j} = p_{0,j} \oplus p_{2,j} \oplus p_{3,j} \oplus s_{0,j}^{(7)} \oplus s_{1,j}^{(7)}$$

$$p_{1,j} = p_{0,j} \oplus p_{1,j} \oplus p_{3,j} \oplus s_{1,j}^{(7)} \oplus s_{2,j}^{(7)}$$

$$p_{2,j} = p_{0,j} \oplus p_{1,j} \oplus p_{2,j} \oplus s_{2,j}^{(7)} \oplus s_{3,j}^{(7)}$$

$$p_{3,j} = p_{1,j} \oplus p_{2,j} \oplus p_{3,j} \oplus s_{3,j}^{(7)} \oplus s_{0,j}^{(7)} \tag{9.3}$$

where $p_{i,j}$ is the parity bit associated with state byte $s_{i,j}$, and $s_{i,j}^{(7)}$ is the most significant bit of $s_{i,j}$.

The question that remains is the granularity at which the comparisons between the generated and predicted parity bits will be made. Scheduling one validation check at the end of the whole encryption process has the obvious advantage of having the lowest overhead in terms of hardware and extra delay. Theoretically, this could result in the error indication being masked during the encryption procedure, yielding a match between the generated and predicted parity bits despite the ciphertext being erroneous. It can be shown, however, that errors injected at any step of the AES encryption procedure will not be masked, and therefore, a single validation check of the final ciphertext is sufficient for error-detection purposes.

Still, not every combination of errors can be detected by this scheme. Parity-based EDCs are capable of detecting any fault that consists of an odd number of bit errors; an even number of bit errors occurring in a single byte will not be detected. Moreover, if errors are injected in both the state and the round key, some data faults of odd cardinality will not be detected, for example, a single bit error in the round key and a single bit error in the state, occurring in matching bytes which are added in the AddRoundKeys step. The reason we do not restrict our discussion to single bit error coverage (as is usually done when benign faults are considered) is that when a malicious fault injection attack takes place, it most likely impacts multiple adjacent bits of the state and/or round key. Still, although we cannot expect a 100% fault coverage when using a parity-based EDC, the fault coverage has been shown to be very high, even when multiple faults are considered.

Parity-based EDCs are suitable for the DES cipher as well, but the situation here is different from that with AES, due to two of the internal operations in the DES encryption process, namely, the expansion (from 32 to 48 bits) and the permutation of the 32 bits. The latter permutation is irregular, and therefore, there is no simple way to predict the individual parity bits of the four bytes. A more practical solution is to verify the correctness of the permutation by duplicating the circuit and comparing the results. In addition, if we wish to detect faults in the remaining steps of the encryption using a parity-based EDC, we must schedule a validation checkpoint within each round prior to the permutation and generate new parity bits afterward. A simple way to overcome the complexity of parity prediction for the 32-bit permutation is to use a single parity bit per 32-bit word. This, however, yields a very low fault coverage and is not recommended.

In a similar way, EDCs can be developed for other symmetric key ciphers. Several such ciphers that rely on modular addition and multiplication will better match residue codes (see Chapter 3). Other symmetric ciphers have been shown to require a very expensive implementation of EDCs, leading to the conclusion that the brute-force duplication is probably a more suitable solution. The cost of providing protection against fault-based attacks should be taken into account when selecting a cipher for a device.

The RSA public key cipher is based on modular arithmetic operations, and as such, it suggests the residue code as a natural choice. First, the check bits for the plaintext are generated based on the selected modulus C for the residue check

```
Decryption_Algorithm_1(S, N, (d_{n-1}, d_{n-2}, ..., d_0))
begin
    a = S
    for i from n − 2 to 0 do
        a = a² mod N
        if d_i = 1 then a = S · a mod N
    end
    M = a
end
```

FIGURE 9.8   A straightforward decryption algorithm for RSA.

($M \bmod C$ where M is the original message). Since all operations performed during the RSA encryption (and decryption) are modular ones, we can apply them to the input check bits and obtain the predicted output check bits. The residue check will fail to detect an error if the faulty ciphertext has the same residue check bits as the correct one. Assuming that the fault injected is random, this match will happen with a probability of $1/C$, and thus, a higher value of C will result in a higher fault coverage (but also a higher overhead).

9.3.3 Are These Countermeasures Sufficient?

The objective of the countermeasures described above is to detect any fault injected during the process of encryption or decryption, and when such faults are detected, prevent the transmission of the erroneous results that may assist the attacker in extracting the secret key. Unfortunately, it has been demonstrated that although the detection of faults is necessary, it is not always sufficient for protecting against fault-based attacks. We illustrate this point through two examples: an RSA decryption and an AES encryption.

Suppose we use for the RSA decryption a straightforward algorithm that consists of raising the input S to the power d (where d is the private key) as shown in Figure 9.8. The inputs to this algorithm are the encrypted message S, the modulus N, and the n-bit private key $d = d_{n-1}, d_{n-2}, \ldots, d_0$.

EXAMPLE

Assume a 4-bit private key $(d_3, d_2, d_1, d_0) = (1011)$ (the decimal 11). The algorithm in Figure 9.8 will calculate $M = ((S^2)^2 \cdot S)^2 \cdot S = S^{11}$. ∎

Fault attacks on this algorithm can be detected either by using a residue code or by calculating $M^e \bmod N$ and comparing the result to S. Even with either of

```
Decryption_Algorithm_2(S, N, (d_{n-1}, d_{n-2}, ..., d_0))
begin
    a = S
    for i from n − 2 to 0 do
        a = a² mod N
        b = S · a mod N
        if d_i = 1 then a = b else a = a
    end
    if (no error has been detected) then M = a
end
```

FIGURE 9.9   A modified decryption algorithm for RSA.

these detection techniques, the algorithm is vulnerable to a power analysis-based attack because a step where $d_i = 0$ will consume less power than a step for which $d_i = 1$. To counter such an attack, the algorithm can be modified so that the power consumed in every step will be independent of d_i. The modified algorithm shown in Figure 9.9 will, as expected, incur higher delay and power penalties compared to the original algorithm. The check at the end of the algorithm intends to make the algorithm resistant to fault injections.

However, a careful examination of the algorithm in Figure 9.9 reveals that it is still vulnerable to fault-based attacks. Since the result b of the multiplication $S \cdot a \bmod N$ is not used if $d_i = 0$, the attacker can inject a fault during this multiplication, and if the final result of the decryption is correct, he can deduce one bit of the secret private key.

Fortunately, a different algorithm can be devised using what is called a Montgomery ladder, as shown in Figure 9.10. In this algorithm, the intermediate values of both a and b are used in the next step, and thus, a fault injected in any intermediate step will yield an erroneous result which will be detected.

◼ EXAMPLE

Assume, as before, a 4-bit private key $(d_3, d_2, d_1, d_0) = (1011)$. The algorithm in Figure 9.10 will calculate M as follows. For $i = 3$, $d_3 = 1$, and thus, $a = S$ and $b = S^2$. For $i = 2$, $d_2 = 0$, and thus, $a = S^2$ and $b = S^3$. For $i = 1$, $d_1 = 1$, and thus, $a = S^5$ and $b = S^6$. Finally, for $i = 0$, $d_1 = 1$, resulting in $M = a = S^{11}$ and $b = S^{12}$.

◼

The Montgomery-ladder-based decryption algorithm for RSA allows another approach to detect faults injected during the decryption. The computed a and b must be of the form (M, SM), and a fault injected during any intermediate step will destroy this relationship. Thus, checking whether a and b satisfy this relationship before providing the final result of the decryption can detect all injected errors,

```
Decryption_Algorithm_3(S, N, (d_{n-1}, d_{n-2}, ..., d_0))
begin
    a = 1
    b = S
    for i from n − 1 to 0 do
        if d_i = 0 then
            a = a² mod N
            b = a · b mod N
            end
        if d_i = 1 then
            a = a · b mod N
            b = b² mod N
            end
    end
    if (no error has been detected) then M = a
end
```

FIGURE 9.10 **A Montgomery-ladder-based decryption algorithm for RSA.**

except those that modify either the bits of the secret private key d or the number of times the loop in Figure 9.10 is performed. By using some EDC for these two, in addition to verifying the relationship between a and b, all injected faults can be detected.

We next describe a fault-based attack on AES encryption that may succeed even if a fault-detection mechanism that prevents erroneous results from being output is incorporated into the design. The attack starts with providing an all-zeroes input to the AES encryption device. In the very first step of the encryption (see Figure 9.4), the initial round key is added, resulting in the state matrix $s_{i,j} = 0 \oplus k_{i,j} = k_{i,j}$, where $0 \leqslant i, j \leqslant 3$. At exactly the same time instant, before the first SubBytes operation, the attacker injects a fault into the ℓth bit ($\ell = 0, 1, \ldots, 7$) of a particular byte $s_{i,j}$ of the state matrix so that the selected bit is set to 0. If the corresponding bit of the key (bit ℓ of $k_{i,j}$) is 1, the output will be incorrect and the detection mechanism will disallow this output. If, however, the corresponding bit of the key is 0, no error will occur and the encryption device will work properly, providing the attacker with the value of that bit of the secret key.

This attack is very simple to understand theoretically but may prove to be quite difficult to mount due to the need for precise timing and location of the injected fault. The secret key can still be extracted even if the strict timing and location requirements of this attack are relaxed, but this may require a larger number of fault injection experiments. The interested reader can find further details in the original paper referenced in the Further Reading section. The simple attack described above shows that implementations of symmetric key ciphers, even those with fault detection capabilities, are not completely immune to fault-based attacks.

9.3.4 Final Comment

A final remark is in order: the topic of this chapter is still a very active area of research and a constant stream of new fault-based attacks on cryptographic devices, and of novel countermeasures to protect the devices against these attacks appears in the literature. The objective of this chapter is to demonstrate the extra difficulties in devising fault-protection techniques to deal with malicious faults injected into cryptographic devices.

9.4   Further Reading

The official descriptions of the DES and AES algorithms appear in [24] and [25], respectively. The AES example that is outlined in Section 9.1.1 is detailed in [25]. A more detailed description of AES appears in [13]. The RSA algorithm was first described in [27]. Javascript AES, DES, and RSA calculators/demonstrators showing intermediate values are available [29]. A considerable number of articles on all aspects of cryptography are posted on the Website of the International Association for Cryptologic Research [17]. Well-written descriptions of key terms in cryptography appear in the online encyclopedia *Wikipedia* [30].

Fault injection attacks were first discussed in [7]. Many other fault attacks on public and symmetric key ciphers have been later presented in [1,2,9,12,14, 16,26,32]. A survey of various fault injection techniques is provided in [3] which also reviews some protection schemes against such attacks. Detailed descriptions of ways to protect ciphers from attacks appear in [4,5,8,11,19–21,23,28]. The derivation of the parity bit prediction rules for AES follows [4]. Simulators for error detection in several ciphers are available online [22]. The insufficiency of fault detection schemes against fault-based attacks on RSA and AES has been demonstrated in [8,31]. The modified RSA decryption algorithm based on the Montgomery ladder is described in [15,18]. New fault injection attacks and countermeasures appear in [10].

9.5   Exercises

1. Construct an RSA encryption scheme using $p = 61$ and $q = 53$. Select the public key $e = 17$, which is obviously relatively prime to $\phi(pq)$. Find the corresponding private key d, and for the message $M = 123$, calculate the ciphertext and show that the private key allows the decryption of the ciphertext.

2. Develop a software implementation of DES (or find one on the Internet) and apply the fault-based attack shown in Table 9-2. Modify the program to inject the faults, and write another program to find the secret key.

3. Complete the example (in the chapter) of injecting a fault into the private key d of an RSA decryption device that uses the public key $(e, N) = (7, 77)$ and

the private key $(d, N) = (43, 77)$. Assume a ciphertext of 37 as in the example. List all possible single-bit errors and all double-bit errors that can be injected into d. For each error on your list find the erroneous plaintext that the device will produce. Are all the erroneous plaintexts unique?

4. Develop a software implementation of RSA (or find one on the Internet), use the prime numbers $p = 7$ and $q = 11$ as in the example in this chapter and select $e = 7$. This yields the public key $(e, n) = (7, 77)$ and the private key $(d, n) = (43, 77)$. Inject single-bit failures in your program, and obtain all the bits of the private key.

5. Use the program and parameters from Problem 4 and add a residue check with the modulus 3. Repeat the single-bit fault attacks. Will the modified program detect all such faults?

6. Show that $x^8 \bmod g(x) = x^4 + x^3 + x + 1$ for the generator polynomial of AES $g(x) = x^8 + x^4 + x^3 + x + 1$.

7. Verify all 16 results of the MixColumns step that are shown in Figure 9.6f.

8. Inject a single-bit error in the state matrix shown in Figure 9.6c, replacing the first byte 19 by 18, and calculate the erroneous state matrix at the end of round 2. Compare your result to the matrix shown in Figure 9.6h. How many bytes are in error?

9. Suppose you are using AES with data blocks and key of size 128 bits. Your messages however are only 50-bit long. What would you put in the unused 78-bit positions?

10. Verify the correctness of the parity prediction equations for the MixColumns step in AES.

References

[1] R. Anderson and M. Kuhn, "Low Cost Attacks on Tamper Resistant Devices," *International Workshop on Security Protocols*, Lecture Notes in Computer Science, Vol. 1361, pp. 125–136, Springer-Verlag, 1997.

[2] C. Aumüller, P. Bier, W. Fischer, P. Hofreiter, and J.-P. Seifert, "Fault Attacks on RSA with CRT: Concrete Results and Practical Countermeasures," *Cryptology ePrint Archive*, Report 2002/073, 2002. Available at: http://eprint.iacr.org/2002/073.

[3] H. Bar-El, H. Choukri, D. Naccache, M. Tunstall, and C. Whelan, "The Sorcerer's Apprentice Guide to Fault Attacks," *Proceedings of the IEEE*, Vol. 94, Issue 2, pp. 370–382, February 2006. Also in the *Cryptology ePrint Archive*, Report 2004/100, 2004. Available at: http://eprint.iacr.org/2004/100.

[4] G. Bertoni, L. Breveglieri, I. Koren, P. Maistri, and V. Piuri, "Error Analysis and Detection Procedures for a Hardware Implementation of the Advanced Encryption Standard," *IEEE Transactions on Computers*, Vol. 52, pp. 492–505, April 2003.

[5] G. Bertoni, L. Breveglieri, I. Koren, P. Maistri, and V. Piuri, "Concurrent Fault Detection in a Hardware Implementation of the *RC5* Encryption Algorithm," *IEEE International Conference on Application-Specific Systems, Architectures and Processors*, pp. 410–419, 2003.

[6] G. Bertoni, L. Breveglieri, I. Koren, and P. Maistri, "An Efficient Hardware-Based Fault Diagnosis Scheme for AES: Performances and Cost," *IEEE International Symposium on Defect and Fault Tolerance in VLSI Systems,* pp. 130–138, October 2004.

[7] E. Biham and A. Shamir, "Differential Fault Analysis of Secret Key Cryptosystems," *17th Cryptology Conference, Crypto 97, Lecture Notes in Computer Science*, Vol. 1294, pp. 513–525, Springer-Verlag, 1997.

[8] J. Blöemer and J.-P. Seifert, "Fault Based Cryptanalysis of the Advanced Encryption Standard (AES)," *Financial Cryptography, Lecture Notes in Computer Science*, Vol. 2742, pp. 162–181, Springer-Verlag, 2003. Available at: http://eprint.iacr.org/2002/075.

[9] D. Boneh, R. DeMillo, and R. Lipton, "On the Importance of Eliminating Errors in Cryptographic Computations," *Journal of Cryptology*, Vol. 14, pp. 101–119, 2001.

[10] L. Breveglieri, I. Koren, D. Naccache, and J.-P. Seifert (Eds.), *Fault Diagnosis and Tolerance in Cryptography (FDTC), Lecture Notes in Computer Science*, Vol. 4236, Springer-Verlag, 2006.

[11] A. S. Butter, C. Y. Kao, and J. P. Kuruts, "DES Encryption and Decryption Unit with Error Checking," US patent US5432848, July 1995.

[12] M. Ciet and M. Joye, "Elliptic Curve Cryptosystems in the Presence of Permanent and Transient Faults," *Cryptology ePrint Archive,* Report 2003/028, 2003. Available at: http://eprint.iacr.org/2003/028.

[13] J. Daemen and V. Rijmen, *The Design of Rijndael: AES—The Advanced Encryption Standard,* Springer-Verlag, 2002.

[14] C. Giraud, "DFA on AES," *Cryptology ePrint Archive,* Report 2003/008, 2003. Available at: http://eprint.iacr.org/2003/008.

[15] C. Giraud, "Fault Resistant RSA Implementation," *Fault Diagnosis and Tolerance in Cryptography (FDTC'05),* pp. 143–151, 2005.

[16] C. Giraud and H. Thiebeauld, "Basics of Fault Attacks," *Fault Diagnosis and Tolerance in Cryptography (FDTC'04)—Supplemental Volume of the Dependable Systems and Networks Conference,* pp. 343–347, 2004.

[17] International Association for Cryptologic Research. Available at: http://www.iacr.org/. ePrint Archive, available at: http://eprint.iacr.org.

[18] M. Joye and S.-M. Yen, "The Montgomery Powering Ladder," Cryptographic Hardware and Embedded Systems—CHES 2002, *Lecture Notes in Computer Science*, Vol. 2523, pp. 291–302, Springer-Verlag, 2002.

[19] R. Karri, K. Wu, P. Mishra, and K. Yongkook, "Fault-Based Side-Channel Cryptanalysis Tolerant Rijndael Symmetric Block Cipher Architecture," *IEEE Symposium on Defect and Fault Tolerance in VLSI Systems*, pp. 427–435, 2001.

[20] R. Karri, G. Kuznetsov, and M. Goessel, "Parity-based Concurrent Error Detection in Symmetric Block Ciphers," *International Test Conference 2003—ITC 2003*, Vol. 1, ISSN 1089-3539, pp. 919–926, 2003.

[21] M. G. Karpovsky and A. Taubin, "A New Class of Nonlinear Systematic Error Detecting Codes," *IEEE Transactions on Information Theory*, Vol. 50, pp. 1818–1820, 2004.

[22] I. Koren, Fault Tolerant Computing Simulator. Available at: http://www.ecs.umass.edu/ece/koren/fault-tolerance/simulator/.

[23] K. J. Kulikowski, M. G. Karpovsky, and A. Taubin, "Fault Attack Resistant Cryptographic Hardware with Error Detection," *Fault Diagnosis and Tolerance in Cryptography (FDTC'06), Lecture Notes in Computer Science*, Vol. 4236, pp. 185–195, Springer-Verlag, 2006.

[24] National Institute of Standards and Technology, "Data Encryption Standard," *FIPS Publication No. 46*, January, 1977.

[25] National Institute of Standards and Technology, "Advanced Encryption Standard," *FIPS publication No. 197*, November 2001. Available at: http://csrc.nist.gov/publications/fips/fips197/fips-197.pdf.

[26] G. Piret and J.-J. Quisquater, "A Differential Fault Attack Technique against SPN Structures, with Application to the AES and Khazad," Cryptographic Hardware and Embedded Systems—CHES 2003, *Lecture Notes in Computer Science*, Vol. 2779, pp. 77–88, Springer-Verlag, 2003.

[27] R. L. Rivest, A. Shamir, and L. Adleman, "A Method for Obtaining Digital Signatures and Public-key Cryptosystems," *Communications of the ACM*, Vol. 21, pp. 120–126, 1978.

[28] A. Shamir, "Method and Apparatus for Protecting Public Key Schemes from Timing and Fault Attacks," US Patent 5991415, 1999.

[29] E. Styer, AES calculator, available at: http://www.cs.eku.edu/faculty/styer/460/Encrypt/JS-AES.html; DES calculator, available at: http://www.cs.eku.edu/faculty/styer/460/Encrypt/JS-DES.html; RSA demonstrator, available at: http://wwwr.cs.eku.edu/faculty/styer/460/Encrypt/RSAdemo.html.

[30] *Wikipedia, The Free Encyclopedia*. Available at: http://en.wikipedia.org/wiki/Cryptography.

[31] S.-M. Yen and M. Joye, "Checking Before Output May Not Be Enough Against Fault-Based Cryptanalysis," *IEEE Transactions on Computers*, Vol. 49, pp. 967–970, September 2000.

[32] S.-M. Yen, S. Moon, and J.-C. Ha, "Permanent Fault Attack on the Parameters of RSA with CRT," *Lecture Notes in Computer Science*, Vol. 2727, pp. 285–296, Springer-Verlag, 2003.

Simulation Techniques

This chapter introduces the reader to statistical simulation approaches for evaluating the reliability and associated attributes of fault-tolerant computer systems.

Simulation is frequently used when analytical approaches are either not feasible or not sufficiently accurate. Simulation, in general, has a deep theoretical foundation in statistics that can take years to master, and to which many books have been devoted. However, learning to write a basic simulation program and to use the fundamental statistical tools for analyzing the output data is much easier. These basic techniques are what we concentrate on in this chapter. Having said that, this chapter is meant primarily for readers with a reasonably strong understanding of probability theory.

We start by explaining how to write a simulation program. We then show how the output can be analyzed to deduce the system attributes. We then consider ways in which the results can be made more accurate by reducing the variance of the simulation output. We end the chapter by considering a different kind of simulation—fault injection, which is an experimental technique to characterize a system's response to faults.

10.1 Writing a Simulation Program

When faced with the need to construct a simulation model, one has three options:

- Write a program in a high-level general programming language, such as C, Java, or C++.

- Use a special-purpose simulation language such as SIMSCRIPT, GPSS, or SIMAN.

■ Use or modify an available simulation package that has been designed to simulate such systems. Examples include SimpleScalar for computer architectures and OPNET for network simulation.

In this section, we will focus on the first option. Readers wishing to follow one of the other approaches should consult the user's manual of the chosen language or package.

The most common form of simulation programs is a *discrete-event* simulation in which the events of interest (changes in the state variables) occur at discrete instants of time. Most events of interest in fault-tolerant computing such as the arrival of jobs at a computer system, error occurrence, the failure of a processor, and its recovery or replacement, are discrete events. By contrast, the flow of water out of a leaky bucket is an example of a continuous-event system: the state variable (water level) is a continuous function of time at the macro level. Of course, if one were to consider it at an atomic level, this would become a discrete-event system as the molecules of water leak one by one out of the bucket. This is an example of a situation in which what is continuous at one level of granularity turns out to be discrete at a finer level.

Let us illustrate the simulation process by an example, after which we will extract some general principles of the approach.

■ EXAMPLE

Suppose we wish to simulate the mean time to data loss (MTTDL) of a RAID Level 1 disk system. This system is so simple that good analytical models exist for its analysis and we do not really need a simulation model to obtain the MTTDLs. Still, this will be a good warm-up exercise in writing simulation programs. Also, the simulation can be used when the analytical model breaks down due to its limiting assumptions that do not always apply in practice (e.g., when the failures deviate significantly from a Poisson process).

RAID Level 1 systems have been covered in Chapter 2: recall that the system consists of two mirrored disks, and that data loss occurs when the second disk fails before the first failed disk has been repaired.

We start by identifying the events of interest to us: these are the *failures* and *repair actions*. Suppose failures occur as a Poisson process with rate λ, and repair time is a random variable R with density function $f_R(\cdot)$. Assuming that the parameters of the failure process and repair time distributions are known to us, we can generate failure and repair times using a random number generator, as described later in Section 10.4. We show in Section 10.2 how the input parameters can be estimated if they are not given to us.

The key data structure in the simulation is a linked list called the *event chain*, which holds the scheduled events (in this case, disk failure and repair instants) in temporal (meaning time) order. We also define a variable called the *clock*, which keeps the current simulated time and has an initial value of 0.

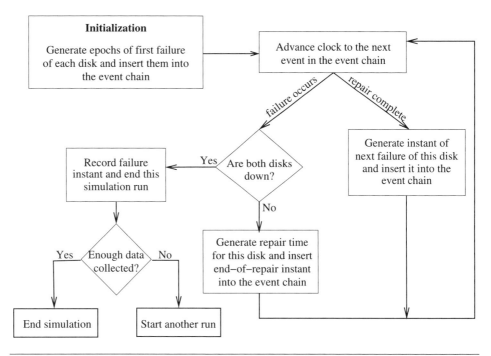

FIGURE 10.1   Simulation of a RAID Level 1 system.

The simulation consists of advancing the clock from one event to the next, recording statistics as we go. The flowchart for the simulation is shown in Figure 10.1. One point of detail is worth mentioning. Since the granularity of the time being measured is not infinitely fine (owing to the finite word length of the computer), it is possible—although highly improbable—that we will have two events: a disk failure and a repair completion (of the other disk) scheduled for the same instant in the event chain. In this case, we must decide in which order the events will be inserted in the event chain. For example, we may decide that the failure event goes in first and the repair completion next. Let us illustrate the operation of the algorithm in Figure 10.1. We begin by generating first-failure epochs for the two disks: suppose they happen at times 28 and 95, respectively. At time 0, the system state is (Up, Up), representing the condition of the two disks. The event chain now is

$$(28, d1, F) \leftrightarrow (95, d2, F)$$

where the three elements in the 3-tuple indicate the epoch of the event, the disk in question ($d1$ or $d2$), and the event (F for failure and R for repair completion). The clock is now advanced to the next event in the event chain which occurs at time 28. The event is the failure of the first disk, and the system state now is $(Down, Up)$. Generate a repair time for this disk: suppose the length of the generated repair time is 10, and the disk will be up again at time 38. Remove the event that we just processed from the event chain, and insert the repair event into the event chain:

$$(38, d1, R) \leftrightarrow (95, d2, F)$$

Advance to the next event in the chain, at time 38. At this point, the first disk is back up, so the state of the system is (*Up, Up*). Generate the next failure time of this disk: suppose this failure is 68 units into the future, which means that the failure will happen at time $38 + 68 = 106$. The event chain is now

$$(95, d2, F) \leftrightarrow (106, d1, F)$$

Advance to the next event at time 95. The system state now is (*Up, Down*). Generate the repair time of this disk: suppose it is 14, so that this disk will come up at time $95 + 14 = 109$. The event chain is now

$$(106, d1, F) \leftrightarrow (109, d2, R)$$

Advance to the next event, at time 106. The system state is now (*Down, Down*), representing data loss. For this simulation run, time to data loss (TTDL) is 106, and a new simulation run can begin. After all the runs are completed, the MTTDL of the system is estimated by calculating the average of the TTDLs of all the runs. If desired, a confidence interval for the MTTDL can be constructed as shown later in Section 10.2.5. ■

More complex simulations require more work, but the principle is the same. We create an event chain that is ordered temporally and advance from one event to the next, recording statistics appropriately. One has to be extremely careful to ensure that all events are captured in the event chain and that the simulation does not skip over any of them.

The following are the key steps to follow when writing a simulation program:

- Thoroughly understand the system being simulated. Not doing so can result in a wrong system being modeled.

- List the events of interest.

- Determine the dependencies between events, if any.

- Understand the state transitions.

- Correctly estimate the distributions of the various input random variables.

- Identify the statistics to be gathered.

- Correctly analyze the output statistics to extract the required system attributes.

10.2 Parameter Estimation

To run a simulation program, the values of certain input parameters are needed, such as failure and repair rates. In addition, we need a way of analyzing the simulation output and extracting parameters such as reliability and mean time to system failure. In this section we will see how such parameter values can be estimated. We will distinguish between point estimation and interval estimation, describe three methods by which to obtain point estimates of parameter values, and show how a confidence interval for the parameter can be constructed. Most of our discussion assumes that we know the underlying shape of the distribution that the data will follow and that this shape depends on one or more parameters whose exact value is unknown to us. For example, we may believe that processors fail according to a Poisson process, which we can characterize by estimating the rate, λ, of this process. In some cases, we will estimate parameters even without knowledge of the exact shape of the distribution, using approximating formulas (most notably, the Central Limit Theorem).

10.2.1 Point Versus Interval Estimation

Suppose we are given a random variable X with a known distribution function characterized by an unknown parameter θ. To estimate θ, we either sample or simulate n independent observations of X, denoted by $X_1, \ldots, X_n$, and use a suitable function $T(X_1, \ldots, X_n)$ as an estimator of θ. Since we will very likely not obtain the exact value of θ, we denote the estimate by $\hat{\theta}$. Note that $\hat{\theta}$ is a random variable and will have a different value if a different sample $X_1, \ldots, X_n$ is selected. In what follows, we denote the expectation of a random variable X by $E(X)$ and its variance by $\text{Var}(X)$. Recall that the standard deviation of X (commonly denoted by $\sigma(X)$) is the square root of the variance. We would like an estimator to be *unbiased*.

Definition. An estimator $\hat{\theta} = T(X_1, \ldots, X_n)$ is called an *unbiased estimator* of a parameter θ if $E(\hat{\theta}) = E(T(X_1, \ldots, X_n)) = \theta$.

Even if the estimator is unbiased, the likelihood that our point estimate is exactly equal to the real parameter is practically zero, although the difference between them is likely to diminish as n increases. We can characterize the confidence in our estimate by calculating an interval in which the parameter is expected to lie. This is *interval estimation*, and the resulting interval is called a *confidence interval*. The wider the interval, the greater is the likelihood that it includes the actual parameter but the less informative it is. The next three sections discuss methods of obtaining point estimators, and Section 10.2.5 deals with constructing confidence intervals.

10.2.2 Method of Moments

Suppose we want to estimate the values of m parameters of the probability distribution of some random variable, X. We define the jth *distribution moment* as $E(X^j)$ $(j = 1, 2, \ldots)$. We then sample or simulate n independent observations of X, namely, $X_1, \ldots, X_n$, and define the jth *sample moment*, M_j, as

$$M_j = \frac{\sum_{i=1}^{n} X_i^j}{n}$$

We now equate the first m distribution moments with the first m sample moments:

$$\hat{E}(X^j) = M_j \quad (j = 1, \ldots, m)$$

The left-hand sides include the m parameters as unknowns, and so we have m equations, the solution of which yields estimators of these parameters.

Let us consider some examples.

■ E X A M P L E

Suppose we believe that the running time, X, of a task has a normal distribution with two parameters μ and σ^2 whose values we do not know. We execute the task n times and record the running times $X_1, \ldots, X_n$. Since $\mu = E(X)$ and $\sigma^2 = \text{var}(X) = E(X - \mu)^2 = E(X^2) - (E(X))^2$, we can use the Method of Moments to write the two equations for our estimates, $\hat{\mu}$ and $\hat{\sigma}^2$, of the mean and variance, respectively:

$$\hat{\mu} = \bar{X} = \frac{X_1 + X_2 + \cdots + X_n}{n}$$

and

$$\hat{\sigma}^2 = \frac{\sum_{i=1}^{n} X_i^2}{n} - \hat{\mu}^2 = \frac{\sum_{i=1}^{n} X_i^2}{n} - \bar{X}^2 = \frac{\sum_{i=1}^{n} (X_i - \bar{X})^2}{n}$$

Although $\bar{X}$ is an unbiased estimate of μ, $\hat{\sigma}^2$ is not an unbiased estimate of σ^2. As shown in almost any basic book on statistics, a small correction will result in an unbiased estimator for σ^2:

$$\hat{\sigma}^2 = \frac{\sum_{i=1}^{n} (X_i - \bar{X})^2}{n - 1} \tag{10.1}$$

When n is large (as it is in most engineering experiments), there is no significant numerical difference between dividing by n or by $n - 1$. ■

■ E X A M P L E

Suppose we know that the lifetime, X, of a processor is exponentially distributed, but do not know the value of the parameter, λ, of that distribution. The density function for the processor lifetime is

$$f(x) = \lambda e^{-\lambda x}, \quad x \geq 0$$

We have one unknown and therefore need just one equation. We start with n processors and run them until they all fail. Let X_i be the lifetime of processor i. Then, our estimate of the first moment of the processor lifetime (its mean value) is the sample average $\bar{X}$. Since $E(X) = 1/\lambda$, we end up with the equation

$$\frac{1}{\hat{\lambda}} = \bar{X}$$

and therefore,

$$\hat{\lambda} = \frac{1}{\bar{X}}$$

Although $\bar{X}$ is an unbiased estimator of $1/\lambda$, $1/\bar{X}$ is *not* an unbiased estimator of λ. Still, it is often a good estimate. ■

■ E X A M P L E

Suppose, instead, that X follows a Weibull distribution. Recall that X has the density function

$$f(x) = \lambda \beta x^{\beta-1} e^{-\lambda x^{\beta}} \quad (x \geq 0) \tag{10.2}$$

The two parameters of this distribution are λ and β, so we need two equations to solve for these two unknowns. We obtain these equations by writing out expressions for the first two moments: $E(X)$ and $E(X^2)$:

$$E(X) = \lambda^{-1}\Gamma(1 + 1/\beta)$$
$$E(X^2) = \lambda^{-2}\Gamma(1 + 2/\beta)$$

where $\Gamma(y) = \int_0^\infty e^{-u} u^{y-1}\, du$ is the Gamma function (see Section 2.2). We can therefore write

$$\hat{\lambda}^{-1}\Gamma(1 + 1/\hat{\beta}) = \bar{X}$$

$$\hat{\lambda}^{-2}\Gamma(1 + 2/\hat{\beta}) = \frac{\sum_{i=1}^n X_i^2}{n}$$

We have two equations in the two unknowns λ and β, which we can solve to obtain the estimates $\hat{\lambda}$ and $\hat{\beta}$. ∎

The method of moments is a fairly simple approach which often works reasonably well, although, as we have seen, it does not always result in unbiased estimators. Still, we can generalize and say that the sample average $\bar{X}$ is always used as an estimate for the expected value $E(X)$.

10.2.3 Method of Maximum Likelihood

The maximum likelihood method determines parameter values for which the *given observations* would have the highest probability. Given a set of observations, we set up a *likelihood function*, which expresses how likely it is that we obtain the observed values of the random variable, as a function of the parameter values. We then find those values of the parameters for which this function is maximized.

■ EXAMPLE

We believe that the intervals between failures of a certain system are exponentially distributed, with parameter λ. Further, these intervals are independent of one another. From experimental observation of the system we obtain the following five values for the interfailure intervals: $10, 5, 11, 12, 15$.

The joint density function of these five observations is the product of the individual observations, since these were made independently of one another. This joint density, conditioned on the parameter being λ, is the likelihood function, $L(\lambda)$:

$$L(\lambda) = \lambda e^{-10\lambda} \cdot \lambda e^{-5\lambda} \cdot \lambda e^{-11\lambda} \cdot \lambda e^{-12\lambda} \cdot \lambda e^{-15\lambda} = \lambda^5 e^{-53\lambda}$$

We now seek that value of λ which will maximize $L(\lambda)$. We can do this using basic calculus:

$$\frac{dL(\lambda)}{d\lambda} = \left(5\lambda^4 - 53\lambda^5\right)e^{-53\lambda} = 0$$

Solving for λ yields $\lambda = 0, 5/53$.

Clearly, $\lambda = 0$ is a minimum while $\lambda = 5/53$ is a maximum. Hence, our estimate of λ based on this set of observations is $\hat{\lambda} = 5/53$. (Note that this is equal to the Method of Moments estimate for the same parameter, which is $\hat{\lambda} = 1/\bar{X} = 1/(53/5) = 5/53$.) ∎

■ EXAMPLE

Suppose now that we believe that the interfailure times are distributed according to the Weibull distribution, which has the probability density function shown in Equation 10.2, and we have to estimate the two parameters λ and β, using the same five observations as in the previous example.
The likelihood function is now given by

$$L(\lambda, \beta) = f(10) \cdot f(5) \cdot f(11) \cdot f(12) \cdot f(15)$$

$$= \lambda^5 \beta^5 10^{\beta-1} 5^{\beta-1} 11^{\beta-1} 12^{\beta-1} 15^{\beta-1} e^{-\lambda(10^\beta + 5^\beta + 11^\beta + 12^\beta + 15^\beta)}$$

When attempting to maximize a function like this, it is easier to proceed by maximizing $\ln L(\lambda, \beta)$ rather than $L(\lambda, \beta)$ itself. Since $\ln(x)$ is a monotonically increasing function of x, this will lead to the same values for $\hat{\lambda}, \hat{\beta}$. Now,

$$\ln L(\lambda, \beta) = 5 \ln \lambda + 5 \ln \beta + (\beta - 1)(\ln 99000) - \lambda(10^\beta + 5^\beta + 11^\beta + 12^\beta + 15^\beta)$$

$$= 5 \ln \lambda + 5 \ln \beta + 11.5(\beta - 1) - \lambda(10^\beta + 5^\beta + 11^\beta + 12^\beta + 15^\beta)$$

To find $\hat{\lambda}, \hat{\beta}$, we differentiate the log-likelihood with respect to λ and β and equate the derivatives to zero:

$$\frac{\partial \ln L(\lambda, \beta)}{\partial \lambda} = 0$$

$$\frac{\partial \ln L(\lambda, \beta)}{\partial \beta} = 0$$

This yields the equations

$$5\lambda^{-1} = 10^\beta + 5^\beta + 11^\beta + 12^\beta + 15^\beta$$

$$5\beta^{-1} + 11.5 = \lambda(10^\beta \ln(10) + 5^\beta \ln(5) + 11^\beta \ln(11) + 12^\beta \ln(12) + 15^\beta \ln(15))$$

These equations can now be solved to obtain the values of $\hat{\lambda}$ and $\hat{\beta}$. ■

We now turn to the issue of experiments which are concluded before they are truly complete. For instance, suppose we are conducting experiments to obtain processor lifetime data. We may have a certain time-limit to our experiment: at that point, we terminate data collection even if not all the processors under test have failed yet. When using such experiments to estimate parameter values, we have to take into account the premature termination of the experiment. We do this by multiplying the joint density of the completed observations by the probability that the non-failed units have lifetimes exceeding the experimental time-limit.

■ E X A M P L E

We carry out experiments to estimate the lifetime of a processor. We believe that the processor lifetime (measured in hours) follows an exponential distribution, with parameter μ whose value we are seeking to estimate. The density function for the processor lifetime is

$$f(x) = \mu e^{-\mu x}, \quad x \geqslant 0$$

and the cumulative probability distribution function is

$$F(x) = 1 - e^{-\mu x}$$

We start with a total of 10 processors and impose a time limit of 1000 hours on our experiment. That is, our experiment will end when 1000 hours have elapsed or all the processors have failed (whichever occurs sooner).

Suppose our observations are that four failures occurred before the experiment is terminated, at times 700, 800, 900, 950 hours. The remaining six processors have lifetimes exceeding 1000 hours.

The likelihood function for the whole sample is given by

$$L(\mu) = f(700)f(800)f(900)f(950)\big(1 - F(1000)\big)^6$$
$$= \mu^4 e^{-\mu(700+800+900+950)} e^{-6000\mu}$$
$$= \mu^4 e^{-9350\mu}$$

We find $\hat{\mu}$ that maximizes the likelihood function by getting the derivative of L and equating it to zero,

$$\frac{dL(\mu)}{d\mu} = \big(4\mu^3 - 9350\mu^4\big)e^{-9350\mu} = 0$$

which results in $\mu = 0; \ 4.3 \times 10^{-4}$.

The maximum likelihood estimate is therefore $\hat{\mu} = 4.3 \times 10^{-4}$. ■

If we terminate the experiment prematurely, we lose information and the quality of the estimate is likely to suffer. This is shown in the following example.

EXAMPLE

Consider again the previous example, except that we decide to set the time-limit of our experiment at some relatively small T, say $T = 500$ hours. Based on the measurements in the previous example, no failures will have occurred over this interval. Applying the maximum likelihood method, we seek the value of μ which maximizes

$$L(\mu) = \left(1 - F(T)\right)^{10} = \left(e^{-\mu T}\right)^{10} = e^{-10\mu T}$$

The maximum likelihood estimate resulting from our experiment is $\hat{\mu} = 0$, which translates to a prediction that the processor lifetimes are infinite. This result is, of course, ludicrous; however, it is the best that we can extract from the maximum likelihood approach and the observation that no failures have occurred. ∎

The maximum likelihood approach can also be used when the data are not observed exactly but are only known to lie in some interval. Once again, this is probably best explained through an example.

EXAMPLE

Similarly to the previous examples, we have 10 processors whose lifetime of X days is exponentially distributed with an unknown parameter μ. The units operate in some remote location, and we can only check on their status at 11 AM every day. We observe the first failure on the 50th day, the second on the 120th day, and the third on the 200th day, at which point the experiment concludes.

When we observe a failure at 11 AM on day i, it means that the lifetime of the processor was greater than $i - 1$ days but less than i days. The probability of such a failure is therefore equal to

$$q_i = F(i) - F(i - 1) = e^{-(i-1)\mu} - e^{-i\mu}$$

The likelihood function associated with our observations is then given by

$$L(\mu) = q_{50} q_{120} q_{200} \left(e^{-200\mu}\right)^7$$

We can now find the value of μ which maximizes this likelihood function. ∎

The greater these sampling intervals, the worse is likely to be our estimate. Indeed, if the time-intervals are too coarse, the maximal likelihood method will make ridiculous predictions. Consider the following modification to our previous example.

■ EXAMPLE

Consider a situation in which the processors are checked every T days, for some large T (say $T = 300$). Suppose we find, on the very first check, that all 10 processors have failed: this means that all 10 have had lifetimes less than T days.
The likelihood function associated with this observation is

$$L(\mu) = \left(F(T)\right)^{10} = \left(1 - e^{-\mu T}\right)^{10}$$

The value of μ that maximizes this function is $\hat{\mu} = \infty$; our estimate is thus that the average processor lifetime is zero! What this means is that T was set so high that we were not able to obtain much information from checking after T days. ■

10.2.4 The Bayesian Approach to Parameter Estimation

The Bayesian approach relies on Bayes's formula for reversing conditional probability, and it works as follows. We start with some *prior* knowledge of the parameter we are estimating, expressed through a probability or density function of the parameter values. We then collect experimental or observational data of the random variable, and construct a *posterior* probability or density of the parameter based on both our prior knowledge and the observations. The parameter estimate is the expected value of this posterior probability.

■ EXAMPLE

We believe that a processor fails according to a Poisson process with rate λ, which is the parameter we wish to estimate. Suppose we know that λ is somewhere in the range $[10^{-4}, 2 \times 10^{-4}]$, and we express this knowledge by considering λ to be a random variable uniformly distributed over that range. Thus,

$$f_{\text{prior}}(\lambda) = \begin{cases} 10^4 & \text{if } 10^{-4} \leqslant \lambda \leqslant 2 \times 10^{-4} \\ 0 & \text{otherwise} \end{cases}$$

The current estimate for λ is its expected value, $\hat{\lambda} = 1.5 \times 10^{-4}$.
Suppose now that we run the processor for τ hours without observing a failure. The posterior density of λ, which incorporates the information gleaned from this experiment is as follows:

$$f_{\text{posterior}}(\lambda) = f_{\text{prior}}(\lambda | \text{lifetime} \geqslant \tau)$$

$$= \frac{\text{Prob}\{\text{Lifetime} \geqslant \tau | \text{Failure rate} = \lambda\}\, f_{\text{prior}}(\lambda)}{\int_{\ell=10^{-4}}^{2\times 10^{-4}} \text{Prob}\{\text{Lifetime} \geqslant \tau | \text{Failure rate} = \ell\}\, f_{\text{prior}}(\ell)\, d\ell}$$

$$= \frac{e^{-\lambda\tau}\, f_{\text{prior}}(\lambda)}{\int_{\ell=10^{-4}}^{2\times 10^{-4}} e^{-\ell\tau}\, f_{\text{prior}}(\ell)\, d\ell}$$

$$= \begin{cases} \dfrac{10^4 e^{-\lambda\tau}}{10^4 \int_{\ell=10^{-4}}^{2\times 10^{-4}} e^{-\ell\tau}\, d\ell} & \text{if } \lambda \in [10^{-4}, 2\times 10^{-4}] \\ 0 & \text{otherwise} \end{cases}$$

$$= \begin{cases} \dfrac{\tau e^{-\lambda\tau}}{e^{-0.0001\tau} - e^{-0.0002\tau}} & \text{if } 10^{-4} \leqslant \lambda \leqslant 2\times 10^{-4} \\ 0 & \text{otherwise} \end{cases}$$

The estimate of λ is now given by the expected value of this new density

$$\hat{\lambda} = \int_{\lambda=10^{-4}}^{2\times 10^{-4}} \lambda\, f_{\text{posterior}}(\lambda)\, d\lambda = \frac{(1 + 0.0001\tau)e^{-0.0001\tau} - (1 + 0.0002\tau)e^{-0.0002\tau}}{\tau(e^{-0.0001\tau} - e^{-0.0002\tau})}$$

Figure 10.2 plots the estimate of λ based on observed values of τ. Note that as τ increases, λ tends to the lower bound of the $[0.0001, 0.0002]$ interval; it can never go outside this interval, however. ■

The Bayesian approach is controversial because it depends on the existence of prior information about the parameter being estimated. In some cases, this information may not be difficult to derive. For instance, if we are asked to evaluate an unknown coin, we can assume that the probability of getting a "head" is uniformly distributed over the entire possible range of $[0, 1]$. In other cases, it may not be possible to express prior information with any confidence.

Note also that if the prior density is zero over any given parameter inter val, it will remain zero for that interval no matter what the experimental results are. In our earlier example, we started with a prior density that was zero outside the interval $[10^{-4}, 2 \times 10^{-4}]$. Since the posterior densities are constructed by multiplying this prior density by some additional terms, all posterior densities will also be zero outside this interval only. When the prior density is zero over some interval I, it means that we already *know* that the parameter cannot fall in that interval. Since this knowledge is assumed to be correct, no amount of posterior information can result in the probability of falling in I being anything but zero.

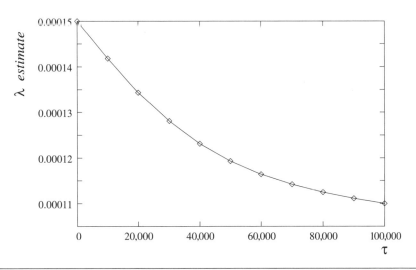

FIGURE 10.2   Estimate of λ based on observed τ.

10.2.5 Confidence Intervals

A *confidence interval* with *confidence level* $1 - \alpha$ for an unknown parameter θ is an interval $[a, b]$ calculated as a function of a sample of size n, $X_1, \ldots, X_n$, in such a way that if we calculate similar intervals based on a large number of samples of size n, a fraction $1 - \alpha$ out of these intervals will actually include the real parameter θ. $1 - \alpha$ is usually selected to be 0.95 or 0.99, also expressed as 95% or 99%.

The most common use of confidence intervals in engineering applications is that of calculating a confidence interval for the expectation, μ, of some random variable, and this is discussed next. Our treatment rests on a fundamental result of probability theory: the Central Limit Theorem. We state it here without proof.

Central Limit Theorem. *Suppose $X_1, X_2, \ldots, X_n$ are independent and identically distributed random variables with mean μ and standard deviation σ. Consider the average of these variables, $\bar{X} = \frac{X_1 + X_2 + \cdots + X_n}{n}$. In the limit, as $n \to \infty$, $\bar{X}$ approaches the normal distribution, with mean μ and standard deviation $\sigma / \sqrt{n}$: this means that for a large n*

$$F_{\bar{X}}(x) = \text{Prob}\{\bar{X} \leqslant x\} \approx \frac{1}{\sqrt{2\pi}\,\sigma / \sqrt{n}} \int_{-\infty}^{x} e^{-\frac{1}{2}\left(\frac{y - \mu}{\sigma / \sqrt{n}}\right)^2} \, dy$$

Stated slightly differently, for a large sample size n

$$\text{Prob}\left\{\frac{\bar{X}-\mu}{\sigma/\sqrt{n}} \leqslant z\right\} \approx \Phi(z) \tag{10.3}$$

where

$$\Phi(z) = \frac{1}{\sqrt{2\pi}}\int_{-\infty}^{z} e^{-y^2/2}\,dy$$

is the probability distribution function of a standard normal random variable (with mean 0 and standard deviation 1). We should stress that this is an approximate result; it gets more exact as $n \to \infty$.

Let us now define Z_p to be the number for which $\Phi(Z_p) = p$. Then, we have from Expression 10.3 that, in the limit as $n \to \infty$,

$$\text{Prob}\left\{\frac{\bar{X}-\mu}{\sigma/\sqrt{n}} \leqslant Z_{1-\frac{\alpha}{2}}\right\} = 1 - \frac{\alpha}{2}$$

and

$$\text{Prob}\left\{\frac{\bar{X}-\mu}{\sigma/\sqrt{n}} > Z_{1-\frac{\alpha}{2}}\right\} = 1 - \left(1-\frac{\alpha}{2}\right) = \frac{\alpha}{2}$$

Since $\Phi(z)$ is symmetric about $z = 0$,

$$\text{Prob}\left\{\frac{\bar{X}-\mu}{\sigma/\sqrt{n}} \leqslant -Z_{1-\frac{\alpha}{2}}\right\} = \frac{\alpha}{2}$$

and therefore,

$$\text{Prob}\left\{-Z_{1-\frac{\alpha}{2}} \leqslant \frac{\bar{X}-\mu}{\sigma/\sqrt{n}} \leqslant Z_{1-\frac{\alpha}{2}}\right\} = 1 - \alpha$$

or stated differently,

$$\text{Prob}\left\{\bar{X} - \frac{\sigma}{\sqrt{n}}Z_{1-\frac{\alpha}{2}} \leqslant \mu \leqslant \bar{X} + \frac{\sigma}{\sqrt{n}}Z_{1-\frac{\alpha}{2}}\right\} = 1 - \alpha \tag{10.4}$$

The interval

$$[a,b] = \left[\bar{X} - \frac{\sigma}{\sqrt{n}}Z_{1-\frac{\alpha}{2}}, \bar{X} + \frac{\sigma}{\sqrt{n}}Z_{1-\frac{\alpha}{2}}\right] \tag{10.5}$$

is called a $1-\alpha$ confidence interval. $1-\alpha$ is called the *confidence level* of the interval. So long as the experiment has not yet been conducted and $\bar{X}$ remains a random variable, there is a probability of $1-\alpha$ that the true mean, μ, will be included in the interval. Once we have calculated $\bar{X}$ (based on simulation or experimentation), it is no longer a random variable; it is a fixed number. Since μ is also a fixed number, it is either inside or outside the calculated confidence interval. The level of confidence $1 - \alpha$ is therefore not the probability that the true mean lies within the calculated interval; it is rather the confidence we have in the method of calculation that was used to generate the interval—it is successful in $1 - \alpha$ of the cases. This is a subtle technical point, which does not affect how we use confidence intervals.

■ **EXAMPLE**

Suppose we wish to estimate the mean lifetime (in months), μ, of a device, by constructing for it a 95% confidence interval. In a sample of $n = 50$ such devices, we obtained an average lifetime of $\bar{X} = 37$ months, with a standard deviation of $\sigma = 5$ months. Looking up a table of the standard normal distribution, we find that $Z_{0.975} = 1.96$. Hence, the 95% confidence interval for μ is

$$[a,b] = \left[37 - 1.96 \cdot \frac{5}{\sqrt{50}} \ , \ 37 + 1.96 \cdot \frac{5}{\sqrt{50}} \right] = [35.61, \ 38.39]$$

We now say with a confidence of 95% that the expected lifetime of a device of the type analyzed is between 35.6 months and 38.4 months.   ■

■ **EXAMPLE**

Suppose the confidence interval obtained in the previous example is too wide for our requirements; we need a 95% interval that is not wider than 1 month. Since we have no control over σ and $Z_{1-\frac{\alpha}{2}}$, the only way to make the interval narrower is by increasing the sample size n. We require that

$$2 \cdot Z_{1-\frac{\alpha}{2}} \sigma / \sqrt{n} \leqslant 1$$

or

$$2 \cdot 1.96 \cdot 5 / \sqrt{n} \leqslant 1$$

which results in

$$n \geqslant (2 \cdot 1.96 \cdot 5)^2 = 384.16$$

We therefore need a sample of at least 385 devices in order to obtain the required accuracy in estimating μ.   ■

◼ EXAMPLE

A given system either fails during the day or it does not. We want to estimate the probability p that it does fail, using a 99% confidence interval. To estimate p based on n experiments or simulation runs (where each experiment represents one day), we define

$$X_i = \begin{cases} 1 & \text{if the system fails in experiment } i \\ 0 & \text{otherwise} \end{cases}$$

Since $E(X) = p$, our estimate of p is

$$\hat{p} = \bar{X} = \frac{\sum_{i=1}^{n} X_i}{n}$$

$\hat{p}$ is actually the fraction of days in the sample on which the system failed. To get a confidence interval for p, note that $\text{Var}(X) = p(1 - p)$ and $\sigma(X) = \sqrt{p(1 - p)}$. Relying once more on the Central Limit Theorem, and using $\hat{p}$ instead of the unknown p, we obtain the approximate confidence interval for p at confidence level $1 - \alpha$

$$[a, b] = \left[\hat{p} - Z_{1-\frac{\alpha}{2}} \sqrt{\frac{\hat{p}(1 - \hat{p})}{n}}, \ \hat{p} + Z_{1-\frac{\alpha}{2}} \sqrt{\frac{\hat{p}(1 - \hat{p})}{n}} \right]$$

Suppose we conducted $n = 200$ experiments out of which the system failed in 12 cases, resulting in $\hat{p} = 0.06$. From tables of the normal distribution we can determine that $Z_{0.995} = 2.57$. Our 99% confidence interval is therefore the interval

$$\left[0.06 - 2.57 \sqrt{\frac{0.06 \times 0.94}{200}}, \ 0.06 + 2.57 \sqrt{\frac{0.06 \times 0.94}{200}} \right] = [0.017, 0.103]$$

We can say with a confidence of 99% that the failure probability is somewhere between 1.7% and 10.3%.

The last interval has a width of 0.086 and is clearly not informative enough for most applications. To get a more accurate result we need to increase n. Say, for example, that we require the width of the confidence interval to be no larger than 0.002 (which implies that the estimate will be removed at most 0.1% from the real failure probability, with a confidence of 99%). What should the number of experiments (or simulation runs) be? Based on our "pilot study" we have $\hat{p} = 0.06$, and therefore

$$2 \times 2.57 \frac{\sqrt{0.06 \cdot 0.94}}{\sqrt{n}} \leqslant 0.002$$

which results in

$$n \geqslant \frac{4 \cdot 2.57^2 \cdot 0.06 \cdot 0.94}{0.002^2} = 3.7 \times 10^5$$

In most instances, it will be impractical to conduct so many experiments. ∎

The last example has highlighted a major problem in high-reliability systems: in most cases, we will need a substantial amount of data to validate statistically the high reliability of the system. Suppose we are trying to validate by experiment that the true failure probability, p, of a life-critical system is 10^{-8}. For such a low failure probability to be validated, we need a very high level of confidence indeed, say 99.999999% (or even higher), requiring a truly astronomical volume of data. We explore this matter further in the Exercises.

10.3   Variance Reduction Methods

As is evident from Equation 10.5, the length of a confidence interval is inversely proportional to $\sqrt{n}$, where n is the number of simulation runs or experiments, and proportional to the standard deviation of the random variable under study. Note that the standard deviation that is used in calculating the confidence interval is itself in practice an estimate obtained from the simulation data and may therefore vary slightly with n. The brute-force way to shrink the confidence interval of an estimate is obviously to increase n. However, in the interest of efficiency, we should also consider the option of somehow reducing the variance (and, consequently, the standard deviation) of the estimate. In this section, we consider several schemes for doing so.

The first two approaches rely on the following facts from elementary statistics:

$$E(X + Y) = E(X) + E(Y) \quad \text{and} \quad \text{Var}(X + Y) = \text{Var}(X) + \text{Var}(Y) + 2\,\text{Cov}(X, Y)$$

where $\text{Cov}(X, Y) = E([X - E(X)][Y - E(Y)])$ is called the covariance of X and Y.

10.3.1 Antithetic Variables

Suppose we run simulations to estimate some parameter (for example, Mean Time to Data Loss [MTDL] in a RAID system). In traditional simulation, we would run n independent simulations and use the results. If Z_1, Z_2 are the outputs from two independent runs, we can expect that

$$\text{Cov}(Z_1, Z_2) = 0$$

so that

$$\text{Var}\left(\frac{Z_1 + Z_2}{2}\right) = \frac{\text{Var}(Z_1) + \text{Var}(Z_2)}{4}$$

When the method of antithetic variables is used, we try to run simulations in pairs, coupled together in such a way that their results (any parameter that is estimated by the simulation, be it reliability, waiting time, etc.) are negatively correlated, and then treat $Y = (Z_1 + Z_2)/2$ as the output from this pair of runs. If the simulation pair produces the outputs Z_1, Z_2 such that $\text{Cov}(Z_1, Z_2) < 0$, the variance of Y will be *smaller* than it would be if the two runs were independent and not coupled.

A good way to couple pairs of simulation runs is to couple the random variables used by them. Suppose the output of the simulation is a monotonic function of the random variables and the first run of the pair uses uniform random variables $U_1, U_2, \ldots, U_n$, then the second run can use $1 - U_1, 1 - U_2, \ldots, 1 - U_n$. The corresponding random variables in the two sequences are negatively correlated: if U_i is large, $1 - U_i$ is small, and vice versa. This applies even when the distributions of the random variables used in the simulation are not uniform. We are assuming that in order to generate such random variables, we will ultimately need to call uniform random number generators (URNGs), described later in Section 10.4.1. We can apply the coupling on the output of these URNGs. For example, if we need to generate exponentially distributed random variables by using $X = -(1/\mu)\ln U$, the coupled simulations will generate U and then use $X_1 = -(1/\mu)\ln U$ and $X_2 = -(1/\mu)\ln(1 - U)$, respectively (see Section 10.4.3).

In particular, if we can write the simulation output as being a monotone function of the uniform random variables used, then it is possible to show that the simulation outputs will indeed be negatively correlated when the method of antithetic variables is used. Showing this is outside the scope of this book; see the Further Reading section for details on where to find the proof.

■ **EXAMPLE**

Consider a structure composed of k elements. Denote by S_i the state of component i: a functional component is denoted by $S_i = 1$, whereas if it is down we have $S_i = 0$. A *structure function* $\phi(S_1, S_2, \ldots, S_k)$ is an indicator function (assumes the values $0, 1$), which expresses the dependence of the functionality of the system on the functionality of its components: it is equal to 1 if the system is functional for $S_1, \ldots, S_k$ and to 0 if it is not.

For instance, if the system consists of k elements connected in series, we have

$$\phi(S_1, S_2, \ldots, S_k) = S_1 \times S_2 \times \cdots \times S_k$$

If it is a triplex system with a perfect voter and S_i denotes the state of the ith processor, then

$$\phi(S_1, S_2, S_3) = \begin{cases} 1 & \text{if } S_1 + S_2 + S_3 \geqslant 2 \\ 0 & \text{otherwise.} \end{cases}$$

Now suppose we want to simulate the reliability R, for some given length of time t, of a system with a very complex structure function that cannot easily be analyzed. Using traditional methods, we would run a simulation by generating random variables that would determine whether individual components were up or not, and then determine whether the overall system was functional during $[0, t]$. Using antithetic variables, we will run the simulations in pairs, with the random variables coupled as described above. If Y_i is the average of the values of the structure function from the two simulation runs in pair i, and we run a total of $2n$ simulations (or n pairs), then the estimated reliability of the system is

$$\hat{R} = \frac{Y_1 + Y_2 + \cdots + Y_n}{n}$$

Furthermore, the variance of the estimate is likely to be far lower than would be obtained if we ran $2n$ independent simulations.

It is important to note that the Y_is are independent of one another. That is, although each run consists of paired simulations, there is no coupling between one pair and another. This allows us to use traditional statistical analysis on the Y_is. ∎

By how much can we expect the variance of the estimate to drop? This depends on the covariance of the two outputs in each pair of runs. In the Exercises, you are invited to determine the usefulness of this approach in a variety of cases.

10.3.2 Using Control Variables

When simulating to estimate the mean value $E(X)$ of a random variable X, select some other random variable, Y, whose expectation is known or can be calculated precisely to be θ_Y. Consider the random variable

$$Z = X + k(Y - \theta_Y)$$

Z has the properties

$$E(Z) = E(X),$$

$$\text{Var}(Z) = \text{Var}(X) + k^2 \text{Var}(Y) + 2k \text{Cov}(X, Y)$$

Hence, if we can pick k suitably, we can exploit any correlation between X and Y to reduce the variance of the estimate of $E(Z)$ (note that $E(X) = E(Z)$), and then use simulation to estimate $E(Z)$ rather than $E(X)$. Because $\text{Var}(Z) \leqslant \text{Var}(X)$, this will result in a narrower confidence interval. Y is called the *control variable* or *control variate*.

It is easy to show that $\text{Var}(Z)$ is minimized when

$$k = -\frac{\text{Cov}(X, Y)}{\text{Var}(Y)}$$

For this value of k,

$$\text{Var}(Z) = \text{Var}(X) - \frac{(\text{Cov}(X, Y))^2}{\text{Var}(Y)}$$

If $\text{Cov}(X, Y)$ and $\text{Var}(Y)$ are not known in advance, we can estimate them by running n simulations (for some initial small n), generating X_i, Y_i for $i = 1, \ldots, n$ and using the following estimates:

$$\widehat{\text{Cov}}(X, Y) = \frac{\sum_{i=1}^{n}(X_i - \bar{X})(Y_i - \bar{Y})}{n - 1}$$

and

$$\widehat{\text{Var}}(Y) = \frac{\sum_{i=1}^{n}(Y_i - \bar{Y})^2}{n - 1}$$

where $\bar{X} = \frac{\sum_{i=1}^{n} X_i}{n}$ and $\bar{Y} = \frac{\sum_{i=1}^{n} Y_i}{n}$.

■ EXAMPLE

We are interested in estimating the reliability (at time t) of a complex system that uses processor redundancy without repair. We can use as control variable the number of processors that are up at that time. ■

10.3.3 Stratified Sampling

The method of stratified sampling is probably best introduced through an example.

■ EXAMPLE

A computer system runs daily from 9 AM to 5 PM and is available for repair only after 5 PM. We wish to simulate the system and estimate the probability, π, that the system survives through a randomly selected day. Because the failure rates of the processors are different on weekdays and on weekends due to different utilizations, the system has two different survival probabilities—π_1 on a weekday and π_2 on a weekend day.

The conventional way to do a simulation experiment is the following: for each run, first select the day at random (weekday with probability $p_1 = 5/7$, weekend with probability $p_2 = 2/7$), apply the appropriate failure rate for that type of day, and then simulate for the behavior of the system over that day. If it fails during run i, set $X_i = 0$; if it survives, set $X_i = 1$. Make n runs for a sufficiently large n and then estimate the survival probability as $\hat{\pi} = (X_1 + X_2 + \cdots + X_n)/n$.

A better approach, which uses the method of stratified sampling, is to carry out two sets of runs. Set 1 consists of n_1 runs in which the system is simulated under weekday conditions (with the failure rates set appropriately), and set 2 consists of n_2 runs (where $n_1 + n_2 = n$) with the failures rates set according to weekend conditions. Then, if the survival probability estimated from set i is $\hat{\pi}_i$ ($i = 1, 2$), the overall survival probability is estimated as

$$\hat{\pi} = (5/7)\hat{\pi}_1 + (2/7)\hat{\pi}_2$$

Denoting

$$V_1 = \text{Var}(X|\text{Weekday}) = \pi_1(1 - \pi_1)$$

and

$$V_2 = \text{Var}(X|\text{Weekend}) = \pi_2(1 - \pi_2)$$

we obtain

$$\text{Var}(\hat{\pi}) = \frac{(5/7)^2 V_1}{n_1} + \frac{(2/7)^2 V_2}{n_2}$$

We claim that this second approach can be expected to yield estimates with a smaller variance if n_1 and n_2 are chosen appropriately. There are two ways of choosing n_1 and n_2:

- The most straightforward way is to set $n_i = np_i$.

- A better approach is to use a pilot simulation to obtain a rough estimate of V_1 and V_2, and select n_i to minimize the variance of the estimate under the constraint $n_1 + n_2 = n$.

■

In general, suppose we are running a simulation to estimate the mean value, $E(X)$, of some random variable X, and that this mean value depends on some parameter, $Q \in \{q_1, q_2, \ldots, q_\ell\}$. Suppose we can accurately calculate $p_i = \text{Prob}\{Q = q_i\}$, $i = 1, 2, \ldots, \ell$.

Using the stratified sampling approach, we first run n_i simulations to estimate $E(X)$ conditioned on the event $\{Q = q_i\}$, for every $i = 1, \ldots, \ell$. Then, we estimate $E(X)$ by applying the Total Probability formula. That is,

$$E(X) = E[E(X|Q)] = E(X|Q = q_1)p_1 + E(X|Q = q_2)p_2 + \cdots + E(X|Q = q_\ell)p_\ell$$

The effectiveness of the stratified sampling approach is based on the identity that you are invited to prove in the Exercises:

$$\text{Var}(X) = E[\text{Var}(X|Q)] + \text{Var}[E(X|Q)]$$

The actual amount of variance reduction will depend on the extent of the correlation between X and Q. In effect, we are using our knowledge of $\text{Prob}\{Q = q_i\}$ to reduce the variance, since Q itself does not need to be simulated any more and the variability introduced by simulating it is eliminated.

10.3.4 Importance Sampling

In the importance sampling approach to simulation, we simulate a modified system in which the chance of failure has been artificially boosted and then correct for that boost. A detailed development of the theory is beyond the scope of this book: we have limited ourselves to providing just an introduction to it. There are three reasons for this.

- Importance sampling is a temperamental technique. If not carefully used, it can end up actually *increasing* the variance of the simulation estimate.

- It is not yet a mature technique. It is, rather, the focus of much current research.

- It is more mathematically complicated than anything else encountered in this book.

The importance sampling approach is based on the following reasoning. Suppose we want to estimate by simulation some parameter $\theta = E[\phi(X)]$ where $\phi(\cdot)$ is some function and X is a random variable with probability density function $f(x)$.

Assume that $g(x)$ is a probability density function with the property that $g(x) > 0$ for all x for which $f(x) > 0$. Then,

$$
\begin{aligned}
E\big[\phi(X)\big] &= \int \phi(x) f(x)\, dx \\
&= \int \frac{\phi(x) f(x)}{g(x)} g(x)\, dx \\
&= \int \psi(x) g(x)\, dx
\end{aligned}
\tag{10.6}
$$

where $\psi(x) = \frac{\phi(x) f(x)}{g(x)}$. Now, $\int \psi(x) g(x)\, dx$ is equal to $E[\psi(Y)]$, where Y is a random variable with probability density function $g(\cdot)$. This suggests that we estimate $E[\psi(Y)]$ rather than $E[\phi(X)]$ (although both are equal to θ).

More precisely, the standard approach to estimating $\theta = E(\phi(X))$ would be to obtain a sample of X, namely, $X_1, X_2, \ldots, X_n$, and estimate θ as

$$
\hat{\theta} = \overline{\phi(X)} = \frac{1}{n} \sum_{i=1}^{n} \phi(X_i)
$$

The importance sampling approach is to obtain a sample of Y (with density function $g(y)$), denoted by $Y_1, Y_2, \ldots, Y_n$, and then estimate θ as

$$\hat{\theta} = \overline{\psi(Y)} = \frac{1}{n} \sum_{i=1}^{n} \psi(Y_i)$$

For this method to be beneficial, it is necessary that

$$\text{Var}\left(\psi(Y)\right) < \text{Var}\left(\phi(X)\right)$$

This will happen if we select some $g(x)$ with the property that $f(x)/g(x)$ is small whenever $\phi(x)$ is large and vice versa. The choice of $g(x)$ is crucial to the reduction of variance: an incorrect choice can render the method of importance sampling counterproductive by actually increasing the variance.

■ **EXAMPLE**

Consider two random variables A and B, each exponentially distributed with parameter μ. That is, their density functions are each of the form $f(x) = \mu e^{-\mu x}$, for $x \geqslant 0$. Then, suppose we want to use simulation to estimate the parameter $\theta = \text{Prob}\{A + B > 100\}$. Assume that $\mu \gg 1/50$, so that it is unlikely that $A + B > 100$ (and θ is therefore very small).

We could obviously solve this problem analytically, without any need for simulation. However, let us use it as a vehicle to explain how the principles of importance sampling could be used here.

Using the conventional approach, we would generate two samples of size n for A and B: $a_1, a_2, \ldots, a_n$ and $b_1, b_2, \ldots, b_n$, respectively. Define

$$\phi(a_i, b_i) = \begin{cases} 1 & \text{if } a_i + b_i > 100 \\ 0 & \text{otherwise} \end{cases}$$

Because $\theta = E(\phi(A, B))$, we can estimate

$$\hat{\theta} = \frac{1}{n} \sum_{i=1}^{n} \phi(a_i, b_i)$$

As we saw in Section 10.2.5, we will need a very large number of observations to accurately estimate a very small value of θ. In the importance sampling approach, we change the density function so that larger values of A and B are more likely. In particular, let us use the density function $g(x) = \gamma e^{-\gamma x}$ for some $\gamma \ll \mu$. Using this density function, we generate values of A and B denoted by

$a_1', a_2', \ldots, a_n'$ and $b_1', b_2', \ldots, b_n'$. We then use the estimate

$$\hat{\theta} = \frac{1}{n} \sum_{i=1}^{n} \phi(a_i', b_i') \frac{f(a_i')}{g(a_i')} \frac{f(b_i')}{g(b_i')} = \frac{1}{n} \sum_{i=1}^{n} \phi(a_i', b_i') \left(\frac{\mu}{\gamma}\right)^2 e^{-(\mu-\gamma)(a_i'+b_i')}.$$

It now remains for us to obtain a suitable value of γ to reduce the variance of the estimate. Denoting the ith term of the above sum by S_i, we note that if $a_i' + b_i' \leqslant 100$, $S_i = 0$. Also, if $a_i' + b_i' > 100$, then

$$S_i = \left(\frac{\mu}{\gamma}\right)^2 e^{-(\mu-\gamma)(a_i'+b_i')} \leqslant \left(\frac{\mu}{\gamma}\right)^2 e^{-100(\mu-\gamma)}.$$

Selecting γ to minimize

$$\left(\frac{\mu}{\gamma}\right)^2 e^{-100(\mu-\gamma)}$$

will minimize the maximum possible value of S_i and thereby reduce the variance of S_i. Simple calculus shows that $\gamma = 0.02$ minimizes the above quantity. Thus, the importance sampling approach to this problem is as follows:

- Generate a_i', b_i' according to the density function $g(x) = 0.02e^{-0.02x}$, for $i = 1, 2, \ldots, n$.

- Define $\phi(a_i', b_i') = 1$ if $a_i' + b_i' > 100$ and 0 otherwise.

- Estimate θ by

$$\hat{\theta} = \frac{1}{n} \sum_{i=1}^{n} \phi(a_i' + b_i') \left(\frac{\mu}{0.02}\right)^2 e^{-(\mu-0.02)(a_i'+b_i')}.$$

Simulating Continuous-Time Markov Chains: Mean Time Between System Failures

Suppose the system we are analyzing can be described by a Markov chain (see Chapter 2) with continuous time t, also called a CTMC (continuous-time Markov chain). Let λ_{ij} be the rate of transition from state i to state j, then, $\lambda_i = \sum_{j \neq i} \lambda_{ij}$ is the total rate of departure from state i. The sojourn time of the system in each state (the time it stays in a state before leaving it) is exponentially distributed with parameter λ_i for state i.

Now, suppose that all the transitions in the chain are either *component failure* or *repair* transitions. A subset of the states, those in which the system is considered to have failed, are called *system-failure* states.

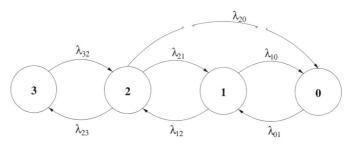

FIGURE 10.3   A continuous-time Markov chain.

■ EXAMPLE

Consider a system of three processors that can fail and be repaired, and suppose the system behaves according to the Markov chain depicted in Figure 10.3. The state is the number of processors that are functional. The failure transitions are $3 \to 2$, $2 \to 1$, $2 \to 0$, and $1 \to 0$. The repair transitions are $2 \to 3$, $1 \to 2$, and $0 \to 1$. The rates of transition are as shown on the arrow labels. From this, we can write

$$\lambda_3 = \lambda_{32}$$

$$\lambda_2 = \lambda_{21} + \lambda_{20} + \lambda_{23}$$

$$\lambda_1 = \lambda_{10} + \lambda_{12}$$

$$\lambda_0 = \lambda_{01}$$

Suppose the system is operational as long as at least one processor is operational, then the set of system-failure states is $\{0\}$. ■

Going back to the general failure-repair Markov chain, we are interested in finding the mean time between system failures (MTBF). Because repair is usually much faster than time between component failures, the chain makes a large number of transitions before it enters one of the system-failure states, and thus the simulation will have to run for a very long time to measure the time until the system fails. We can use importance sampling to speed up the simulation as follows.

Let us define state N as the initial state with all components functional, and let $t = 0$ be the time at which the simulation starts. By definition, there are no repair transitions out of state N; there can only be failure transitions. Let F be the set of system-failure states. Since we are considering systems with repair, there will be one or more repair transitions out of each state with any failed components. Ultimately, the system will return to state N. Let this time of return be τ_R, the *system regeneration* time. (At this point, the system is as good as new). Let τ_F be the time until the system first enters a system failure state. Then, you are invited in the Exercises to show that

$$E[\tau_F] = \frac{E[\min(\tau_R, \tau_F)]}{\text{Prob}\{\tau_F < \tau_R\}} \tag{10.7}$$

In most systems, where repair rates are much greater than failure rates, we can expect that $E[\min(\tau_R, \tau_F)]$ will be only slightly smaller than $E(\tau_R)$, since the system can be expected to return to state N many times before it enters a system-failure state. We can expect the system to return to state N fairly quickly. So, traditional simulation can be used to estimate $E[\min(\tau_R, \tau_F)]$: just calculate the average length of time it takes the system to return from state N to state N.

Estimating $\theta = \text{Prob}\{\tau_F < \tau_R\}$, on the other hand, should be done using importance sampling because $\tau_F < \tau_R$ is the rare event in which the system fails before returning to state N. Notice that we no longer need to keep track, in our simulations, of the time it takes to make the transitions, or of how long τ_F or τ_R may be; all we need to record is the fraction of times that $\tau_F < \tau_R$. This means that we do not need to change the sojourn time of the system in any of its states, just the transition probabilities.

The technique we will follow to implement importance sampling is called *balanced failure biasing*. Before presenting it, we have to introduce some notation. Each transition out of any state represents either a failure or a repair event. In state N, since everything is functional, there can only be failure events. Conversely, in a state in which everything is down, there can only be repair events. Let $n_F(i)$ be the number of failure transitions (the number of outgoing transitions denoting component failure events) out of state i.

Since we are not interested in finding out the amount of time the system spends in each state, we need only simulate a discrete-time Markov chain (DTMC) embedded into the continuous-time chain. This is a DTMC that studies just the progress of the system from one state to the next, without recording the sojourn time in each state.

Suppose we have a CTMC that has the following events: It starts from state N, moves to state i_1 at time t_1, to state i_2 at time t_2, etc. The sample-path for the corresponding embedded discrete-time Markov chain will be N, then i_1, then i_1, etc.

We now define a probability transition function for the DTMC, p_{ij}, which is the probability that the system moves to state j given that it was in state i. It can be shown that

$$p_{ij} = \frac{\lambda_{ij}}{\sum_k \lambda_{ik}}$$

Intuitively, the probability that the system will transit from state i to state j is the rate of going from i to j as a fraction of the total rate of leaving state i.

Define by $p_R(i)$ the probability of making a repair transition out of state i. Now, pick some p^* (usually 0.2 to 0.4 works well) and define a new DTMC characterized by transition probabilities $\tilde{p}_{ij}$ defined as follows:

- *Case 1.* $i = N$

$$\tilde{p}_{ij} = \begin{cases} \frac{1}{n_F(i)} & \text{if } i \to j \text{ is a failure transition and } p_{ij} > 0 \\ 0 & \text{otherwise} \end{cases}$$

- *Case 2.* i is neither N nor a system-failure state and $p_R(i) > 0$

$$\tilde{p}_{ij} = \begin{cases} \dfrac{p^*}{n_F(i)} & \text{if } i \to j \text{ is a failure transition and } p_{ij} > 0 \\ \dfrac{(1-p^*)p_{ij}}{p_R(i)} & \text{if } i \to j \text{ is a repair transition and } p_{ij} > 0 \\ 0 & \text{otherwise} \end{cases}$$

- *Case 3.* i is not a system-failure state but $p_R(i) = 0$

$$\tilde{p}_{ij} = \begin{cases} \dfrac{1}{n_F(i)} & \text{if } p_{ij} > 0 \\ 0 & \text{otherwise} \end{cases}$$

- *Case 4.* i is a system-failure state

$$\tilde{p}_{ij} = p_{ij}$$

We have only modified transition probabilities out of states that are not system-failure states. For these, we have done the following:

- The total probability of making a failure transition is now p^*.
- This probability is equally divided among all the failure transitions.

We now perform n simulation runs of the modified system, recording for each the likelihood ratio of the sample path (where the sample path is the sequence of states that are visited). The likelihood ratio for simulation run k, L_k, is defined as

$$L_k = \frac{\text{Probability of the original DTMC having this sample path}}{\text{Probability of the modified DTMC having this sample path}}$$

Let

$$I_k = \begin{cases} 1 & \text{if simulation run } k \text{ ends with system failure} \\ 0 & \text{if simulation run } k \text{ ends with the system back in state } N \end{cases}$$

Then, we estimate

$$\hat{\theta} = \widehat{\text{Prob}}\{\tau_F < \tau_R\} = \frac{\sum_{k=1}^{n} I_k L_k}{n}$$

Let us now relate this to Equation 10.6. The transition probabilities that we use to simulate the system (the $\tilde{p}_{ij}$ values) are a realization of $g(x)$. L_k is a realization of $f(x)/g(x)$. Finally, I_k is a realization of $\phi(x)$. Because failure is a discrete event, we replace the integral in Equation 10.6 by a sum.

■ E X A M P L E

Consider the system shown in Figure 10.4a: its embedded DTMC is shown in Figure 10.4b. The labels for the CTMC arrows are the transition rates, and those for the embedded DTMC arrows the transition probabilities. By defi-

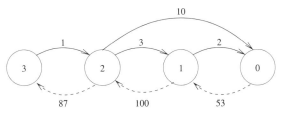

(a) Continuous-time Markov chain

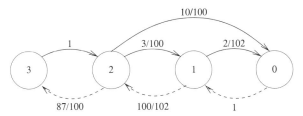

(b) Embedded discrete-time Markov chain

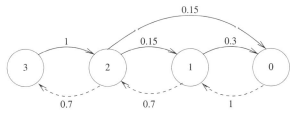

(c) Modified discrete-time Markov chain

FIGURE 10.4   A continuous-time Markov chain (CTMC) and its embedded discrete-time Markov chain (DTMC). Solid lines indicate failure transitions; dashed lines indicate repair transitions.

nition, the transition probabilities out of each state must add up to 1. (In a general DTMC, it is permissible for a state to transit to itself; this will never happen here since each transition represents either a failure or a repair event). State 0 is the only system-failure state.

Now, suppose we select $p^* = 0.3$. Consider the transitions out of each state, one by one.

- *State 3*. There is only one transition out of this state, to state 2. We therefore have $\tilde{p}_{32} = 1$.

- *State 2*. There is one repair transition out of state 2 and $n_F(2) = 2$ failure transitions. Each of these failure transitions will have probability $p^*/2 = 0.15$ of happening; the single repair transition will happen with probability $1 - p^* = 0.7$.

- *State 1*. There is one repair transition and one failure transition out of this state: $n_F(1) = 1$, the failure transition will happen with probability $p^* = 0.3$, and the repair transition with probability $1 - p^* = 0.7$.

- *State 0*. This is a system-failure state: there is no change to the transition probabilities out of this state.

Figure 10.4c depicts the modified DTMC. We will now simulate this chain, to estimate $\text{Prob}\{\tau_F < \tau_R\}$ under the new transition probabilities. Suppose we decide to make a total of three simulation runs and average them to find an estimate for this probability. (In reality, one would carry out perhaps thousands or even millions of such simulation runs, but we are just illustrating the technique here.) We will simulate the system starting from state 3. The simulation will end when the system enters either state 3 (in which case, we have $\tau_F > \tau_R$), or the system-failure state 0 (in which case, $\tau_F < \tau_R$). Table 10-1 shows possible results for these runs.

Consider the first of the three runs. The sequence of states is $3 \rightarrow 2 \rightarrow 3$. The probability of such a sequence of transitions taking place in the modified DTMC is $\tilde{p}_{32} \times \tilde{p}_{23} = 1 \times 0.7$; the corresponding probability for the original DTMC is $p_{32} \times p_{23} = 1 \times 0.87$. The likelihood ratio is therefore $\frac{1 \times 0.87}{1 \times 0.7}$. (Recall

TABLE 10-1 ■ Three sample paths and the associated likelihood ratios

Run No.	Sample path	Likelihood ratio	$\tau_F < \tau_R$?
1	3, 2, 3	$L_1 = \frac{1 \times 0.87}{1 \times 0.7}$	No
2	3, 2, 1, 2, 1, 0	$L_2 = \frac{1 \times (3/100) \times (100/102) \times (3/100) \times (2/102)}{1 \times 0.7 \times 0.15 \times 0.7 \times 0.15 \times 0.7 \times 0.3}$	Yes
3	3, 2, 1, 2, 3	$L_3 = \frac{1 \times (3/100) \times (100/102) \times (87/100)}{1 \times 0.15 \times 0.7 \times 0.7}$	No

that this is the factor that corrects for our modification of the transition probabilities to get $\tilde{p}_{ij}$).

Similarly for the remaining runs.

Run 2 of the three simulation runs is the only one that has resulted in the event $\tau_F < \tau_R$. Therefore, $I_1 = 0$, $I_2 = 1$, $I_3 = 0$, and our simulation estimate is

$$\hat{\theta} = \widehat{\text{Prob}}\{\tau_F < \tau_R\} = \frac{0 \times L_1 + 1 \times L_2 + 0 \times L_3}{3} = \frac{L_2}{3} = 0.0025$$

∎

Simulating Continuous-Time Markov Chains: Reliability

To find reliability by simulation, the conventional way is to run the system until it enters a system-failure state and then find the total elapsed time to system failure. From these times we can obtain the probability distribution function of the time to first failure, whose complement is the reliability function.

Balanced failure biasing can be used for shortening the simulation time for this case as well. There is, however, an important difference between calculating the reliability function and estimating the MTBF that we showed in the previous section. For the latter, we were able to avoid the task of actually storing durations and just counted the number of times the system failed before getting back to state N. In our present case, we have to maintain time information in our simulation. Also, we would like to force at least one transition out of state N.

Doing the latter is quite simple. In a conventional simulation, we would use the density function $f(t) = \lambda_N e^{-\lambda_N t}$ for simulating the sojourn time of the system in state N. In the forcing technique, we use instead the density function

$$\tilde{f}(t) = \begin{cases} \frac{\lambda_N e^{-\lambda_N t}}{1 - e^{-\lambda_N T}} & \text{if } 0 \leqslant t \leqslant T \\ 0 & \text{otherwise} \end{cases}$$

for some predetermined T. This forces at least one transition out of N prior to time T.

The likelihood ratio associated with this choice is obviously $f(t)/\tilde{f}(t)$. In practice, we will combine forcing with balanced failure biasing, in which case the overall likelihood ratio will be the product of the likelihood ratios of the two.

It is important to note that the forcing technique should only be used if $1 - e^{-\lambda_N T}$ is a relatively small quantity, and transitions out of state N are rare over the interval $[0, T]$.

10.4 Random Number Generation

At the heart of any simulation of probabilistic events is the random number generator, whose job it is to generate independent and identically distributed (i.i.d.) random variables according to some specified probability distribution function. The quality of such a generator is often critical to the accuracy of the results that the simulation produces, so that choosing a good generator is of considerable practical importance. We discuss in this section how to create random number generators and test their quality.

When faced with the need to generate a stream of i.i.d. random numbers according to some probability distribution function, we usually proceed in two steps. In the first step, we generate a stream of i.i.d. random numbers that are uniformly distributed in the range $[0, 1]$; in the second, we transform these to fit the desired probability distribution.

10.4.1 Uniformly Distributed Random Number Generators

In an ideal world, we would be able to generate truly random numbers that were both distributed uniformly over $[0, 1]$ and statistically independent of one another. If we can identify some physical process that displays the appropriate stochastic properties, we could simply take measurements of that process. For example, one commercially available generator amplifies the shot noise plus the thermal noise in transistors and then uses a thresholding function to convert that noise to bits (if the noise is above the threshold, it is a 1, otherwise it is a 0). This stream of bits is then processed to produce a sequence of numbers that satisfy quite stringent tests of randomness.

In most instances, however, we have to make do with random numbers generated by a computer program. Herein lies a fundamental contradiction. Typically, such a sequence of random numbers $X_1, X_2, \ldots$ satisfies some function $f(\cdot)$ such that $X_{i+1} = f(X_i)$. Given the *seed*, X_0, we can therefore predict what the numbers are going to be: there is nothing truly random about them. This is why numbers generated in such a way are called *pseudo-random*. We hope when we generate them that they look sufficiently random that we can get away with using them, rather than truly random numbers, in our simulations. In effect, we are trying a variation of the well-known Turing test for intelligence on the random number sequences. The Turing test for artificial intelligence is as follows. Have people interact with either a computer or a human being, without being told which. If they cannot make out from the responses they get to questions whether they are talking to a computer or a human, then the computer has intelligence. The variation that applies to random number sequences states that if we generate a pseudo-random sequence and give it to a statistician without telling her how it was obtained, she should not be able to distinguish between such a sequence and one generated truly randomly. This is an extremely stringent test, and one that most generators will fail. All that is realistic to hope for is that the pseudo-random numbers generated will be sufficiently close to the real thing to make our simulations sufficiently accurate for our purposes. A major source of error in simulations is using poor quality random number generators. Later in this section, we will see how to test such sequences to determine if they satisfy statistical properties of randomness.

A commonly used set of URNGs generate *linear congruential sequences* of the form:

$$X_{i+1} = (aX_i + c) \bmod m, \quad 0 \leqslant a, c < m$$

where a, c, m are constants. m is called the modulus of the generator, a the multiplier, and c the increment. If $c = 0$, this is known as a multiplicative generator. We start this iterative process by specifying X_0, the seed of this sequence. The properties of the generator depend on the values of these constants. Given such a sequence of integers (which must clearly be in the set $\{0, 1, \ldots, m - 1\}$), we define the sequence of fractions $U_i = X_i/m$, which are supposed to be uniformly distributed and mutually independent in the range $[0, 1]$.

Because the sequence $X_1, X_2, \ldots$ must consist of numbers from a finite set, the sequence will repeat with time. That is, given any such generator, there always exists some M such that $X_i = X_{i+M}$. The smallest such M is called the *period*, P, of the generator, and clearly $P \leqslant m$.

■ EXAMPLE

Consider the generator $X_{n+1} = (aX_n + c) \bmod 8$. (We use an unrealistically small modulus just for illustration: in practice as we will see, very large moduli are used). We will show that the values of a and c are critical to the functioning of the generator.

Start by considering the following set of results:

seed	0	1	2	3	4	5	6	7
X_1	1	4	7	2	5	0	3	6
X_2	4	5	6	7	0	1	2	3
X_3	5	0	3	6	1	4	7	2
X_4	0	1	2	3	4	5	6	7
X_5	1	4	7	2	5	0	3	6
X_6	4	5	6	7	0	1	2	3
X_7	5	0	3	6	1	4	7	2

$a = 3; c = 1; m = 8$

Note that for this sequence, every value of the seed results in a sequence of numbers with period 4. Let us now try another set of constants.

seed	0	1	2	3	4	5	6	7
X_1	2	4	6	0	2	4	6	0
X_2	6	2	6	2	6	2	6	2
X_3	6	6	6	6	6	6	6	6
X_4	6	6	6	6	6	6	6	6
X_5	6	6	6	6	6	6	6	6
X_6	6	6	6	6	6	6	6	6
X_7	6	6	6	6	6	6	6	6

$a = 2; c = 2; m = 8$

The result is quite disastrous. a very non random and correlated stream of numbers. This generator gets trapped into producing a stream of 6s, irrespective of the seed. Let us try yet another set of constants.

seed	0	1	2	3	4	5	6	7
X_1	1	6	3	0	5	2	7	4
X_2	6	7	0	1	2	3	4	5
X_3	7	4	1	6	3	0	5	2
X_4	4	5	6	7	0	1	2	3
X_5	5	2	7	4	1	6	3	0
X_6	2	3	4	5	6	7	0	1
X_7	3	0	5	2	7	4	1	6

$a = 5; c = 1; m = 8$

For these values of a and c, we have, for every seed, a sequence of numbers with the maximum period of 8. We should caution that it does not automatically follow that this is a good generator, just that it passes a basic sanity check.

■

The Linear Congruential Generator (LCG) has a period of m if and only if each of the following properties hold:

■ c and m are relatively prime (their highest common factor is 1).

■   For every prime number p that divides m, $a - 1$ is a multiple of p.

■   If m is a multiple of 4, then $a - 1$ is also a multiple of 4.

The proof of this result is outside the scope of this book; see the Further Reading section for where to find it.

Since random number generators are so important in simulation, many researchers have carried out extensive searches in the parameter space to find generators with good properties. One widely used generator with fairly good statistical properties uses the parameters $a = 16807$, $m = 2^{31} - 1$, $c = 0$.

The periods of LCGs are limited by m, and that can be a problem for running very long simulations. In simulating fault-tolerant systems, in which a very large number of events must be generated for each system failure that is encountered, the periods of such generators are often much too small. For example, in the generator mentioned above, $m = 2^{31} - 1 = 2{,}147{,}483{,}647$, and it is entirely possible to have in a simulation more than two billion calls to a random number generator. Because we want the number of calls to be much less than the generator period, we can use combined generators. One way of doing this is to select parameters a_{ij},

m_1, m_2, k and define

$$X_{1,n} = (a_{11}X_{1,n-1} + a_{12}X_{1,n-2} + \cdots + a_{1k}X_{1,n-k}) \bmod m_1$$

$$X_{2,n} = (a_{21}X_{2,n-1} + a_{22}X_{2,n-2} + \cdots + a_{2k}X_{2,n-k}) \bmod m_2$$

Now, if these parameters are carefully chosen, the sequence

$$U_n = \left(\frac{X_{1,n}}{m_1} - \frac{X_{2,n}}{m_2} \right) \bmod 1$$

(by mod 1 we mean the fractional part of this expression) will have properties close to those of i.i.d. uniformly distributed random variables.

After a long computer search for suitable parameters for such a generator, the following has been recommended as having good statistical properties: $k = 3$, $m_1 = 2^{32} - 209$, $(a_{11}, a_{12}, a_{13}) = (0, 1403580, -810728)$, $m_2 = 2^{32} - 22853$, $(a_{21}, a_{22}, a_{23}) = (527612, 0, -1370589)$. Such a generator has main cycles of length approximately 2^{191}. See the Further Reading section for details.

10.4.2 Testing Uniform Random Number Generators

All tests for URNGs ask the following question: How faithfully does the output of the URNG follow the properties of a uniformly distributed stream of random numbers that are statistically independent of one another? To answer this question, we must first identify some of the key properties of interest.

The most obvious property is that of uniformity. That is, we would like to calculate the extent to which the output is uniformly distributed over the range $[0, 1]$. Suppose we generate 1000 numbers and find that all of them are in the range $[0, 0.7]$. Now, it is *not impossible* that a set of 1000 numbers selected independently and uniformly from the unit interval should all fall in the range $[0, 0.7]$: the probability of this event is $0.7^{1000} = 1.25 \times 10^{-155}$, which, although very small, is certainly not zero. Thus, if we get such a sequence from the URNG that we are testing, we cannot say *for sure* that the URNG is bad: all we can say is that it is *very unlikely* that a good generator will produce a sequence like that, and consequently we declare the generator bad.

We present next some ways of testing the goodness of a URNG. As with any statistical test, there is an interplay between sensitivity and specificity in the following tests. Looking for too high a sensitivity can result in a high chance of declaring a generator bad when it is actually good.

The χ^2 Test

Use the URNG to generate a large sequence of numbers. Define $a_0, a_1, a_2, \ldots, a_{k-1}, a_k$ for some suitable k such that

$$0 = a_0 < a_1 < a_2 < \cdots < a_{k-1} < a_k = 1$$

and define intervals $I_i = [a_i, a_{i+1})$ for $i = \{0, \ldots, k-1\}$. Then, let O_i and E_i be the observed and expected frequencies, respectively, of generated numbers to fall within interval I_i, and define the quantity S, which measures the deviation of the observed frequencies from the expected ones, as

$$S = \sum_{i=0}^{k-1} \frac{(O_i - E_i)^2}{E_i}$$

Clearly, a good URNG will result in a small value of S. It can be shown (the Further Reading section has a pointer to where you can find this derivation) that if the random numbers were the output of a perfect URNG, and we have a large number of them (with at least five expected to fall within each of the intervals I_i), S approximately follows the χ^2 distribution with $k-1$ degrees of freedom.

It is easy to find tables of the χ^2 distribution in books on statistics or on the Internet. We reject the URNG if S is so large that the probability that a true URNG would generate such a deviation (or a larger one) is very small (say, less than 5%).

■ EXAMPLE

Let us break up the interval $[0, 1]$ into 10 equal subintervals, each of length 0.1. Thus, $I_i = [0.1i, 0.1i + 0.1)$, for $i = 0, 2, \ldots, 9$. Suppose that after generating 1000 random numbers, we get the results shown in Table 10-2. Let us pick 0.05 as our significance level; this means that we will reject the URNG if it results in a sum S such that the probability of an ideal URNG generating such a sum or larger is less than 0.05. Referring to a χ^2 table with 9 degrees of freedom we see that, at a significance level of 0.05, we should reject the URNG if $S > 16.9$. Because in this example, we have $S = 331.98$, we reject this generator—it deviates too much from the expected behavior. There is a very small probability

TABLE 10-2 ■ Illustrating the χ^2 test

i	O_i	E_i	$(O_i - E_i)^2$	$(O_i - E_i)^2/E_i$
0	15	100	7225	72.25
1	100	100	0	0.00
2	200	100	10000	100.00
3	88	100	144	1.44
4	100	100	0	0.00
5	100	100	0	0.00
6	90	100	100	1.00
7	80	100	400	4.00
8	27	100	5329	53.29
9	200	100	10000	100.00
TOTAL				331.98

(much smaller than 0.05) that a good URNG will produce a sequence of numbers like this one. ∎

Serial Test

To test whether a URNG produces uniformly distributed random numbers is necessary but certainly not sufficient. To see why, consider the following generator (this is an extreme, contrived example whose sole purpose is to make a point). Generate $Y_1, Y_2, \ldots, Y_n$ using any URNG that closely follows the uniform distribution. Then, generate a sequence $Z_1, Z_2, \ldots, Z_n$, such that for some $k > 1$,

$$Z_1 = Z_2 = \cdots = Z_k = Y_1$$
$$Z_{k+1} = Z_{k+2} = \cdots = Z_{2k} = Y_2$$
$$\vdots$$
$$Z_{(n-1)k+1} = Z_{(n-1)k+2} = \cdots = Z_{nk} = Y_n$$

If $Y_1, \ldots, Y_2$ follows the uniform distribution sufficiently closely, the sequence Z_i will pass the χ^2 test. However, the Z_is would certainly not be acceptable because they are highly correlated. So, we need to test for lack of correlation as well: in other words, we have to test for the statistical independence of successive numbers. Such an independence is really a fake: the nth random number is a function of the $(n-1)$st. All that we are really testing for is whether the sequence of generated numbers *looks* like an independent sequence. Similarly, it is entirely possible (though unlikely) that we would independently generate random numbers that *appear* correlated. The best we can realistically do is ask the question: Is the probability sufficiently high that such a sequence of numbers would be generated by an ideal generator that produced numbers independently of one another?

To test for correlation between successive numbers, we can use the serial test. In k dimensions, the test is as follows. Generate a sequence of random numbers and then group them together into k-tuples as follows:

$$G_1 = (X_1, X_2, \ldots, X_k)$$
$$G_2 = (X_{k+1}, X_{k+2}, \ldots, X_{2k})$$
$$G_3 = (X_{2k+1}, X_{2k+2}, \ldots, X_{3k})$$
$$\vdots$$

Then, divide the k-dimensional unit cube into n equal subcubes, count the number of k-tuples that fall into each of the subcubes, and check (using the χ^2 test) whether the k-tuples are uniformly distributed among the subcubes.

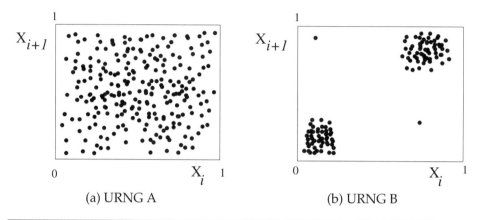

(a) URNG A   (b) URNG B

FIGURE 10.5   Comparing two generators.

■ E X A M P L E

Suppose we are testing for correlation in two dimensions. To do this, we generate pairs (X_1, X_2), (X_3, X_4), ... We then subdivide the two-dimensional unit cube (the unit square) into, say, 100 squares (call them mini-squares), each of area 0.01. We count the number n_i of pairs that fall into mini-square i, and use the χ^2 test to check if these pairs are uniformly spread through the unit square. If correlation exists, some of the mini-squares will have a significantly higher concentration of pairs than the others (see Figure 10.5). ■

Permutation Test

Given a certain sequence of numbers, divide them into non-overlapping subsequences, each of a chosen length, k. Each of these subsequences can be in one of $k!$ possible orderings. If the URNG is good, we expect these orderings to be equally likely to occur, which can be checked using the χ^2 test.

■ E X A M P L E

Consider the case $k = 3$. Denote a subsequence by u_1, u_2, u_3. This subsequence has $3! = 6$ possible orderings: $u_1 \leqslant u_2 \leqslant u_3$; $u_1 \leqslant u_3 \leqslant u_2$; $u_2 \leqslant u_1 \leqslant u_3$; $u_2 \leqslant u_3 \leqslant u_1$; $u_3 \leqslant u_1 \leqslant u_2$; and $u_3 \leqslant u_2 \leqslant u_1$. If we generate a large number of such sequences, we expect a good URNG to generate each of these six orderings with a frequency of $1/6$. If the frequency of at least one ordering differs significantly from $1/6$ (as measured by the χ^2 test), the URNG will fail this test. ■

The Spectral Test

This is probably the most powerful test available. The approach followed by the spectral test is perhaps easiest to understand in two-dimensional space. Let us try to draw parallel lines in such a way that each point in the scatter plot is on one of these lines. Then, find the maximum distance between any two adjacent parallel lines. Let d_2 be the maximum of this quantity, taken over all possible ways in which such parallel lines can be drawn (the subscript refers to the fact that we are working in two dimensions). We define $v_2 = 1/d_2$ as the two-dimensional accuracy of the URNG. The larger this quantity the better: the intuition behind this is that for large values of v_2, the points are spread out more "randomly" in two-dimensional space.

This approach can be generalized to higher dimensions. In k-dimensional space (where we would plot $(X_i, X_{i+1}, \ldots, X_{i+k-1})$), we can replace the parallel lines by $(k-1)$-dimensional parallel hyperplanes and repeat the distance calculation. The quantity $v_k = 1/d_k$ (where d_k is defined for k dimensions as d_2 was for two) is the k-dimensional accuracy of the URNG.

It has been recommended to study the scatter up to about six dimensions and require that $v_i \geqslant 2^{30/i}$ for $i = 2, 3, 4, 5, 6$ to accept a generator as good.

The only issue left is how to compute v_i. The theory behind this is beyond the scope of this book; the user can download routines for running the spectral test from the Internet.

10.4.3 Generating Other Distributions

Given a URNG, we can easily generate random numbers that follow other distributions. There are a handful of standard methods for doing this.

Inverse-Transform Technique

This technique is based on the fact that if a random variable X has a probability distribution function $F_x(\cdot)$, the random variable $Y = F_X(X)$ is uniformly distributed over $[0, 1]$. This can be easily proved as follows:

Denote by F_X^{-1} the inverse function of F_X, that is, $F_X^{-1}(F_X(y)) = y$. (If the inverse does not exist because there are multiple such quantities y, use the smallest such y). Then, for $0 \leqslant y \leqslant 1$,

$$\text{Prob}\{Y \leqslant y\} = \text{Prob}\{F_X(X) \leqslant y\}$$
$$= \text{Prob}\{X \leqslant F_X^{-1}(y)\} \quad \text{(because } F_X(\cdot) \text{ is nondecreasing)}$$
$$= F_X\big(F_X^{-1}(y)\big)$$
$$= y$$

Therefore, if we generate random numbers $Y_1, Y_2, \ldots$ that are uniformly distributed over $[0, 1]$, we will get random variables distributed according to $F_X(\cdot)$ by generating $X_i = F_X^{-1}(Y_i)$.

■ EXAMPLE

Suppose we want to generate instances of X, an exponentially-distributed random variable with parameter μ. The probability distribution function of X is

$$F_X(x) = 1 - e^{-\mu x}, \quad x \geqslant 0$$

Now, define

$$Y = F_X(X) = 1 - e^{-\mu X}$$

and

$$e^{-\mu X} = 1 - Y$$

hence

$$-\mu X = \ln(1 - Y)$$

and finally

$$X = -(1/\mu) \ln(1 - Y)$$

Thus, to generate exponentially distributed random numbers, first generate uniformly distributed random numbers y over $[0, 1]$ and then output $x = -(1/\mu) \ln(1 - y)$. The computation can be speeded up a little by recognizing that $-(1/\mu) \ln y$ will also work; see the Exercises for details. ■

Working with discrete random variables is similar, as shown by the following example.

■ EXAMPLE

We are asked to generate a discrete-valued random variable V with the following probability mass function:

$$\text{Prob}\{V = v\} = \begin{cases} 0.1 & \text{if } v = 1 \\ 0.3 & \text{if } v = 2 \\ 0.6 & \text{if } v = 2.25 \\ 0 & \text{otherwise} \end{cases}$$

The only values that V can take are $1, 2, 2.25$. The corresponding probability distribution function is clearly

$$F(v) = \text{Prob}\{V \leqslant v\} = \begin{cases} 0.0 & \text{if } v < 1 \\ 0.1 & \text{if } 1 \leqslant v < 2 \\ 0.4 & \text{if } 2 \leqslant v < 2.25 \\ 1.0 & \text{if } v \geqslant 2.25 \end{cases}$$

This distribution function has jumps at $v = 1, 2$, and 2.25 and is flat otherwise. Now, generate a uniformly distributed random variable, U, over the interval $[0, 1]$, and output

$$V = \begin{cases} 1 & \text{if } 0 \leqslant U \leqslant 0.1 \\ 2 & \text{if } 0.1 < U \leqslant 0.4 \\ 2.25 & \text{if } 0.4 < U \leqslant 1.0 \end{cases}$$

Why is this an example of the inverse transform approach? See Figure 10.6, which contains the distribution of the function. Suppose we get $U = 0.70$ from our URNG. We then find the interval $(F(2), F(2.25))$ into which U falls and output $V = 2.25$.

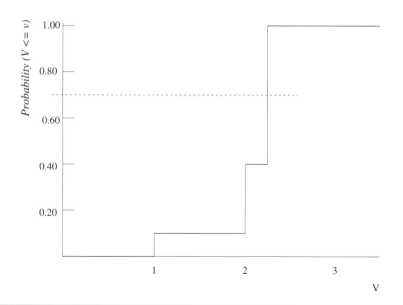

FIGURE 10.6   Generating a discrete random variable.

■ E X A M P L E

Suppose we are asked to generate a *nonhomogeneous Poisson process*. This is a generalization of the well-known Poisson process; the only difference is that the rate of event occurrences is not a constant λ but a function of the time t, denoted by $\lambda(t)$. The probability of an occurrence during the interval $[t, t + dt]$ is given by $\lambda(t) \, dt$. Nonhomogeneous Poisson processes are useful in modeling components with failure rates that change with age.

Our task now is to generate times at which events occur in such a process. We will do so by generating the time of the first event, then the time of the second event based on the time of the first event, and so on.

To do this with the inverse-transform technique, we first need to compute the probability distribution function of the time between successive event occurrences. The probability of *no* event occurrence in the time interval $[t_1, t_2]$ is given by $e^{-\int_{t_1}^{t_2} \lambda(\tau) \, d\tau}$, and therefore, if the ith event occurred at time t_i, the interval to the next event occurrence has the following probability distribution function

$$F(x|t_i) = 1 - e^{-\int_{t_i}^{x+t_i} \lambda(\tau) \, d\tau}$$

Suppose, as an example, that $\lambda(t) = at$, which means that the failure rate increases linearly as a function of time. Then, the distribution function of the time interval between the ith and $(i+1)$st events will be

$$F(x|t_i) = 1 - e^{-\int_{t_i}^{x+t_i} a\tau \, d\tau} = 1 - e^{-a[x^2 + 2xt_i]/2}$$

To use the inverse-transform technique, we set

$$u = 1 - e^{-a[x^2 + 2xt_i]/2}$$

solving for x

$$x = -t_i + \sqrt{t_i^2 - 2\ln(1 - u)/a}$$

This is the length of the interval separating t_i and t_{i+1}. Thus, we will generate event times as follows. Generate $U_1, U_2, \ldots$, uniformly distributed over $[0, 1]$.

1. Set $t_1 = \sqrt{-2\ln(1 - U_1)/a}$

2. Set $t_2 = t_1 - t_1 + \sqrt{t_1^2 - 2\ln(1 - U_2)/a} = \sqrt{t_1^2 - 2\ln(1 - U_2)/a}$

3. Set $t_3 = t_2 - t_2 + \sqrt{t_2^2 - 2\ln(1 - U_3)/a} = \sqrt{t_2^2 - 2\ln(1 - U_3)/a}$

and so on. ■

■ E X A M P L E

Suppose we want to generate positive random variables distributed according to the Weibull distribution (see Equation 10.2), for which

$$F(x) = 1 - e^{-\lambda x^{\beta}} \quad (\text{for } x \geqslant 0)$$

We now have

$$u = 1 - e^{-\lambda x^{\beta}}$$

and consequently,

$$x = \left[-\ln(1-u)/\lambda \right]^{1/\beta}$$

■

Rejection Method

Suppose we are given a random number generator that produces random numbers according to a probability density function $g(\cdot)$, and would like to generate random numbers according to a probability density function $f(\cdot)$ such that $f(x) \leqslant cg(x)$ for all x and for some finite constant, c. Then, the rejection method proceeds as follows:

1. Generate a random number, Y, according to the probability density function $g(\cdot)$.

2. Generate U, uniformly distributed over $[0, 1]$.

3. If $U \leqslant \frac{f(Y)}{cg(Y)}$, output Y; otherwise go back to step 1 and try again. The output has the required probability density function, $f(\cdot)$.

The role of the constant, c, is to ensure that the $f(Y)/cg(Y)$ is never greater than 1. We would like to select a function $g(\cdot)$ such that c is not very large; as you are invited to prove in the Exercises, the average number of times we have to loop through the above procedure to generate one output is c.

We next prove that this method produces the desired results.

$$\text{Prob}\{X \leqslant x\} = \text{Prob}\left\{ Y \leqslant x \,\middle|\, U \leqslant \frac{f(Y)}{cg(Y)} \right\}$$

$$= \frac{\text{Prob}\left\{ Y \leqslant x \text{ and } U \leqslant \frac{f(Y)}{cg(Y)} \right\}}{\text{Prob}\left\{ U \leqslant \frac{f(Y)}{cg(Y)} \right\}}$$

$$\text{Prob}\left\{Y \leqslant x \text{ and } U \leqslant \frac{f(Y)}{cg(Y)}\right\} = \text{Prob}\left\{U \leqslant \frac{f(Y)}{cg(Y)} \middle| Y \leqslant x\right\} \text{Prob}\{Y \leqslant x\}$$

$$= \frac{F(x)}{c} \text{ (fill in the missing steps as an exercise)}$$

$$\text{Prob}\left\{U \leqslant \frac{f(Y)}{cg(Y)}\right\} = \frac{1}{c} \quad \text{(showing this is another exercise)}$$

Hence, $\text{Prob}\{X \leqslant x\} = F(x)$, which completes the proof.

■ EXAMPLE

Suppose we want to generate random variables Z according to the normal distribution, with mean 0 and variance 1. The desired density function is

$$h(z) = \frac{1}{\sqrt{2\pi}} e^{-z^2/2}, \quad -\infty < z < \infty$$

We need to find a suitable function $g(\cdot)$. A URNG will not do: its density function goes to 0 beyond a finite interval. However, we know how to generate an exponentially distributed random variable (with parameter 1): it has density $g(x) = e^{-x}$ for $x \geqslant 0$. The only problem is that the normal distribution is nonzero for both positive and negative z, and the exponential is only defined for $x \geqslant 0$.

This difficulty can be easily overcome: observe that $h(z)$ is symmetric about the origin and $h(z) = h(-z)$. Let us generate a random variable $X = |Z|$: it has twice the density of the normal over the non-negative half of the interval. This results in the density function

$$f(x) = \frac{2}{\sqrt{2\pi}} e^{-x^2/2}, \quad 0 \leqslant x < \infty$$

Then, we set $Z = X$ with probability 0.5 and $Z = -X$ with probability 0.5.

We start by finding a c such that $f(x) \leqslant cg(x)$. To do this requires us to maximize $f(x)/g(x)$ over $x \geqslant 0$: simple calculus shows that this happens when $x = 1$, so we can use

$$c = \frac{f(1)}{g(1)} = \sqrt{\frac{2e}{\pi}}$$

After some algebraic manipulation, we get

$$\frac{f(x)}{cg(x)} = e^{-(x-1)^2/2}$$

Therefore, to generate X, we carry out the following steps:

1. Generate Y, with probability density function $g_Y(y) = e^{-y}$.

2. Generate U_1 uniformly distributed over $[0,1]$.

3. If $U_1 \leqslant e^{-(Y-1)^2/2}$, output $X = Y$; otherwise go back to step 1 and try again.

To generate Z from X, we do the following:

1. Generate U_2 uniformly distributed over $[0,1]$.

2. If $U_2 \leqslant 0.5$, output $Z = X$, otherwise output $Z = -X$.

Composition Method

When the random variable to be generated is the sum of other random variables, we can generate each of the latter and then add them up.

▪ EXAMPLE

We want to generate a random variable Z which is defined as $Z = V + X + Y$, where:

1. V is uniformly distributed over the interval $[0,10]$.

2. X is exponentially distributed with parameter μ.

3. Y has the normal distribution, with mean 5 and variance 23.

We generate V and X using the inverse transform technique, and Y using the rejection method. We then add them up and output the result. ▪

10.5 Fault Injection

As mentioned previously in this chapter, simulating a system to obtain its reliability or similar attributes requires the knowledge of parameters such as the components' failure rates. These can be obtained either through lengthy observations, or much faster through fault injection experiments. In such experiments, various faults are injected either into a simulation model of the target system or a hardware-and-software prototype of the system. The behavior of the system in the presence of each fault is then observed and classified. Parameters that can be estimated based on such experiments include the probability that a fault will cause an error, and the probability that the system will perform successfully the actions required to recover from that error (the latter probability is often called *coverage factor*, see Chapter 2). These actions consist of detecting the fault, identifying the system component affected by the fault, and taking an appropriate recovery action which may involve system reconfiguration. Each of these actions takes time that is not a constant but may change from one fault to another and may also depend on the current workload. Thus, fault injection experiments, in addition to providing estimates for the coverage factor, can also be used to estimate the distribution of the individual delay associated with each of the above actions.

In addition, fault injection experiments can be used to evaluate and validate the system dependability. For example, errors in the implementation of fault-tolerance mechanisms can be discovered, and system components whose failure is more likely to result in a total system crash can be identified. Also, the effect of the system's workload on the dependability can be observed.

10.5.1 Types of Fault Injection Techniques

Initially, fault injection studies involved injection of physical faults into the hardware components of the system. This necessitates being able to modify the current value of almost every circuit node, thus mimicking a fault that may occur there. With the considerable increase in circuit density in current VLSI technologies and the associated reduction in device size, this technique is now limited in its capabilities because only the pins of integrated circuits can be easily accessed.

Accessibility can be improved by taking advantage of scan chains, which connect a large number of internal circuit latches in a sequential manner, and are currently included in many designs of complex integrated circuits. Scan chains are normally constructed to simplify the debugging and manufacturing test of the circuit by allowing the user to shift out the current values (for observation purposes) and shift in new values. By shifting in erroneous bits, the scan chain can be used to inject faults as well.

Even so, injecting faults into all internal circuit nodes is not practically feasible due to the very large number of circuit nodes in even a moderately complex system, which makes exhaustive insertion prohibitive. Instead, a subset of these insertion points must be carefully selected.

Several alternative schemes have been developed to allow the injection of faults without having direct access to internal nodes. One such scheme is to subject the hardware to particle radiation (for example, heavy-ion radiation). Such radiation can clearly inject faults into otherwise inaccessible locations, but on the other hand it can only inject transient faults, because the effect of the particle hit will disappear after a brief delay. This technique has the additional advantage of closely resembling what might happen in real life. As device feature sizes in current integrated circuits get smaller, errors due to neutron and alpha particle hits become more common. Such particle hits (also called soft errors or single event upsets) are abundant in space but also appear at ground level due to cosmic rays that bombard the earth and to radioactive atoms that exist in trace amounts in the packaging materials.

A different method for fault injection is through power supply disturbances. The supply voltage is briefly dropped to levels below the nominal range. Unlike the radiation method which usually generates single event upsets, this scheme affects many nodes in the circuit simultaneously, producing multiple transient faults. Moreover, the exact location of these faults cannot be controlled. The effect of power supply disturbances does, however, resemble a real-life situation that may be experienced by computer systems in industrial applications.

Another approach to fault injection is through electromagnetic interference. The system is subjected to electromagnetic bursts, which can be either allowed to affect all components or be restricted to individual ones. Here too, the injected faults are transient.

The above-mentioned physical injection techniques rely on having a working prototype of the target system. If the designers wish to test some fault-tolerance features in their design and modify them if the observed dependability is insufficient, then the use of a physical injection technique may prove to be too costly. An alternative would be to inject faults through the software layer. This technique, known as Software Implemented Fault Injection (SWIFI), can be applied either to a prototype of the target system or to a simulation model of it. SWIFI also overcomes some of the problems with physical fault injection such as repeatability and controllability. It provides easy access to many internal circuit nodes in the system (but not to all of them) and allows the control of the location, time, duration, and type of the injected faults much more easily than does physical injection. An important advantage of the SWIFI approach is that it is not restricted to hardware faults but allows the injection of software faults as well.

If SWIFI is applied to a simulation model of the target system rather than a prototype, then mixed-mode simulation techniques can be used, supporting several levels of system abstraction including architectural, functional, logical, and electrical. In mixed-mode simulation, the system is decomposed in a hierarchical manner, allowing us to simulate various components at different levels of abstraction. Thus, an injected fault can be simulated at a low abstraction level and the propagation of its effect through the system can be simulated at higher abstraction levels, greatly reducing the simulation time. Although simulation-based fault injection has several desirable properties, injecting faults into a hardware-software prototype provides more realistic, credible, and accurate results.

Software fault injections can be performed either during compilation or during run time. To inject faults during compile time, the program instructions are modified and errors are injected into the source code or assembly code to emulate the effect of hardware (permanent or transient) and software faults. To inject faults during run time, one can use either timers (hardware or software) to determine the exact instant of the injection, or a software trap that will allow determining the exact time of the injection relative to some system event. This technique requires only minor modifications, if any, to the application program. A third method of timing the fault injection through software is by adding instructions to the applica-

TABLE 10-3 ■ Comparing the properties of four approaches to fault injection

Property	Hardware direct injection	Hardware indirect injection	Software during compilation	Software during runtime
Accessibility	low	high	low	low to medium
Controllability	high	low	high	high
Intrusiveness	none	none	low	high
Repeatability	high	low	high	high
Cost	high	high	low	low

tion program. This will allow faults to be injected in predetermined time instances during the execution of the program.

10.5.2 Fault Injection Application and Tools

Fault injection has been applied for measuring the coverage and latency parameters, for studying error propagation, and for analyzing the relationship between the workload of the system and its fault handling capabilities. Another interesting application of fault injection schemes has been to evaluate the effect of transient faults on the availability of highly dependable systems. These systems were capable of recovering from the transient faults but still had wasted time doing that, thus reducing the availability.

Various fault injectors have been developed and are currently in use. Some are mentioned in the Further Reading section. Studies comparing several fault injectors have been conducted, concluding that two fault injectors may either validate each other or complement each other. The latter happens if they cover different faults.

The different approaches to fault injection result in quite different properties of the corresponding tools. Some of these differences are summarized in Table 10-3.

All fault injection schemes require a well-defined fault model, which should represent as closely as possible the faults that one expects to see during the lifetime of the target system. A fault model must specify the types of faults, their location and duration, and, possibly, the statistical distributions of these characteristics. The fault models used in currently available fault injection tools vary considerably, from very detailed device level faults (for example, a delay fault on a particular wire) to simplified functional level faults (such as an erroneous adder output).

10.6 Further Reading

Two textbooks on simulation [12,29], provide useful information on how to write simulation programs. Another, more elementary and limited, source is the operations research book [19]. A large number of topics related to simulation models can be found in [4]. Many simulations are written in special-purpose simulation languages such as GPSS; for a good source for this language, see [30]. In our treatment, we did not discuss parallel simulation: this is a very promising approach to speeding up simulation. For details, see [14].

The topic of parameter estimation is covered in many books. See for example, [10,31]. [33] provides a readable section on the subject.

Perhaps the best sources for variance reduction methods are the two above-mentioned books [13,29]. For importance sampling, see [15,18,26,27]. These also contain a useful bibliography. [25] provides an early source for the technique of forcing. A case study of the use of importance sampling in evaluating real-time system dependability is presented in [11].

An excellent source of information about uniform random number generators is [23]. You can find there a detailed mathematical treatment of the properties of the linear congruential generator, including the relationships that must hold in order to have $P = m$. Especially valuable is the detailed treatment of statistical tests of randomness that is provided. The theoretical basis for the χ^2 test is explained in detail, and the most powerful test of all—the spectral test—is covered extensively. This book also has an outstanding set of references to the literature. Additional sources of information on empirical statistical tests are [5] and [21].

The recent work in [24] is useful for good random number generators with extremely long periods.

Generating random numbers with distributions other than uniform is discussed in many books. For example, see [5,29].

Several survey papers reviewing the uses of fault injectors and the various available tools have been published [9,20]. Some of the fault injection tools that have been developed rely on hardware fault injection, e.g., Messaline [2], FIST [16], Xception [8], and GOOFI [1]. Other are based on software fault injection, for example, Ferrari [22], FIAT [6], NFtape [32], and DOCTOR [17]. A good comparison of several tools for evaluating the dependability of a fault-tolerant system was presented in [3]. Another use of software fault injection is to assess the risk involved in using a software product [34,35]. This scheme uses code that modifies the program state by injecting anomalies in the instructions to see how badly the software can behave.

10.7 Exercises

1. You are given a set of 10 processors that are believed to follow a Poisson failure process, with failure rate λ per hour per processor. You run the processors for a week, and obtain the following numbers of failures for each processor: 2, 4, 2, 1, 1, 2, 3, 2, 0, 2.

   a. What is your estimate for the value of λ?

    b. Construct a 95% confidence interval for λ using Equation 10.1.

    c. Construct a 95% confidence interval for λ using the fact that for the Poisson distribution $E(x) = \text{Var}(x) = \lambda$.

    d. Explain the difference between the results of parts b and c.

2. You are given a set of 10 processors that are believed to follow a Poisson failure process, with failure rate λ per hour per processor. The prior density of λ is a uniform distribution over the range $[0.001, 0.002]$.

    a. You run these processors for 100 hours without any of the processors failing. What is the best estimate for the value of λ (the mean of the posterior density of λ)?

    b. You continue the experiment for a total of 10,000 hours without observing any failures. What is your best estimate for λ?

    c. Suppose you were to run this experiment for a *very* long time without any processor failing. What do you think the posterior density function for λ would be?

3. This question follows up on our comments on the difficulty of validating the reliability of a life-critical system to a sufficiently high level of confidence.

    Suppose you were calculating the confidence interval for the reliability of a life-critical system whose true failure probability over a given interval of operation is 10^{-8}. (Of course, you don't *know* that this failure probability is 10^{-8}, which is why you are gathering statistics). Obtain an estimate of the number of observations you would require to show with 99.999999% confidence that the true failure probability is in the range $[0.9 \times 10^{-8}, 1.1 \times 10^{-8}]$.

    You will need, for this question, an algorithm to calculate the values of the normal distribution with sufficient accuracy. It should not be difficult to find one through an Internet search; see, for example, [7].

4. Evaluate RANDU, which was a routine widely used many years ago to generate uniform random numbers. Its recurrence is $X_{n+1} = (65539X_n) \bmod 2^{31}$. Pick $X_0 = 23$ and use each of the testing methods described in Section 10.4.2. Software for the spectral test can be found on the Internet.

5. Repeat Problem 4 for the random number generator that is included in your favorite computer system or spreadsheet.

6. Given a uniform random number generator, obtain a generator for continuous-valued random variables with the following probability density functions. Assume that the densities are 0 outside the specified ranges, and that μ_1, μ_2 have known values.

    a. $f_1(x) = 0.25, \quad 16 \leqslant x \leqslant 20$

b. $f_2(x) = 0.4\mu_1 e^{-\mu_1 x} + 0.6\mu_2 e^{-\mu_2 x}, \quad x \geqslant 0$

c. $f_3(x) = \frac{1}{24} x^4 e^{-x}, \quad x > 0$

d. $f_4(x) = \begin{cases} x & \text{if } 0 \leqslant x \leqslant 1 \\ 2 - x & \text{if } 1 \leqslant x \leqslant 2 \\ 0 & \text{otherwise} \end{cases}$

7. Generate discrete random variables with the following probability mass functions (assume that the parameters have known values):

   a. $\text{Prob}\{X = n\} = p(1 - p)^{n-1}, \quad n = 1, 2, 3, \ldots; \quad 0 < p < 1$

   b. $\text{Prob}\{X = n\} = e^{-\lambda} \lambda^n / n!, \quad n = 0, 1, 2, \ldots; \quad \lambda > 0$

   c. $\text{Prob}\{X = n\} = \begin{cases} 0.25 & \text{if } n = 1 \\ 0.50 & \text{if } n = 2 \\ 0.25 & \text{if } n = 3 \\ 0 & \text{otherwise} \end{cases}$

   d. $\text{Prob}\{X = n\} = 0.7 e^{-\lambda} \lambda^n / n! + 0.3 e^{-2\lambda} (2\lambda)^n / n!$

8. When deriving the generator for exponentially distributed random variables, we showed that $-(1/\lambda) \ln(1 - U)$ would work. However, we pointed out that $-(1/\lambda) \ln U$ would also yield exponentially distributed random variables. Prove that this is the case.

9. When proving the correctness of the rejection method, we omitted some steps. Complete the proof with these steps in place.

10. Write a simulation program to obtain the MTTF of the system shown in Figure 10.4a.

11. Write a simulation program to find the MTTDL of a RAID Level 3 system, consisting of eight data disks and one parity disk. The disks fail independently, according to a Poisson process with rate 10^{-7} per hour. The repair time (in hours) has an exponential density with mean 2 hours.

   a. Estimate the mean time to data loss, MTTDL.

   b. Derive the 99% confidence interval for the MTTDL after running a total of 1000 simulation runs.

   c. Determine how many runs are required to make the width of the 99% confidence interval less than 10% of the estimated MTTDL (from part a).

   d. Vary the number of simulations from 1000 to 10,000, and plot the width of the confidence interval over this range.

12. Repeat the above simulation, using the method of antithetic variables. Compare the width of the 99% confidence interval you obtain with the two approaches, for an identical total number of simulations ranging from 1000 to 10,000.

13. Repeat the above simulation, using the method of importance sampling. Use the balanced failure biasing technique. Vary the value of p^* from 0.1 to 0.9, in steps of 0.1, and run 1000 simulations for each such value. Plot the width of the 99% confidence interval as a function of p^*.

14. Consider the example discussed in Section 10.3.3. Suppose you carry out a few runs to get a rough estimate of π_1 and π_2, and end up with $\hat{\pi}_1 = 0.9$ and $\hat{\pi}_2 = 0.98$. Your simulation time budget allows you to carry out a total of 1000 simulation runs, so that $n_1 + n_2 = 1000$. What values should you select for n_1 and n_2 to minimize the variance of your estimate of the survival probability, π.

15. Consider the system shown in Figure 10.7. Each block suffers failure independently of the others, according to a Poisson process with rates $\lambda_A = 0.001$, $\lambda_B = 0.002$, $\lambda_C = 0.005$, $\lambda_D = 0.01$, $\lambda_E = 0.009$, $\lambda_T = 0.005$, and $\lambda_P = 0.00001$ per time unit. The subscripts refer to the block labels. The blocks marked 3 are perfectly reliable and never fail. The nodes *In* and *Out* represent the input and output points, and not blocks: they do not fail.

    Each node takes an exponentially distributed amount of time to repair: the mean time to repair is 1 time unit for all nodes.

    Failure happens when there is no longer a path from the *In* node to the *Out* node.

    a. Write a simulation program to obtain the mean time to failure for this system. Plot the width of the 99% confidence interval associated with simulation runs ranging from 500 to 10000.

    b. Use the method of control variables and repeat part (a).

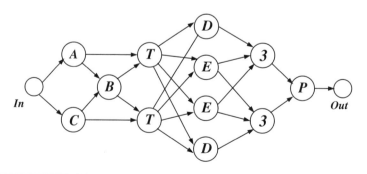

FIGURE 10.7   Non-series parallel system.

   c. Repeat part (a) by using importance sampling with balanced failure biasing ($p^* = 0.2$).

16. Repeat part (a) of the previous problem, with the blocks now suffering failure according to a nonhomogeneous Poisson process, in which the failure rates are increasing functions of time. Use $\lambda_i(t) = t^{1/3}\lambda_i$, for $i \in \{A, B, C, D, E, P, T\}$. Assume that upon node repair, the effective age of that node becomes 0, i.e., that upon repair we reset its t to 0.

References

[1] J. L. Aidemark, J. P. Vinter, P. Folkesson, and J. Karlsson, "GOOFI: A Generic Fault Injection Tool," *Dependable Systems and Networks Conference (DSN-2001)*, pp. 83–88, 2001.

[2] J. Arlat, A. Costes, Y. Crouzet, J. C. Laprie, and D. Powell, "Fault Injection and Dependability Evaluation of Fault-Tolerant Systems," *IEEE Transactions on Computers*, Vol. 42, pp. 913–923, August 1993.

[3] J. Arlat, Y. Crouzet, J. Karlsson, P. Folkesson, E. Fuchs, and G. H. Leber, "Comparison of Physical and Software-Implemented Fault Injection Techniques," *IEEE Transactions on Computers*, Vol. 52, pp. 1115–1133, September 2003.

[4] J. Banks (Ed.), *Handbook of Simulation*, Wiley, 1998.

[5] J. Banks, J. S. Carson II, B. L. Nelson, and D. M. Nicol, *Discrete-Event System Simulation*, Prentice Hall, 2001.

[6] J. H. Barton, E. W. Czeck, Z. Segall, and D. P. Siewiorek, "Fault Injection Experiments Using FIAT," *IEEE Transactions on Computers*, Vol. 39, pp. 575–582, April 1990.

[7] B. D. Bunday, S. M. H. Bokhari, and K. H. Khan, "A New Algorithm for the Normal Distribution Function," *Sociedad de Estadistica e Investigacion Operativa Test*, Vol. 6, pp. 369–377, 1997.

[8] J. Carreira, H. Madeira, and J. G. Silva, "Xception: A Technique for the Experimental Evaluation of Dependability in Modern Computers," *IEEE Transactions on Software Engineering*, Vol. 24, pp. 125–136, February 1998.

[9] J. A. Clark and D. K. Pradhan, "Fault Injection: A Method for Validating Computer-System Dependability," *IEEE Computer*, Vol. 28, pp. 47 56, June 1995.

[10] A. C. Cohen and B. J. Whitten, *Parameter Estimation in Reliability and Life Span Models*, Marcel Dekker, 1988.

[11] G. Durairaj, I. Koren, and C. M. Krishna, "Importance Sampling to Evaluate Real-Time System Reliability," *Simulation*, Vol. 76, pp. 172–183, March 2001.

[12] G. S. Fishman, *Discrete Event Simulation*, Springer-Verlag, 2001.

[13] G. S. Fishman, *A First Course in Monte Carlo*, Duxbury, 2006.

[14] R. M. Fujimoto, *Parallel and Distributed Simulation*, Wiley, 2000.

[15] A. Goyal, P. Shahabuddin, P. Heidelberger, V. F. Nicola, and P. W. Glynn, "A Unified Framework for Simulating Markovian Models of Highly Dependable Systems," *IEEE Transactions on Computers*, Vol. 41, pp. 36–51, January 1992.

[16] U. Gunneflo, J. Karlsson, and J. Torin, "Evaluation of Error Detection Schemes Using Fault Injection by Heavy-ion Radiation," *19th IEEE International Symposium on Fault-Tolerant Computing (FTCS-19)*, pp. 340–347, June 1989.

[17] S. Han, K. G. Shin, and H. A. Rosenberg, "DOCTOR: An Integrated Software Fault Injection Environment for Distributed Real-time Systems," *International Computer Performance and Dependability Symposium (IPDS'95)*, pp. 204–213, April 1995.

[18] P. Heidelberger, "Fast Simulation of Rare Events in Queuing and Reliability Models," *ACM Transactions on Modeling and Computer Simulation*, Vol. 5, pp. 43–55, January 1995.

[19] F. S. Hillier and G. J. Lieberman, *Introduction to Operations Research*, McGraw-Hill, 2001.

[20] M. C. Hsueh, T. K. Tsai, and R. K. Iyer, "Fault Injection Techniques and Tools," *IEEE Computer*, Vol. 30, pp. 75–82, April 1997.

[21] R. Jain, *The Art of Computer Systems Performance Analysis*, Wiley, 1991.

[22] G. A. Kanawati, N. A. Kanawati, and J. A. Abraham, "FERRARI: A Flexible Software-Based Fault and Error Injection System," *IEEE Transactions on Computers*, Vol. 44, pp. 248–260, February 1995.

[23] D. E. Knuth, *The Art of Computer Programming*, Vol. 2, Addison-Wesley, 1998.

[24] P. L'Ecuyer, "Random Numbers," *International Encyclopedia of Social and Behavioral Sciences*, Elsevier, 2001.

[25] E. E. Lewis and F. Bohm, "Monte Carlo Simulation of Markov Unreliability Models," *Nuclear Engineering and Design*, Vol. 77, pp. 49–62, 1984.

[26] M. K. Nakayama, "Fast Simulation Methods for Highly Dependable Systems," *Winter Simulation Conference*, pp. 221–228, 1994.

[27] M. K. Nakayama, "A Characterization of the Simple Failure-Biasing Method for Simulations of Highly Reliable Markovian Systems," *ACM Transactions on Modeling and Computer Simulation*, Vol. 4, pp. 52–86, January 1994.

[28] D. Powell, E. Martins, J. Arlat, and Y. Crouzet, "Estimators for Fault Tolerance Coverage Evaluation," *IEEE Transactions on Computers*, Vol. 44, pp. 261–274, February 1995.

[29] S. M. Ross, *Simulation*, Academic Press, 2002.

[30] T. J. Schriber, *An Introduction to Simulation using GPSS/H*, Wiley, 1991.

[31] H. W. Sorenson, *Parameter Estimation: Principles and Problems*, Marcel Dekker, 1980.

[32] D. T. Stott, G. Ries, M.-C. Hsueh, and R. K. Iyer, "Dependability Analysis of a High-Speed Network Using Software-Implemented Fault Injection and Simulated Fault Injection," *IEEE Transactions on Computers*, Vol. 47, pp. 108–119, January 1998.

[33] K. S. Trivedi, *Probability and Statistics with Reliability, Queuing and Computer Science Applications*, John Wiley, 2002.

[34] J. M. Voas and G. McGraw, *Software Fault Injection*, Wiley Computer Publishing, 1998.

[35] J. Voas, G. McGraw, L. Kassab, and L. Voas, "Fault-Injection: A Crystal Ball for Software Liability," *IEEE Computer*, Vol. 30, pp. 29–36, June 1997.

Index